THE *RELACIÓN DE MICHOACÁN* (1539–1541) AND THE POLITICS OF REPRESENTATION IN COLONIAL MEXICO

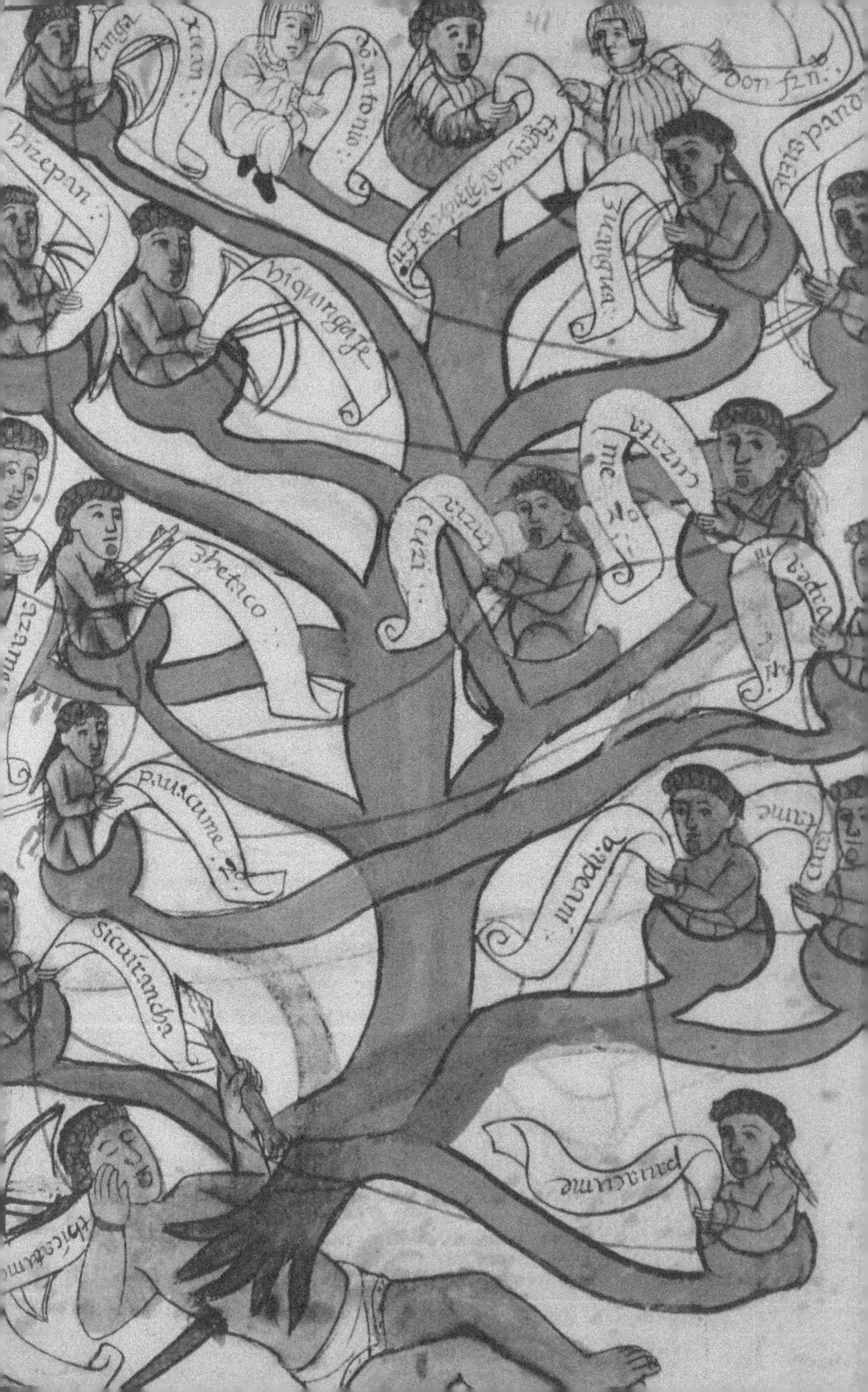

do antonio
hiquingare
zhetaco
sicuirancha
paucacume

THE Relación de Michoacán (1539–1541) AND THE *Politics of Representation in Colonial Mexico*

ANGÉLICA JIMENA AFANADOR-PUJOL

UNIVERSITY OF TEXAS PRESS *Austin*

This book is a part of the Recovering Languages and Literacies of the Americas publication initiative, funded by a grant from the Andrew W. Mellon Foundation.

Printed in the United States of America
First edition, 2015
Second paperback reprint, 2025

♾ The paper used in this book meets the minimum requirements of ANSI/NISO Z39.48-1992 (R1997) (Permanence of Paper).

LIBRARY OF CONGRESS CATALOGING-IN-PUBLICATION DATA
Afanador-Pujol, Angélica Jimena, 1973– author.
The Relación de Michoacán (1539–1541) and the politics of representation in colonial Mexico / Angélica Jimena Afanador-Pujol. — First edition.
pages cm
Includes bibliographical references.
ISBN 978-0-292-77138-3 (cloth : alk. paper) — ISBN 978-1-4773-0239-2 (pbk. : alk. paper)
1. Relación de Michoacán. 2. Illumination of books and manuscripts—Mexico—Michoacán de Ocampo. 3. Indians of Mexico—Ethnic identity. 4. Indians of Mexico—Mexico—Michoacán de Ocampo—History. 5. Art—Political aspects—Mexico—Michoacán de Ocampo. 6. Michoacán de Ocampo (Mexico)—History—16th century. I. Title.
F1219.1.M55A35 2015
972′.3701—dc23 2014038312

doi:10.7560/771383

A Camilo, pequeño acompañante

Contents

Acknowledgments

A large number of friends and colleagues have joined me in this project, which first started as a PhD dissertation and has since evolved into this book. I thank the many people in Michoacán who opened their homes, libraries, and archives to me. I thank Viera Sairán Monfón for her friendship, keen eye, and delightful company during many road trips to see Michoacán's breathtaking convents, small towns, and pre-Columbian cities. Her drawings have brought to life many of the pages of this book. In addition to engaging in our intellectually stimulating conversations, Ricardo Aguilar worked with me on the transcription of the document "Información de méritos y servicios de don Antonio Huitzimengari, hijo del último cazonci de Michoacán, 1553–1554." I am grateful to him and his beautiful family, Liz, León Matías, and my *ahijado* Santiago, for their companionship through the years. Alicia Mateo's and Benjamín Lucas's courage, generosity, and dedication in sharing their knowledge of P'urhépecha culture have been an inspiration through the years. They have provided much-needed support with linguistic materials and in 2006 invited me to the "Diplomado de Medicina Tradicional" they co-taught at the Universidad Intercultural Indígena de Michoacán. I am grateful to the medicine women and men whom I met there and who so patiently explained P'urhépecha concepts to me, *diosï meiamu.* I am grateful to Nana Josefina Chávez for her healing hands and for expanding my definition of the *imaginario.* J. Benedict Warren and the late Patricia Warren provided meals, conversations, road trips, and their love and support while I lived in Mexico and after my return to the United States. I met Carlos Paredes Martínez early during my research and benefited much from his openhearted generosity. He introduced me to the scholarly group Kw'anískuyarhani de Estudiosos del Pueblo Purépecha and shared his enthusiasm, library, and wealth of knowledge about Michoacán. He kindly agreed to join my dissertation committee and has provided much valuable feedback.

While I was living in Spain, Graciela Bernal gave me a home away from home in Seville, and Juan Jesús Molina, one in Madrid. Consolación Fernández, Magdalena Díaz, Katia Souza Machado, and Esther González provided a breath of fresh air during the oppressing summer heat while I conducted archival research in Seville.

My years at UCLA provided me with much personal and professional growth. I am grateful for the teachings and the intellectual challenges my dissertation committee members bestowed on me: Charlene Villaseñor Black, Kevin Terraciano, and the late Albert Boime. Above all, I am grateful to my adviser, Cecelia F. Klein. It is difficult to express in words the gratitude I feel for everything Cecelia has done for me over the years. Her intellectual guidance, honesty, friendship, and generosity have made this book possible. Her unwavering support, even as I struggled to obtain visas to conduct research in three different countries, inspired me to finish.

Many have been the friends who read previous versions of these chapters, provided valuable comments, and helped me think through my ideas. I thank a few of them: Almila Akdag, Susan Gagliardi, and Simon Kenrick. I particularly express my gratitude to Dustin W. Leavitt, whose keen comments and edits helped this project come to fruition. I am also grateful to Elizabeth Coughlin, my research assistant at the University of Minnesota, whose enthusiasm and hard work were invaluable to completing the manuscript. My friends Melia Belli, Lisa Tom, Rhonda Jones, and Miranda Brady encouraged me to finish and provided much-needed relief after long days of work over the years. Louis Mendoza's companionship, encouragement, and helpful editorial comments have helped me finish revising the book.

For their cooperation with my research, I enthusiastically acknowledge Héctor Álvarez Contreras, previously at the Secretaría de Cultura, Michoacán; Eugenio Mercado López, former director of the Museo Regional Michoacano, Morelia, and Carlos Reyes Galván, also at that institution; Carmen Alicia Dávila Murguía, former director of the Museo de Arte Colonial, Morelia; María del Rosario Ortiz Marín, former director of the Ex-Convento de Tiripetío, and the Ex-Convento's former staff, Igor Cerda Farías, Francisco Ávalos, Francisco Tapia, and Dzoara López; the staff at the Archivo Histórico de la Ciudad de Pátzcuaro; the staff of the Library of the Museo Nacional de Antropología in Mexico City; the staff of the Archivo General de Indias, Seville, Spain; the staff of the Biblioteca Nacional de España; and Father Marcelino de Otero and director José Luis del Valle Merino of the Real Biblioteca del Monasterio, San Lorenzo de El Escorial, Spain.

The original research was made possible thanks to the generous funding of a UC MEXUS Dissertation Research Grant and two Edward A. Dickson Fellowships from the Department of Art History at the University of California, Los Angeles. Writing was made possible thanks to an Andrew W. Mellon Foundation/American Council of Learned Societies Dissertation Completion Fellowship. I was able to revise my manuscript thanks to an Andrew W. Mellon Foundation/ACLS Early Career Fellowship Program Recent Doctoral Recipients Fellowship, 2009–2010, while in residence at the John Hope Franklin Humanities Institute, Duke University. The institute's stimulating atmosphere and the support of fellow post-docs made it a delightful year. A College of Liberal Arts Single Semester Leave Award, University of Minnesota, fall 2012, gave me much-needed time to address the insightful comments of the UT Press anonymous reviewers. A Grant-in-Aid of Research, Artistry, and Scholarship from the Office of the Vice President for Research at the University of Minnesota (2014) paid for the copyrights of many of the images included in this book. I am grateful to Michele Ciaccio from the Getty Research Institute, who generously shared with me several images. The support of the faculty and staff of the School of Art, Herberger Institute for Design and the Arts, at Arizona State University, allowed me to make the final edits to the manuscript.

THE *RELACIÓN DE MICHOACÁN* (1539–1541) AND THE POLITICS OF REPRESENTATION IN COLONIAL MEXICO

Introduction

Spanish invasion and colonization of the Americas was a slow process that frequently involved war, careful planning, and the crafting of political alliances. Competing expeditions of conquistadors to unexplored areas often fought for claims to land, labor, and bounty. Spanish factions found it necessary to collaborate with indigenous noble families to collect tribute, direct building projects, and maintain settlements in working order. Indigenous people were equally divided along kinship and ethnic lines, cultural practices, and centuries-old rivalries. Spaniards used to their advantage the rivalries among indigenous groups. Likewise, indigenous nobles quickly learned to work with the intricacies and politics of the different Spanish factions. These nobles learned to use the colonial court system to defend their claims to land and ancestral privileges. Theirs was a rapidly changing world.

In the winter of 1539, Spanish viceroy Antonio de Mendoza left the viceregal capital Mexico-Tenochtitlan (today Mexico City) and traveled by horse westward approximately 193 miles through valleys and forested mountains to the city of Tzintzuntzan on the shore of Lake Pátzcuaro in the present-day state of Michoacán. This journey took him across the political border separating the Aztecs of central Mexico, who spoke Nahuatl, from their P'urhépecha-speaking enemies.[1] On his way to Tzintzuntzan, the viceroy must have seen the lands of Otomís, Matlatzingas, Nahuas, and other groups that inhabited this expansive territory. He took this long and arduous trip to Tzintzuntzan in the hopes of settling what would be one of the most notorious labor and land disputes involving Spaniards and indigenous people in all of colonial Mexico—or, as it was known at the time, New Spain.

Key to resolving this and other disputes was gaining an understanding of P'urhépecha political and territorial organization and history prior to the first arrival of Europeans in 1521. Mendoza, who had come to occupy the post of viceroy four years before his trip, probably knew little about Michoacán. This may have been his reason for commissioning a Spanish Franciscan friar at this time to record the customs of the region. The "Prologue" of the illustrated manuscript containing this account, *Relacion de las çerimonias y rrictos y poblaçión y gobernaçion de los yndios de la provinçia de Mechuacán hecha al yllustrisimo señor don Antonio de Mendoça, virrey y governador desta Nueva España por su majestad, etcétera* (from here on referred to as the *Relación de Michoacán* or *Relación*), states explicitly that the friar created it at the viceroy's request to help him govern the area more efficiently.[2] Around this time, the viceroy also commissioned other indigenous documents, possibly including the *Codex Mendoza*, to help him govern, and to send along to Crown officials back in Spain.[3]

The *Relación de Michoacán* is one of the earliest surviving illustrated manuscripts from colonial Mexico. It predates even the better-known works by Franciscan friar Bernardino de Sahagún about the Aztec people of central Mexico, the *Primeros memoriales* (ca. 1558–1561) and the *Florentine Codex* (1578–1580).[4] The *Relación* now resides in the Royal Library of the Monastery of San Lorenzo de El Escorial, Spain, where it presumably arrived sometime in the sixteenth century. A small book, approximately 20.5 × 14.5 cm, the *Relación* was written and illustrated on European handmade linen-fiber paper.[5] Today, it contains 139 pages combining alphabetic script and 44 hand-painted images.

According to the friar's words in the "Prologue," he determined the general contents of the manuscript and originally envisioned it as a three-part book. Previous studies have noted that the manuscript does not survive in its entirety. Someone removed pages from the manuscript before it was bound. Part 1, containing descriptions of religious ceremonies, was removed; only one of its pages survives. Part 2, containing a historical account of pre-Columbian times, is complete. Part 3, describing ethnographic practices and a history of the events that transpired after the arrival of the Spaniards in the region, seems also to have undergone a purge, for many of its pages have been rearranged.[6]

Upon its arrival at El Escorial, the manuscript was bound. The binder added white sheets of paper at the front and back of the manuscript, trimmed and gilded the edges of the pages, and added a fine honey-colored leather cover, which bears the monastery's emblem, a cartouche containing a grill (the instrument of Saint Lorenzo's torture).[7] Unfortunately, the manuscript was bound out of order. The binder placed the prologue first, part 3 directly following it, with the only page from part 1 mistakenly among the folios of part 3, and part 2 after part 3. At the end of part 2, on pages originally left blank by the artists and scribes, another hand at a later date and using a different ink (most likely after the manuscript was bound) wrote a text entitled "Calendario de toda la índica gente por donde han contado sus tiempos hasta oy agora nuevamente puesto en forma de rueda para mejor ser entendido" (Calendar of all indigenous people by which they have counted all of their time up until today, now again put in the shape of a wheel to be better understood). After the manuscript was bound, someone removed at least two pages containing text and possibly one more containing an image. Then a couple of hands numbered its pages using two different systems and two more numbering systems for its images.[8] The manuscript has also undergone several restoration efforts.[9]

In the prologue of the manuscript, the friar tells the viceroy that to accomplish his task, he employed indigenous noble informants, whose oral contributions formed the text. He remains silent about who created the forty-four illustrations of the manuscript. In chapter 1 of this book, I propose these were four native artists, who worked closely with the friar revising the final contents. We see in chapters 1, 3, and 4 that these artists added images when necessary, edited others, and overall illuminated (in the figurative and literal sense) a rather complex text.[10] The friar, who also remains anonymous throughout the manuscript, tells us he translated the narrators' accounts into Spanish and presented the manuscript to the viceroy in their name.

The interests of these different officials and collaborators gave the *Relación* a complex final form. The literary scholar Herón Pérez Martínez has pointed out that the *Relación* brings together different traditions: the epistolary, religious, and epic, as well as that of the *Informe*. *Informes* were executed at the request of Spanish authorities and were generally structured by the desire to obtain particular information, to answer official requests, and, often, to address particular questions.[11] In epistolary fashion, the *Relación* reads as a letter to an official containing an epic story, yet it also contains an ethnographic section. Throughout its pages the different contributors express their own interests and desires. The combination of these traditions makes it a fascinating project, yet one that presents many challenges for its analysis.

Studies of colonial-era manuscript paintings have often divided manuscripts by patronage and read them accordingly. Broadly speaking, the main distinction being made is between ethnographic documents produced by Spanish officials and works produced by indigenous people. For the communities of central Mexico, for example, scholars have pointed out that indigenous patrons often produced histories, tribute lists, maps, and genealogies to legitimize their power and fight against the encroachment of Spaniards, other indigenous groups, and even other members of their own families.[12] Ethnographic manuscripts produced by Spanish clerics and officials with the collaboration of indigenous painters, like the works of Sahagún and Diego Durán, are often seen as serving the interests of Europeans who sought to gain useful information for their religious, economic, personal, and political enterprises. Analysis of these manuscripts has for the most part focused on the contributions of Spaniards, their background, and the value of the information they collected for understanding the pre-Columbian past. Art historians Dana Leibsohn and Carolyn Dean have pointed out that when scholars have analyzed the function of indigenous collaborators, they have done so to understand what survives of the pre-Columbian past or what represents a European influence. They notice that many studies deny the intricacies of the process and ways in which they came to be produced in the colonial period.[13] In his recent study of the accounts of the Spanish conquest of central Mexico, the historian Kevin Terraciano has begun to unravel how indigenous contributors shaped the accounts of the conquest that Sahagún collected. My study takes this approach one step further by looking at how two different and competing ethnic and political factions of indigenous artists and informants working on one ethnohistoric manuscript shaped its content to promote their own interests.[14]

To better situate the *Relación*, archival research has been key in understanding the complex picture in which different Spanish and indigenous factions sometimes collaborated and sometimes fought for resources and status in the colonial socioeconomic hierarchy. These documents reveal that oversimplified views of colonizer versus colonized present an obstacle when analyzing the intricacies of colonial-era society. Ethnic and political factions often crossed such a neat divide and shaped much of colonial life.

While scholars have assumed that the indigenous contributors of the *Relación* held the same interests, careful analysis of the *Relación* and archival documents reveals that the contributors were in fact members of two distinct ethnic groups and their agendas were not uniform. To collect information, the friar worked with noble members of two ethnic factions. One was a ruling elite family of Michoacán called the Uanacaze, who claimed descent from their tutelary god Curicaueri. The Uanacaze were members and the leaders of a larger ethnic group sometimes referred to in the *Relación* as the Uacúsecha, a P'urhépecha name meaning "the eagles." Elsewhere in the manuscript the Uacúsecha are called Chichimecs, a Nahuatl name generally used for nomadic groups from northern Mexico. According to the *Relación*, the Uanacaze and their group had allegedly migrated to Michoacán from elsewhere. The manuscript tells us that upon their arrival to the shores of Lake Pátzcuaro in Michoacán's highlands, the Uanacaze conquered its local residents and settled in three cities along the lakeshore: Tzintzuntzan, Ihuatzio, and Pátzcuaro. From there they launched the conquest of the region all the way to the lowlands along the Pacific coast. By the time Spaniards arrived in this area, Tzintzuntzan had become the politically dominant city.

Another contributor to the *Relación* was a non-Uanacaze noble known as Don Pedro Cuiniarangari. Even though in the pages of the *Relación*, the Uanacaze ruler refers to Don Pedro as his "brother," a word used as a term of endearment among friends in other documents, Don Pedro identifies himself as a descendant of high priests from one of the islands in Lake Pátzcuaro, that is, as a noble *isleño* (Islander). These so-called Islanders had held sway over the islands and basin of Lake Pátzcuaro until the Uanacaze conquered the region.

At the time the *Relación* was completed in 1541, however, Don Pedro was governor of the region. Because the governorship was the highest post in the colonial government that could be held by an indigenous man, there was understandably the potential for tension between Don Pedro and the Uanacaze. To ease this tension, Don Pedro, in his contribution to the *Relación*, focused, among other things, on his past role as an intermediary between the Uanacaze ruler and the Spanish forces. Significantly, he took credit for having helped facilitate the area's peaceful submission to the European newcomers in the 1520s.

This book examines the *Relación*'s illustrations in relation to the differing agendas of Don Pedro, the Uanacaze, and colonial authorities, including the viceroy. Ultimately, it seeks to reveal how the indigenous artists and nobles who worked on the manuscript developed differing visual strategies for representing themselves and the ethnic identities of their ancestors in the face of competing claims and changing values in order to shape their future in colonial society. To communicate with their colonial audience, the artists of the *Relación* had to reinterpret and reimagine the past. They did so by conscientiously adapting selected pre-Columbian and European iconographic prototypes, thus becoming active agents in the creation of knowledge about the region. Through their visual images they represented ethnic identity and history in ways that not only reflected their own interests but also could be understood by the colonial authorities.

The work of anthropologists and social theorists such as Fredrik Barth, Michel Foucault, Arjun Appadurai, Elizabeth Brumfiel, and Ann Stoler on social classifications such as race and ethnicity provides ways to better comprehend how the illustrations of the *Relación* served to shape the viceroy's views. These scholars point out that socially constructed classifications help create and shape identities that are class affirming and thus fundamental to acquiring and maintaining political power.[15] In the case of the *Relación*, the images served to allocate desirable attributes to the Uanacaze elite while representing other ethnic groups in less desirable terms. However, ethnic identities had to be carefully crafted, since Don Pedro, a non-Uanacaze noble, occupied the most important political post. His self-image had to be codified in ways that justified his position to the Spanish authorities at the same time that he and the Uanacaze were striving to present a united front against the encroaching interests of the Spaniards in the region.

While the interests of these contributors often come together in the *Relación*, sometimes their differences manifest as incongruities between text and images. Because the images were inserted in the manuscript after the text was completed and highlight different aspects of it, they act upon and create a constant dialogue with it. The text they illustrate provides a way to read the images by helping to convert indigenous concepts into ideas that could have been understood by a colonial audience.

My investigation builds on the work of previous scholars in order to further our understanding of how ethnic differences in the colonial period shaped the images and content of colonial narratives of the pre-Columbian past. Since the *Relación*'s first publication in 1869, it has received copious scholarly attention. Twelve editions, two of which are facsimiles, have made this work widely available. Additionally, the text of the *Relación* has been translated into, and published in, English, French, and Japanese.[16] To date, however, the manuscript has been largely used as a primary source for understanding the pre-Columbian life of the region, serving as a window into pre-Columbian beliefs and practices, history, and socioeconomic organization.[17] When scholars have analyzed the significance of ethnic divisions in the *Relación*, they for the most part have focused on what these divisions reveal about pre-Columbian times. For example, in his study "Los antiguos habitantes de Michoacán," written between 1902 and 1923 but not published until 1960, the Mesoamericanist Eduard Seler used the *Relación*'s text and other colonial-era documents to determine that before the arrival of the Spaniards, the inhabitants of Michoacán had been a multiethnic society governed by the Uanacaze.[18] Following Seler, the anthropologist Paul Kirchhoff wrote an introduction to the 1956 facsimile of the *Relación* in which he divided the characters in the *Relación*'s narrative according to their ethnic affiliations in order to ease our reading of the text.[19]

Since then, the *Relación*'s text has served as a primary ethnohistorical source for studies of P'urhépecha social and ethnic classifications and interactions prior to the conquest.[20] Nevertheless, studies in the last fifteen years have questioned the veracity of the *Relación*'s contents and pointed to the contradictions with the archaeological record.

The archaeologist Dominique Michelet has warned against taking the *Relación* at face value, pointing to the incongruity between the manuscript's "mythical qualities" and modern-day concepts of history.[21] He notes the parallels between the *Relación* and Aztec migration stories, the *Relación*'s deviation of narrative time from "real" time, the unlikely nature of some of the sequences of events, the numerous political interventions of the god Curicaueri, and the moralizing nature of the narrative.[22] However, as the art historian Elizabeth Boone has noted of studies of Nahuatl and Mixtec histories, while the distinction between mythical and historical narratives highlights the discrepancies among modern, colonial, and indigenous notions of history, it obscures the arbitrary nature of our own modern historical practices and implicitly discredits other forms of history.[23] Rather than attempt to investigate the veracity or lack thereof of the *Relación*'s contents, this book aims to investigate the choices the indigenous contributors made in the colonial context.

Over the course of the last fifty years, studies of the *Relación* have begun to shed light on the colonial context of the manuscript's narrative. Scholars such as Cynthia Stone, Hans Roskamp, Miguel León-Portilla, J. Benedict Warren, and Herón Pérez Martínez have focused on the contributions of the Spanish friar and his role as an early ethnographer.[24] Warren has tracked down and identified the friar as Jerónimo de Alcalá.[25] Pérez Martínez and Stone, as well as Moisés Franco Mendoza and Jean Marie Le Clézio, have begun to unravel the relation of the indigenous contributions to the *Relación*'s text to a P'urhépecha oral tradition that survived into the early colonial period.[26] Recently, the historians James Krippner-Martínez and Claudia Espejel Carbajal have begun to inquire about the impact of Spanish practices and beliefs on the contents of the *Relación*.[27] Some scholars, such as Carlos Paredes Martínez and Otto Schöndube, have noted that the *Relación*'s text privileges the history of the larger ethnic group known as Uacúsecha, which, according to Roskamp, would have helped their descendants position themselves advantageously in colonial society.[28] However, how this group's responses to its colonial context shaped the manuscript's text remains to be explored. The contributors to the *Relación* did not belong to one indigenous group but two, a fact that has not been taken into account when analyzing how the manuscript reflects their diverging strategies for accessing colonial authorities.

The images have not received the same kind of critical analysis as the text and are often assumed to simply illustrate it. In the 1956 facsimile edition of the *Relación*, the scholars José Tudela and José Corona Núñez go to great lengths to identify iconographic details in the pictures, correlating them with material culture items such as ceramics and architecture.[29] Anthropologists such as Patricia Anawalt and Helen P. Pollard, in addition to using the images to help interpret archaeological findings, have used them to reconstruct elements of Michoacán's pre-Columbian material culture such as dress, palaces, and tools.[30] While this reciprocity among text, images, and material culture has served to validate the manuscript as a resource for understanding pre-Columbian life, it has tended to obscure the complexity of the situation.

The assumption that the images are only straightforward illustrations of the text has often gone hand in hand with the belief that the artists in Michoacán had had no previous experience in conveying information through images. This derives in part from the friar's prologue to the *Relación*, in which he states that the people of Michoacán lacked books. Whether he meant books using alphabetic writing (as in the case of European books) or pictographic books like those produced in Mesoamerica is not stated, but his assertion was not uncommon in the early sixteenth century. European clergy often failed to see the pictographic writing of Mesoamerican books as a viable source of information because they upheld alphabetic writing as a mark of civilization.[31] The friar's statement has triggered a discussion about whether or not there was a pre-Columbian pictographic writing system in Michoacán and what kinds of writing may have existed there.[32] This debate, however, has contributed little to our understanding of the *Relación*'s images as products of the colonial period.

The belief that during the colonial period the artists of the *Relación* lacked visual literacy has meant that until now little agency has been attributed to them. Their ability to make choices and encode complex thoughts in their visual imagery has gone unrecognized for the most part. In the influential 1956 edition of the *Relación*, José Tudela, who praises the manuscript's illustrations for their innovative qualities, nevertheless characterizes them as "childlike" and "without tricks or conventions that are preestablished or inherited."[33] Although scholars have criticized this paternalistic approach, they continue to perceive the images as lacking complexity.

In a recent study of the images and their relevance to the pictographic tradition in Michoacán, Juan José Batalla Rosado concludes that even though the images include some pre-Columbian Mesoamerican iconographic conventions, such as footprints representing movement and direction of travel, they do not contain logosyllabic writing. He therefore concludes that in Michoacán more complex thoughts must have been transmitted orally.[34] Similarly, Nora Jiménez, who fails to see any phonetic or logographic information in the *Relación*'s paintings, concludes that they serve only to illustrate the text.[35]

Rather than analyze the images as anachronistic tools for understanding the pictographic writing of the pre-Columbian period, I propose to look at them as colonial products, the result of the artists' deliberate selections from a repertoire of both European and Mesoamerican motifs, formats, and illusionistic techniques made to convey rich meanings and encode complex thoughts. Scholars have long recognized that in other parts of Mesoamerica, pre-Columbian and early colonial pictographic writing and visual imagery encoded many layers of information about religious, sociopolitical, and economic practices. Mesoamerican artists did not necessarily make clear-cut distinctions between "art" in the European sense of the word and what we call writing.[36] Boone has pointed out that recording speech was often not the goal in Mesoamerican writing systems of the sixteenth century; rather, Mesoamerican pictography expressed complex ideas that were represented either directly or through abstract conventions.[37] Since for the most part there is no dependency on sound in these visual representations, they have the ability to cross language and ethnic barriers.

Although, as was the case for the Aztec-dominated Valley of Mexico, no known pre-Columbian illustrated manuscripts survive from Michoacán, indigenous pictographic writing was commonly known and widely used during the colonial period. Archival documents reveal that indigenous nobles from Michoacán presented *pinturas* (paintings) depicting tribute, territories, and historical information to prove their claims before the Spanish authorities. Most of these paintings no longer exist, but accounts of them can be found in the court records now housed in Mexican and Spanish archives.[38]

The existence of these colonial documents is significant not only because they attest to pictographic literacy in Michoacán but also because they reveal that this system shared elements with other writing systems in Mesoamerica. This is not to say that no iconographic differences existed between P'urhépecha and other Mesoamerican writing systems. Rather, it is to point out that they must have shared enough elements to be read across cultural and language barriers. In a court case from the 1550s, for example, the plaintiff, who was Don Pedro's son, presented as evidence a painting, now lost, that several indigenous witnesses "read" at trial. If witnesses did not speak Spanish, somebody else translated their testimony in P'urhépecha or Nahuatl into Spanish, and a scribe recorded it. Thus, speakers of both P'urhépecha and Nahuatl could "read" the same painting even though the verbal form of their reading varied linguistically.[39]

Recent approaches have gone beyond a literal and iconographic reading of the images of the *Relación*. Roskamp has looked at some of the iconography used in the images and their parallels with Mesoamerican writing systems, pointing to some of the more complex ideas the artists may have represented.[40] Stone, taking a structuralist approach, has interpreted the images as "echoing" a pre-Columbian cosmovision organized according to principles of duality and a belief in an axis mundi. Stone has ignored, however, the fact that some of the images show evidence of European prototypes. Furthermore, she has interpreted the illustrations without reference to the text they accompany.[41] On the other end of the spectrum, Espejel Carbajal has claimed that none of its iconographic elements can be safely attributed to a pre-Columbian tradition. She sees the illustrations as representing a solely Spanish pictographic system.[42] The range of the interpretations offered by these scholars signals the difficulty in recognizing the variety of sources that the artists drew upon, as well as understanding the motives behind their choices.

Rather than look at the images as repositories of one tradition to the exclusion of another, I look at what the adaptation of aspects of both pre-Columbian and European pictorial traditions reveals about the interests of and strategies employed by the two indigenous ethnic groups involved in the making of the *Relación*. Most of the surviving illustrations of the *Relación* deal with ethno-political conflicts that took place before the arrival of the Europeans. Yet how the political motives of the indigenous artists working during the colonial period shaped those images remains to be explored. My work goes beyond previous scholarship by analyzing the images within the context of archival colonial documents to reveal the conflicts that engulfed the indigenous collaborators. The *Relación* provides an important opportunity for study because its indigenous collaborators represented the interests of two distinct indigenous ethnic groups.

My analysis attempts more than this, however. It also shows how the contributors to the *Relación* shaped its images to make them understandable to its intended recipient. This necessitates discussion of the challenges Spaniards faced in Michoacán during the early colonial period; for example, this area did not have a homogeneous population. Numerous ethnic groups lived in the Lake Pátzcuaro area. The region was multilingual, with Nahuatl, Otomí, and P'urhépecha speakers often struggling for resources and political leverage, as shown across the pages of archival records.[43] By the onset of the colonial period, the Uanacaze ruled over communities described by the *Relación* as enemies conquered during pre-Columbian times.[44] Furthermore, the Spanish conquest and colonization efforts had fomented the relocation of indigenous populations, many of which had traveled with the Spaniards as allies in the war of conquest.

Colonial documents attest to mixed populations within individual towns but also to Nahua and Otomí settlements whose populations were homogeneous.[45] People with Nahuatl names abound in court records: they are listed as *caciques* (chiefs), noblemen and noblewomen, sculptors, interpreters, and employees of the church.[46] Many of them played key roles during the early colonial period and formed powerful, yet shifting, alliances.[47] It is not always easy to decipher the tensions that existed among these groups because the Spanish Crown had ordered, although this was not always observed, that no legal procedures were to take place among the indigenous peoples. The latter, in turn, often preferred to keep the Spaniards out of their affairs.[48]

To make matters even more complex, Spaniards sometimes appointed indigenous town authorities from different ethnic groups, thus altering preexisting hierarchies.[49] Spaniards also encroached on indigenous lands and placed pressure on limited resources and labor. Indigenous nobles from different groups found themselves having to form unexpected alliances both among themselves and with some Spaniards to fight other Spaniards. The *Relación* provides a unique view on how some of these alliances played out during the colonial period and on how ethnic identities were represented and mobilized.

The circumstances that first brought the Spanish viceroy to Michoacán speak to the context in which the *Relación* was conceived. According to the historian J. Benedict Warren, the viceroy presumably commissioned the manuscript on December 31, 1539, during his first visit to Tzintzuntzan in order to settle an intense legal dispute involving the Spanish Crown, Spanish settlers, the newly appointed bishop, and several members of the indigenous nobility of Michoacán.[50] This dispute, several years in the making, was centered on the distribution of *encomiendas* (allocations of indigenous labor and its products), which often brought to the forefront the interests of various Spaniards and the indigenous nobility.

Tzintzuntzan, which was also called the City of Michoacán and the City of Uchichila in sixteenth-century documents, was at first the encomienda of Hernán Cortés, but in 1528 it passed into the hands of the Crown. Encomienda distributions were based on geopolitical units (i.e., towns, *barrios* [wards], etc.), but little is understood of the City of Michoacán's geographical limits. The indigenous nobility and their Spanish supporters would argue that it covered the entire lake basin and its islands and had been the Uanacaze ruler's *señorío* (kingdom).[51] On the other side, Spanish *encomenderos* (holders of an encomienda grant), who were quickly encroaching on the basin and its islands, would argue that the indigenous settlements around and on the lake were independent of the city and therefore part of their own encomiendas.[52] The conflicts between the indigenous nobility and the encomenderos escalated over the years, even leading to armed conflict and the trial and execution in 1530 of the Uanacaze ruler Zinzicha Tangaxuan. Under Cortés's administration, Tangaxuan had been allowed to continue as lord of the region as long as he did not collect tribute for himself. Under the Crown this arrangement was kept, since, at least in principle, the Crown respected the privileges and territory of indigenous rulers, although it reserved jurisdiction for itself.[53] Yet when Nuño de Guzmán, president of the Primera Real Audiencia (First Royal Audience), the highest judiciary body in the colonies, took Tangaxuan and other nobles prisoner for the purpose of obtaining their gold, the encomenderos took advantage of the nobles' absence by extending their own encomienda boundaries. Eventually, they would accuse Tangaxuan of obstructing their work, and in 1530, the First Royal Audience would convict Tangaxuan of idolatry, sodomy, collecting tribute, interfering with the work of Spaniards, and even killing some of them. Nuño de Guzmán sentenced Tangaxuan to death and seized his land and worldly possessions to pay for the trial, allocating the remainder to the Spanish Crown.[54]

After Tangaxuan's death, the Islander Don Pedro, who had provided the most incriminating testimony against Tangaxuan in his trial, became governor of the city, as previously mentioned. This unprecedented situation would create many tensions between Don Pedro and the Uanacaze heirs. Nevertheless, they had to come together to defend common interests. Regarding territorial claims, Don Pedro would have to defend the integrity of the physical boundaries of the City of Michoacán to maintain his own privileges as its governor. To keep the basin and its islands together, he and the Uanacaze nobles would call it Tangaxuan's señorío in order to keep it under the jurisprudence of the Crown.

By 1539, thousands of court folios had been produced around these conflicts. All sides had presented witnesses, paintings, and legal arguments. In October of that year, the conflict escalated almost to point of an armed confrontation between a particular encomendero by the name of Juan Infante and the indigenous nobility supported by Bishop Vasco de Quiroga. The viceroy had traveled to Michoacán in hopes of settling this dispute and most likely during this visit commissioned the *Relación*. To the indigenous nobility and its supporters, the making of the *Relación* presented a unique opportunity to speak directly to the viceroy and present their claims of legitimacy as rulers over the region.

This book explores how the *Relación*'s indigenous contributors made use of such an opportunity. Chapter 1 examines how the manuscript was made and what this process reveals about the relationship between the viceroy, the friar, the indigenous nobility, and the indigenous painters. The *Relación* contains several emendations, including images inserted where none was originally intended. These emendations reveal the aspects of the narrative that the friar and artists sought to highlight, as well as the discrepancies among some of their intentions.

Through the analysis of court documents, I have been able to determine that indigenous artists enjoyed many favors from the Uanacaze family, such as paid servants and free goods. Not surprisingly, in return artists painted maps representing land limits, genealogies, and historical events that were used in colonial courts to defend the privileges of the indigenous nobility. This relationship of mutual dependency joined the interests of the Uanacaze to those of the artists, making visual imagery the political medium by which the former legitimated their interests.

Chapters 2 through 6 are organized thematically around a selection of images from the *Relación*. They investigate how indigenous artists used representations of justice and history to re-create the identity of the indigenous nobility during the colonial period. Since much of the *Relación* focuses on the Uanacaze conquering and overcoming other indigenous ethnic groups, the construction of ethnic identity is central to the manuscript.

Chapter 2 explores paintings of the administration of justice in the *Relación* and the function of the body in sixteenth-century Michoacán. In these images, the artists used the body to represent the individual's relationship to society. Punishments focus on specific body parts to mark transgressions against the Uanacaze social system. In these scenes, the Uanacaze, with a governor as their intermediary, penalize crimes such as adultery and witchcraft, which were strongly condemned in the eyes of Spaniards. In this way, these scenes present the Uanacaze as the moral choice for rulership in the region, while including the non-Uanacaze governor (i.e., Don Pedro) within that judicial hierarchy and justifying his post.

In Chapter 3, I study the visual representation of landscape in part 2 of the *Relación*, which narrates the conquest of the region by the Uanacaze and their allies. In these scenes, the artists represent landscape by combining European Renaissance conventions for realism, such as one-point perspective, with indigenous pictographic conventions, such as toponyms. In this way, the artists presented a landscape that was readable to European eyes and simultaneously evoked a sense of authenticity and insider knowledge. Through this valuable visual strategy the artists represented the Lake Pátzcuaro basin as a unified region while tying it specifically to the Uanacaze and their allies' rise to power. Ultimately, this visual strategy legitimized the indigenous administration of the region while countering the interests of Spaniards.

Chapter 4 studies the Uanacaze reconstruction of their identity to conform to a Christian paradigm. The artists included images that represented the Uanacaze's Chichimec ethnicity in terms of Christian motifs and Christian values. Many of the traits generally associated with Chichimec behavior, such as hunting and an austere life, were reconstituted to be aligned with the new Christian norms. The viceroy could have easily recognized the moral qualities required of rulers in the Uanacaze lineage. Furthermore, the artists carefully selected scenes in which the new Chichimec identity could be contrasted with the lax behavior of non-Uanacaze peoples. In order to explain the place of Don Pedro in this moral/ethnic dichotomy, however, he had to be defined as a servant to the Uanacaze's interests and as an intermediary between the ruler and the new colonial order.

In Chapter 5, I analyze the image in the *Relación* based on the European Tree of Jesse, a common European motif used to diagram the genealogy of Christ, to demonstrate that indigenous artists used European prototypes in their capacity not only of encoding indigenous beliefs but also of serving the nobility's political needs. By using a European motif, the artist could communicate clearly and effectively with the manuscript's European audience. The artist substituted the Uanacaze genealogy for that of Christ, presenting their heirs as the legitimate rulers of the region.

Chapter 6 analyzes the ethnographic image depicting a ruler's funeral. My research shows that contrary to what at first may seem to be an objective and generalized representation, this painting responds to a specific circumstance, that is, the death of the Uanacaze ruler at the height of Uanacaze political domination in the region. In this image, the artist made careful use of body paints and clothing to differentiate the ancestors of the *Relación*'s collaborators. While the Uanacaze ancestors are dressed as upstanding Chichimec warriors, have their bodies painted in black pigment, and are represented as the unmistakable successors to the throne, Don Pedro's ancestors sport yellow body paint and are sacrificed to serve the Uanacaze ruler for eternity. In other words, while Don Pedro, a non-Uanacaze nobleman, had come to occupy the highest political post after the death of the Uanacaze ruler in the aftermath of the conquest, the artist shows that the *rightful* successor should have been a member of the Uanacaze family, more specifically, the ruler's son. Upon the death of Don Pedro Cuiniarangari, a year or two after the *Relación* was completed, the viceroy gave the governorship of the area to the Uanacaze heirs.

The way the manuscript was made, the selection of images, and the relationship of the images to the text reveal the collaboration between the Spanish friar and the native narrators and artists in creating knowledge for this region. In the course of representing the past, the artists became agents in constructing the new colonial order. They transformed a vision of the past to present the Uanacaze as the preferred choice for rulership over all of the other ethnic groups in the region. At the same time, they justified the Islander Don Pedro's position as governor in order to present a united indigenous front before colonial authorities. By carefully selecting and adapting European and pre-Columbian motifs, the artists made their claims in ways that would have been understandable to the manuscript's European audience, particularly Viceroy Antonio de Mendoza. They used the images to counter the interests of those Spaniards who were encroaching on the ways of life and resources of people living in the Lake Pátzcuaro basin.

1

The Making and the Makers of the Relación de Michoacán

Turning the honey-colored leather cover that binds the *Relación* today reveals carefully written text and delicately executed images on select papers imported from Europe to the colonies. On the frontispiece an artist envisioned, before the fact, the presentation of the manuscript to the viceroy (fig. 1; see plate 1).[1] A barefoot friar, accompanied by a group of four indigenous men, hands over a manuscript to a bearded viceroy, who wears a robe with the cross of the Order of Santiago. The friar wears a long brown robe cinched at the waist by a cord with three knots, indicating he belongs to the Franciscan Order. A nobleman wearing a short green robe with a ruffled collar, tights, a turquoise-blue lip plug, a hat with a small fish on it, and black shoes stands behind the Franciscan friar. Directly behind the nobleman, three indigenous men stand wearing brown robes and carrying staffs in their hands and gourds on their backs. In the upper right-hand corner of the frontispiece, behind the viceroy, stands a figure with short hair and wearing a long red robe. After the artist had completed this figure, he decided to cover it with a green leaf-patterned square that resembles a wall hanging. Chips of green pigment falling off the manuscript have revealed its hidden secret.

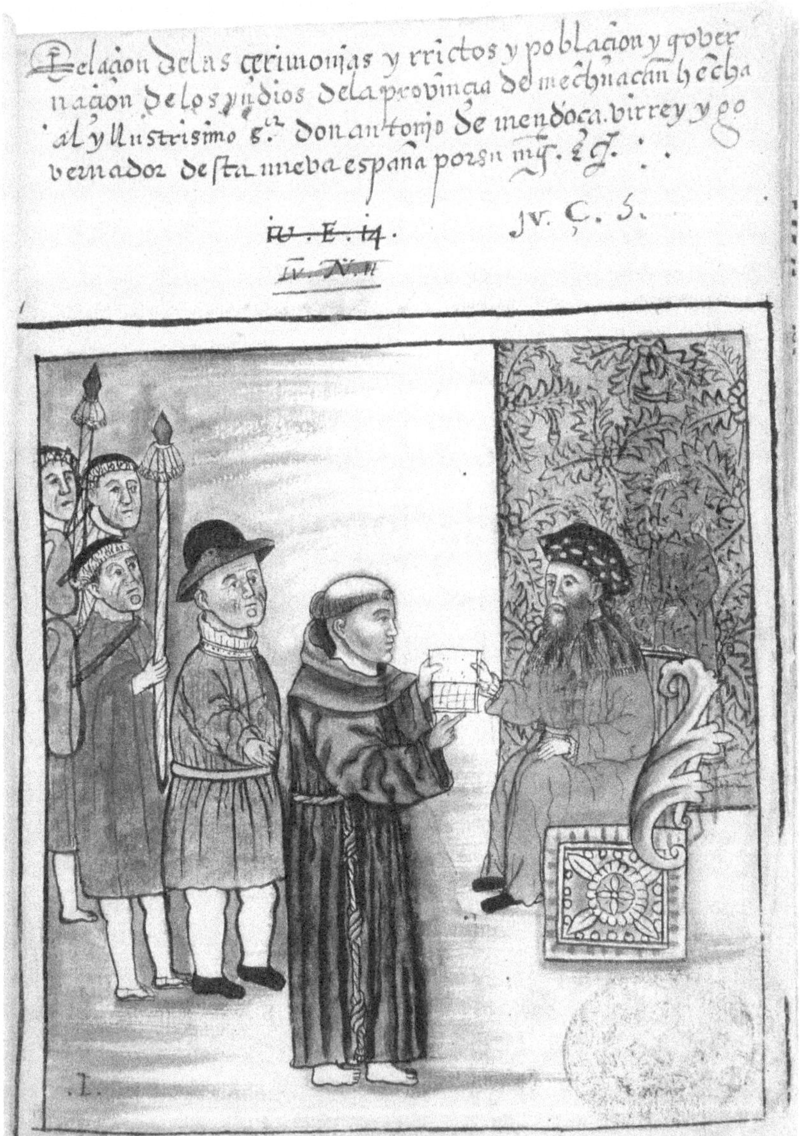

FIGURE 1. Artist 1. *Relación de las ceremonias y ritos y población y gobernación de los indios de la provincia de Michoacán*, fol. 1r, frontispiece. Real Biblioteca del Monasterio de El Escorial, San Lorenzo de El Escorial, Spain, C IV 5. Photograph © Patrimonio Nacional, Spain.

Even if a projection into the future, the frontispiece not only reveals part of the process of creation but also provides the artist's view about who the contributors to the *Relación* may have been. Even though the prologue of the *Relación* explains the manuscript was produced at the incentive of the viceroy and coordinated by the Spanish friar, much can be learned about the surviving version of the manuscript by examining the different hands that shaped it and studying the sociopolitical position of the painters and their possible connection to the indigenous elite of the area. This chapter studies the process through which the images were created and seeks to provide a framework for analyzing them in relationship to the artists' agency. To this end, I study the production of the manuscript, and the images in particular, in relation to the interests of the artists and of others who collaborated in the making of the manuscript.

Modern scholarship has often focused on the identity of the anonymous friar, his role, and the way his work fits in with similar ethnographic enterprises of the colonial period. Some early candidates included Bernardino de Sahagún, Martín Jesús de la Coruña, and Maturino Gilberti.[2] Most recently, through painstaking archival research, J. Benedict Warren has identified him as a little-known Franciscan, Jerónimo de Alcalá. According to Warren, Alcalá first lived at the Franciscan convent in Tzintzuntzan, and when the political and ecclesiastical capital moved from Tzintzuntzan to Pátzcuaro in 1538, he moved there.[3] Alcalá later accompanied Viceroy Mendoza to the Mixtón War in 1541.[4]

Viceroy Mendoza has also received considerable attention in scholarly circles. Several books have been dedicated to his function as viceroy, his life, and legacy. Mendoza's commissioning of the *Relación* speaks in part to his aristocratic upbringing and his duties as viceroy.[5] He was part of a powerful Castilian family renowned as book lovers, art patrons, and collectors. He had been appointed first viceroy of New Spain and president of its First Royal Audience on April 17, 1535. New to his job and this part of the world, he had to figure out how to govern the indigenous peoples of New Spain. The viceroy was responsible for spreading the Catholic faith, policing and regulating conduct, maintaining peace, overseeing regional governments, and developing the colonial economy.[6] He had to navigate the many disputes between the indigenous people and the different factions of Spaniards living there. He also had to combat indigenous uprisings west of Michoacán, particularly in the Mixtón War. The manuscript would have provided valuable information to this novice viceroy.

Although Mendoza had only recently arrived in New Spain, he was not unfamiliar with multicultural societies. His grandfather and father had fought the Moorish government in Granada, and, once Granada had been conquered, his father had been named mayor of the Alhambra and captain general of Granada. Granada was a diverse city with a Moorish, Jewish, and Christian population. Mendoza grew up watching his father govern this polyglot and multifaith population.[7] He also witnessed his father's evangelization efforts with the assistance of the Franciscan Order.[8] Not surprisingly, the viceroy chose a Franciscan friar to assist him in collecting information from such a sensitive region. Mendoza's role as the patron and audience of the manuscript invited the self-interest of its other participants. This added layers of complexity to his request.

For the Franciscan, the commission to assemble the *Relación* was an opportunity to find favor in the eyes of the viceroy. In part 1 of the *Relación*, the friar placed himself and his order at the center of the viceroy's evangelization efforts by documenting religious practices as a means of eradicating them.[9] In fact, the literary scholar Cynthia Stone has pointed out that the friar's edits to the text often highlight the role of missionaries, and his order in particular, in introducing the Christian faith to the region.

The friar promoted the Franciscan Order's role in evangelization efforts and made it known that the order and he were willing to cooperate with civil authorities. The Franciscans' relationship with members of the colonial government had not always been the best and included heated confrontations with Nuño de Guzmán, who had preceded Mendoza as president of the First Royal Audience.[10] The friar's collaboration with Mendoza was a way to improve relationships with civic authorities. Through the text, as Stone has pointed out, the friar became an intermediary, a cultural interpreter of the history, behaviors, and practices of the people of Michoacán. The viceroy was to govern the people of Michoacán through and by means of the friar's knowledge.

The friar, as a European man of letters, also lent legitimacy to the indigenous account. First he converted what were once oral and possibly pictorial histories into a narrative that could be written down using alphabetic script. He also helped shape this account in ways that made sense, or "spoke," to a European audience.[11] For example, while he explains in the introduction to part 2 of the *Relación* that all events and wars were attributed to the Uanacaze god Curicaueri, in the main body of the text they are usually attributed to rulers and noblemen.[12] In addition, by adding glosses, titles, and corrections, the friar showed his approval of the manuscript's contents each step along the way.

In order to compile the information for the manuscript, the friar worked with indigenous collaborators. Unlike Mendoza and Alcalá, little is known about them. The text of the *Relación* provides scant—and sometimes contradictory—information about who these men may have been. The friar explains that his informants were indigenous *viejos* (elders), even though he complains there were almost no viejos alive in this region. He mentions only one by name, Don Pedro Cuiniarangari, the indigenous governor at the time the *Relación* was compiled. In acknowledging his own role, the friar humbly (or coyly) states that he submits the manuscript in the name of the viejos and that he is only their translator.

Selecting whom to work with must have been a careful and highly strategic decision. This was the friar's opportunity to consolidate alliances with powerful indigenous nobles. Indigenous people had almost succeeded in expelling the Franciscans from Michoacán before, and given the tensions between the Franciscan Order and Spanish civil authorities, careful negotiations were in order. According to the historian Mary Ann Hedberg, conflicts among Spaniards would often be resolved on the basis of who could negotiate better with indigenous people.[13] Furthermore, much of the land in central Michoacán remained in the hands of the indigenous nobility, who gathered and administered the labor and resources to build convents, churches, and other religious structures.[14] The friar's personal success, like that of his order in the region, depended on his ability to negotiate with the indigenous elite.

In choosing to work with a particular group of nobles, he was also supporting their interests. This would not be the only time Alcalá had chosen to support them. During the heated encomienda dispute between Tzintzuntzan's nobles, Bishop Vasco de Quiroga, and encomendero Juan Infante, Alcalá served as translator to cross-examine the indigenous witnesses presented by Infante because the Tzintzuntzan's nobles and Quiroga argued that Infante's witnesses and translators were not reliable.[15]

Although the friar names only the Islander Don Pedro, he also worked with elders representing the interests of the Uanacaze, thus collecting the testimonies of at least two ethnic groups. Previous scholars have pointed out that Don Pedro may be represented on the frontispiece as the man standing directly behind the friar, wearing a lip plug, Spanish clothing, and on his hat sporting a small fish, possibly denoting that he is an Islander, since in the *Relación* the Islanders introduce fish to the Uanacaze diet. The other contributors are possibly represented by the three elderly men wearing brown tunics and carrying gourds and staffs. During the colonial period, the staff identified indigenous men who worked closely with the Catholic Church, helping in the process of evangelization by teaching Christian doctrine and denouncing sins.[16] The gourd and staff may also indicate that they had served as the main Uanacaze priests before the arrival of Europeans, since these are some of the accoutrements that those priests carry in other images in the *Relación* (fig. 2; see plate 2).

The relationship between Don Pedro and the Uanacaze and their supporters rippled with tensions. Some of these tensions were based on pre-Columbian precedents. According to part 2 of the *Relación*, the Islanders had previously dominated the islands and basin of Lake Pátzcuaro but had been conquered by the Uanacaze, possibly as far back as the fourteenth century. Part 2 presented the Uanacaze as the legitimate ruling house.

During the colonial period, not only did these groups continue to distinguish themselves from one another but their divisions seem to have played a significant role in the outcome of events and the ways in which indigenous people viewed and recounted them. Don Pedro claimed in the *Relación* that he had facilitated the peaceful submission of the area to Spanish forces in the 1520s and had saved the Uanacaze ruler Tangaxuan from drowning himself in the waters of Lake Pátzcuaro in despair. Yet in 1530, on the shores of the Lerma River, Don Pedro provided the most incriminating testimony during Tangaxuan's trial, which resulted in the ruler's execution.[17] Also in the *Relación*, he would later maintain that none of the indigenous witnesses testified against their ruler, thus reinforcing his own loyalty. When Don Pedro returned to the City of Michoacán from this ordeal, he did so as the city's governor.

Given this situation, it may be difficult to imagine how the Uanacaze and Don Pedro could have worked together on the *Relación*. Key to understanding their collaboration is the fact that the *Relación* was being produced for the viceroy. At this very moment in history, the indigenous nobility of the City of Michoacán had to present a united front to fight the encroachment of Spanish encomenderos. Uanacaze nobles depended on Don Pedro, as the current governor, to protect their land. Don Pedro had to justify his role and present the legitimacy of his authority before the newly appointed viceroy. These various tensions play out in the subtext of the manuscript as well as in its images.

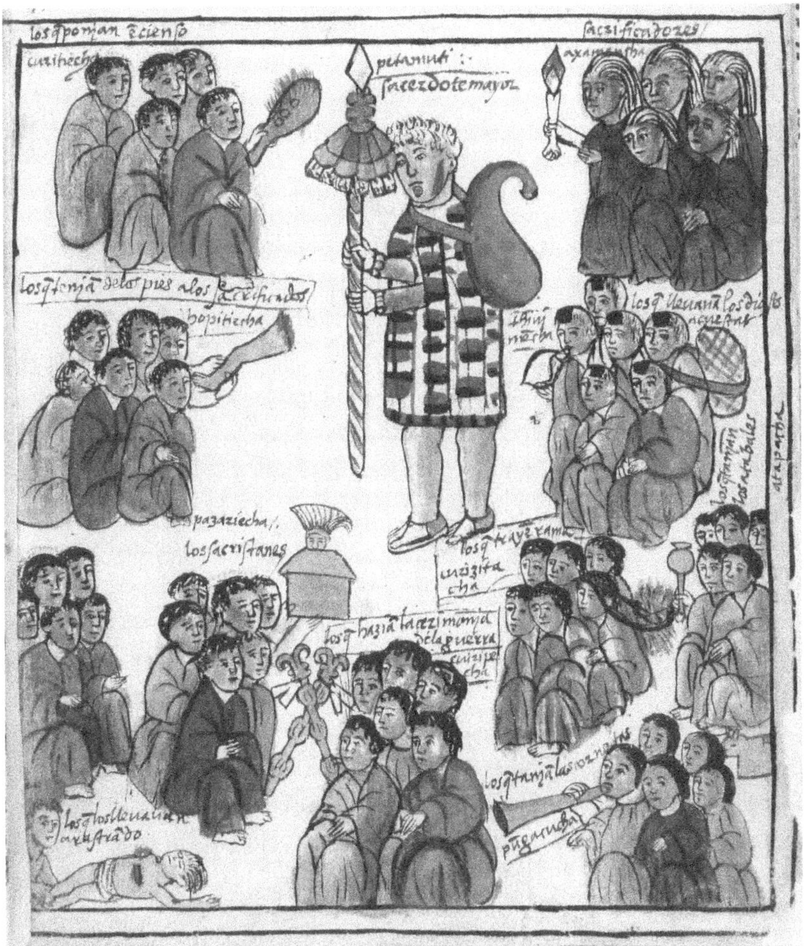

FIGURE 2. Artist 1. "Estos son los sacerdotes officiales de los cúes" (These are the official priests of the temples). *Relación de Michoacán*, fol. 9r. Real Biblioteca del Monasterio de El Escorial, San Lorenzo de El Escorial, Spain, C IV 5. Photograph © Patrimonio Nacional, Spain.

Don Pedro and his contribution to the *Relación* have puzzled scholars for some time. Warren has characterized him as a traitor, based on the incriminating testimony he provided during the trial of the Uanacaze ruler. In analyzing the text of the *Relación*, Stone has interpreted Don Pedro's contribution as both a message to the viceroy and as a public speech he would have given to the indigenous nobility. To the viceroy, Stone argues, Don Pedro presents himself as an intermediary between the Spaniards and the Uanacaze ruler, and to the indigenous nobility, he explains the difficulties he faced at the onset of the Spanish invasion and apologizes for his role in the execution of the ruler.

While Don Pedro may have represented himself as an intermediary official, one must note that in 1530, when the Uanacaze ruler Tangaxuan was executed, the post of governor of the City of Michoacán became the most significant position held by an indigenous nobleman in the region.[18] The city was a vast territory that included neighborhoods and subject towns around the Lake Pátzcuaro basin. At the time the *Relación* was compiled, Don Pedro was between forty and forty-seven years of age and one of the most powerful men in Michoacán.[19] In addition to being governor, he was captain of the indigenous army.[20] When a new Franciscan convent was built in Tzintzuntzan in 1535, he supervised its construction.[21] He had even eventually married several of Tangaxuan's widows. Since Don Pedro administered much of the labor and land of the region, it was in the friar's best interest to reinforce his alliance with the indigenous governor.

Spaniards were not blind to the ethnic and political differences that divided indigenous groups in Michoacán. Nuño de Guzmán would claim in his *Memoria* that after Tangaxuan's death, he had given back the governorship of all towns in Michoacán to the people who had governed them before the Uanacaze conquered them.[22] Given that Don Pedro descended from Islander nobility, he would have fallen within that category. By 1539–1541, when the *Relación* was produced, Guzmán had fallen out of the good graces of the Spanish Crown and had been removed from his post. For the new viceroy, lineage, as in his own case, would have played a more significant role in the selection of officials. For these reasons, Don Pedro was left to justify his position as Islander and governor. At the same time, Don Pedro had to fight the encroachment of Spaniards in the region. His contribution to the manuscript can be analyzed as the strategic defense of his post and actions but also as an attempt to show a united front with the Uanacaze in order to combat Spanish interests.

The relationship between Don Pedro and the Uanacaze heirs deserves some attention. Scholars have often believed Don Pedro was intended to serve as governor until Tangaxuan's children reached their age of majority.[23] However, by 1541 the eldest son, Don Francisco Tariacuri, was at or was nearing that age.[24] By April 20, 1542, Don Francisco was already married and owned land, the two prerequisites for reaching the age of majority. He had already fought successfully to recoup lands and jewels that once had belonged to his family.[25] He had even presented a *probanza*—a document explaining his worth and merits in order to receive royal grants—which generally took several months to prepare. Additionally, in 1543 Don Francisco presented a petition (including a painting) to Viceroy Mendoza to recoup land that, according to him, Don Pedro had "usurped."[26] His desire to reverse Don Pedro's actions, as well as his accusation of usurpation, reveals the tensions that existed between the Uanacaze heirs and Don Pedro. However, the Uanacaze heirs also had to present a united front with Don Pedro, who in court was defending Tangaxuan's señorío as a way to preserve indigenous sovereignty over the City of Michoacán.

It is possible that these young nobles also contributed to the making of the *Relación*. Don Francisco and his brother Don Antonio Huitzimengari are mentioned by name and depicted in it, and documentary evidence locates them in the same place and time as the production of the manuscript. Stone has proposed that the figure that once stood next to the viceroy and was later covered by the wall hanging, shown in figure 1, may represent one of the Uanacaze heirs, based on the similarities between it and these two heirs depicted in a genealogical tree included later in the *Relación*. Furthermore, the tree presents them as next in line to Tangaxuan to rule.

The privileged position of these heirs in the manuscript may at least in part be explained by their possible affiliation with the other contributors. We know that Don Francisco and Don Antonio had been schooled at the convent in Tzintzuntzan when Jerónimo de Alcalá was there.[27] They had served as pages to Viceroy Mendoza. And at least Don Francisco had accompanied the viceroy to the Mixtón War.[28] The brothers also moved to Pátzcuaro along with the other political and ecclesiastic authorities, and Don Antonio attended the Colegio de Pátzcuaro.[29] This sequence of circumstances places them at the same locations where the manuscript would have been produced and, together with their proximity to the viceroy, could explain their privileged inclusion in the *Relación*'s images.

The affiliations of some of the other contributors can be deduced from the contents of the manuscript. According to the friar, part 2 of the *Relación* is based on a speech given by the main indigenous priest, or *petamuti* (pl. *petamutiecha*). The petamuti speaks in the name of the Uanacaze tutelary god Curicaueri. The Franciscan friar's voice interferes only occasionally and only to explain or highlight certain things. It is likely that the words spoken by the petamuti are based on a speech or speeches given by several elderly informants (i.e., the elderly men represented in the frontispiece and Don

Pedro). The petamuti is thus a composite character, a literary device that enables the consolidation of multiple views. In his speech, the petamuti identifies the Uanacaze as the legitimate rulers of the region; therefore, it would have been most beneficial to the Uanacaze heirs (e.g., Don Francisco Tariacuri and Don Antonio Huitzimengari) and to those with close ties to them.

It is difficult to know who were the elders giving the speech. Warren has mentioned that some of them may have included nobles and *naguatlatos* (translators of Nahuatl), who figure so prominently in court cases.[30] This may account for the presence of Nahuatl words and names in the *Relación*.[31] I have also been able to locate the names of two indigenous governors of the City of Michoacán before 1540, who may have contributed to the *Relación*.[32] One was Don Alonso de Ávalos, named Acanyçante in P'urhépecha, and the other was known only as Don Francisco. Acanyçante had been translator for the viceroy and for the Uanacaze ruler Tangaxuan before his death. He had accompanied Tangaxuan during his ordeal with Nuño de Guzmán and during the subsequent trial. Acanyçante was one of the few noblemen who, even under severe torture, did not testify against him.[33]

During Tangaxuan's trial, Don Pedro, under torture, had accused Acanyçante of dancing in the skins of Christians who had been sacrificed, an accusation that could have cost Acanyçante his life.[34] It seems that in spite of the seriousness of the accusations and their underlying causes, these men had to overcome their differences for the sake of the creation of the *Relación*. Acanyçante's contribution is apparent in Don Pedro's account of the events that led to the Uanacaze ruler's death. According to Don Pedro, during the few instances when he left Tangaxuan's side, Acanyçante stayed with him. In Don Pedro's account, Tangaxuan speaks to Acanyçante; but given that Don Pedro was not present, Tangaxuan's words must have survived only as told by Acanyçante.

After Tangaxuan's death, Acanyçante returned to Michoacán, where he served as governor until Don Pedro, who was being held by Nuño de Guzmán, returned from his ordeal.[35] Acanyçante continued to have much sway in the City of Michoacán and often defended the interests of Tangaxuan's children, to the extent that in 1532 he was accused of lying to Spanish authorities in order to do so.[36] Acanyçante also worked in the convent at Tzintzuntzan, where Jerónimo de Alcalá resided for a period of time.

The record does not provide Don Francisco's full name, but it is possible that he, too, contributed to the making of the manuscript. He could have been one Don Francisco, the legal representative of the Uanacaze heir, who is mentioned in a document from 1530, or even the heir himself, who was named Don Francisco Tariacuri.[37]

Presumably, then, Don Pedro, the Uanacaze heirs, and various elders and/or other members of the nobility, with all of their conflicting interests, narrated the history of the region in the voice of a single, anonymous Uanacaze petamuti. Through this voice they invoked the legitimacy of the Uanacaze and their right to rule and at the same time made room to explain Don Pedro's position.

Once the friar collected the information from them, and possibly from previously written sources, he and possibly five scribes wrote from one to several drafts, then transcribed the text into what is now the surviving version of the *Relación*.[38] The process of copying from a previous version of the existing *Relación* can be appreciated in folios 71r and 90v, in which the scribes began to copy text that had already been transcribed. Realizing their mistakes, the scribes covered with white wash the duplicated text and proceeded to rewrite the text at the appropriate place in the narrative. The differences in handwriting styles suggest that most likely five scribes worked on copying the contents of the manuscript. Scribe 1 copied the prologue, and scribe 2 copied the sole surviving page from part 1. Scribes 3 and 4 copied part 2, leaving space for only a few images. Then scribe 5 copied part 3, leaving spaces for images below the titles of almost every chapter.

In the pages that survive, the process of creation emerges not as monolithic or linear but rather as one in which meaning was revised multiple times as the *Relación* was produced and altered by its various contributors. After the scribes of the *Relación* had finished transcribing the text, the friar embarked on a careful editorial process, presumably with the assistance of the artists. First, he read the text and made some corrections to it.[39] Then, he went back and decided to make room for a few images. A white wash was then carefully applied over the titles of selected chapters. The editorial hand rewrote them, carefully creating an empty space between them and the text immediately following so that small images could be painted directly below the titles. From what can be seen, the new titles were identical—or at least very close—to the original ones, but their new placement allowed them to function simultaneously as titles of both the images and the chapters. This, in many cases, dictated the content of the illustrations and has often shaped the viewer's interpretation of them. The artists painted small scenes in the new spaces, as well as in some spaces the scribes left blank at the end of the chapters.

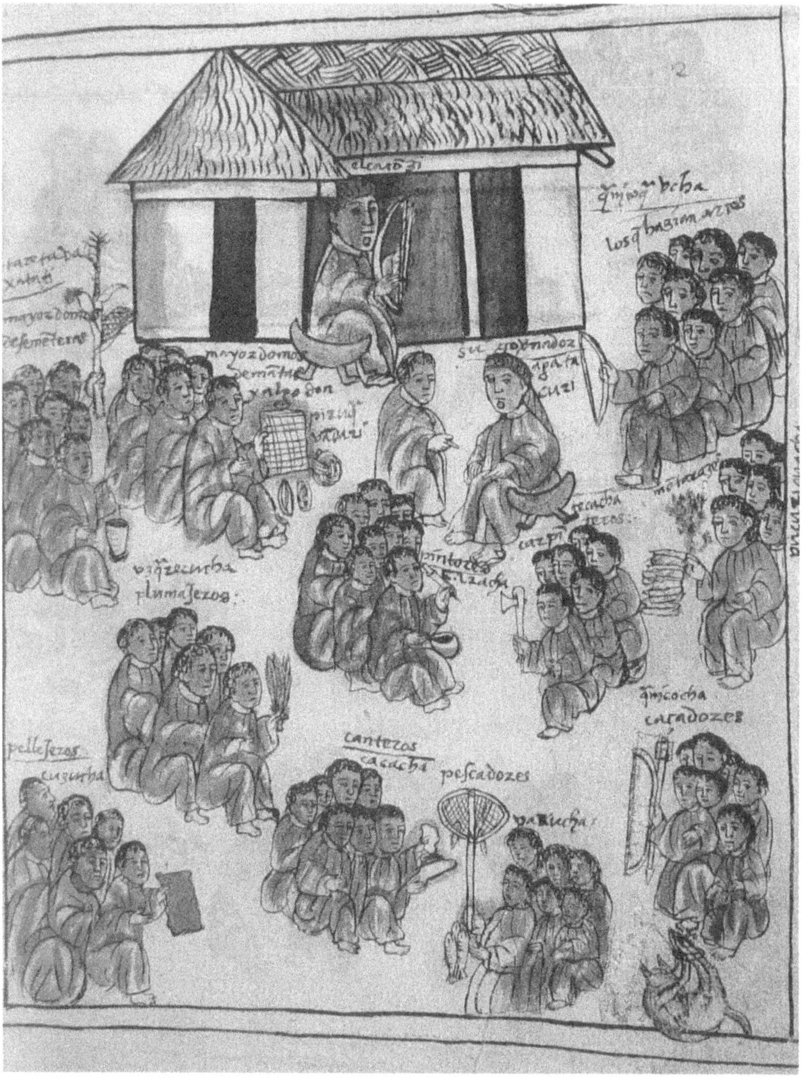

FIGURE 3. Artist 1. *Relación de Michoacán*, fol. 5r. Real Biblioteca del Monasterio de El Escorial, San Lorenzo de El Escorial, Spain, C IV 5. Photograph © Patrimonio Nacional, Spain.

It seems that the artists also made choices about when and where to include images. In one case in part 2, and in four more in part 3, when these artists presumably felt the space provided was inadequate, they added an image on a full sheet of paper (figs. 3, 4; see plates 3, 4 and also figs. 2, 49, 53, plate 24). They also were selective about which images to include; for example, the scribe of part 3 left nine spaces for images that were never filled (folios 25v, 40v, 41v, 43r, 44r, 48v, 53v, 56r). The unpainted spaces are not consecutive: the artists painted the first ten images, left one space blank, then painted another six images, left another five spaces blank and inserted one image on a separate sheet of paper, and left the last three spaces for images in that section blank, which indicates that the artists were selective about which scenes to paint even when the scribes had previously left spaces for them.

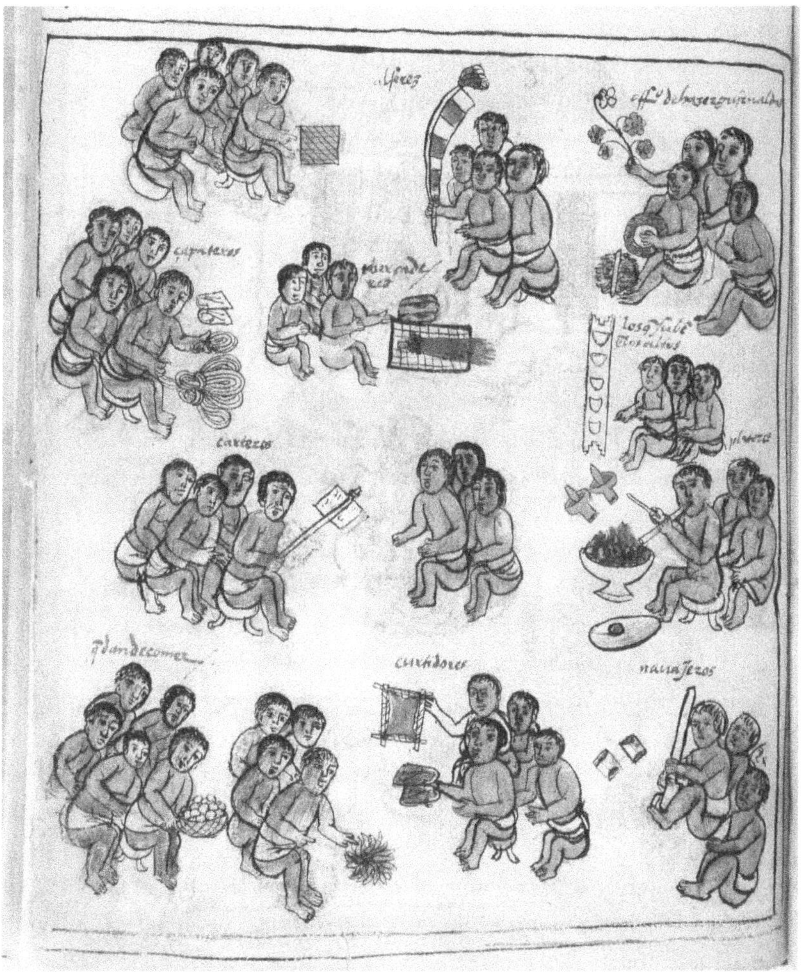

FIGURE 4. Artist 2. *Relación de Michoacán*, fol. 5v. Real Biblioteca del Monasterio de El Escorial, San Lorenzo de El Escorial, Spain, C IV 5. Photograph © Patrimonio Nacional, Spain.

Once the spaces for images had been decided, the artists carefully planned out their images. Careful observation of the manuscript indicates that four artists worked together. Most of the time, they drew a frame around the drawing area. Then, like the artists of pre-Columbian Maya codices and those of colonial central Mexico, three of the four artists sketched out their images.[40] Thin charcoal lines can still be seen in some of the drawings (for artist 1, see, for example, figs. 3, 53; for artist 2, see fig. 4; and for artist 4, see figs. 12, 41, plate 17). We can even see a set of figures drawn in charcoal in one image that the artist decided not to paint (see fig. 4). In some instances, these artists decided to work together on a single plate, each one drawing a particular facet of the narrative and parceling out the space accordingly (see figs. 8, 22).

The four artists drew the contour lines of figures, architectural features, and some elements of the landscape in ink. They applied gray and color washes to the scenes. In some instances, they decided to edit their own images, whiting-out parts and then repainting them (see figs. 1, 53). In one instance, an artist emended the work of another (see fig. 29). Finally, the friar went back one more time, adding captions to some images, and in one case adding text to a chapter/image title so it would match the image better (see figs. 2, 3, 4, 53, and 44, plate 19, respectively).

The friar remains silent about the identity of the painters and scribes of the *Relación*. Like the people of central and southern Mexico, the indigenous people of Michoacán did not make a distinction between writing and painting. Elizabeth Boone has pointed out with respect to the former that they saw both of these activities as ways to encode information. In P'urhépecha, they called both activities *carani* and painters and scribes *carariecha* (sing. *carari*). These carariecha, much like their Maya and central Mexican counterparts of pre-Columbian and early colonial times, had close ties with the ruling class.[41] Upon the arrival of Europeans, carariecha learned the Latin alphabet and began to use it to record information. In Spanish-language records, Spanish officials distinguished between *escribanos* (scribes) and *pintores* (painters) and tell us that often they were both exempt from paying tribute and performing mandatory labor.[42]

At this point, it is not possible to determine the identity of the carariecha who contributed to the making of the *Relación*, yet it as well as other colonial documents can provide useful information about them and their office. According to the *Relación*, during pre-Columbian times all people with specialized skills, including the carariecha, were classified on the basis of their *oficios* (trades), each trade having an official to oversee it. An official known as the *chunicha*, who in turn was under the direct supervision of the Uanacaze ruler, oversaw the carariecha. The chunicha post was held for life and upon this official's death would pass to a member of his family. The role of the chunicha seems to have been to organize the carariecha and collect the fruits of their labor. At least during the colonial period, the chunicha seem to have been skilled painters in their own right. The *Relación geográfica* from Pátzcuaro mentions that many of them were *oficiales primícimos* (very good/talented officials) and goes on to describe them as very wealthy.[43]

The individuals Spaniards called scribes worked in convents and became part of the governing staff of *hospitales* (institutions that served the poor and sick during colonial times) and members of city and town governments.[44] In spite of the distinctions introduced by Spaniards, in P'urhépecha documents scribes used the title of carariecha.[45] Unlike most colonial government posts, which rotated, theirs did not. In this way, the carariecha acquired experience and institutional memory beyond that of other officials. Their erudite knowledge made them essential to governing officials, and they often acted as legal advisers.[46] Some would in fact simultaneously occupy other important posts, including those of translator and even governor.[47] Members of the Uanacaze family, including Don Antonio Huitzimengari, his son, and grandson, reportedly worked as scribes.[48]

It is possible that some of these carariecha made the paintings that once accompanied many legal procedures, but this remains unverified and most of these paintings have disappeared. Some of the nobles who narrated the contents included in the *Relación* could have acted, likewise, as scribes and painters. But the text remains silent about this, and the illustrations were done after the text was completed and do not match specific scribal hands.

Regarding individuals whom Spaniards referred to as painters, it seems that they too were held in high esteem and enjoyed many of the privileges reserved for the indigenous nobility, and some in fact were members of the nobility—one indigenous painter was the grandson of Zinzicha Tangaxuan.[49] In some cases, they were allowed to wear Spanish-style clothing, a privilege that in the early colonial period was restricted by sumptuary laws and granted only to members of the indigenous nobility. The *principales* (officials) of the painters were even granted the right to ride small horses.[50]

During the colonial period, evidence shows that Uanacaze heirs continued to exact services from indigenous painters. On July 5, 1547, the nobles of the City of Michoacán presented to the Uanacaze governor Don Antonio Huitzimengari a painted list of the tribute and labor they had once given to his elder brother Don Francisco. Only an alphabetic record of this list survives, but according to it, the original document showed that painters, feather workers, carpenters, and shoemakers, as well as officials, had been obliged to serve Don Francisco. Don Antonio, as the new governor, requested the same privileges.[51]

The Uanacaze heirs also controlled or administered many of the materials necessary for the completion of paintings and other artworks. When Don Francisco was governor, he collected tribute from the Province of Ávalos in western Mexico, a place to which painters from as far as Toluca in central Mexico would travel to find pigments.[52] When the Uanacaze were not directly in charge of the artists' resources, they collected tribute in order to acquire them. For example, the people of Tzintzuntzan and its subject towns accused Don Antonio Huitzimengari of exacting too much tribute in order to obtain the pigments and tin for the Humilladero Chapel he was building in Pátzcuaro.[53]

Although painters and officials had to serve the Uanacaze heirs, their relationship with these nobles seems to have been somewhat reciprocal. In 1590, Don Antonio Huitzimengari's son Don Constantino Huitzimengari, who at the time was governor of the City of Michoacán, was accused of abusing his subjects by exacting too much tribute in order to give it to officials such as "painters, carpenters, feather workers, etc.," so that they would produce for him.[54] Painters were in charge of such delicate matters as keeping records of tribute items and contributions made to building projects. They also painted maps, genealogies, and coats of arms often used to defend the rights of indigenous nobles in colonial courts (a few of these survive on large *lienzos* [canvases] and European paper). In the course of legal proceedings, indigenous nobles would often present paintings to the Spanish authorities as evidence, together with witnesses capable of reading such records. This seems to have become the modus operandi, and Spanish officials would often request such paintings from the indigenous nobility during the course of litigations.[55] The position of indigenous painters in colonial society depended on the indigenous elite they serviced. To further the interests of their patrons was in fact to further their own interests.

It seems that service to the elite did not preclude painters from working as freelancers. The best documentation on these painters comes from an unlikely source, a 1590 adultery case involving a freelancer from the City of Michoacán. The Spaniard Francisco de Arévalo, presumably a wealthy man, since he rode a horse and carried a sword, found the indigenous painter Francisco Lorenzo seminude and under the bed of his wife, María Avaldes. Arévalo attacked the painter, stabbing him six times. Once Spanish authorities came to detain Arévalo for his actions, he accused the painter of adultery and demanded the death penalty. Spanish officials initiated an investigation, questioning both sides, calling in witnesses, and confiscating the property of the accused. Although the witnesses were mostly interested in Francisco Lorenzo's extracurricular activities, the court record reveals some insightful information about him and his work.[56]

Francisco Lorenzo made a living as a freelance painter and enjoyed many privileges. He was an educated man who knew how to sign his name and presumably could read, because he owned a book written in P'urhépecha.[57] He was bilingual, giving his testimony in Spanish without the need of an interpreter. He was Catholic, married, and wore Spanish-style clothing—which he was forced to leave behind when he fled the scene! It seems Spaniards in the area held him in high esteem and commissioned numerous works from him. Arévalo, the offended husband, went so far as to mention in his statement that he considered him his friend.[58]

After interviewing Francisco Lorenzo at the hospital, Spanish officials inspected his place and made an inventory of its contents. His bed, a box, a few things the Spaniards found of little value (and did not take the time to list individually in the inventory), and his house were given to his mother. However, his works were confiscated and deposited with a Spanish official, presumably until the case could be resolved. The inventory reveals that Francisco Lorenzo was a prolific artist. He was in high demand and painted for Spanish officials (including the man who confiscated the contents of his studio), the Jesuit Order, and the indigenous nobility. He painted on a variety of grounds that ranged from gourds (*tecomates*), bowls (*jícaras*), boudoirs, tables, large and small desks (*escritorios*, *escritorillos*, and *escrivanías*), to canvas, wood, and parchment.

The inventory does not specify what Francisco Lorenzo painted on the gourds, bowls, and furniture. On canvas and wood grounds, he was working on religious themes, one a Saint Francis and the other a Saint John with angels and God the father. On parchment, he painted a coat of arms.

When given a chance to comment about the contents of the inventory, Francisco Lorenzo listed the patrons of each piece and mentioned that most of them had paid in advance for his work. Some still owed him, and in one other case he and the patron still had to set the amount. Francisco Lorenzo did not provide a price for the coat of arms he painted for a man listed only by the honorific title "Don" and the first name Constantino. One can safely assume this was Don Constantino Huitzimengari, Uanacaze heir and indigenous governor of the City of Michoacán in 1590, the same noble who that year had been accused of demanding too much tribute in order to give it to painters.

Not all painters worked as freelancers. Some worked exclusively for church projects. Some may have charged for their work, but others were excused from mandatory labor (a privilege colonial officials often sought to limit). It seems that even when they painted for the church, they did so at the request of indigenous authorities who directed the building projects. In 1633, indigenous painter Miguel Francisco Sira, who was over sixty years of age, claimed that he had worked since he was a child painting the church of Uruapan, Michoacán. At that late age, he had been called to mandatory labor, which he refused. In his defense, the witnesses he called argued that he had saved the town's indigenous authority the cost of his specialized labor for the many years he had served as painter.[59]

While colonial documents provide some insightful information about the status, working methodologies, and social networks of artists, to date no information about the specific artists who worked on the *Relación* has been located. For this, only the close observation of the *Relación* can provide some clues about the different artists' hands and training based on their choices, but this is less than an exact science. In the past, José Tudela concluded that only one artist illustrated the manuscript, and the historian Juan José Batalla Rosado suggested three.[60] They, as well as Hans Roskamp and Stone, identify the many pre-Columbian elements present in the images and see them as the product of indigenous painters. Recently, the art historians Nuria Salazar Simarro and Espejel Carbajal have separately proposed that between four and five different hands worked on the images.[61] Moreover, Espejel Carbajal has concluded they are mere illustrations of the text and has questioned whether it was in fact indigenous artists and not Europeans who created them, because of their use of Renaissance representational techniques and motifs.[62] In my analysis of the original manuscript, and to some extent of the 2000 facsimile, I have identified the work of four different artists. Although some aspects of my analysis coincide to some extent with Espejel Carbajal's, my work further reveals that these artists did more than illustrate the text; they often complemented it, added information, and went so far as to change some of the narratives. Furthermore, I contend that the images express an in-depth knowledge of pre-Columbian concepts and therefore indigenous artists produced them.

Previous studies of early colonial paintings throughout Mexico have used the degrees to which artists incorporated pre-Columbian and European styles and iconography to determine their educational backgrounds and help identify different artists' hands. I urge that we see these stylistic differences not as unmediated European or indigenous training but as a matter of choice on the artists' part. By carefully selecting from both European and pre-Columbian visual repertoires, these artists conveyed complex meanings and lent authenticity to the contents of the manuscript while seeking to communicate to colonial authorities.

The art of Europe during the late fifteenth and sixteenth centuries focused on the representation of visible qualities. The flat surfaces of canvases, panels, walls, and manuscript pages were transformed by means of illusionistic techniques into three-dimensional scenes. Space was conceived of as a three-dimensional continuum.[63] European artists used single-point perspective and empirical and multiple-point perspectives to give the illusion of depth. The use of lines and shading gave the illusion of volume and weight.[64] European friars and colonial authorities introduced many of these techniques to Michoacán and the rest of New Spain through European prints, books, and paintings. These images were often used to educate indigenous pupils in the Christian doctrine and the new ways of conceiving the world. In turn, indigenous artists copied many of them on the walls of newly built convents and often used them as models for images in manuscripts.

According to the art historian Donald Robertson, this European way of conceiving pictorial space was quite different from the pictorial traditions of postclassic Mesoamerica (fourteenth through sixteenth centuries) before the arrival of Europeans. In the late 1950s and 1960s, through a study of surviving manuscripts and mural paintings, Robertson defined an international painting style for Mesoamerica.[65] Mesoamerican painters used contour lines (which Robertson called frame lines) to enclose areas of flat color; the lines had very little variation and do not indicate volume. Pre-Columbian landscape, he notes, is composed of a vocabulary of standardized, discrete natural and architectural two-dimensional forms (temples, fortifications, ballcourts, mountains, caves, springs, etc.), which are differentiated by qualifying signs and neatly delimited by contour lines.[66] Unlike their European counterparts, pre-Columbian landscapes appear not to

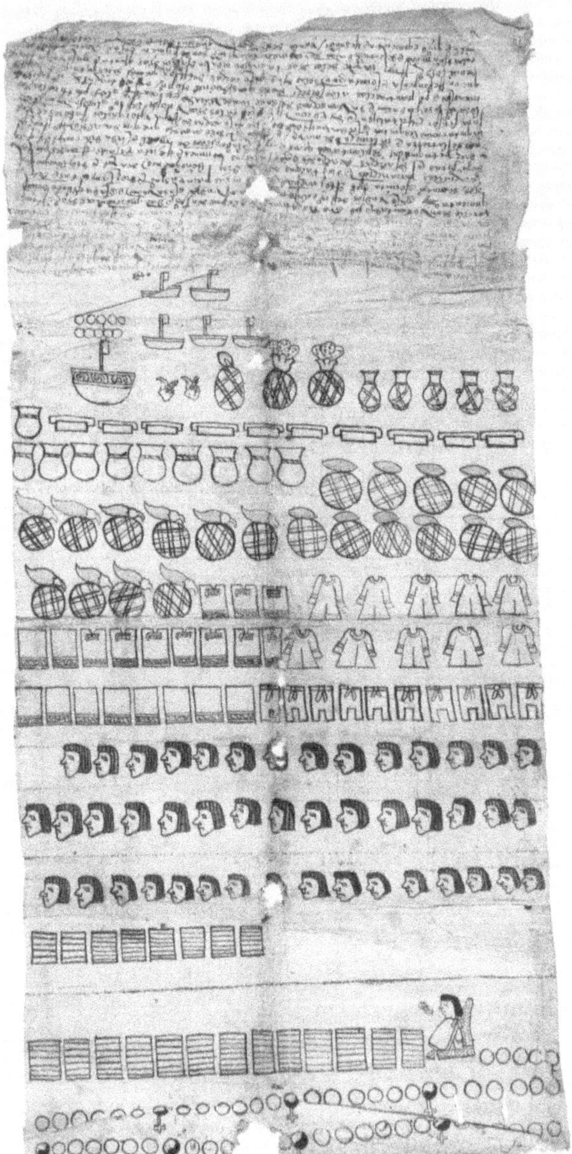

FIGURE 5. "Tributes of Tzintzuntzan and Tlalpujava, recto, [1542–1552]." Garrett Mesoamerican Manuscripts, No. 7. Princeton University Library (now missing). Even though the labeling at the Princeton Library identifies this document as coming from Tzintzuntzan and Tlalpujava, through careful analysis of surviving copies, the scholar Hans Roskamp has identified it as coming from the town of Cutzio in southeast Michoacán. This folio contains many pictographic elements that appear in codices from other regions, such as the flags to signify the number 20, dots to indicate numbers and/or days of the week, and a man with a speech scroll to indicate he is the ruler.

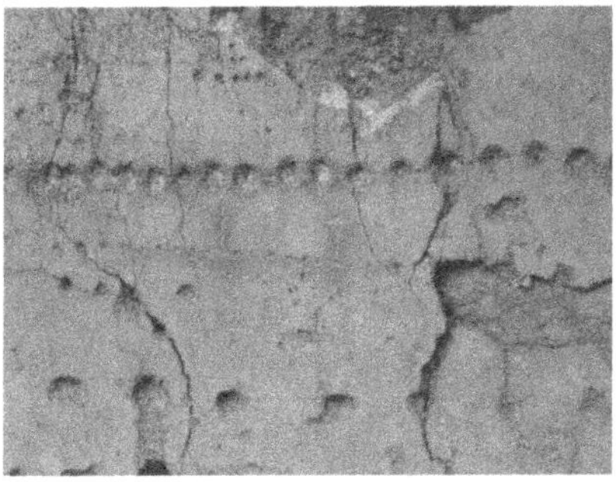

FIGURE 6. Graffiti in the courtyard of the former Colegio de Pátzcuaro, now the Museo de Artes Populares, Pátzcuaro, Michoacán. Dots represent numbers in Mesoamerican writing of the sixteenth century. In the middle line in this picture, they probably stand for days of the week, and the crosses over the seventh dot, for Sundays. Photograph by the author.

integrate actions with settings, and landscape features and human figures do not necessarily adhere to ground lines and often seem to float in space.

Many elements depict details that would not be seen in plain view but are integral to the narrative or the function of the object being depicted (e.g., the roots of plants). Different objects are sized in proportion to each other according to their importance in the story, not necessarily in accordance with their actual physical dimensions. Artists often represent human bodies in isomorphic form with torsos usually turned forward and faces, and often legs, in profile. They frequently disregard the difference between right and left feet. Arms and hands are generally expressive and add meaning and vitality to the figures.

Robertson's typology is still very much in use today.[67] Recently, Elizabeth Boone and Michael Smith have revisited it and pointed out the symbols that generally accompany it.[68] Furthermore, they mention that this style was probably started along the coasts during the epiclassic period and was widespread throughout Mexico by the sixteenth century, with many regional variations. As is the case with most scholars who discuss Mesoamerican styles, Robertson, Boone, and Smith do not include Michoacán in their discussion; thus it is important to note that the *Relación*, several other manuscripts from colonial Michoacán, and the graffiti on the walls of colonial buildings share some of the stylistic and iconographic elements of the Mesoamerican international style (figs. 5, 6).

Defining a regional style for areas like the Valley of Mexico and Michoacán where no pre-Columbian manuscripts survive can be a challenge, and as Boone has pointed out for central Mexico, we may not have a complete picture of the different stylistic repertoires available to pre-Columbian artists, some of which may have included those visual techniques we now attribute to European traditions. Adding to this conundrum, in regard to architecture and sculpture, artists often chose stylistic traditions that created connections to people and places. The art historian Eduardo Douglas has pointed out that artistic style in the early colonial period was more likely a matter of choice than the unmediated product of training or instinct.[69] In the case of colonial manuscripts, and the *Relación* in particular, I would add that artists chose from European and Mesoamerican repertoires as part of a selective and calculated effort to convey a particular meaning in the hopes of better communicating with their audience while conveying their knowledge of the pre-Columbian past.

I have identified four artists' hands based on their treatment of lines, space, and figures. I have numbered them in the order in which they appear in the manuscript as it is currently bound. It is important to keep in mind that sometimes one sees variation in the same artist based on the size of the image and, to a lesser or greater degree, as the artists copied European prototypes.

All four artists shared common elements, such as the representation of women wearing knee-length skirts and the way they proportioned their figures in relationship to one another and to the buildings in the scene, but on some occasions they would vary sizes according to their importance in the narratives. Nevertheless, their work exhibits much differentiation, and it is in the differences that I have identified the different hands.

Three of the artists' hands can be discerned in the ways in which they distinctly painted the petamuti. Generally speaking, artist 1's figures vary from portraitlike paintings, such as the frontispiece, to generalized representations with oval-shaped heads. He bestowed on the petamuti a greater luxury of detail than he even gave to the ruler. His petamuti often wears a white garland on his oval-shaped head; a lip plug in his lower lip; bracelets on his arms; a turquoise-encrusted gourd on his back; and a white, maroon, and black patterned robe that stops just short of his knee. The petamuti holds a lance-shaped staff painted with diagonal stripes in a candy cane pattern. Just below the arrowhead on his staff hangs a skirt of multicolored feathers and shells (fig. 7; see also figs. 2, 25, 30, plate 9). In some of these scenes, the petamuti wears a large pendant in the shape of tweezers on his chest and delicately drawn sandals on his feet, even though this artist did not differentiate right and left feet, and at times red paint covers his sideburns.

Artist 3 provided the elements necessary to identify the petamuti, his

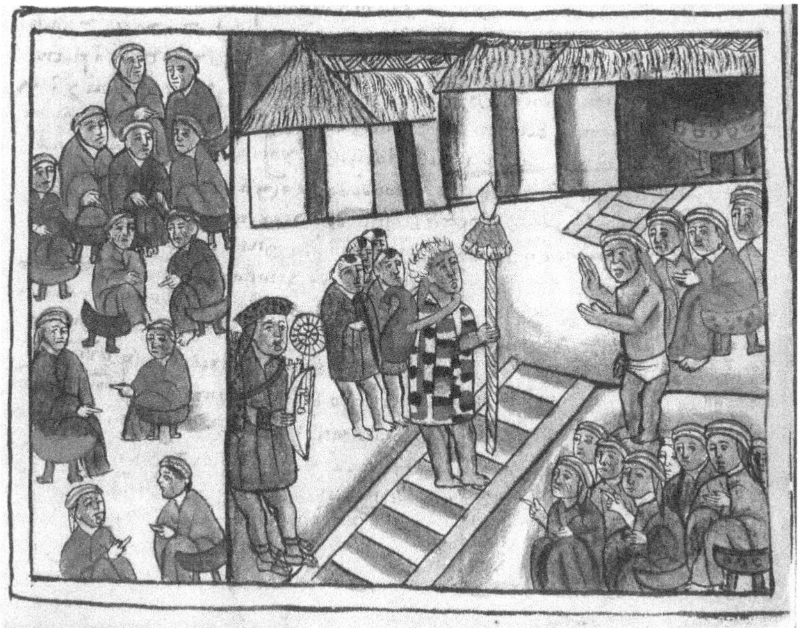

FIGURE 7. Artist 1. "Como hazían otro Señor y los parlamentos que hací[an]" (How they selected another lord and the speeches they gave). *Relación de e Michoacán*, fol. 32r. Real Biblioteca del Monasterio de El Escorial, San Lorenzo de El Escorial, Spain, C IV 5. Photograph © Patrimonio Nacional, Spain.

staff and gourd, and omitted smaller details such as tweezers, sandals, and red sideburns (bottom left side of fig. 8). This is common in artist 3's figures, which are largely standardized and show little variation in personal features. Their heads are large in proportion to their bodies, and they hold stiff poses. The eyes of his figures are characteristically large, with dark pupils (he leaves out this detail in his smaller figures; see figs. 34, 38, plate 12).

Artist 4 bestowed on the petamuti some of the same accoutrements as artist 1: the garland on his head; a pendant in the shape of tweezers on his chest; a lip plug; a lance-shaped staff painted with diagonal stripes and topped with feathers and shells; a turquoise-encrusted gourd on his back; and a white, maroon, and black patterned robe. He paid close attention to details, outlined the turquoise inlays of his gourd, drew a pattern of swirls on the flaps he attached to the gourd, and carefully showed the design of the sandals. Of the *Relación*'s artists, artist 4 was the most comfortable with Renaissance techniques. His figures move swiftly through the pages of the

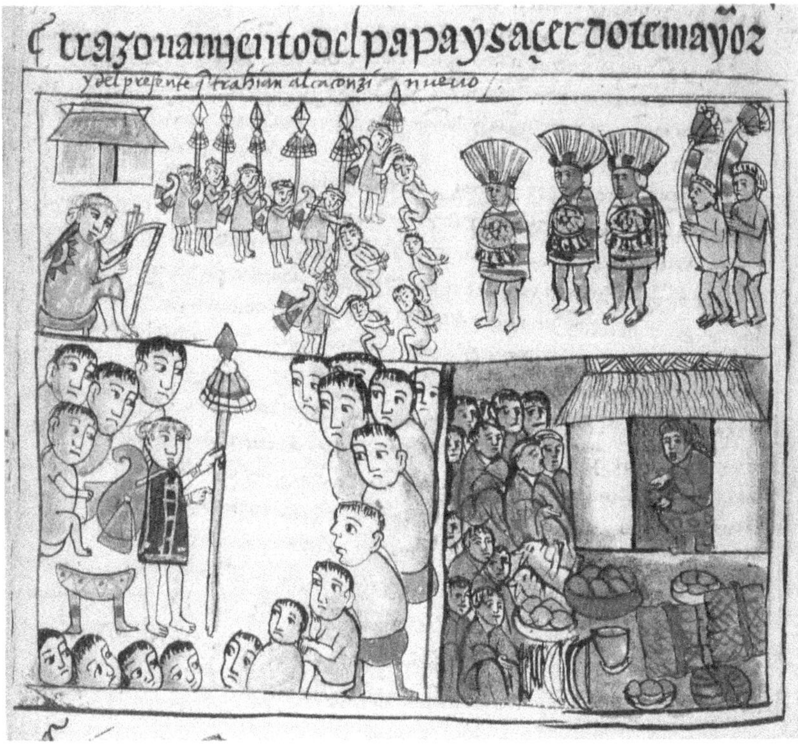

FIGURE 8. Artists 1 and 3. "Razonamiento del papa y sacerdote mayor y del presente que trahían al Caçonzi nuevo" (The speeches of the pope and main priest and the gifts they brought to the new cazonci). *Relación de Michoacán*, fol. 33v. Real Biblioteca del Monasterio de El Escorial, San Lorenzo de El Escorial, Spain, C IV 5. Photograph © Patrimonio Nacional, Spain.

Relación. Unlike artist 1, who did not differentiate between the left and right foot, artist 4 depicted his petamuti walking with his right foot forward and the left one close behind, pointing toward an audience listening to his speech (see fig. 31, plate 10).

Other details such as breechcloths can also help distinguish the hands of the *Relación*'s four artists. Artist 1's male figures wear briefs (fig. 9; see also figs. 13, 53); artist 2's wear loincloths rendered as a narrow curve of cloth around the hips (fig. 10; see also figs. 4, 50, 52, plate 23); artist 3's wear white loincloths that tightly hug the hips, looking like two small triangles that slightly overlap in the front and have thin red or black stripes at the edges and tiny black stitches (fig. 11; see also figs. 38, 56, plate 25); and artist 4's wear loincloths similar to those of artist 3, but his fit the figures more loosely (fig. 12; see also fig. 41).

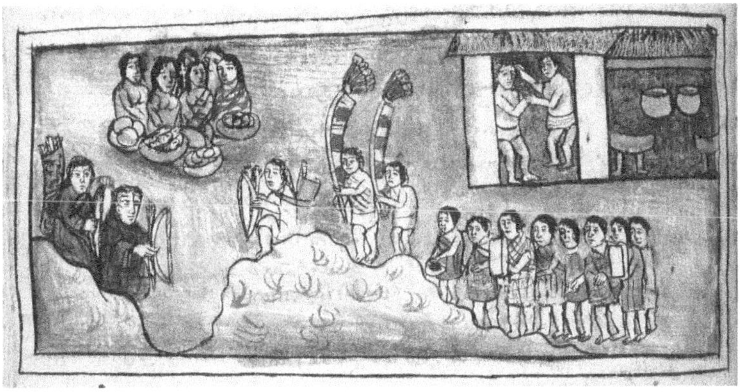

FIGURE 9. Artist 1. "Como Tariacuri embió a llamar su hijo Curatame de Curinguaro y de las differencias que tuvo con él" (How Tariacuri sent for his son Curatame from Curinguaro and of the differences he had with him). *Relación de Michoacán*, fol. 105v. Real Biblioteca del Monasterio de El Escorial, San Lorenzo de El Escorial, Spain, C IV 5. Photograph © Patrimonio Nacional, Spain.

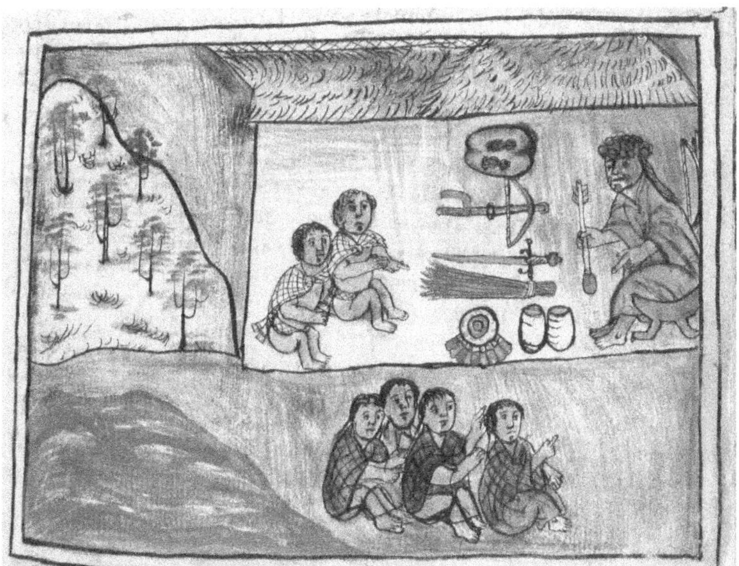

FIGURE 10. Artist 2. "De la benida de los españoles a esta provincia, segund me lo contó don Pedro, que es agora Governador, y se halló en todo, y como Montezuma, señor de México ynbió a pedir socorro al Caçonçi Zuangua, padre del que murió agora" (Of the arrival of the Spaniards to this province, according to Don Pedro's account, who is now governor and who was around all of it, and how Montezuma, lord of Mexico, sent a request for help to the cazonci Zuangua, father of the one who died recently). *Relación de Michoacán*, fol. 39r. Real Biblioteca del Monasterio de El Escorial, San Lorenzo de El Escorial, Spain, C IV 5. Photograph © Patrimonio Nacional, Spain.

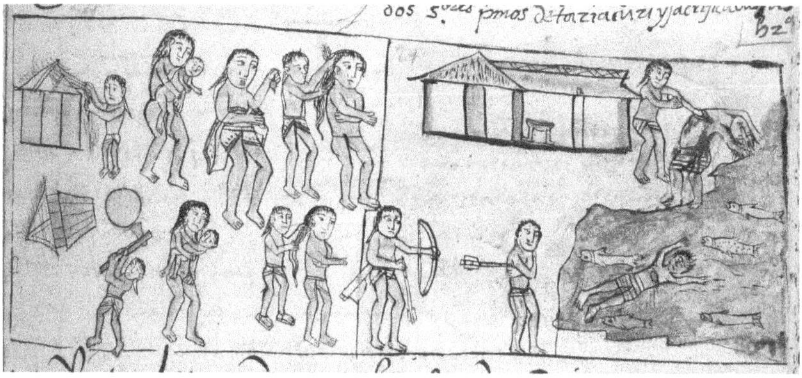

FIGURE 11. Artist 3. "Como Zurunban hizo deshazer las casas a los de Tariacuri, y cómo fueron flechados dos señores, primos de Tariacuri, y sacrificadas sus hermanas" (How Zurunban had the houses of Tariacuri's people destroyed, and how two lords, cousins of Tariacuri, were shot with arrows and his sisters sacrificed). *Relación de Michoacán*, fol. 85r. Real Biblioteca del Monasterio de El Escorial, San Lorenzo de El Escorial, Spain, C IV 5. Photograph © Patrimonio Nacional, Spain.

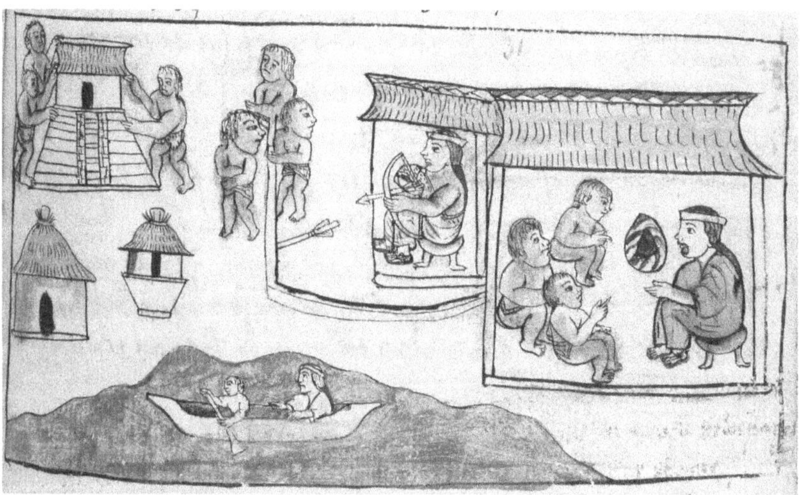

FIGURE 12. Artist 4. "Como Tariacuri dio a sus sobrinos e hijo una parte de su dios Curicaueri, y como los quiso flechar, por unos cúes que hizieron y de la costunbre que tenían los señores entre sí, antes que muriesen" (How Tariacuri gave to his nephews and his son a part of his god Curicaueri, and how he tried to shoot them because of some temples they made, and of the customs the lords had among them before they died). *Relación de Michoacán*, fol. 118r. Real Biblioteca del Monasterio de El Escorial, San Lorenzo de El Escorial, Spain, C IV 5. Photograph © Patrimonio Nacional, Spain.

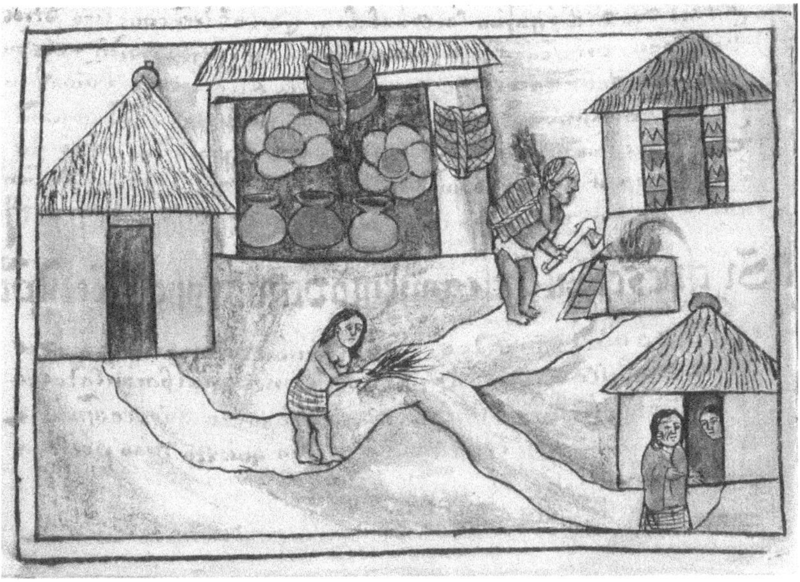

FIGURE 13. Artist 1. "De la manera que se casaba la gente baxa" (Of the way the lower-class people married). *Relación de Michoacán*, fol. 27r. Real Biblioteca del Monasterio de El Escorial, San Lorenzo de El Escorial, Spain, C IV 5. Photograph © Patrimonio Nacional, Spain.

The four artists produced images of their own. Artists 1 painted several plates on his own (see figs. 1, 2, 3, 7, 9, 13, 25, 26, 30, 32, 36, 53, 57, plates 11, 14, 26), sometimes editing them after completion (see figs. 1, 3, 9, 53). Artist 2 painted six images on his own (see figs. 4, 10, 46, 50, 51, 52, plate 22). Artist 3 painted some illustrations on his own (see figs. 11, 19, 34, 38, 39, 44, 45, 49, 56, plates 20, 21) and edited one of his own images (see fig. 56). Artist 4 was the sole author of several paintings (see figs. 12, 28, 37, 41, plate 15).

Artist 1's familiarity with European prototypes and techniques seems to have granted him a prominent role in the manuscript. He painted the frontispiece (the first image a reader would have seen), basing it on European presentation scenes, which usually portray a manuscript author and/or an artist presenting a finished work to his patron, in this case Viceroy Mendoza.[70] He also painted the genealogical tree picturing the Uanacaze family (based on the European Tree of Jesse), an image meant to summarize the Uanacaze history of the region, to which the entire second part of the manuscript is dedicated (see fig. 53). When he was not copying from European prototypes, he often used European techniques. He sometimes anchored elements in space using shadows cast on the ground (e.g., fig. 13; see

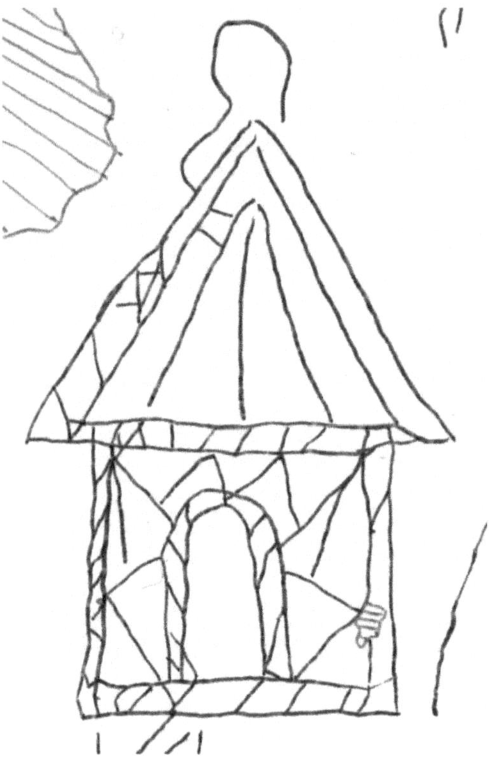

FIGURE 14. Graffito of a house. Second floor, Convent of Tzintzuntzan, Michoacán. Possibly seventeenth century. Drawing by the author.

also fig. 1). He created the illusion of volume by varying the width of contour lines and applying gray washes to people and structures (e.g., figs. 1, 7).

In addition, one can recognize artist 1's hand in his use of fairly standardized architectural features. Square entrances lead to the interiors of palaces and temples. These have stylized thatched roofs with rows of comma-shaped lines representing the dangling straw (see figs. 3, 13). A rim of woven lines in a twill pattern tops the trapezoidal roofs of temples and all but three houses (see figs. 3, 7, bottom right side of 8, 25, 32, 36). A small circle sometimes tops triangular roofs (see figs. 7, 13). A similar device also appears on the top of some of the houses by artist 3 and is a feature present in the houses in the graffiti incised in the plaster of the Franciscan convent at Tzintzuntzan (fig. 14).

Artist 1 often used body parts to indicate actions and/or emotions but omitted them when they were unnecessary. A hand on the side of a woman's face indicates sorrow or anguish (see fig. 57), and pointing hands, speaking (see figs. 3, 7, 36). Figures sitting in profile or three-quarter view often show only one of their legs (see figs. 2, 3).[71]

He took great liberty with the clothing of the figures. Some of his male figures wear briefs (see figs. 32, 53), and the humiliated or poor are nude (see fig. 29 center). Artist 1 sometimes used ankle-length robes to indicate rank—see, for example, figure 32, where only the Uanacaze ruler wears a long robe. However, he also dressed figures in long robes indiscriminately, even the majority of the figures in a given scene (e.g., see fig. 36). These robes may be full length or come halfway down the thigh (see figs. 1, 3). He is the only artist who paints a female figure wearing a shirtlike garment (see fig. 13).

In addition to knowing and using European techniques and prototypes, artist 1 knew indigenous conventions and used them selectively. For instance, he depicted the hoofprints of a deer as hooves seen from the side (see fig. 26), a convention used in the pre-Columbian *Codex Fejérváry-Mayer* from central Mexico, rather than use the European convention of depicting deer hoofprints as seen from above (figs. 15a, 15b, respectively).

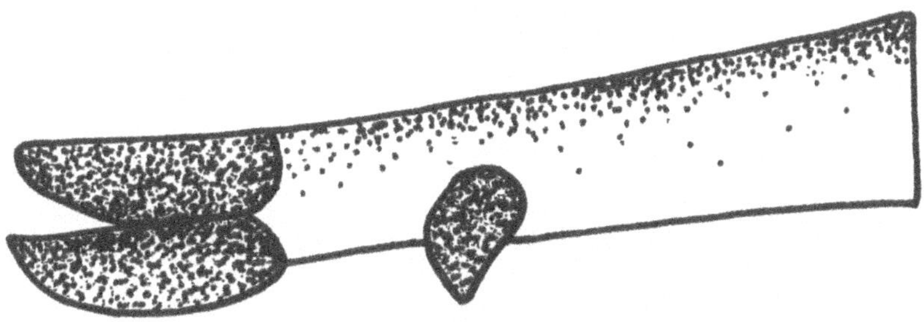

FIGURE 15A. *Codex Fejérváry-Mayer,* plate 21 (detail). After León-Portilla, "El tonalámatl de los pochtecas," 61. Drawing by Viera Sairán Monfón.

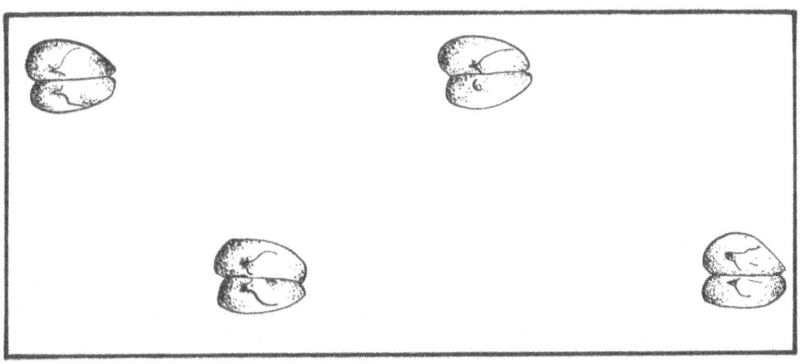

FIGURE 15B. Study of deer-tracks diagram (detail). Hohenlohe archive, Neuenstein, Germany. After J. Cummins, *The Hound and the Hawk.* Drawing by Viera Sairán Monfón.

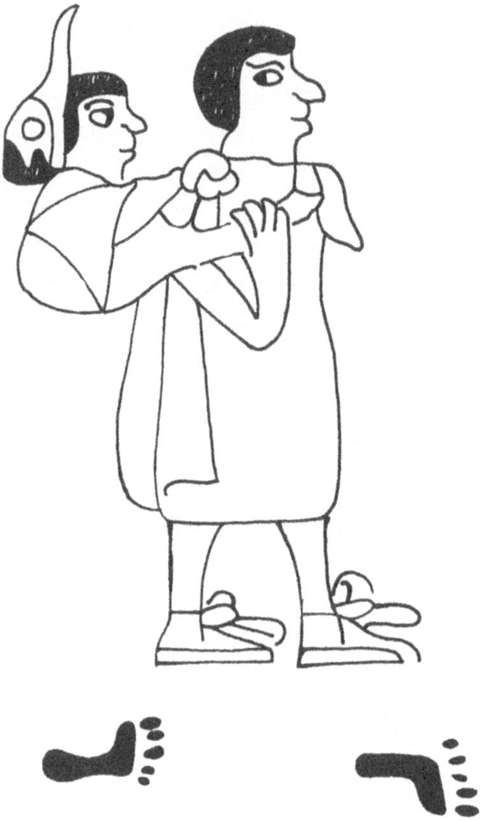

FIGURE 16A. *Tira de la peregrinación*, plate 2 (detail). After Johansson, "*Tira de la peregrinación*," 25. Drawing by Viera Sairán Monfón.

To identify the offices of priests, he used accoutrements (a god bundle, a conch shell, trumpets, etc.) that either refer to P'urhépecha material culture or appear in pre-Columbian and colonial painted sources from other areas in Mexico (figs. 16a, b, c; see also fig. 2).

Scenes painted by artist 1 sometimes add information absent in the text, and at times contradict it, probably to show a more accurate representation of indigenous practices and history. For example, in his representation of the Uanacaze genealogy in figure 53, he shows how the nobleman Zetaco died, information missing in the text. Also, some of the differences between the text and his images may refer to ideograms.

Like artist 1, artist 2 was familiar with European prototypes. He created the only grisaille in the *Relación*, which in all likelihood he copied from a printed source (see fig. 46). He used contour lines to give the illusion of volume and shaded the ground with gray washes to indicate a continuous

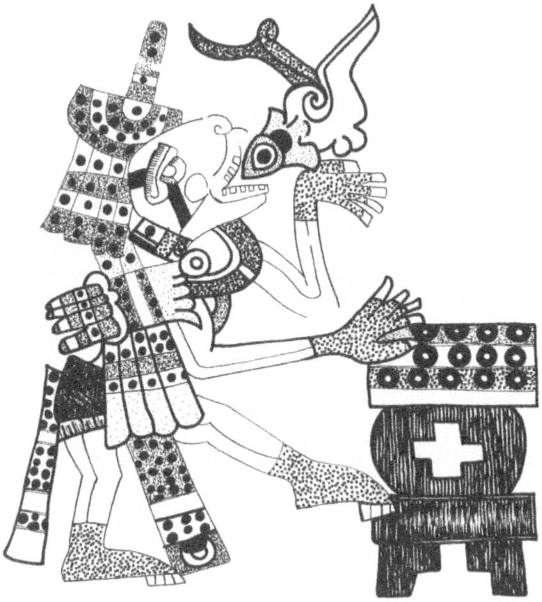

FIGURE 16B. *Codex Borgia*, plate 24 (detail). After Díaz and Rodgers, *Codex Borgia*, 54. Drawing by Viera Sairán Monfón.

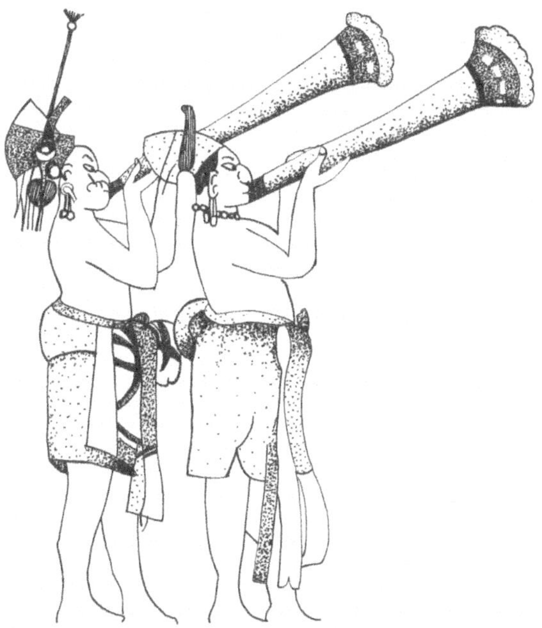

FIGURE 16C. Trumpet players (detail). North wall, room one, Templo de las pinturas, Bonampak, Chiapas, Mexico. Drawing by Viera Sairán Monfón.

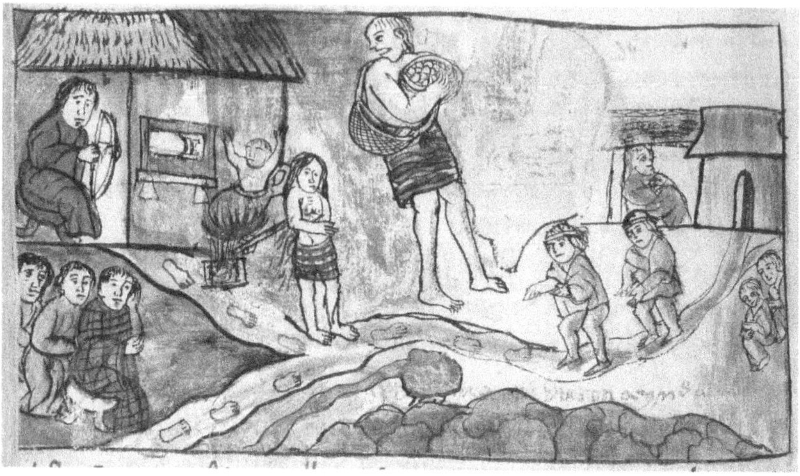

FIGURE 17. Artists 2 and 4. "Como los del pueblo de Yziparamucu pidieron ayuda a los de Coringuaro y del agüero que tuvieron los de Yziparamucu" (How the [people] from the town of Yziparamucu asked those from Coringuaro for help, and of the omen those from Yziparamucu had). *Relación de Michoacán*, fol. 124v. Real Biblioteca del Monasterio de El Escorial, San Lorenzo de El Escorial, Spain, C IV 5. Photograph © Patrimonio Nacional, Spain.

landscape (e.g., see figs. 50, 51). He often painted his figures in three-quarter view and seated in small groups.

He was also acquainted with Mesoamerican pictographic systems and incorporated them into his landscapes. For example, he painted a flowing spring by a gate in a stone wall to represent the toponym of Itziparámuco (variously spelled Yzí Parámuco), which means "water by the shore or the entrance."[72] This is the place where, according to the accompanying text, the events illustrated took place (fig. 17; see plate 5).

Of all the artists, artist 3 used the most Mesoamerican motifs, a plethora of elements that can be found in other Mesoamerican codices and that refer to items in Michoacán's preconquest material culture, such as drinking jars (see figs. 45, 49, 56), jewelry, clothing, and even a sacrificial stone (see fig. 35, plate 13). He sometimes painted trees and plants with their roots showing (fig. 18; see also figs. 45, 49), a common convention in pre-Columbian codices but absent in the paintings of the other three artists of the *Relación*, whose drawings of vegetation are limited to patches of tall grasses and slender inked trees without roots (for artist 1, see figs. 9, 25; artist 2, fig. 51; and artist 4, fig. 28).[73]

Even when using European motifs, artist 3 transformed them by adding indigenous elements. For example, Espejel Carbajal has noticed the resemblance between figure 19, in which human body parts are boiled in a large pot, and an illustration in the 1494 Italian publication *La leyenda dorada*, in which two men boil a third in a large pot over an open fire.[74] The cooking fire in the *Relación*, however, is transformed by adding three stones to the hearth. The three-stone hearth was and is still used among many Mesoamerican peoples and is known among P'urhépecha speakers as *parhangua*.[75]

Artist 3 came up with creative solutions to the small spaces allowed for many of his plates. To accommodate complex narratives, he used synecdoche, one figure standing in for the action of several (e.g., see fig. 27). He combined European techniques for rendering three-dimensional space, such as bird's-eye views and overlapping figures, with pre-Columbian spatial techniques (e.g., see left side of fig. 22, plate 6). He provided X-ray views of buildings, partially removing walls and roofs to allow the viewer to see events inside (see figs. 45, 56). Much like pre-Columbian representations,

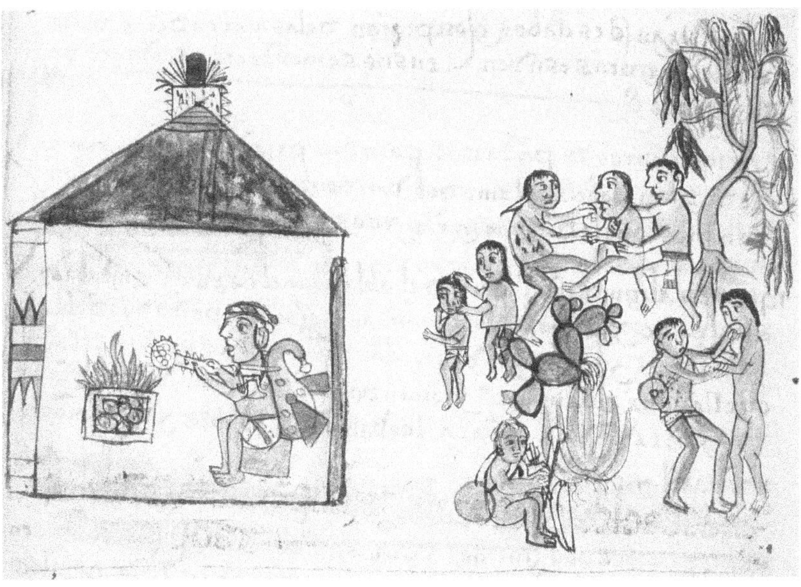

FIGURE 18. Artists 3 and 4. "De las entradas que hazían en los pueblos de sus enemigos" (Of the forays into the towns of their enemies). *Relación de Michoacán*, fol. 13v. Real Biblioteca del Monasterio de El Escorial, San Lorenzo de El Escorial, Spain, C IV 5. Photograph © Patrimonio Nacional, Spain.

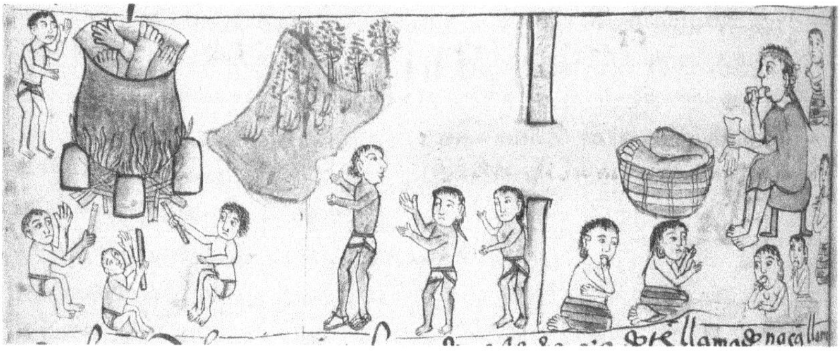

FIGURE 19. Artist 3. "Como Tariacuri mandó cozer a Naca y le dio a comer a sus enemigos" (How Tariacuri had Naca cooked and fed him to his enemies). *Relación de Michoacán*, fol. 83v. Real Biblioteca del Monasterio de El Escorial, San Lorenzo de El Escorial, Spain, C IV 5. Photograph © Patrimonio Nacional, Spain.

many of his figures float in space (e.g., see figs. 11, 18, 19). Sometimes he did include a ground line but did not always attach the figures to it.

Dress, accoutrements, and postures differentiate male and female figures and indicate the different roles played by characters. Like artist 1, artist 3 used a pointing hand to show that a figure is speaking (see figs. 34, 40). Female figures wear skirts and sometimes appear nude to indicate their humiliation (see fig. 11). Their elongated ears often have thin bars across the lobes. Like women in pre-Columbian codices, they kneel while men sit (see fig. 56). They often express anguish or sadness with one hand over their abdomen and the other on the side of their face (see figs. 38, 45, 56, plate 16). Noblemen wear jewels and have their hair braided. In social settings, they wear robes that hang halfway down their thighs. Artist 3 dressed them for battle in white loincloths and occasionally in cotton armor depicted as a line along the waistline or as lines around both the waistline and the arms. Sometimes small black dots or lines show the texture of the cotton armor (see fig. 18 and left side of fig. 22). These warriors hold bows and arrows in their hands and wear quivers filled with small arrows on their backs.

The figures of artist 4, the last artist to contribute to the *Relación*, move gracefully through the pages of the manuscript in a variety of poses and perspectives. He even took a stab at foreshortening his figures (the left side of fig. 20). His contour lines are not solid, but feathery, and indicate volume. He depicted the Uanacaze men wearing loincloths and both short and long robes. Sometimes the ruler is differentiated from others by his long robe, which comes all the way to the ankles. Artist 4 rarely depicted women, but in the one instance he did, the woman wears the same knee-length wrap-around skirt that the other artists gave to their female figures (fig. 21).

Artist 4 was well aware of European conventions and mathematical projections. He often shaded architectural and landscape features with a gray wash to give them the illusion of volume and to define different spaces (see figs. 12, 28). Architectural structures show a certain level of standardiza-

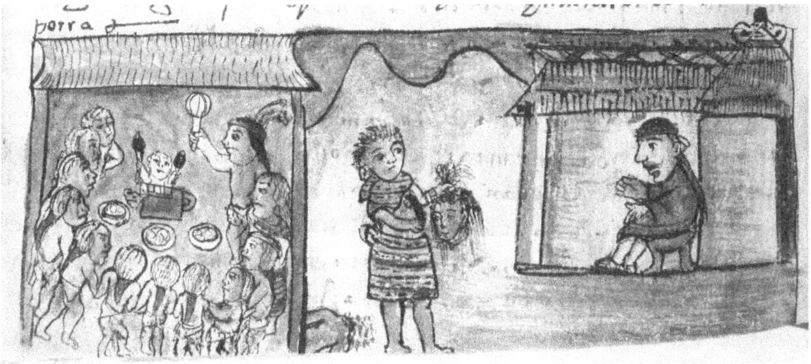

FIGURE 20. Artists 3 and 4. *Relación de Michoacán*, fol. 135v. Real Biblioteca del Monasterio de El Escorial, San Lorenzo de El Escorial, Spain, C IV 5. Photograph © Patrimonio Nacional, Spain.

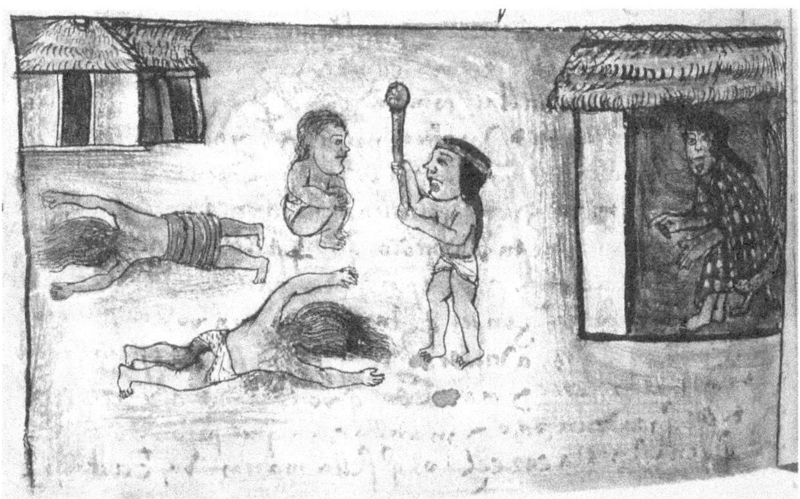

FIGURE 21. Artists 2 and 4. *Relación Michoacán*, fol. 134v. Real Biblioteca del Monasterio de El Escorial, San Lorenzo de El Escorial, Spain, C IV 5. Photograph © Patrimonio Nacional, Spain.

tion. He carefully delineated thatched roofs and drew the dangling straw in neatly organized rows. The entrances to his houses and palaces are midpoint archways, and he used single-point perspective to represent the interior of one of his structures (see fig. 28).

It seems that these artists' knowledge of European techniques, at least in part, determined their role in the making of the manuscript. Artists 1 and 4, the most adept at these techniques, collaborated with the other two artists to create images that balance the use of pre-Columbian techniques and motifs with European conventions, stylistic preferences, and the use of three-dimensional representations. These images, while conveying an extensive knowledge of local elements, would have given the illusion of reality for a European audience. In figure 22 (see also plate 6), for example, artist 3 drew a scene on the left-hand side of the picture frame in which the Uanacaze are planning the conquest of a town while viewing a map on the ground. On the right-hand side, artist 4 drew the actual conquest of the town, thus turning a two-dimensional plan into a full-blown three-dimensional battle.

Artist 4 also collaborated with artists 2 (see figs. 17, 21) and 3 (see figs. 18, 20, 27, 31 [petamuti by artist 4], 35, 40, 43, plate 18). Artist 1 not only collaborated with artist 3 in one plate but went so far as to edit another plate by artist 3 (see figs. 8 and 29, respectively).

Their carefully selected use of Mesoamerican motifs indicates that the artists were also conversant in rich Mesoamerican pictographic traditions. Therefore, their images should be studied for their potential to convey complex meanings, as do other Mesoamerican pictorial traditions. Mesoamerican pictographs work both as pictures in the European sense of the word and as writing. As a way of understanding them, scholars have categorized them into direct/pictorial representation, logograms/ideograms (which represent a concept or idea), transparent ideograms (the idea they represent comes close to the representation), and phonetic transcriptions/referents. These categorizations are not rigid and allow for some overlap, as well as for the fact that many glyphs can have more than one function.[76]

The artists of the *Relación* not only used pre-Columbian motifs but also chose pictographic over naturalistic representations that often carried both direct and logographic meaning. For example, artists 1, 3, and 4 represent temple-pyramids as a frontal stepped pyramid with balustrades running along the sides of the steps leading to a thatched roof temple structure on the top (see figs. 25, 39, 12, plate 7). We must note that these are not realistic representations.[77] Temple-pyramids during the postclassic period in Mi-

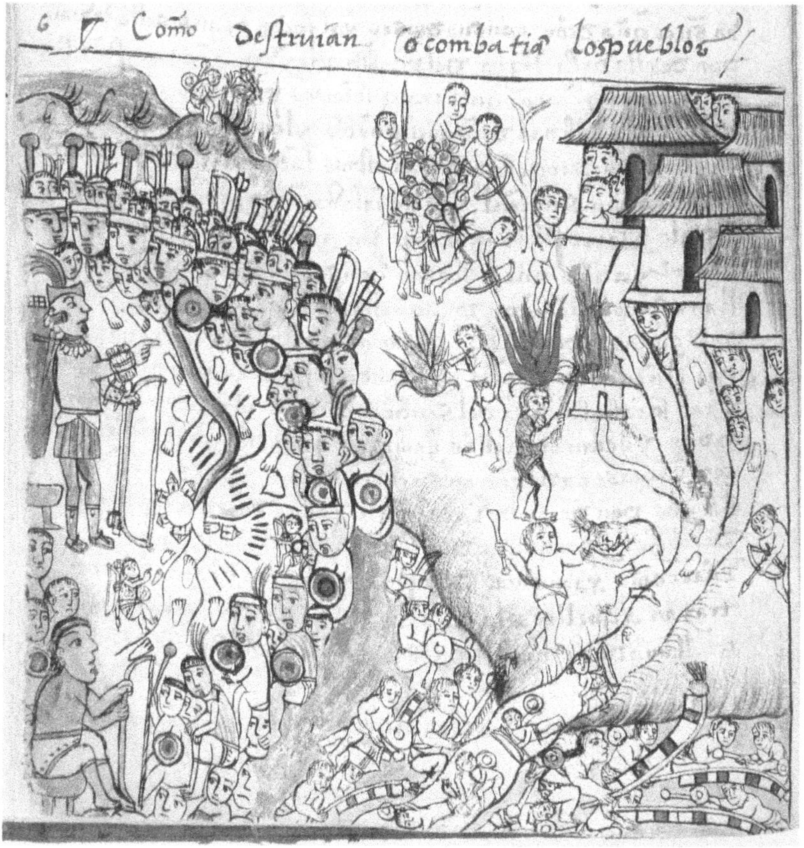

FIGURE 22. Artists 3 and 4. "Como destruían o combatían los pueblos" (How they destroyed or fought the towns). *Relación de Michoacán*, fol. 15v. Real Biblioteca del Monasterio de El Escorial, San Lorenzo de El Escorial, Spain, C IV 5. Photograph © Patrimonio Nacional, Spain.

choacán were generally of two types: (1) rectangular-plan stepped pyramids, which often appear in pairs (e.g., the pyramids at the Plaza de Armas in Ihuatzio); and (2) composites in which a trapezoidal platform is attached to a round one, known today as *yacatas* (figs. 23, 24).[78] Thus, rather than opt for a realistic representation, the artists chose a pictograph.

The temples in the *Relación*, besides serving as iconographic representations, serve as ideograms invoking not just a ceremonial structure but also a community's political power. Much as in other Mesoamerican codices, the dismantling and burning of a temple stands for the conquest of a community.[79] One of the images of the *Relación* depicts the gods' prediction of

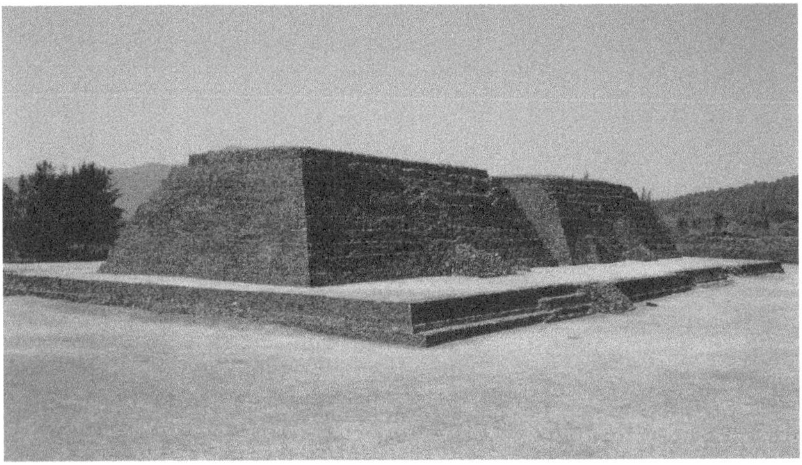

FIGURE 23. Pyramids at the Plaza de Armas, Ihuatzio, Michoacán. Photograph by the author.

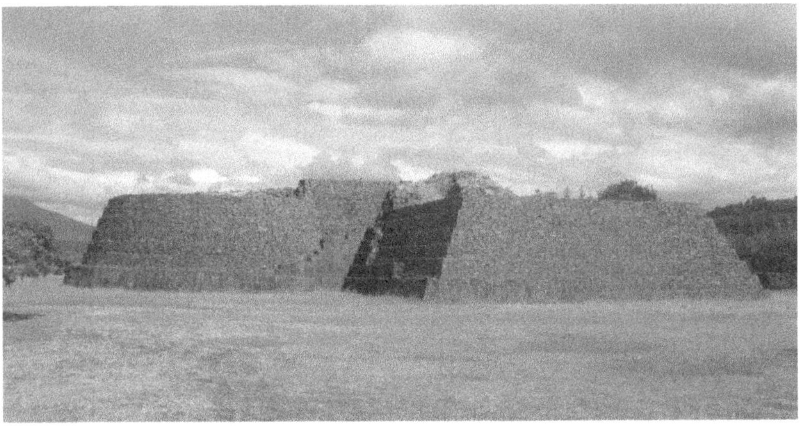

FIGURE 24. Yacatas, Tzintzuntzan, Michoacán. Photograph by the author.

the arrival of the Spaniards (fig. 25; see plate 7). In it, the destruction of the temple, as shown by the stones falling off their platform, signals not just the end of indigenous religion but also the end of Uanacaze rule. Thus, the temple as a symbol encodes multiple layers of meaning.

The *Relación*'s artists also used other ideograms to refer to other Mesoamerican concepts. All four artists use the motif of a man sitting in a house to represent the P'urhépecha concept of *yrecha* (ruler). As Mesoamericanist Eduard Seler has pointed out, the root of *yrecha*, *yre-*, means "to live in or inhabit a place."[80] The man sitting in the house thus becomes the yrecha. This convention was employed in other areas of Mesoamerica, as well, as exemplified by the *Codex Baranda* from Oaxaca.[81]

Other complex ideograms may have gone unnoticed because at first sight they appear to be only slight variations of the text. For example, according to the text the Uanacaze captured an Islander priest who was recruiting supporters to fight against them and sacrificed him at the temple. However, artist 1 shows the Islander priest being held by a single Uanacaze noble, and another one, facing him, has shot the Islander with an arrow (fig. 26). After killing the priest, according to the text, the Uanacaze nobles returned his

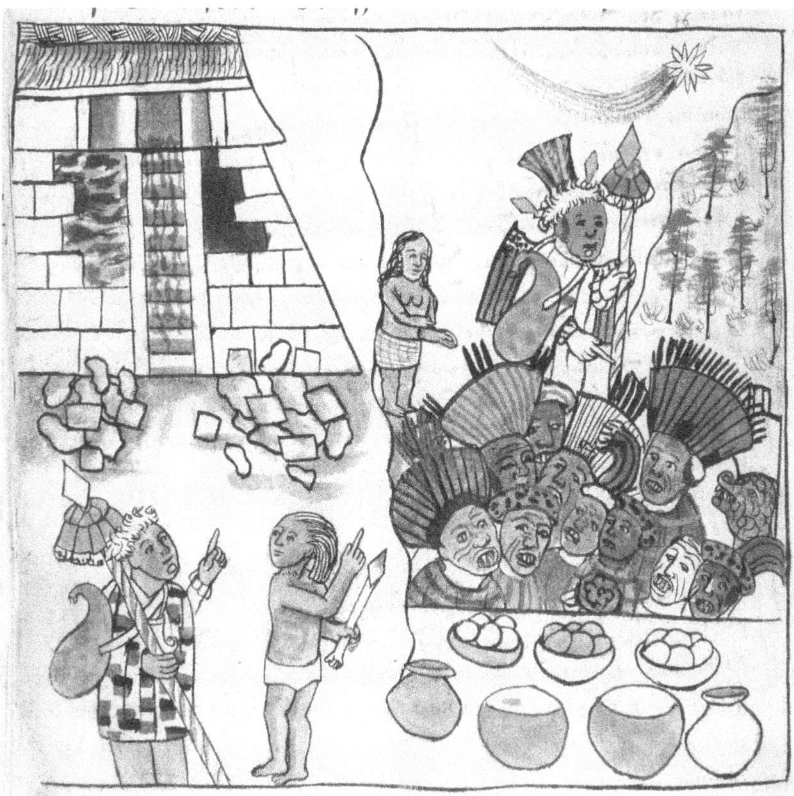

FIGURE 25. Artist 1. "De los agüeros que tubo esta gente y sueños, antes que viniesen los españoles a esta Provincia" (Of the omens and dreams these people had before the Spaniards came to this province). *Relación de Michoacán*, fol. 35v. Real Biblioteca del Monasterio de El Escorial, San Lorenzo de El Escorial, Spain, C IV 5. Photograph © Patrimonio Nacional, Spain.

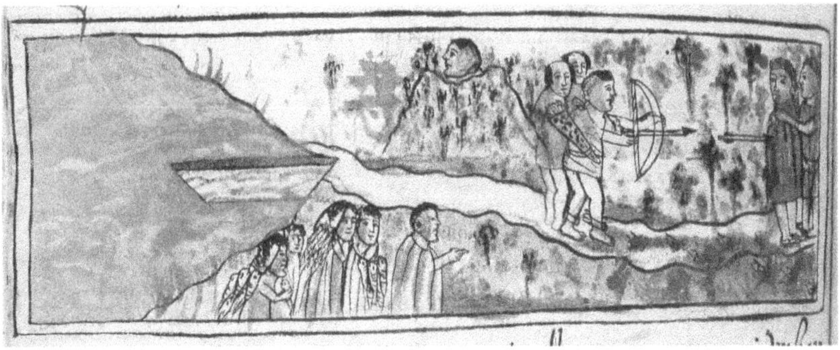

FIGURE 26. Artist 1. "Como Quaracuri avisó a Tariacuri y fue tomado este sacerdote Naca en una celada" (How Quaracuri warned Tariacuri and he captured the priest Naca in an ambush). *Relación Michoacán*, fol. 80v. Real Biblioteca del Monasterio de El Escorial, San Lorenzo de El Escorial, Spain, C IV 5. Photograph © Patrimonio Nacional, Spain.

body to the Islander lord who had sent the priest on his unfortunate mission. The priest's death served as a warning to his lord for his ill-conceived plans. The discrepancy between text and image may signal that the latter refers to the concept of *quaningarintstani* (to forewarn and consider).[82] The word *quaningarintstani* comes from the root *qhuani-*, meaning "to throw something," and is used to construct words such as *qhuanicuni* (to shoot with arrows); the particle *-ngari-*, meaning "to face somebody"; and *-ntsta-*, a reiterative particle. Thus, the image showing the Uanacaze lord facing and shooting the Islander priest may in fact be a visual representation of *quaningarintstani*, here meaning "to forewarn the Islander noble."

Some of the direct representations the artists used can also be read beyond their literal meaning, for example, the depiction of human footprints, which are often found in indigenous manuscripts from other parts of Mexico.[83] According to Batalla Rosado, in the *Relación* they serve only to signal directional movement.[84] Close observation reveals that the artists used them to represent conquest.[85] Artist 3 used them to indicate the impending conquest of enemy towns (see left-hand side of fig. 22 and fig. 38). He replicated this concept in a scene showing the arrival of the Spaniards in the area (see fig. 49). In it, the horses carrying the Spaniards do not leave hoofprints; instead, human footprints signify the Spaniards' impending takeover of Michoacán. Artist 4 used footprints to depict the actual advance of the Uanacaze troops on enemy towns (see right-hand side of fig. 22). The

P'urhépecha noun for footprint, *atzicata*, shares the root of the verb *atzicani* (stepping on something) and is closely related to the verb *angaxurhini* (to stand somewhere). These verbs can signify conquest, governance, and possession of a given space.[86] The text of the *Relación* confirms this reading by using the metaphor "step on one side on the water and on the other the land" to indicate that the Uanacaze and the Islanders together will conquer both the islands in Lake Pátzcuaro and the mainland.[87]

The artists' use of ideograms shows their knowledge of Mesoamerican pictography and their ability to convey complex meaning. However, the *Relación*'s images seldom possess the iconographic complexity of manuscripts from other areas. Pictographs for people's names, dates, and even most place-names are conspicuously absent. The *Relación*'s compositions seem streamlined, and the story line can be followed without the erudition of an indigenous reader. Given that the artists did know and use indigenous pictographic conventions in the *Relación*, the incidental omission of such conventions suggests that both inclusion and exclusion were deliberate, indicating that the artists carefully chose elements from both Mesoamerican and European iconography.

To understand the reasoning behind these choices, it is important to note that the artists of the *Relación* had a very difficult task at hand. They did not simply seek to represent a past that was significant to them but one that was accessible to Spanish viewers. Spanish officials often lacked the skills to read indigenous paintings, so in judicial cases indigenous witnesses were enlisted to interpret the contents of pictorial documents. If necessary, a translator would be used during their testimony.[88] Viceroy Mendoza maintained that indigenous paintings could lead to confusion over time and therefore had all information from court cases recorded in a journal using alphabetic text.[89] By carefully choosing the contents of the images and pairing them with alphabetic text, the friar and artists created a document they hoped the viceroy could understand.

If the *Relación*'s images were to work on their own, that is, to be understood by a European audience without the need of indigenous interpreters, clarity without sacrificing readability was important. While the *Relación*'s artists may have chosen some pictographs that added nuances and complexities to the text, more often they chose pre-Columbian motifs that could be understood on their own or paired them with corroborating or explanatory text.

They selected some of these pictographic elements from the indigenous tradition because they paralleled elements in European iconography. This was not unique to the *Relación*. For example, Jeanette Peterson has noted that a person pointing his or her hand at another in both Nahuatl and European images indicates that the former is speaking to the latter. This gesture shows up in colonial paintings from central Mexico, indicating that the meaning of these gestures overlapped across cultures.[90] This is also the case in the *Relación*, in which indigenous leaders are often shown "pointing/speaking" to their audiences (see figs. 36, 40, 46). In addition, all four artists' depictions of the yrecha as a man sitting in a house are comparable to the European convention of representing rulers in their palaces.

Other indigenous iconographic elements, while they may not have had close parallels in European art, were probably easily understood because they exhibit clear associations with the ideas they depict. For example, an arrow sticking into the ground next to a fire symbolizes a declaration of war. Even among those not visually inclined, a show of weapons implies bellicose intentions. Footprints symbolizing movement and conquest would probably have been well understood by the Spanish audience, because Spanish and Nahua colonial rituals of taking over somebody else's land included walking on the newly acquired possessions.[91]

The contributors of the *Relación* paired those pictographs that might have been hard for the Spaniards to understand with explanatory text. For example, artist 3's depiction of a broken tree indicating the rift between allies, a convention that appears in other indigenous manuscripts, is placed in a chapter in which the text explains that the tree was rotten and broke when a Uanacaze lord climbed it, and that, upon falling, the Uanacaze lord lost consciousness (fig. 27).[92] When he regained it, he remembered previous insults from some of his allies and decided to wage war on them. A cave, which often represents a place of origin or, among Texcocan manuscripts from central Mexico, the founding of a polity, is explained in the text of the *Relación* as the place where three Uanacaze lords met to discuss their plans to consolidate the region under their rule (i.e., consolidate their own polity; fig. 28, and see plate 8).[93]

When the artists of the *Relación* reviewed the manuscript, they changed some of the compositions by deleting some pre-Columbian motifs and less clear iconography and aligning the content of the images closer to the story of the text. In the image in folio 124v, for example, a rectangular icon, which remains to be identified by scholars, was originally placed in the middle of

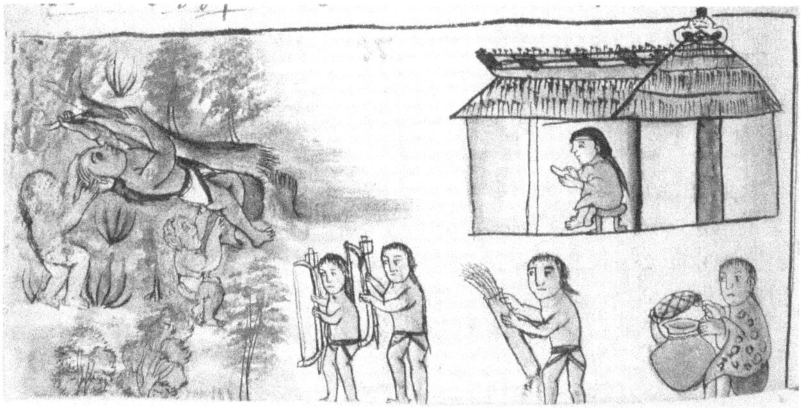

FIGURE 27. Artists 3 and 4. "Como Tariacuri enbió sus sobrinos amonestar y avisar un cuñado suyo, que no se emborrachase, y como los rescibió mal y a la buelta lo que le aconteció a Hirepan con un árbol en el monte" (How Tariacuri sent his nephews to admonish and warn one of his brothers-in-law not to get drunk, and how he mistreated them, and on the way back what happened to Hirepan with a tree in the forest). *Relación de Michoacán*, fol. 126v. Real Biblioteca del Monasterio de El Escorial, San Lorenzo de El Escorial, Spain, C IV 5. Photograph © Patrimonio Nacional, Spain.

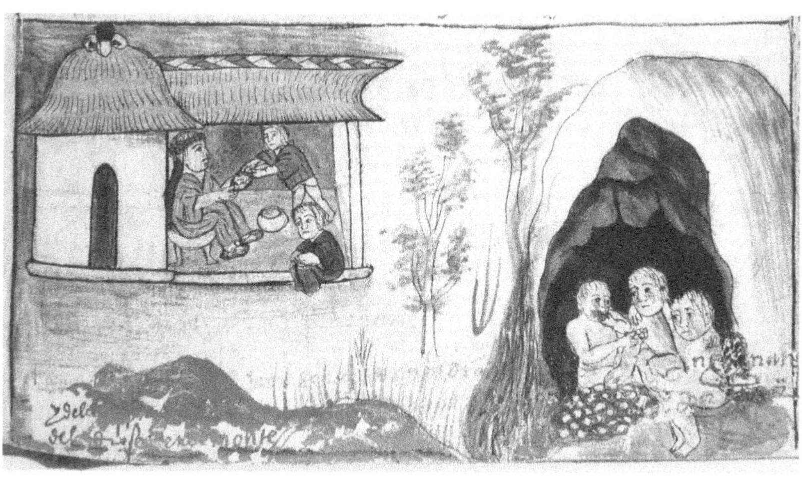

FIGURE 28. Artist 4. "Como Curatame enbió por Hirepan y Tangaxoan que hazían penitencia en una cueva y de la respuesta que dieron" (How Curatame sent for Hirepan and Tangaxoan, who were doing penance in a cave, and the answer they gave). *Relación de Michoacán*, fol. 116r. Real Biblioteca del Monasterio de El Escorial, San Lorenzo de El Escorial, Spain, C IV 5. Photograph © Patrimonio Nacional, Spain.

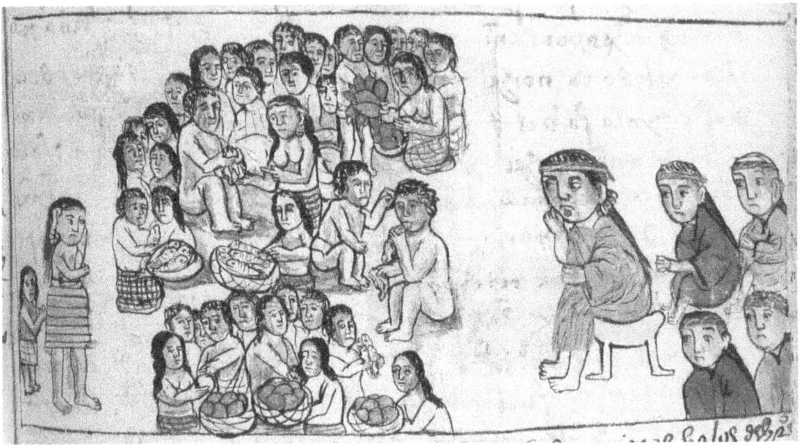

FIGURE 29. Artists 1 and 3. "Como Tariacuri buscava sus sobrinos Hirepan y Tangaxoan que se avían ydo a otra parte, y de la pobreza que tenía su madre con ellos" (How Tariacuri was looking for his nephews Hirepan and Tangaxoan who had gone elsewhere, and of the poverty their mother endured with them). *Relación de Michoacán*, fol. 101r. Real Biblioteca del Monasterio de El Escorial, San Lorenzo de El Escorial, Spain, C IV 5. Photograph © Patrimonio Nacional, Spain.

the composition in front of a large female figure and was later whited-out and not replaced (see fig. 17). Likewise, artist 1, one of the artists most familiar with European conventions, corrected the illustration in folio 101r, which artist 3 had originally painted. Artist 1 deleted a small group of unidentified figurines in the center and replaced them with an easily recognizable market scene, complete with sellers of fish and other goods (fig. 29). This brought the illustration into line with the text, which mentioned the market scene, so an uninitiated audience could easily understand it.

In summary, careful analysis of the images reveals that four artists worked on the images of the *Relación*. They sometimes worked alone and sometimes as a team, collaborating on some scenes and even editing each other's work. They carefully selected motifs from the pre-Columbian visual vocabulary and went one step beyond tradition by using Renaissance visual techniques to represent events predating the arrival of Europeans in this region. This choice would not only have made it easier for the European viewer to understand the images but would have found a ready audience in the viceroy, whose family had played an important role in bringing the taste of the Italian Renaissance to Spain.[94]

Conclusion

Even though many of the manuscript's pages are missing, the surviving sections of the *Relación* reveal a complex working relationship among its various contributors. After collecting the information, the friar and his scribes produced from one to several drafts that were then copied to the surviving manuscript; the mistakes of the copyists can be discerned in duplicated lines of the text that had to be whited-out. The friar read the text once again and decided to make a few more corrections. He edited it, crossing out some words, and rewrote the titles in such a way as to make room for more images. The artists then painted the images in some of the spaces originally left for them by the scribes, in the new spaces created by the friar-editor, at the end of chapters where the scribes had left a blank space to mark the end of one chapter and the beginning of the next, and on separate sheets of paper. For the most part, the artists illustrated the events mentioned in the titles but also added a few images that did not match the titles. The artists then went back and corrected a few of the images. The artists carefully selected from a wide repertoire of pre-Columbian and European imagery to both convey complex meaning and communicate effectively with the manuscript's intended audience. Finally, the friar-editor went over the manuscript one more time, added explanatory glosses to some of the illustrations, and changed one of the titles to make it match an image. This process of creation reveals a constant negotiation of meaning.

The agendas of the *Relación*'s contributors were not uniform. Astutely, the friar had chosen to work with both the Uanacaze family and its allies and the current governor. The Uanacaze family and its allies sought to present themselves as the legitimate rulers of the region. However, Don Pedro Cuiniarangari, the non-Uanacaze governor of the City of Michoacán, had to explain how he had managed to acquire that post. The following chapters explore how the images and text in the *Relación* had to carefully weave these stories together to present a united indigenous front to the Spanish viceroy, since the various collaborators had to fight together in the courts against the Spanish encomenderos in the region. The manuscript became a filter through which to understand the past and apply its lessons to present circumstances. It connected both time and space to the living contributors of the manuscript.

2

Unfaithful Lovers and Malicious Sorcerers

JUSTICE, PUNISHMENT, AND THE BODY

In language inflated with praise for the mission of the viceroy and his own Franciscan Order, the friar-editor asserted in the prologue to the *Relación* that the people native to Michoacán lacked books and moral virtues. The viceroy's duty to govern the people of Michoacán was an arduous one, the friar explained, as their only virtue was generosity. They had no concept of chastity, temperance, or justice, and in P'urhépecha, their native tongue, they had to articulate such concepts in a roundabout way. Yet, contrary to the friar's claims, the *Relación* includes three images whose titles indicate that they depict ceremonies during which justice was being administered.

In this chapter, I argue that the first two images show indigenous justice as intricately connected to concepts of speaking, listening, and obeying (figs. 30 and 31; see plates 9, 10). The artists represented the Uanacaze as arbiters of a judicial system in pre-Columbian times and hoped for the continuation of their privileged position into the colonial period.

The third image supported the need for a Uanacaze-controlled judicial system by depicting the punishment of crimes that were of particular

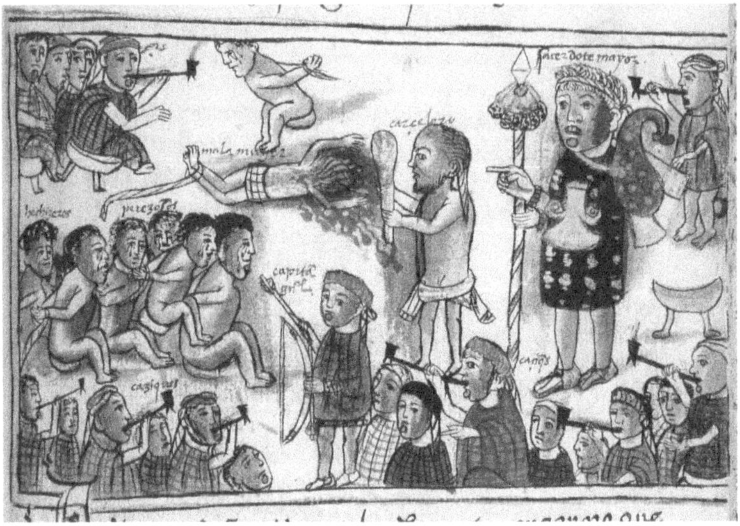

FIGURE 30. Artist 1. "Síguese la historia, como fueron señores el Caçonçi y sus antepasados en esta Provincia de Mechuacan y de la justicia general que se hazía" (Here follows the history of how the cazonci and his ancestors were lords in this province of Michoacán and of the general justice carried out). *Relación de Michoacán*, fol. 61r. Real Biblioteca del Monasterio de El Escorial, San Lorenzo de El Escorial, Spain, C IV 5. Photograph © Patrimonio Nacional, Spain.

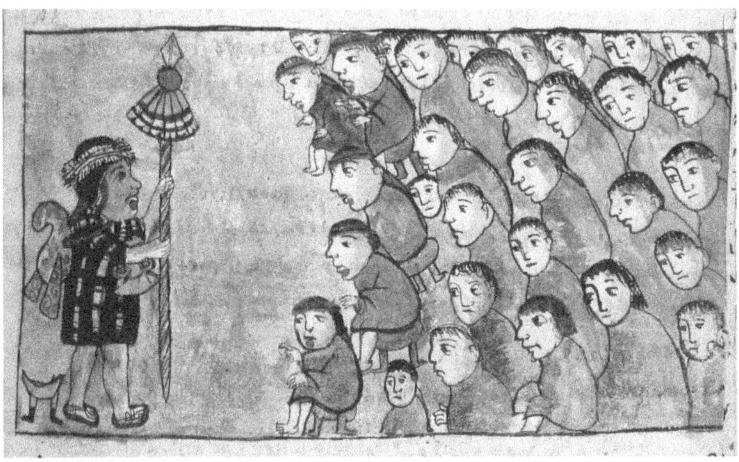

FIGURE 31. Artists 3 and 4. "De la plática y razonamiento que hazía el Sacerdote Mayor a todos los Señores y gente de la provincia acabando esta historia pasada, diziendo la vida que avían tenido sus antepasados" (Of the speeches and reasoning that the main priest would give to all the nobles and people of the province upon finishing this past history, telling the life that their ancestors led). *Relación de Michoacán*, fol. 133r. Real Biblioteca del Monasterio de El Escorial, San Lorenzo de El Escorial, Spain, C IV 5. Photograph © Patrimonio Nacional, Spain.

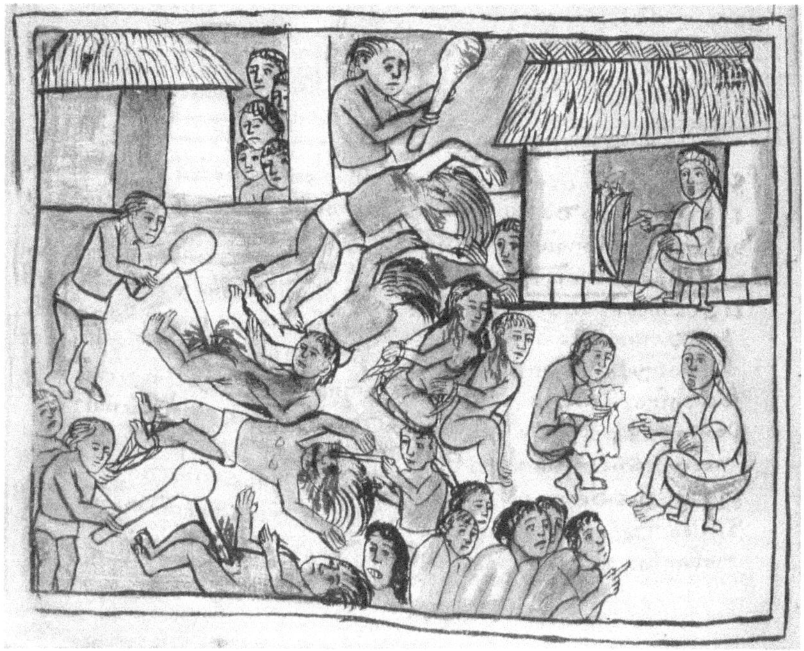

FIGURE 32. Artist 1. "De la justicia que hazía el Cazonçi" (Of the justice done by the cazonci). *Relación Michoacán*, fol. 20v. Real Biblioteca del Monasterio de El Escorial, San Lorenzo de El Escorial, Spain, C IV 5. Photograph © Patrimonio Nacional, Spain.

interest to Spaniards, such as adultery and witchcraft (fig. 32; see plate 11). Its painter connected specific crimes to the punishment of specific body parts, for example, lacerating the ear for unfaithful lovers and lacerating the mouth and gouging the eyes for sorcerers. Interestingly, these particular punishments seem to have responded to P'urhépecha concepts of the body. Thus, the artist created an image that responded to Spanish interests while using P'urhépecha concepts. These three images, by different means, manifested and supported the power of the Uanacaze nobility.

To understand how these justice images sought to speak to the viceroy, the work of Michel Foucault can be of help. In his analysis of medieval society, Foucault has pointed out that during their rise, monarchic institutions represented themselves as new agencies of arbitration, replacing feudal societies that existed in states of conflict.[1] Western monarchies expressed themselves through a system of laws, which were the language of power and helped justify the very presence of the monarchy. In Spain, the judicial reforms of King Fernando III and his son Alfonso X's legislative work, mainly the *Siete Partidas*, slowly replaced other systems and gave arbitration of judicial matters to the royal house.[2] This transformation of European society impacted the way in which Europeans interacted and perceived the peoples they encountered outside Europe. During colonizing expeditions in the Americas, the presence or perceived absence of justice systems often became for Europeans one of the measures used to judge the civilized nature of the peoples they encountered. Indigenous artists often included images of justice among their historical accounts (e.g., *Codex Mendoza* and *Mapa Quinatzin*). These representations, visual and otherwise, of a pre-Columbian justice system in ways that Spanish officials could have comprehended would have helped indigenous leaders validate their continuation in power during colonial times.[3]

In the *Relación*, the first two images of justice bracket the historical narration, which constitutes most of part 2, and depict the main priest giving a speech at a ceremony for administering justice. The main priest addresses an audience while holding his jeweled and feather-crested staff. In the first scene, he stands before an audience, while the accused are receiving or await punishment. The second scene comes at the end of his speech in the manuscript when the priest again speaks to an audience. The first serves as the opening scene of part 2 and of the historical narration it contains; the second closes the historical narration. The third scene, located in part 3 of the *Relación*, provides an ethnographic depiction of justice by the ruler.

The first two images depict the main priest heading a ceremony for administering justice. The opening image appears below the title "Here Follows the History of How the Cazonci [main ruler] and His Ancestors Were Lords in This Province of Michoacán and of the General Justice Carried Out" (fig. 30).[4] Inside a rectangle that occupies about half the page, the artist provides a view of an open-air ceremony. The main priest stands with his mouth slightly open while holding his jeweled and feather-crested staff. He wears a maroon, black, and white cloak. On his back, he carries a turquoise-encrusted gourd with a red tip and golden plates on the sides. He sports bracelets on his arms and golden tweezers on his chest. Carefully written glosses identify him as the *sacerdote mayor* (main priest).

The other characters in the picture are also labeled. The main priest points to a *carcelero* (jailer), who stands in the center of the picture. The jailer is clubbing a *mala mujer* (bad woman), who lies on her stomach with her hands stretched over her head and her feet tied by a rope, blood spattering from her head. Above her, a nude man sits on a small stool with his hands tied behind his back, tears flowing from his eyes. Below the woman stands a male figure identified as *capitán general* (captain general), who with an arrow in his right hand points to a group of naked, crying figures. The captions identify them as *perezosos* (lazy ones) and *hechiceros* (sorcerers). Gathered at the edges of the image, the attentive audience watches the spectacle. Lip plugs, stools, and smoking pipes identify many of them as members of the upper classes.[5] Small glosses corroborate this, identifying a group in the upper left corner as *señores* (lords) and two groups along the bottom edge of the image as *caciques* (chiefs).

In the second image illustrating this justice ceremony, the priest also wears a maroon, black, and white cloak, carries a turquoise-encrusted gourd with small golden plates on his back, and sports golden tweezers on his chest. He wears red and black sandals, painstakingly drawn, and carries in his hands a striped staff with a blue disk surmounted by a pointed arrowhead from which dangle feathers and shells. He addresses an audience, which includes a row of noblemen, identified by their lip plugs, green garlands on their heads, and stools (fig. 31).

The bracketing of the historical account by the justice ceremony and its images has been the subject of some debate. In the facsimile edition of the *Relación* from 1956, the editors note that this ceremony, identified in the text as *Equata-Cónsquaro* (fiesta of the arrows), appears at the beginning of the historical account rather than in the now missing part 1, which contained a discussion of the religious ceremonies. To them, the ceremony appears to be misplaced since they see it as being unrelated to the historical narrative that follows.[6] From another point of view, however, the placement of this ceremony can help unfold the intricate relationship that exists in the *Relación* between history, the administration of justice by a centralized power, and the public celebration of religious rites.

First, one must note that the inclusion of this fiesta and its illustrations stands in stark contrast not only to the friar's complaint that these people lacked justice but also to the sixteenth-century Spanish-P'urhépecha *Diccionario grande de la lengua de Michoacán*, which at first glance seems to confirm the friar's assertion. Lacking an exact equivalent for "justice" in P'urhépecha, the *Diccionario grande* translates it as "cez atsiperaqua justicia," which still includes the Spanish word for "justice," *justicia*.[7] "Cez atsiperaqua justicia" literally means the "well doing or having of justice."[8] The *Diccionario grande* also translates "to carry out sentences" (*justiciar*) as "justicia himbo curanditahpeni," which literally means "to make them obey through justice."[9] *Curanditahpeni* comes from the verb *curani* (to listen), and *curanditahpeni* can be translated as "to make somebody listen." The connection between listening and good behavior (i.e., obeying) in sixteenth-century P'urhépecha is reinforced by terms such as *curandini*, which means both "to understand a language" and "to lead a peaceful life, to not harm anybody."[10] Interestingly, the word *curanditahpeni* shows up again in the *Diccionario grande* as the definition for the Spanish words *castigar* and *punir* (to punish).[11] Thus, while Spaniards understood indigenous justice as a matter of judgment and punishment (physical and otherwise), the P'urhépecha concept seems to focus on the acts of making somebody listen and obey (i.e., behave according to social norm), which the threat of physical punishment only reinforces. Since specific concepts probably did not cross cultural and language barriers unaltered, in all likelihood visual representations did not aim at a simple parity. One therefore should not expect to see a direct correlation in the *Relación* between the indigenous images and the Spanish text.

The images of justice bracketing the historical account show the main priest with his mouth partially opened and his audience in the process of listening. The first scene deliberately captures the main priest at the very moment in which he is verbally narrating the history of the Uanacaze rise to power. The close attention given to his costume and accoutrements makes him the focal point of the scene, as does his size in proportion to other figures. According to the text accompanying the image, for twenty days prior to this fiesta the priest had sat on his stool from morning to noon as he listened to the charges against the accused and made the appropriate decisions concerning their cases. On the day of the fiesta, it says, he stood up, took his staff, and recounted the history of the Uanacaze, just as he does in the illustration; the stool on which he had previously sat is still visible in the background.

The main priest as represented in this image is simultaneously a religious leader, a judge, and the guardian of oral history. It is the act of speaking that fuses these roles and brings him center stage. While in the Aztec world the title used to identify the ruler was *tlatoani* or, in the case of the emperor, *huey tlatoani* (speaker or great speaker, respectively), in Michoacán this title/role seems to have been reserved for the main priest. The P'urhépecha word for the main priest was *petamuti*, meaning "the one who pronounces/speaks or determines with authority."[12] He is the one in charge of making his audience listen and obey. His title derives from his ability to deliver, narrate, or speak, and his authority from his ability to recount history. History, the artist seems to say, is indivisible from speaking and making the audience listen and obey. The indigenous narrators and artists of the *Relación* presented history as a selective and purposeful narrative that seeks to generate a pattern of response: obedience. The recounting of history and making people listen and obey join forces as a complex concept in the *Relación* (and in this image in particular), which the friar, for lack of a more comprehensive word, translated for the Spanish audience as *justicia*.

The image and its glosses further reinforce the union between historical events and making people obey by depicting the main priest giving his speech and the so-called jailer simultaneously clubbing a "bad woman," even though the text specifies that sentences were carried out *after* the main priest had finished his speech. Thus, the scene unites the oral narration of history with the punishment of criminals, both temporally and conceptually. Several sixteenth- and seventeenth-century documents use the P'urhépecha word *catape* for "jailer." According to the historian Felipe Castro Gutiérrez, *catape* may be an abbreviation of *catahpeti* or *catahperi*, meaning "the one who captures or makes someone prisoner."[13] Among pre-Columbian peoples—and those living in Michoacán were no exception—the goal of warriors in battle was often to capture prisoners. In his sixteenth-century chronicle, Francisco Cervantes de Salazar explains that "brave men" dispensed the punishment of criminals throughout Mexico, and in the *Relación*, the term "brave men" is used to describe warriors.[14] It is therefore possible that the so-called jailer in the image stands as a brave man, a warrior who sacrifices the enemies of the Uanacaze. The text of the *Relación* states that people captured in war, when not sacrificed, became slaves. Furthermore, the text accompanying this image mentions that slaves intended for sacrifice who had not yet met their fate were sacrificed on this date, thus equating criminals and prisoners of war.

The conceptual union between previous wars and current criminals is further achieved by the presence of the captain general at the bottom center of the image. He points at the criminals with an arrow in his right hand. According to the *Relación*, the captain general helped carry out the Uanacaze ruler's conquests. The bow and arrows he holds connote war and the conquest of territories. In several images of the *Relación*, burning arrows announce the Uanacaze conquest of their enemies, and colonial documents often mention that arrows marked the rulers' lands (see figs. 22, 38). Therefore, the caption and the image join historical conquests with the administration of justice.

In addition to representing P'urhépecha concepts, the illustration addresses a Spanish-speaking audience through its small glosses. Written by the editorial hand of the manuscript, presumably the friar-editor, these glosses serve as bridges between P'urhépecha and Spanish concepts of justice. Pierre Bourdieu's analysis of the process of communication through which an artwork is deciphered can help clarify the function of these glosses. Bourdieu explains that when "reading" an image, *seeing* is a function of *knowledge*. Viewers must name visible things, expressing verbally what is otherwise coded visually. They must possess the cultural competence to know the specific visual code in order to be effective readers in the process of communication. If they lack knowledge of the specific code, they may feel lost and may not understand it.[15] In the case of this illustration, the glosses provide viewers with sufficient knowledge to decode it in a particular way. They structure the picture according to the participants in a Spanish trial. The glosses identify a "jailer," his victim as a "bad woman," and the group of otherwise unidentified criminals as "lazy ones" and "sorcerers." These glosses serve the function of interpreter of this image for Viceroy Mendoza and, by extension, do the same for the modern viewer. The editorial hand gains cultural capital by interpreting otherwise unrecognizable events. He makes the unfamiliar familiar by joining P'urhépecha and Spanish concepts of justice.[16] To borrow Roland Barthes's word, these captions seek to "anchor" the image's meaning.[17]

The bad behavior of women, sorcery, and laziness that the petamuti—and by extension the Uanacaze—condemns in this image were of particular interest to the Spanish authorities. The historian Claudia Espejel Carbajal has previously noticed the similarities between the crimes prosecuted in the *Relación* and some of those mentioned in Spanish king Alfonso X's *Siete Partidas*, which were brought to and implemented in the Americas.[18] The bad woman being clubbed at the top of the picture in all likelihood represents an adulteress, since the *Relación* often refers to adulteresses as bad women. Unfaithful women were a recurrent concern in Spanish law and literature of the time.[19] The *Siete Partidas* gave detailed descriptions of adultery and sorcery and their respective punishments.[20] Colonial ecclesiastical and civil authorities frowned upon and prosecuted these behaviors, as well as laziness.[21] In colonial Michoacán, adulterers and people living together outside marriage or with multiple partners were often persecuted, since the Spanish authorities sought to control sexuality among indigenous peoples.[22] The 1579 *Relación geográfica* from Chilchota, Michoacán, by the Spaniard Pedro de Billela, mentions that indigenous doctors were really "sorcerers" who tricked people into believing them.[23] These individuals cured, but also caused, ailments and professed the ability to look into past and future events by means distrusted by Spaniards, who associated them with idolatrous practices and "pacts with the devil."[24] In effect, royal edicts prohibited indigenous people from practicing medicine.[25] Laziness, or as the historian Felipe Castro Gutiérrez described it, the unwillingness of the indigenous population to participate in recently introduced forms of labor (i.e., working in Spanish-run mines and plantations), was prosecuted because it hampered the development of the colonial economy.[26] This is not unusual in colonial ideologies. Thus, guided by the glosses, the audience of the manuscript may interpret the image of the Uanacaze priest as a punisher of transgressors of the Spanish code. By focusing on these crimes, the Uanacaze gained status in the eyes of the viceroy.

Part 2 of the *Relación* further blurs the line between past and current criminals in the Uanacaze priest's historical account. At the end of his speech, he reminds the indigenous nobles in his imaginary audience that because their lives had been spared by the Uanacaze, they had become *indebted* to the Uanacaze god Curicaueri.[27] According to the main priest, they were "the low people of Michoacán" and had to maintain Curicaueri's fires and fields and carry out war in his name.[28] Curicaueri was there to punish those who had not fulfilled their duties. It is this social contract benefiting the Uanacaze that the justice system sought to enforce, and punishment was the result of its violation. In the Uanacaze priest's own words: "Why don't you look to your backs, to the past, when you were slaves? Why did they conquer you? Now you do not keep what you promised. . . . Now Curicaueri feels sorry for himself, this current year in which we are, that is why he has you here to do justice to you."[29]

In addition, the petamuti's version of history created a dichotomy between the virtuous Uanacaze and their misbehaving enemies. The Uanacaze priest accuses some of the Uanacaze's enemies of quarreling among themselves, others of impious behavior, some of excessive drinking, and the noblewomen of those groups of sexual misconduct. This speech, as recorded in the *Relación*, helped the Uanacaze nobility gain advantage by representing themselves as having replaced previous rulers who possessed the same moral flaws the Spaniards sought to correct.

Depicting and retelling this history during colonial times was no inconsequential rhetorical act. Indigenous elites throughout Mexico were very much aware of the connection between judicial authority and the ability to govern after the arrival of Europeans. In central Mexico, for example, Don Antonio Pimentel Tlahuiloltzin, one of the colonial heirs to the Tetzcocan ruler Netzahualcoyotl, would likewise have the judicial system of his great ancestor represented in the *Mapa Quinatzin* as a way to advocate for his privileges during colonial times.[30] Portraying the Uanacaze bringing justice to the people of Michoacán would have helped their colonial heirs validate their political power.[31]

In the sixteenth and seventeenth centuries, much of the indigenous authorities' ability to govern depended on their capacity to administer justice, punish criminals, and enforce Christian morals. Town officials had the authority to arrest criminals and to ensure that children received a Christian education and attended Christian rites. They also informed civil and ecclesiastical authorities of perpetrators of moral misconduct (single pregnant women, adulteresses, etc.).[32] In effect, indigenous governors and mayors fought Spanish functionaries for the right to judge crimes, arguing that otherwise they (the governors and mayors) would "lose all of their authority."[33] To present the Uanacaze as the bearers and arbiters of justice and moral standards was to argue for their return to the rulership of Michoacán.

These first two images, then, depict the delivery of a historical speech intended to make people obey, thus conveying the P'urhépecha concept of justice. The Spanish glosses in the first image made it accessible to a Spanish-speaking audience and transformed the image into a Spanish-like trial. The kinds of crimes identified by the glosses were prosecuted in colonial courts. On the one hand, the friar-editor gained cultural and political capital by allying himself with the indigenous nobility. On the other hand, the Uanacaze, represented by the Uanacaze priest, stood as arbiters of justice and guardians of appropriate conduct very much in tune with that of the Spanish colonial system. The main priest's speech presented Viceroy Mendoza with the narration of a familiar history, that of a society that had gone through a transformation and self-validation through a judicial system very much like Spain's. To deny the validity of Uanacaze rule would, by extension, negate the monarchical system the viceroy represented. Thus, the Uanacaze priest's narration reveals itself as a strategy aimed at justifying the Uanacaze return to power in Spanish eyes.

Justice by the Main Ruler

In contrast to the first two images of justice, in which the main priest and his speech are the focus, a third image, titled "Of the Justice Done by the

Cazonci," depicts the main ruler administering justice at the center of a bloody scene of corporal punishment (fig. 32).[34] The friar-editor explains that because not all crimes were included in the previous section, he has included them in part 3 of the *Relación*, the ethnographic section. The artist depicts the courtyard of the ruler's house. The ruler, identified by his blue stool and headdress, appears twice, once inside his house and again in front of it, in the right-hand corner of the image, while pointing at a figure who shows him a cloth. Behind this person sit a woman and a nude man, both bleeding from their ears. Counterclockwise from them, a figure who has lost an arm (held by another individual) lies on his stomach. Above him, one individual clubs another. Continuing in a counterclockwise direction, a man employs a club with a spike protruding from it to puncture the anus of a contorted figure lying on the ground. Next to him, a victim whose mouth has been cut at the corners is being poked in the eyes with a narrow stick and dragged with a rope tied to his left foot by yet another figure. Directly below them, an individual punctures the genitalia of a figure lying on his back with another club-and-spike weapon. The audience in this image is limited to two small groups of five people. One group is at the bottom edge of the image, diagonal and to the left of the ruler. The first person in the group points to the ruler. The other group peeks from the side of a small building on the left-hand side of the picture. The following analysis will show that the artist reinforced the sociopolitical power of the Uanacaze by depicting crimes and punishments in which the Spanish legal system was also invested and by connecting the crimes to punishments that drew upon indigenous concepts of the body.

According to the text of the *Relación*, within this justice system criminals were disciplined for their first three offenses; death punished the fourth. Although, according to the text, the Uanacaze ruler judged only the most serious of cases, some of which resulted in death sentences, the *Relación* artist has chosen to portray a variety of punishments for criminals who had not yet been dealt the death sentence. This busy image, with its bright reds and contorted bodies, is far from self-explanatory. The text of the *Relación* reveals that the castigation of specific body parts marked specific crimes, thus creating a culturally identifiable visual language. Once again, it is only through the narrator's voice, as recorded in the text, that the viewer can begin to understand the relationship between specific crimes and specific physical punishments. For example, the text mentions that sorcerers had their mouths lacerated and were dragged around by the foot, as seen in the bottom left corner of the image. Adulterers had their ears lacerated and were stripped of their cloaks. Slightly off center and to the right, an offended husband, presumably having caught his wife and her lover in flagrante delicto, holds the lover's cloak up to the ruler as evidence of their affair, while sitting behind him the unfaithful pair bleed from the ears.

As noted previously, the specific crimes the text identifies, sorcery and adultery, were both prosecuted by Spanish authorities. In addition, the spectacle of physical punishment would have resonated with Viceroy Mendoza, who had commissioned the manuscript. Michell Merback has pointed out that during medieval and Renaissance Europe, the public spectacle of punished bodies conveyed the power and presence of dynastic rule.[35] Spain was no exception to this, and the royal laws contained in the *Siete Partidas*, which regulated Spanish life (at least in writing), provided for the public, corporal punishment of criminals. Sentences varied depending on the nature of the offense and the social status and even gender of the accuser and the accused. These included lashing, forced labor, exile, amputation of a limb, and death. Those who had killed or intended to kill somebody would receive the same form of execution as their victims or intended victims in an eye-for-an-eye system.[36]

In central Mexico, where the viceroy resided, he would have likewise encountered justice systems in which physical punishment was part of the sentences administered. In the *Codex Mendoza*, an illuminated indigenous manuscript purportedly commissioned by the viceroy roughly at the same time as the *Relación*, death by stoning was used to punish adulterers and thieves.[37] According to the *Mapa Quinatzin* (also contemporary with the *Relación*), the Tetzcocan artists depicted a pre-Columbian judicial system that punished adultery by stoning or hanging and burning, while thieves, prodigal rulers, and judges who abused their authority were punished by strangulation.[38] In 1546 (only about five years after the *Relación* was finished), the viceroy and the members of the Royal Audience wrote a set of laws for the indigenous population listing specific crimes and their respective sentences, consisting for the most part of a combination of prison time and public lashing (including the punishment of adultery and sorcery).[39] Thus, the image in the *Relación* represented crimes and procedures (i.e., physical punishment) that in a large sense were familiar to Viceroy Mendoza and of much interest to his judicial ambitions.

Like the punished body would have in European judicial systems, in the *Relación*'s scene it seems to convey the authority of the ruling house. It functions as the physical expression of justice. It serves as a communication tool. The mutilated bodies work as mnemonic devices. They register in the memory of the viewer the consequences of transgressing a social order that benefited the Uanacaze. Pain, torture, public humiliation, and their spectacle become the connecting experience for the audience of the manuscript, as it would have for those present at such an event. In viewing and imagining the pain, the audience experiences the meaning of the P'urhépecha word *chechexequa* (authority and majesty), which literally translates as "that which induces much fear in the body."[40] Thus, this image not only conveys a judicial code but also seeks to communicate Uanacaze authority, an authority justified by the main priest's politically motivated historical speech.

Among modern-day and sixteenth-century P'urhépecha people the body seems to also represent a rather complex relationship between the individual and society. The linguists Mauricio Swadesh, Paul Friedrich, and Paul de Wolf have persuasively argued that modern-day P'urhépecha speakers use body-related words to describe personal and social space.[41] Furthermore, the anthropologist Tricia Gabany-Guerrero has pointed out that P'urhépecha speakers also use the body as a model or plan for the ideal construction of social relations and institutions.[42] According to Gabany-Guerrero, in one of the modern-day oratory modes that very much resembles the petamuti's speech, the P'urhépecha speaker uses the human body as a model or "point of departure" for analogies about the world.[43]

As in other parts of Mexico and Central America, the body in sixteenth-century P'urhépecha thinking not only served as an analogy for social relations but in fact seems to have embodied them.[44] The P'urhépecha words to express physical health refer not to a state of being but to an individual's relationship with society. In the sixteenth century, the words for health referred to an individual's ability to follow expected behaviors. *Vraquan piquareraqua*, one of the terms used for health, translates as *vraquan*, meaning "to be frank, magnanimous, and brave," and *piquareraqua*, "to feel intellectually those qualities."[45] When characterizing health, modern-day P'urhépecha people use words such as *cesi piquareraqua*, which they define as "to feel well with society, with the people of one's own town." Likewise, they use *cesi nitamani* and *cesi jangua*, translating them respectively as "to be well, to live well together with others" and "to behave well morally, to be respectful."[46] These words indicate that physical well-being depends on the individual's behavior and ability to relate to others following preestablished social norms.

The body's well-being is not a fixed concept. It is a fluid one and it encompasses an ever-changing relationship between the individual and the community. Representations of the body fix in space and time what are otherwise fleeting interactions between the individual and his or her community. These body representations can be explored as the codification of social norms. That is, one can read them as metonyms that refer to the interaction between an individual and society, while addressing the manuscript's audience.

For the image "Of the Justice Done by the Cazonci," the text of the *Relación* mentions that sorcerers were punished when they had put spells on or killed people.[47] The image shows a sorcerer with his eyes being gouged and the corners of his mouth cut open. To understand how this punishment embodies the harm he has inflicted upon society, one must look at the role of sorcerers in sixteenth-century Michoacán. According to the 1579 *Relación geográfica*, in order to cure people, sorcerers (indigenous doctors) would fill a gourd with water, look into it, blow in it, and look at the sky. Then they would blow around the house, utter a few indecipherable words, and squeeze the flesh of the patient to force the ailment out.[48] Don Pedro Cuiniarangari, one of the narrators of the *Relación*, may be forgiven for having confused the Catholic friars with indigenous doctors when he first saw them look into the wine chalice during mass.[49] The *Relación* also mentions that indigenous doctors were able to see crimes committed by thieves by looking into a gourd full of water and that they settled the fate of troubled marriages by throwing grains of corn into a gourd with water and examining them.[50] The sixteenth-century *Diccionario grande* tells us that this practice was known as *ytsi eramanstani* (to see in the water) and gives *eramansri* (the one who looks into water) as one of the words for sorcerer.[51] These indigenous doctors'/sorcerers' role, then, depended on their ability to see illness and past conducts and foresee the outcome of future events. It was their sight that gave them their power over society and allowed them to inflict good or evil. The act of uttering not only indecipherable words but also sentences and diagnoses allowed them to bring their powers to fruition.

Because the body was seen as the material reflection of the individual's relationship to society, the sorcerer's eyes and mouth embodied an aspect of this relationship. In this image, the sorcerer's mutilated eyes and mouth thus correspond to his transgressions against society. The Uanacaze ruler, in ordering the damage to these specific body parts, ensured that the correspondence between individual and society would be materialized in the physical world, in effect causing the restoration of the "natural" order.

Of all the crimes being punished in this image, text and iconography come together again only in the representation of adultery. In the illustration, adultery is represented by a man holding a piece of cloth and a couple bleeding from their ears. The text explains:

> And the husband who found his woman with another would lacerate the ears of both her and the adulterer as a sign that he had found them in adultery. And he would take away their cloaks and he would come to complain, and he would show them [the cloaks] to the one in charge of carrying out justice, and he was believed with that sign he brought.[52]

The Uanacaze interest in this particular crime relates to the recurrent concern throughout the manuscript with the control of sexuality. In the strictures laid out in the *Relación*, marriages among people outside the ruler's family were arranged within the same ethnic group. These strictures limited women to one sexual partner of the same ethnic group by criminalizing adultery and regulating marriage, ensuring the perpetuation of distinct ethnic and filial lines. Those who had had sex before marriage, which was considered a disgrace, were allowed to marry only if their spouse came from the same ethnic group.[53] Community members were to carefully watch out for adultery, and during marriage ceremonies, women of both the noble and lower classes were reminded to be faithful to their husbands.[54] Although men could practice polygamy, only those who slept with married women were punished for having multiple sex partners, whereas women were always limited to only one.[55]

Nevertheless, the *Relación* tells us that the Uanacaze rulers married women from other ethnic groups, thus establishing powerful political liaisons. The narrative implies that they assured themselves the government seat as long as only they could claim direct descent from their god Curicaueri, who they believed was destined to rule the land.[56] Hence, they carefully watched over sexual conduct as a way of ensuring the survival of their hierarchical power during colonial times. This suggests that the Uanacaze's presumption that they controlled sexuality along ethnic lines was really a political tactic aimed at demonstrating the existence of lineages that enforced their political power.

Accordingly, in the pages of the *Relación*, adultery is not punished evenly across social classes, revealing a great deal about the desire of the Uanacaze to prove the legitimacy of their line. Adultery committed by one of the ruler's wives meant the immediate death of her consort, his family, and all those who lived in his house, as well as the confiscation of all property, fields, and insignia of nobility.[57] Meanwhile, adulterers among all other classes were let off for their first three offenses, and death punished only the fourth. Thus, it appears that the legitimate birth of Uanacaze rulers was far more important than the faithful or unfaithful behavior of most women.

While "Of the Justice Done by the Cazonci" focuses the viewer's attention on adultery, a conduct of much interest to Spanish authorities, it does it through a visual vocabulary of indigenous practices. The artist portrayed a man, presumably the husband, holding a seized cloak; behind him, the naked lover. During the colonial period, indigenous husbands throughout Mexico would seize the cloaks, hats, or any other piece of clothing belonging to a daring lover and present it to the authorities as evidence of adultery. In a Mixtec account of a murder in 1684 in Oaxaca, Mexico, a man who had killed his allegedly unfaithful wife skipped town, leaving behind as evidence of her affair a cotton cloak that had belonged to her lover. The husband specified in a note he left with the cloak that he had taken it when he had found them in flagrante delicto.[58] In Michoacán, in 1597, when Pedro Cuiris found his wife with another man, he hit him in the head with a stone and took his hat, which he presented to the Spanish court as evidence of the affair.[59] While Spanish regulations required only the verbal account of the offended husband as evidence, we know of at least one Spaniard who resided in Pátzcuaro, Michoacán, and apparently followed local customs when in 1590 he found his wife with the indigenous painter Francisco Lorenzo and took the painter's clothes to the authorities as evidence of the affair.[60]

In the *Relación*, representing the adulterous pair bleeding from the ears seems to respond to P'urhépecha practices that predated the arrival of Spaniards. In sixteenth-century Spain, the law stipulated that adulterous women should be punished by lashing, confiscation of their property, payment of punitive fines, placement in convents, and death, and, in Mexico, colonial officials punished adultery with jail time and public lashes.[61] However, the artist of the *Relación* depicted the adulterous couple bleeding from the ears. In Michoacán, ears and their adornments functioned as social symbols of religious devotion, markers of noble status and political allegiance. Most likely, the artist's choice indicated that this punishment divested the offenders of their social status.

For the people of central Michoacán, the ear was the focus of religious devotion in the form of bloodletting to the gods. In 1530, when the president of the First Royal Audience, Nuño de Guzmán, prosecuted a trial against Uanacaze ruler Zinzicha Tangaxuan, Guzmán asked Tangaxuan if the blood on two idols was from human sacrifices, to which the ruler responded: "[T]he blood on the aforementioned idol is blood from the ears of Indians."[62] While Guzmán sought to determine only whether or not a human sacrifice had been performed, the ruler's response specifically identified the source of the blood as someone's ears. In one of the few glimpses of childhood provided by the *Relación*, a council of elderly priests constantly urges a young child, who is the future ruler, to let blood from his ears.[63] This ruler and his successors, as well as their subjects, would draw blood from their ears many times throughout their lives in the course of religious and war ceremonies.[64] Through bloodletting, they fulfilled their duties to their god and divinized ancestor Curicaueri. In the words of the aforementioned ruler, "he fed the god."[65] This metaphor also appears in pre-Columbian images from central Mexico, such as one in the *Codex Borgia*, which shows a man piercing his ear, the blood flowing into the mouth of a death divinity (fig. 33). The Uanacaze describe their ancestors in the *Relación* as having "ears fat and swollen from auto-sacrifice."[66] Pricked and inflamed ears marked them as devout and religiously upstanding.

This association between the ear and religious thought seems to have permeated Christian belief after the Conquest. In the later part of the sixteenth century, a Jesuit priest living in Pátzcuaro, Michoacán, recorded an indigenous creation story that combines local and Christian elements, complete with earth deities, the Flood, and humankind being created from ashes. In the story, rather than blow onto the ashes, one of the gods sprinkles them with blood from his ears.[67] As late as the seventeenth century, the Franciscan friar and chronicler Alonso de la Rea could note that people in pre-Columbian Michoacán wore small "plates" in their ears in imitation of a god.[68]

These ear decorations helped identify people with their gods and marked people's noble status. The narrators of the *Relación* held earspools in great esteem and described a revered elder ruler as wearing golden earspools.[69] The primary gods Xaratanga and Curicaueri appeared in dreams to offer golden earspools to Uanacaze lords in exchange for favors and offerings.[70] A number of the *Relación*'s images depict noblewomen with their earlobes stretched and pierced by thin bars, and high-ranking men, such as the ruler and his war captain, wearing large earspools (see figs. 22, 44, 49).

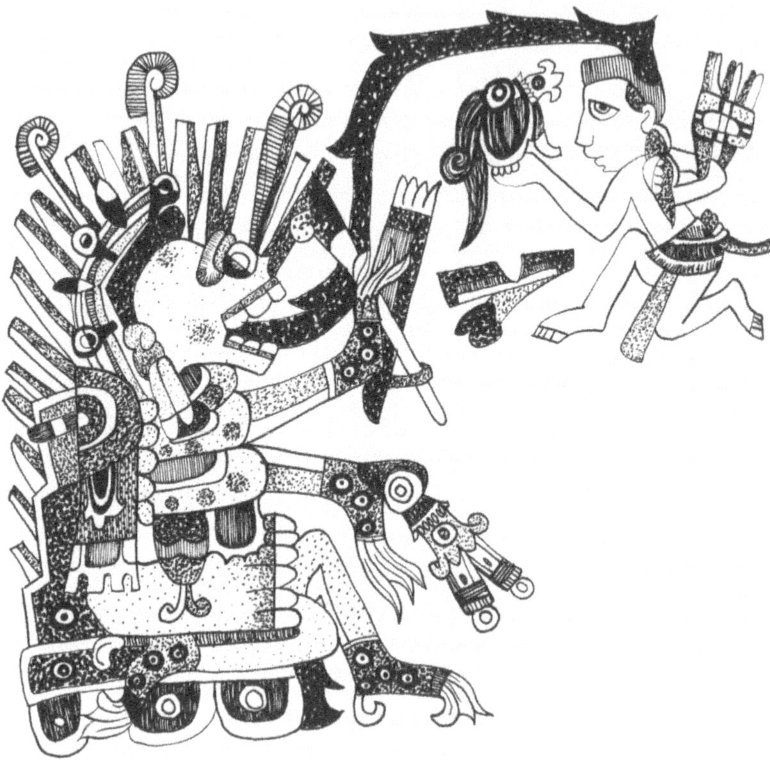

FIGURE 33. *Codex Borgia*, plate 75 (detail). After Díaz and Rodgers, *Codex Borgia*, 3. Drawing by Viera Sairán Monfón.

During pre-Columbian times sumptuary laws controlled the wearing of earspools. According to the *Relación*, the materials from which earspools were made varied, wood being used for those of lower economic status, gold and turquoise, as well as obsidian and turquoise, for the upper classes. Socioeconomic status alone did not automatically result in the right to wear earspools. Friar Isidro Félix de Espinosa, a Franciscan writing on Michoacán in the later part of the seventeenth century, reports that during pre-Columbian times lords could not wear jewels, expensive clothing, or feathers, "symbols of brave men," until they had killed or captured their first prisoner of war.[71] The so-called brave men in the *Relación* wear lip plugs and earspools. Furthermore, the *Relación* explains that the Uanacaze ruler controlled the wearing of earspools and other jewels by municipal rulers. After a municipal leader died, his relatives returned the deceased's earspools, lip plugs, and bracelets, considered his insignia of authority, to the Uanacaze ruler (fig. 34; see plate 12). The Uanacaze ruler would then appoint a successor, to whom he would give these symbols of office.[72]

In early colonial exchanges, the precious earspools of the nobility held their value. On May 4, 1532, in a court document, the Spaniard Antonio de Terán priced the Uanacaze ruler's earspools at the considerable amount of more than three hundred gold pesos. In the same document, Don Pedro Cuiniarangari stated that he had given a Spanish interpreter golden earspools with green stones of the kind "the Christians wanted."[73]

It seems that the ear was more than just a bodily appendage to be decorated. Through it one announced and performed one's devotion, social status, accomplishments, and even one's allegiance. To portray someone's ear as divested of its ornaments or damaged was to show that person's position in society being threatened and, possibly, permanently diminished. This

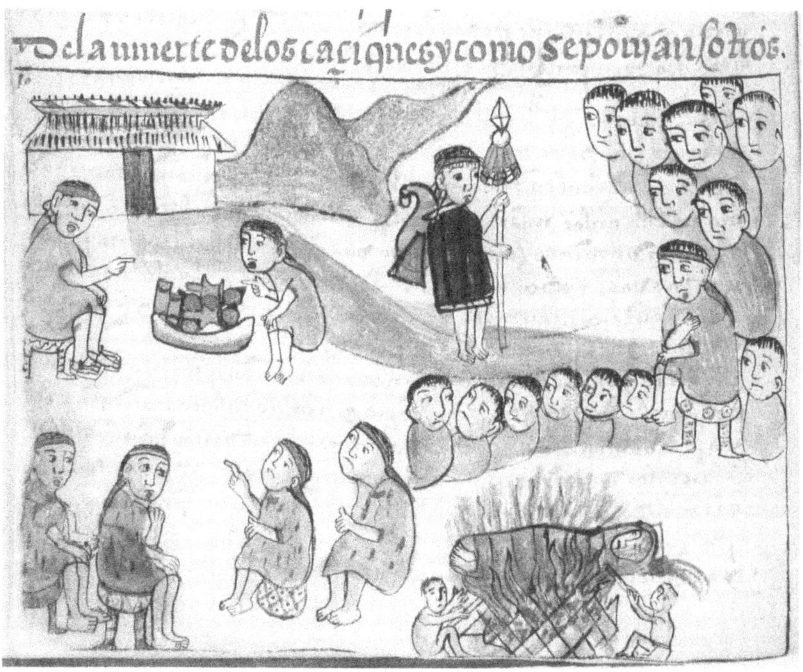

FIGURE 34. Artist 3. "De la muerte de los caciques y como se ponían otros" (Of the deaths of the caciques and how they were replaced). *Relación de Michoacán*, fol. 21v. Real Biblioteca del Monasterio de El Escorial, San Lorenzo de El Escorial, Spain, C IV 5. Photograph © Patrimonio Nacional, Spain.

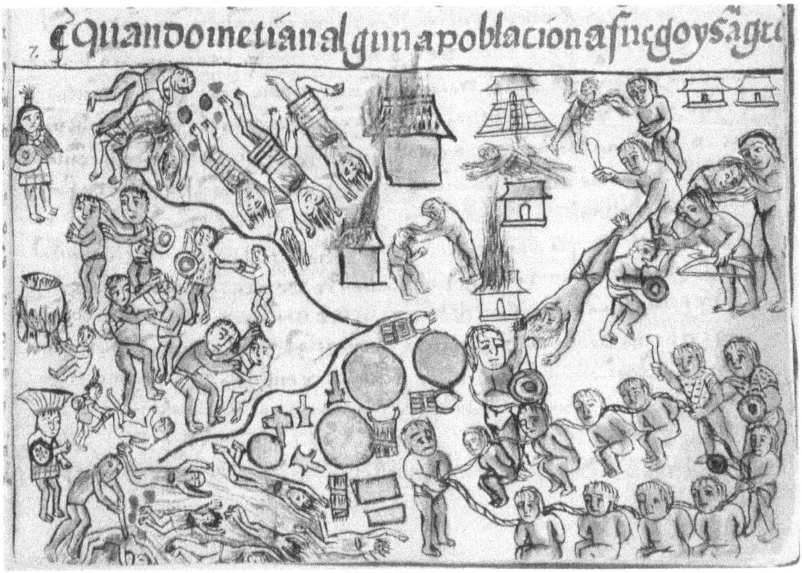

FIGURE 35. Artists 3 and 4. "Quando metían alguna población a fuego y sangre" (How they destroyed a town through fire and blood). *Relación de Michoacán*, fol. 19r. Real Biblioteca del Monasterio de El Escorial, San Lorenzo de El Escorial, Spain, C IV 5. Photograph © Patrimonio Nacional, Spain.

is exemplified in the *Relación* in the depiction of people in enemy towns who fell to the Uanacaze ruler's army. In the image "How They Destroyed a Town through Fire and Blood," which illustrates such an event, the Uanacaze army takes a group of enemies captive in the bottom right-hand corner (fig. 35).[74] These enemies are shown naked with their hands bound behind their backs, a rope tied around their necks, and their insignia of rank—their lip plugs, earspools, and breastplates—lying on the ground.[75] Their political independence, like their accoutrements, has been removed. Like the divestment of the ear's ornament, the disfigurement of the ear, as seen in the image of justice being dispensed by the ruler, announces not just the transgression of social norms but also the precarious situation of the accused within the Uanacaze social system. Since adultery threatened the social system described in the *Relación*, the depiction of its peculiar form of punishment represented a direct attack on the adulterers' social status. Those who did not listen and carefully obey the Uanacaze priest's advice would have to pay with the disfigurement of their ears.

Images representing the Uanacaze judicial system codified the authority of the Uanacaze into an intelligible visual language. In indigenous thought, the body served as a metaphor for the relationship of the individual to society, allowing the artist to use it as a semiotic tool through which he could express the moral codes of the Uanacaze. When disfigured, the body marked transgressors of social and sexual taboos.

Conclusion

While colonial authorities grappled with the idea of how to better control indigenous bodies, the Uanacaze represented themselves as arbiters capable of controlling and enforcing a judicial system very much like the Spanish one. The three images depicting the delivery of justice by members of the Uanacaze elite placed the Uanacaze at the top of this centralized judicial system, a key requisite for their return to colonial government. The first two images focus on the indigenous concept of justice, which combines the narration of history with acts that made people conform to a preestablished social system. In the first image, the main priest recounts history while a jailer punishes criminals. It conflates historical enemies with the contemporary transgressors of the social order, reenacting the bringing of justice to the area by the Uanacaze. In the image of the Uanacaze ruler delivering justice, physical punishment, such as lacerating the ears of adulterers or gouging the eyes and cutting the mouths of sorcerers, marked the bodies of transgressors of a social order that presupposed the restoration of centralized rulership to the Uanacaze.

The glosses inside figure 30 and the text that accompanies figures 30, 31, and 32 transform highly complex indigenous thoughts into judicial concepts understandable to the Spaniards. These glosses and text lead their Spanish-speaking audience to focus on crimes such as adultery, sorcery, and laziness, which greatly concerned Spanish authorities, thus arguing the legitimacy of the Uanacaze rulership in terms relevant to the Spaniards' own interests and values.

3

Making and Emending Landscape in the Petamuti's Speech

Between the two images depicting the petamuti at the justice ceremony discussed earlier (see figs. 30, 31), the folios record the speech the petamuti allegedly gave after determining the sentences criminals would receive at this annual event. His speech is a migration story in which the ancestors of the Uanacaze migrate to central Michoacán. The petamuti's story has many resemblances to the migration stories of other indigenous groups from central and southern Mexico recorded during the colonial period (i.e., the *Mapa Quinatzin* and the *Codex Xolotl*).[1] Like other migration stories, it begins with the migrant group entering a desired homeland and then staging the events leading to the foundation of its community and the consolidation of its territory, including the conquest of local groups, marriage alliances, and the parting of ways among allies. The petamuti's narrative is distributed among thirty-two chapters and is accompanied by twenty-three images.

Even though the petamuti speaks to an imaginary audience, the intended viewer of the manuscript was Viceroy Antonio de Mendoza. The work of the literary critic Michel de Certeau can be of help in understanding the purpose of the story.[2] Certeau explains that stories in general organize indistinct geographical locations into socially experienced spaces and help shape the way an audience relates to the landscape. The speech given by the petamuti would have helped shape the landscape of Michoacán into the Uanacaze's political domain in the mind of the viceroy, who was new to this area. Still, the account is extremely complex, naming almost three hundred places and ninety characters, and it is hard to imagine how it could actually have helped the novice viceroy govern this region. Thus, the images help the reader navigate the story by focusing his attention on particular places and events.

Close observation of part 2 reveals that most of the images were not originally planned but were added by four artists after two scribes had finished transcribing the text. These paintings not only illustrate but subtly emend the accompanying text. In her discussion of colonial images, the art historian Cecelia F. Klein has encouraged people to look at images as cultural stratagems, "as combinations of often subtle and complex devices and tactics" that help negotiate place and power.[3] Expanding upon this framework and applying it to these images, this chapter analyzes the images in part 2 of the *Relación* to reveal how the carefully selected scenes and European spatial techniques sought to highlight the Uanacaze and their Islander allies' ownership of the Lake Pátzcuaro basin, in spite of competing claims from Spanish colonists. The particular landscape that the painters chose to portray laid claim to a territory that was vigorously contested—on-site, in the courts, and, most significantly, in legal paintings.[4]

With the exception of Cynthia Stone, few scholars have noticed the painstaking process by which the images were added to the manuscript or the alterations many of them underwent.[5] Through detailed analysis, Stone has shown that the emendations to the frontispiece conveyed extratextual meaning and can attest to the interests of its contributors. Furthermore, Stone has noted that most of the spaces in part 2 were created after the text was written. However, unlike her insightful analysis of the frontispiece, her explanation for the insertion of new images in part 2 dismisses them as insignificant and as a simple matter of practical necessity, not as conveying extratextual meaning.[6] Additionally, Hans Roskamp has noted that the images do not always match the titles and has attributed the discrepancies to mistakes on the part of the artists.[7] Rather than dismiss these emendations and discrepancies as mere practical corrections or errors as Stone and Roskamp have done, I argue that they should be analyzed in terms of the aspects of the narrative the artists sought to emphasize.

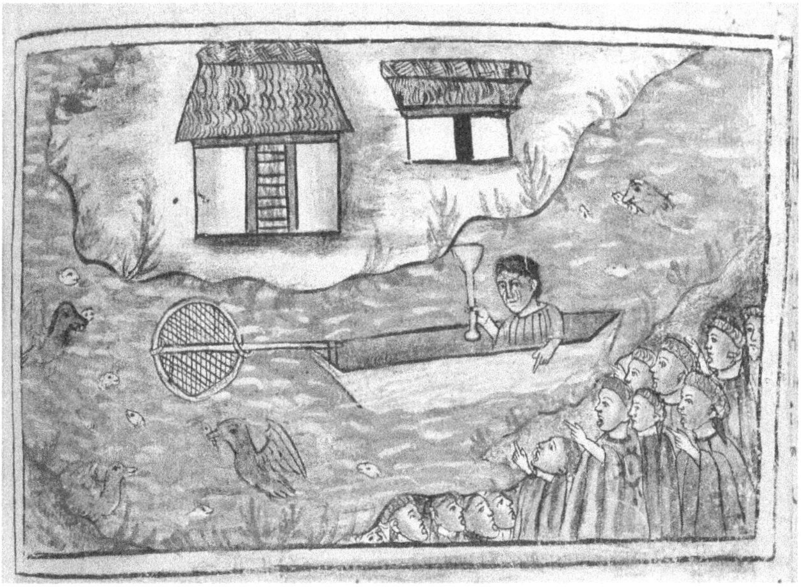

FIGURE 36. Artist 1. "Como los señores de la laguna supieron de la muger que llevaron los chichimecas, y cómo les dieron sus hijas por mugeres" (How the lords of the lake found out about the woman the Chichimecs took, and how they gave them their daughters for wives). *Relación de Michoacán*, fol. 71r. Real Biblioteca del Monasterio de El Escorial, San Lorenzo de El Escorial, Spain, C IV 5. Photograph © Patrimonio Nacional, Spain.

Scribes 3 and 4 wrote this section of the text. Scribe 3 wrote the first five chapters, leaving room only for the initial image of the petamuti giving his speech. Scribe 4 followed suit but inadvertently began to transcribe part of the last chapter that scribe 3 had already copied. About halfway down the page, scribe 4 realized his mistake; he applied a white wash to cover the duplicated text and wrote the title of the new chapter at the top of the page. If the manuscript is held against a light, a bit of the original text can still be seen.[8] Rather than immediately copy the text of the new chapter, scribe 4 left space below the title for an image (fig. 36 and table 1; see plate 14). He then wrote the text of the chapter below the whited-out area.

He left room for only one more image, which can be seen in the last chapter documenting the petamuti's speech between the title and the text (fig. 37 and table 2; see plate 15).

When the painters and editor (presumably the Spanish friar) reviewed the manuscript, they changed the layout the scribes had originally provided. They relocated titles and painted new images below the titles and at the

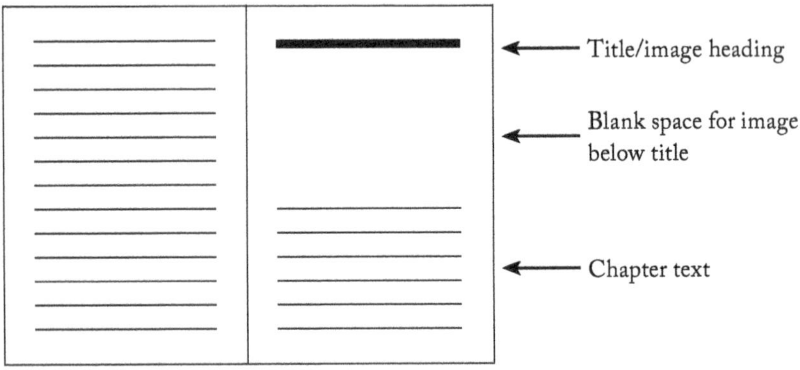

TABLE 1. Folios 70v and 71r: Sketch of scribe's layout after his own correction

ends of the chapters. In one case, when the space provided was inadequate, they added the image of a genealogical tree on a full sheet of paper (see fig. 53). These new images highlight different aspects of the narrative.

The petamuti's speech covers a vast geographical area, focusing on the deeds of the Uanacaze's ancestors. He tells his audience that the Uanacaze ruling family members were the leaders of an invading migratory group variously known as Chichimecs and Uacúsecha, the latter a P'urhépecha term meaning "the eagles." The migration story begins with them arriving in the northern highlands of Michoacán, where they spend four generations, and eventually leads to the Lake Pátzcuaro basin. The petamuti tells his audience that at the basin, they managed to unify the independent cities into one subject state by conquering different ethnic groups, forming political allegiances, marrying local women, and even using divine intervention. In the process, the Uanacaze conquer other Chichimecs, including their in-laws.

Aware that they are about to be conquered, a small group of Islanders submit to the Uanacaze and become their allies—they are none other than the ancestors of the Islander governor Don Pedro Cuiniarangari. They assist the Uanacaze in defeating another Chichimec faction and Islander nobles living on the lake's islands and in mainland cities. At this point, Uanacaze dominance of the area becomes clear in the narrative, and the Uanacaze settle in three cities on the shores of Lake Pátzcuaro: Cuyuacan-Ihuatzio, Pátzcuaro, and Tzintzuntzan (also called Ciudad de Michoacán [City of Michoacán] in the text). From there, together with Don Pedro's ancestors, they launch their conquest of lands outside the Lake Pátzcuaro region, including lands to the east that border Aztec territories and the southern part of Michoacán known as the Hot Lands, or Tierra Caliente.

The speech by the petamuti, as recorded in the *Relación*, has received much attention. As mentioned in the introduction, it has been used to reconstruct the pre-Columbian history and socioeconomic organization of

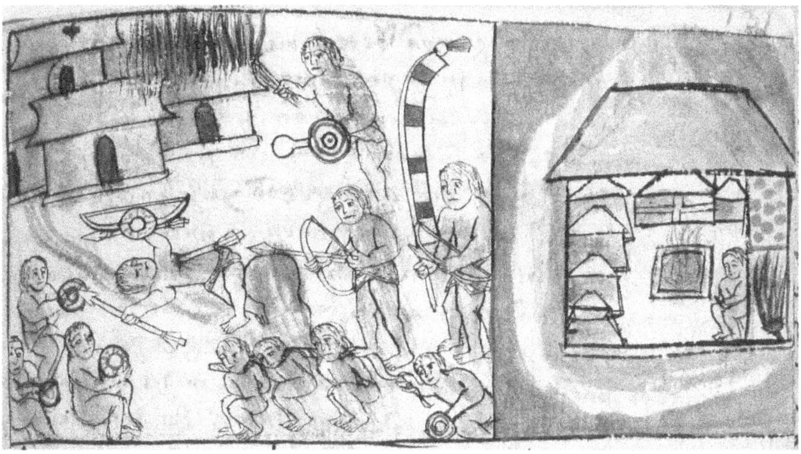

FIGURE 37. Artist 4. "Como Hirepan y Tangaxoan y Hiquingaje conquistaron toda la provincia con los ysleños, y como la repartieron entre sí, y de lo que hordenaron" (How Hirepan and Tangaxoan and Hiquingaje conquered all the province with the Islanders, and how they divided it among themselves, and what they ordered). *Relación de Michoacán*, fol. 131r. Real Biblioteca del Monasterio de El Escorial, San Lorenzo de El Escorial, Spain, C IV 5. Photograph © Patrimonio Nacional, Spain.

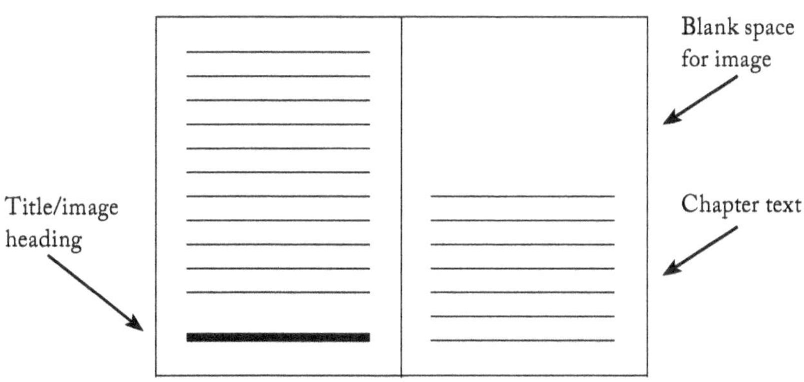

TABLE 2. Folios 130v and 131r: Layout at the end of the petamuti's speech

the area, as well as its oral and literary traditions. Yet the reliability of its contents for modern historic and archaeological practices has been questioned. Previous scholars have attributed the *Relación*'s choice of a migration story to diverging interests, such as the indigenous contributors' desire to connect with Aztec migration stories and consequently their political might, as well as the friar's desire to justify the Spanish invasion of this region.[9] However, migration stories were widespread throughout Mexico during the early colonial period and were often recorded without the intervention of friars.[10] They were written using alphabetic writing and graphically represented as annals and maps known as cartographic histories. For example, the *Lienzo de Jucutacato*, which was painted not far from the place where the *Relación* was produced, records the migration and settlement of a Nahua population in Michoacán.[11] Regardless of the veracity of the Uanacaze migration story, what matters is that among all possible stories, the Uanacaze chose to retell this particular one.

Looking at the impact of narrating the Uanacaze's migration story during the colonial period, Stone has suggested that the petamuti's speech was a call to his native audience to adapt to the demands of the colonial era while acknowledging the first bishop to Michoacán, Vasco de Quiroga, as the creator of the new Catholic order.[12] However, Quiroga is not mentioned by name in the *Relación*, and the most important member of the *Relación*'s audience was to be Viceroy Mendoza. How the indigenous artists presented their political interests to *him* remains to be explored.

The study of other migration stories can shed some light on the motivation for the indigenous deployment of such stories during the colonial period. The art historians Barbara Mundy and Elizabeth Boone have noted that during the colonial period, migration stories often focused on a particular area, highlighting the interests of their makers. Heirs among the elite might focus on their ancestors' claims to a particular land. Their stories not only fixed the territory of their forebears in the past but also allowed them to maintain independent status or even reclaim territories during the colonial period.[13] Migration stories tied together places, historical events, and the deeds of elites.[14]

Analyzing the time line of this section of the manuscript provides some insight into what exactly the contributors of the *Relación* sought to emphasize. Dominique Michelet and James Krippner-Martínez have noticed that the narrative both compresses and stretches time, yet they have arrived at different conclusions. Michelet points out that while the first four generations of the Uanacaze receive limited attention, the narrative focuses primarily on the pre-Columbian ruler known as Tariacuri and two of his nephews and a son, who together conquered the Lake Pátzcuaro area.[15] Michelet suggests that this corresponds to a storyteller's ability to remember recent history better than ancient history. However, James Krippner-Martínez notes that the descendants of Tariacuri's son and nephews, including the living Uanacaze heirs, also receive limited attention. He has attributed this to the narrator's desire to focus on the long genealogy of the current Uanacaze heirs rather than on their actions.[16] The significance of the time line then remains controversial; what we can conclude is that it focuses on the middle section of the narrative, which was originally left without illustrations. The scenes, painted after the text was completed, were used to bring out certain aspects of the narrative and can provide greater insight into the contributors' motivations for focusing on this middle section.

Inserting a Landscape

As noted previously, the scribes of this section left room for only two images to illustrate the petamuti's speech. These would have shown first the pact between the Uanacaze and the Islander nobles, then their conquest of Michoacán outside the Lake Pátzcuaro basin. The first image heading, "How the Lords of the Lake Found Out about the Woman the Chichimecs Took, and How They Gave Them Their Daughters for Wives," which also serves as a chapter title, indicates that the image would have depicted the forging of a marital alliance between two groups of nobles.[17] The second image heading is "How Hirepan and Tangaxoan and Hiquingaje Conquered All the Province with the Islanders, and How They Divided It among Themselves, and What They Ordered."[18] Thus, this second image would have shown the conquest of what during colonial times became the "Province of Michoacán"—roughly corresponding to the modern-day state of Michoacán, which stretches far beyond the Lake Pátzcuaro basin.

When the editor and artists went to work, they guided the viewer through a highly politicized landscape by adding new images. The analysis of these paintings shows that they join landscape with historic events, providing a narrative strategy aimed at establishing the historical rights of the Uanacaze to the Lake Pátzcuaro basin.[19] The makers of the *Relación* were careful about which images to include. They neglected some events and highlighted others, especially the Uanacaze conquest of non-Uanacaze groups (except Don Pedro's ancestors) in the Lake Pátzcuaro region. The editor and artists left the first five chapters without illustrations. As a consequence, no paintings depict what one might expect to be key moments or places in the migration story, such as the arrival of the first Uanacaze ancestors to northern Michoacán, the first union of a Uanacaze man with a local noblewoman, mother of their entire line, or even the wandering of the next four generations through northern Michoacán.

Only when in the story the Uanacaze reach the shores of Lake Pátzcuaro did artist 1 paint the first image (see fig. 36). The image he chose for the first space left blank by scribe 3 does not depict the Islander nobles giving their daughters in marriage to the Uanacaze, as was intended by the scribe in the title he provided. Instead, artist 1 depicted the arrival of the Uanacaze on Lake Pátzcuaro's shores and their meeting with a fisherman from one of the islands in the lake, a meeting that had been described in the text of the previous chapter. The marital alliance between the Uanacaze and the Islander nobles, apparently important to the original scribe, does not appear in any of the *Relación*'s images.

The next few images focus on the Uanacaze conquest of non-Uanacaze groups in and around the basin, including the lake's islands. The first one shows the opening battle between the Uanacaze and Islander nobles for control of the Lake Pátzcuaro basin (fig. 38; see plate 16). Artist 3 depicted the Uanacaze warriors standing next to a burning fire and an arrow (both symbols of war) at the shores of the lake and the distressed-looking Islander leader in his palace, surrounded by his people, observing the Uanacaze at the shores of the lake. The title of the chapter, however, indicates the events surrounding the conquest and not the battle per se: "How the Lord of the Island, Called Caricaten, Asked for Help of Another Lord, Called Zurunban, against Tariacuri, Who Had Him Surrounded in His Island, and a Priest Called Naca Was Sent to Gather People for War."[20] In fact, the description of the Uanacaze burning fires and surrounding the Islanders, to which the illustration refers, appears in the text of the previous chapter.

The following images and their corresponding titles continue to portray the struggle between the Islander and Uanacaze nobles for control of the Lake Pátzcuaro area (see, e.g., fig. 26). The Islanders seek the assistance of one of their own, named Zurumban, who has moved to the mainland. After some initial setbacks, Zurumban manages to defeat the Uanacaze and displace them from their current location next to the lake (see fig. 11).

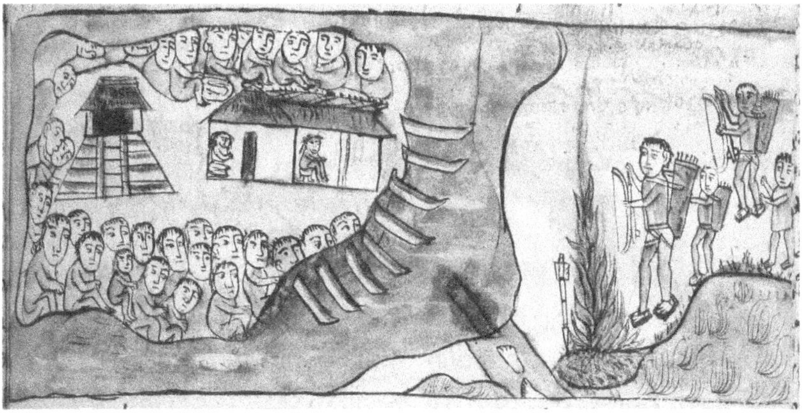

FIGURE 38. Artist 3. "Como el señor de la ysla, llamado Caricaten, pidió socorro a otro Señor llamado Zurunban contra Tariacuri, que le tenía cercado en su ysla, y fue enbiado un sacerdote llamado Naca a hazer gente de guerra" (How the lord of the island, called Caricaten, asked for help of another lord, called Zurunban, against Tariacuri, who had him surrounded on his island, and a priest called Naca was sent to gather people for war). *Relación de Michoacán*, fol. 79r. Real Biblioteca del Monasterio de El Escorial, San Lorenzo de El Escorial, Spain, C IV 5. Photograph © Patrimonio Nacional, Spain.

With the Uanacaze defeated and humiliated, the text and images diverge into a vignette about the Uanacaze ruler Tariacuri and his unfaithful wife. The vignette exemplifies the moral qualities of the Uanacaze and the reasons why they should rule (figs. 39, 40; see also figs. 44, 45; see chapter 4 for an analysis of these images). Interestingly, when the story takes the viewer beyond the basin, the artists omit most geographical features.

Once the fortunes of the Uanacaze improve, the narrative returns to the Lake Pátzcuaro region. The artists once again included the lake basin and the islands in their images to signal the location of events (fig. 41; see also plate 17, figs. 12, 28, 50). The paintings show, among other things, Don Pedro's Islander ancestors submitting to the Uanacaze (see fig. 50). Don Pedro's ancestors then become the allies of the Uanacaze in the conquest of the basin and beyond. It is noteworthy that although the Lake Pátzcuaro basin is quite large and many communities lived around its shores and on its islands, often no recognizable features identify specific communities. The basin and the islands indicate only the general locations of events. Even in the last image, which was meant to show the conquest of the province beyond the Lake Pátzcuaro area, the artist divided the picture into two frames, depicting on the left a battle scene at an unidentified location and on the right Cuyuacán-Ihuatzio at the shores of Lake Pátzcuaro with the war booty being kept there (see fig. 37).

The images that the artists and editor decided to include do not illustrate every single chapter. Instead, each selectively underscores a particu-

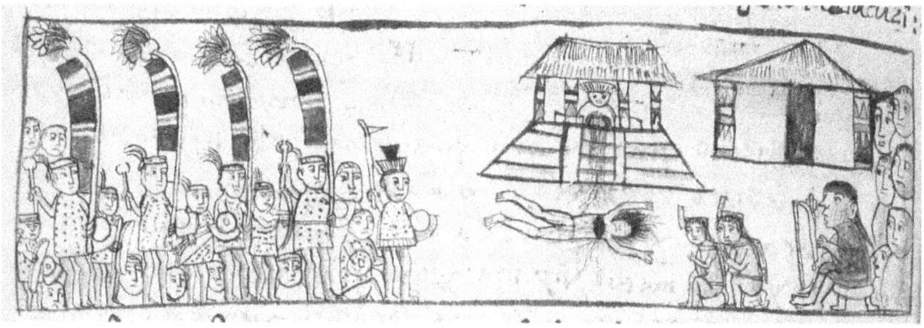

FIGURE 39. Artist 3. "Como se sintió afrentado el suegro primero de Tariacuri porque dexó su hija, y le tomó un cú y fueron sacrificados los enemigos de Tariacuri" (How Tariacuri's first father-in-law was offended because [Tariacuri] left his daughter, and he seized a temple from him [Tariacuri], and the enemies of Tariacuri were sacrificed). *Relación de Michoacán*, fol. 96v. Real Biblioteca del Monasterio de El Escorial, San Lorenzo de El Escorial, Spain, C IV 5. Photograph © Patrimonio Nacional, Spain.

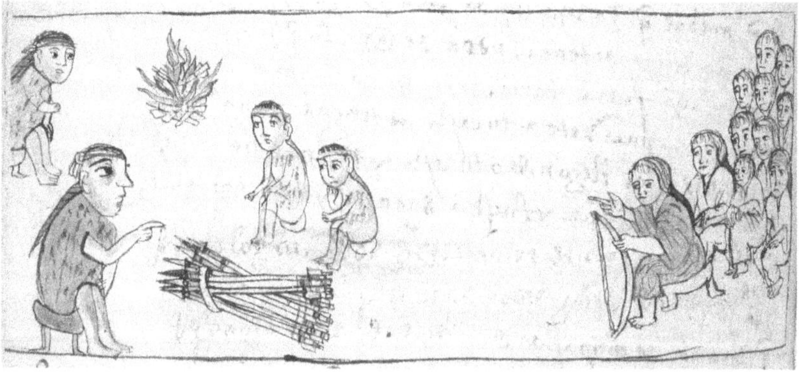

FIGURE 40. Artists 3 and 4. "Como los cuñados de Tariacuri, de la muger primera de Coringuaro, le enviaron a pedir plumajes ricos, y oro, y plata, y otras cosas, y de la respuesta que dio a los mensajeros" (How Tariacuri's brothers-in-law, from his first wife from Coringuaro, sent a message asking for rich feathers, and gold, and silver, and other things, and the answer he gave to the messengers). *Relación de Michoacán*, fol. 98v. Real Biblioteca del Monasterio de El Escorial, San Lorenzo de El Escorial, Spain, C IV 5. Photograph © Patrimonio Nacional, Spain.

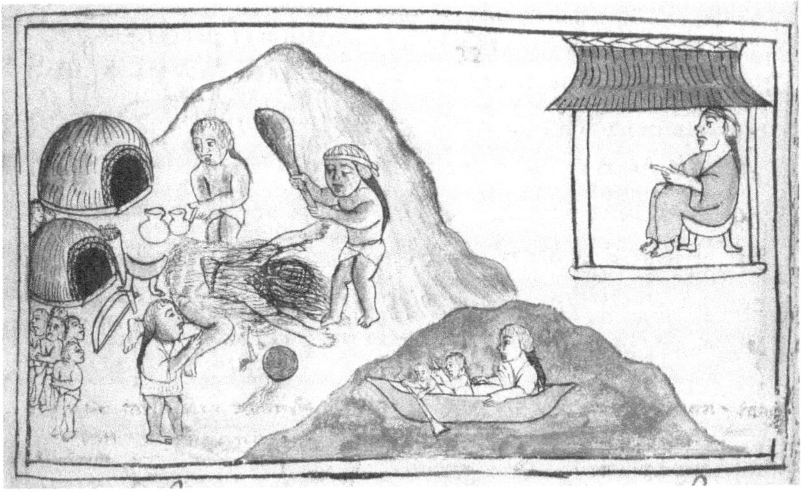

FIGURE 41. Artist 4. "Como Tariacuri mandó matar su hijo Curatame; a Hirepan y Tangaxoan, porque se enborrachava: y le mataron después de borracho" (How Tariacuri ordered Hirepan and Tangaxoan to kill his son Curatame because he was a drunkard, and they killed him after he got drunk). *Relación de Michoacán*, fol. 121r. Real Biblioteca del Monasterio de El Escorial, San Lorenzo de El Escorial, Spain, C IV 5. Photograph © Patrimonio Nacional, Spain.

lar segment of the narrative. The spaces originally left by the scribe would have been filled with images intended to emphasize the allegiances between the Uanacaze and Islander nobles and their conquest of the Province of Michoacán, beyond the Lake Pátzcuaro basin. However, as the editor and artists went through the text a second time, they reshaped the narrative by focusing the viewer's attention on the geography and conquest of the Lake Pátzcuaro basin.

A Delicate Selection: Defining the Landscape

The *Relación* artists were careful not only about which geographical region to emphasize but also about how to represent it. The four artists who worked on this section of the *Relación* all employed the same pre-Columbian visual vocabulary, such as footprints and arrows to depict movement and conquest. Yet the ways in which these elements were depicted, that is, the stylistic choices the artists made, sought to provide a vision of the region that was accessible to a European audience, while representing the Lake Pátzcuaro basin as a unit indivisible under Uanacaze and Islander control.

The art historian Erwin Panofsky's analysis of representations of space is helpful for understanding the choices these artists made. He sees representations of space as "'symbolic forms' that structure the world according to specific cultural demands."[21] A painting of a particular space reflects and enhances the significance and meaning of that space. In Panofsky's view, elements that are useful are included and those that are not deemed necessary are eliminated. The careful selections made by the *Relación*'s artists can be analyzed to understand the demands they sought to meet through their pictures.

The artists of the *Relación* carefully selected the pre-Columbian elements they included. Then they incorporated the elements into the landscape using European spatial techniques to provide a vision of space that was familiar to a European audience. As discussed previously, generally speaking, pre-Columbian landscapes are composed of a vocabulary of two-dimensional natural formations (mountains, caves, springs, etc.) neatly delimited by contour lines and filled in with flat fields of color.[22] These two-dimensional features are combined to provide geographical information.[23] Pre-Columbian representations often have no ground lines, and the features of the landscape and the figures seem to float in space.

In the *Relación*, Mesoamerican pictographs seldom appear as isolated elements, two-dimensional features, or floating toponyms. Rather than use them as the defining elements of a landscape, the artists included them as naturalistic details of European-style landscapes.[24] For example, in the painting on folio 79r, arrows and fire, indicating the declaration of war, are placed on a hill next to the Uanacaze, whose encroachment is indicated by footprints inscribed in neatly delineated paths seen from above, thereby making the Uanacaze's declared intention part of the landscape (compare fig. 38 with fig. 42 from a Mixtec codex representing the conquest of towns). When indigenous toponyms do appear in the *Relación*, they are fully incorporated into European-style landscapes. The town of Itziparámuco, meaning "water by the shore or the entrance," is represented by a spring next to the entrance of the town's stone wall.[25] The water emanating from this spring follows the path of the road, as it would in a European-style landscape (see fig. 17).

The artists also transformed pictographs into three-dimensional representations of objects, figures, and structures. They employed single- and

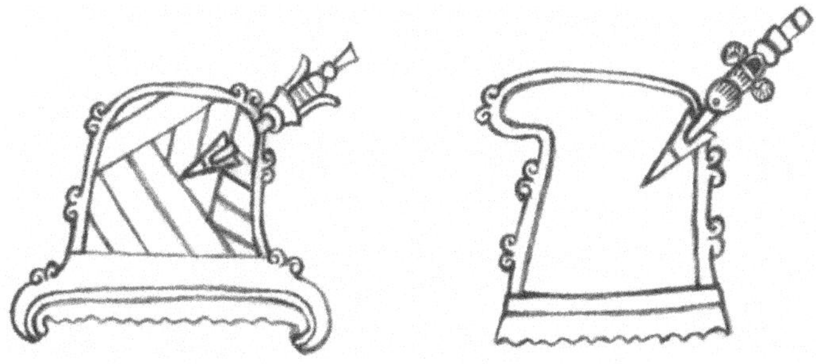

FIGURE 42. *Codex Nuttall* (details). After Zelia Nuttall, *Codex Nuttall*, 77. Drawing by Elizabeth Coughlin.

multiple-point perspectives, bird's-eye views, and shading to indicate an object's volume and location in relation to the viewer, thereby transforming the two-dimensional picture plane into a three-dimensional space. In figure 28, for example, the ideogram for *yrecha*, a house with a man sitting inside it, is transformed into a full-fledged living space. On the left-hand side, an arched door serves as the entrance, and inside the room, to the right, three individuals face each other. Floor lines lead to a vanishing point in the distance, and gray wash on the floor and back wall accentuates the sense of depth in the room. The ruler portrayed sitting on his stool is larger than the other two figures, and of those two, the one in the background is drawn smaller to indicate his distance from the observer. In the right-hand corner of the picture, a cave, pre-Columbian symbol of origin and transformation, is converted into a three-dimensional object through the application of curved, light gray brushstrokes on the outside and a solid jet-black on the inside.[26] Through the application of three-dimensional techniques, the viewer is given the unique opportunity to see, so to speak, beyond the circumscriptions of pre-Columbian spaces.

The work of the cultural geographer Denis Cosgrove can be of help in understanding the significance of this reinvention of pre-Columbian pictographs through European visual techniques. According to Cosgrove, sixteenth-century Europeans privileged the sense of sight as objective over all other senses and ways of relating to the land. Cosgrove asserts that the rise of single-point perspective in Europe coincided with a desire on the part of Europeans to "see" their newly discovered lands and the people that inhabited them.[27] Championed by art theorists such as Leon Battista Alberti, single-point perspective became the most significant tool in European art's kit for rendering "realistic" representations of the world.[28] It structured space and the people and events within it according to the eyes of a single spectator, while at the same time, by locating the viewer outside the pictorial space, stressing the objectivity of the events depicted. Far from being realistic or objective, however, single-point perspective yielded an illusory image of history as static and unchanging. Nevertheless, during the sixteenth century, this illusion of reality lent a sense of truth to painting.[29]

While Cosgrove focuses on single-point perspective as the European technique par excellence for creating the illusion of reality, in fact, the Renaissance saw illusionist techniques flourish. Netherlandish artists also used bird's-eye views and multiple-point and empirical perspective, as well as elaborate details that dazzled viewers with the lifelike appearance of their paintings. These likewise allowed artists to depict a patron's lands and possessions in realistic terms and were well liked by Spanish officials. Bartolomeo Fazio, a humanist at the court of Alfonso V (1396–1458), king of Aragón and Naples (today Spain and Italy, respectively), professed his admiration for Jan van Eyck's *Map of the World* because of its optical strategies in representing a realistic appearance of places and regions.[30] And Spanish king Philip II (1527–1598) hired Flemish artist Anton van den Wyngaerde to create topographical views of Spanish cities that used multipoint perspectives.[31] Thus, lending a sense of reality to events and places was closely linked to representing them three-dimensionally on paper.

At the time the *Relación* was being crafted, nearly twenty years had passed since the arrival of the Spaniards, and Michoacán's landscape had already been significantly altered. Many pre-Columbian temples and buildings had been destroyed, and the seat of government was being transferred from Tzintzuntzan to Pátzcuaro.[32] To be able to visually represent places and past events in ways that not only were legible but also seemed *real* to European eyes lent credibility to the story being narrated. Rather than paint two-dimensional pictographs, the artists created three-dimensional scenes that would have allowed the European viewer to imagine the past.

Even though the *Relación*'s scenes may give the illusion of reality, they represent a rather limited view of the past. The rulers' homes are placed unrealistically close to the lake's shores, and they often serve to represent entire communities, such as Tzintzuntzan and Pátzcuaro. Archaeological records of these locations have shown that they were made up of a number of wards, and their administrative centers contained many temples and precincts. In the absence of many toponyms or distinctive features, the lake basin as portrayed in the *Relación* stands as an indivisible entity, the historical locus of Uanacaze conquest and the seat of their government as represented by the ubiquitous presence of the Uanacaze ruler.

The Lake Pátzcuaro Basin as a Contested Region

By combining iconographies and spatial techniques, the *Relación*'s artists were able to emphasize particular elements of both history and location while simultaneously lending the pictures a sense of reality that transcended the present to reinvent the past. To represent the basin as a geographical and social unit was of particular advantage to the indigenous nobility, who fought against its division by some of the Spanish newcomers.

The impact of court disputes on the contents of the *Relación* has for the most part been overlooked. They involved Spanish newcomers, the Spanish Crown, the newly appointed Spanish bishop Vasco de Quiroga, the Uanacaze heirs, their allies, and the Islander governor Don Pedro Cuiniarangari. While court procedures took into account all sides of the story and numerous rebuttals could follow anyone's claims, the *Relación*, through its migration story and images, gave participants the exceptional opportunity to present their views about the basin and its rightful owners to the viceroy without the intervention of opposing parties.

The political circumstances of the Lake Pátzcuaro basin when the *Relación* was being compiled were rather complex. Members of the indigenous nobility were involved in lengthy and costly legal disputes with Spanish newcomers. One concerned the move of ecclesiastical and political authorities from Tzintzuntzan to nearby Pátzcuaro in 1538 and early 1539, which was orchestrated by Bishop Vasco de Quiroga. José Bravo Ugarte and Rodrígo Martínez Baracs have argued that the *Relación* takes a "Tzintzuntzanist" position by naming Tzintzuntzan rather than Pátzcuaro the "City of Michoacán." This would have afforded Tzintzuntzan a Spanish legal title that conferred certain privileges.[33] It should be noted that in other colonial documents, those nobles who had moved to Pátzcuaro and who had collaborated in the making of the *Relación* continued to call Tzintzuntzan the "City of Michoacán" and Pátzcuaro one of its barrios.[34] Even Vasco de Quiroga had argued that the move was not from one city to another, but from Tzintzuntzan to a barrio within its confines. The naming of Pátzcuaro as a barrio of Tzintzuntzan was part of an effort to proclaim the basin a political unit. This protected the basin's autonomy and sought to stop the encroachment of Spaniards who were attempting to divide it for their own profit.

Through the study of colonial documents, the historian J. Benedict Warren has proposed that the City of Michoacán included the entire tributary area of the Lake Pátzcuaro basin, the towns of Huaniqueo, Tuxpan, Amula, Zapotlan, Tamazula, and possibly Mazamitla.[35] Colonial documents reveal, however, that much was at stake when determining the political and territorial reach of the City of Michoacán. Originally, Spanish authorities understood little of its political organization, and the ensuing litigations made it ever more difficult to define.[36] Those Spaniards who would benefit from the division of the basin saw the City of Michoacán's subdivisions as independent units in their own right.[37] However, the indigenous nobility sought to keep the basin and its islands together.

Indigenous witnesses who testified in favor of the city's nobility argued that the City of Michoacán covered the entire lake basin and its islands. The situation became complicated partly because they (or their translators) used various political terminology, indiscriminately referring to the city's subdivisions in Spanish as *ciudad* (city), *pueblo* (town), *barrio* (ward), and *sujeto* (subject town). Sixteenth-century documents often use the P'urhépecha word *vapatzequa* to refer to these subdivisions, a word that the *Diccionario grande* translates as *barrio* and *colación*.[38] According to the sixteenth-century *Tesoro de la lengua castellana o española* by Sebastián de Covarrubias, a *colación* refers to the people, or *vecinos*, who belong to the same chapel or tribe.[39] In the case of Michoacán, since wards often had their own temples and marked ethnic divisions, and because towns were at times settled by distinct ethnic groups, one can see how the word *vapatzequa* could apply to both.[40] However, for disputes during the colonial period, the Spanish classification of these subdivisions would be key.

Shortly after the arrival of the Spaniards in this area, around 1524, Hernan Cortés divided Michoacán into encomiendas and distributed them among his political allies and cronies. He kept the most valuable for himself: the City of Michoacán, with its heart in Tzintzuntzan and its wards and subject towns reaching far and wide. However, he did not enjoy his possession for long, since even the Spanish Crown became interested in this jewel.

Cortés left for Honduras at the end of 1524. By 1525, he was presumed dead, and the Crown issued instructions to confiscate his encomienda for its own benefit in April 1528. Later that year, under pressure from Cortés, who had reappeared, the Crown reversed its orders. However, the First Royal Audience, headed by Nuño de Guzmán, decided to leave the encomienda in the hands of the Crown—at least on paper. In practice, what the encomienda produced went to support Guzmán's slaves in the mines of Zacatula.[41]

The City of Tzintzuntzan and its nobility faced serious challenges in the following years and had to present a united front. Even though the city was under the Spanish Crown, encomenderos quickly encroached on its territories. The best-known case is that of Juan Infante, who had been given the small partial encomienda of the town of Comanja, but in late 1528 claimed to possess a *cédula* (decree) granting him possession of more than twenty-five towns. Not all of these towns have been identified today, but many were on the shores of Lake Pátzcuaro and on the islands that were considered subjects of Tzintzuntzan (e.g., Uricho, Erongaricuaro, Xaracuaro, Guayangareo). The existence of this cédula was questioned, as most witnesses could only attest to having seen copies of the document or hearing about it from others, but in the next few decades, it would be the source of much litigation.[42] By the following May, the residents and noblemen of Tzintzuntzan were already complaining that not just Juan Infante but also the Spanish encomenderos Juan de Alvarado, Francisco de Villegas, and Gonzalo Gomes had taken over land that belonged to the city and its ruler.[43]

Under Cortés's administration Zinzicha Tangaxuan had been allowed to rule but not to collect tribute for himself (although without an economic basis his reign would seem nearly impossible). Other encomenderos, however, grew weary of Tangaxuan, accused him of receiving tribute from the towns in the region, and eventually took him to court. In 1530, the First Royal Audience tried and sentenced Tangaxuan to death. Nuño de Guzmán allocated his land and worldly possessions to pay for the trial and to provide revenue for the Spanish Crown.[44]

After Tangaxuan died, the Islander Don Pedro became governor of the city. From then on, he had to represent the city's interests and protect its boundaries. Beyond the lake basin, *cabeceras* (head towns) and sujetos were administered by the local nobility, who paid tribute to their corresponding Spanish encomenderos.

Between 1530 and 1535, the Royal Audience went back and forth about to whom the towns belonged, but finally, in 1535, it ruled in favor of the city's nobility. Infante then appealed to the Council of the Indies in Spain, which ruled in his favor in 1538, apparently thanks to the influence of Infante's wife, who was a relative of the royal secretary.[45] In 1539, Viceroy Mendoza, together with the Second Royal Audience, ratified the council's decision, giving the land back to Infante.[46]

In view of this conundrum, the city's nobility must have decided to join forces with the recently elected first bishop of Michoacán, Vasco de Quiroga. Quiroga previously had been *oidor* (judge) for the Second Royal Audience, knew their case, and had founded a hospital in Santa Fe–Uayameo, a town that figures prominently in the *Relación* and that Infante claimed belonged to his encomienda. Together with the bishop, the nobles took Infante back to court. They argued for the reunification of the basin, because according to them it had been Tangaxuan's señorío, and now it was the City of Michoacán, encomienda of the Crown and see of the Bishopric.[47] This alliance provided many lucrative advantages to Quiroga and his legal expertise to the indigenous nobility.

The conflict escalated when Infante attempted to take possession of his alleged encomienda on October 1, 1539. On his way to Santa Fe–Uayameo, where Quiroga had his pueblo-hospital, Infante was met by Quiroga and a group of armed Spaniards; several thousand indigenous warriors were said to be waiting to kill Infante if he should attempt to take possession. Infante retreated and complained to the authorities.

On December 31, 1539, Viceroy Mendoza went personally to Tzintzuntzan, where he met with the indigenous nobility and tried to reason with them regarding the basis for his and the Audiencia's decision. Presumably, it was at this point that he also commissioned the *Relación*.[48] In addition, Mendoza met with Don Pedro, who complained that the ruling in favor of Infante was an injustice against the city (which he described as formerly Tangaxuan's señorío) and against him personally. Don Pedro must not have had much luck with the viceroy, for Mendoza requested that Don Pedro pay back the tribute he had taken from the lands now allocated to Infante.[49]

Infante took possession of his encomienda between January 3 and 5, 1540, and a month later Michoacán's nobility and Quiroga appealed to the Royal Audience. So infamous were the accusations against Infante that in 1542, when the Spanish Crown issued the Leyes Nuevas (New Laws), with which to better rule their colonies in the Americas, they singled out Infante's encomienda as excessively large and demanded that it be redistributed.[50] Quiroga and the indigenous nobility's appeal was forwarded to the Council of the Indies in Spain in 1544, but the council did not rule in their favor until 1553, when Quiroga, making use of the New Laws, pointed out that the Crown had previously commanded that Infante's encomienda be redistributed.[51] Between 1539 and 1542, the years in which the *Relación* was produced, the conflict between Infante and the indigenous nobility was at its peak. Complete with physical confrontations and thousands of folios being produced in the courts, this was a costly and perilous endeavor for all parties involved.

From early on, paintings of the area in dispute were at the heart of the argument. In 1529 (Tangaxuan was still alive), when the residents and noblemen of the City of Michoacán complained to Nuño de Guzmán about the encomenderos trying to take over their land, his response was to request a map of the city portraying its perimeter so that he could settle the dispute.[52] In 1530, indigenous witnesses testified against Infante and presented yet another painting.[53]

One particular painting produced for the conflict with Infante exemplifies how crucial the representation of the Lake Pátzcuaro basin was. In October 1540, both parties had to present paintings and agree on the contents of a final version. When the indigenous nobility and the bishop presented their version of the lake basin, Juan Infante complained that it was poorly painted and "neither true nor right."[54] Infante then presented his own version, to which the Michoacán party added and revised information. Infante took it back and added new information, apparently by pasting pieces of paper over parts of the map. This was not well received by the opposition, who then complained to the authorities. The president and judges of the Royal Audience subsequently ordered that Infante's additions be removed in spite of his complaints and only the names of towns and sujetos be applied directly to the painting. Once the painting was agreed upon, both parties were to present indigenous witnesses who would then read it and answer questions based on its contents.

Unfortunately, this painting has since disappeared, but the associated questionnaire developed by Michoacán's nobility and Quiroga reveals what it intended and, most important, the strategy used to argue their case to the viceroy and the Royal Audience. The questionnaire asked if the towns and wards were all part of the City of Michoacán and if the governor and nobles had owned the barrios peacefully for the last forty years. The questions sought to demonstrate that the communities around Lake Pátzcuaro were not independent towns.

The witnesses in turn responded that the barrios, sujetos, and islands were subjects of the Uanacaze ruler, and that they had, since the death of Tangaxuan, also served the city.[55] The witnesses differentiated between the towns around the lake and the rest of the province, making sure to identify the land around the lake as the property of the Uanacaze ruler Tangaxuan after the arrival of Spaniards.[56] A witness from Capula, Michoacán, named Cristobal would go so far as to testify that after the arrival of the "Christians and before the province [of Michoacán] had been distributed," Tangaxuan had said that "this land [the Province of Michoacán] shall be distributed among the Christians, and each should have his own piece, and I will keep this city and all the towns around the lake, and this shall be my kingdom."[57] The witnesses indicated that Infante had taken advantage of the absence of Tangaxuan to encroach on their lands.[58] They also argued that if the barrios were taken away from the city, it would not be able to pay the required amount of tribute to the Crown.

The *Relación*, requested by the viceroy and given directly to him, unlike the court painting, could and did represent this contested landscape without the revisions and interventions of Infante. The Uanacaze, Don Pedro, and their allies were given and took advantage of an unprecedented opportunity. They portrayed an area conquered and unified by the Uanacaze's ancestors and their Islander allies and, through images, indelibly connected the Lake Pátzcuaro basin to themselves.

In fact, the way maps are used in some of the *Relación*'s scenes reveals that these spatial representations served as the visual expressions of territorial intentions. In the first image showing a map (fig. 43; see plate 18), artist 4 depicts Uanacaze leader Tariacuri giving a speech to his nephews and son in which he instructs them how they are to conquer the land and govern it from three major cities. He points to three small mounds beside which, on the ground, the artist has drawn a small house and lines possibly representing agricultural fields.[59] This map depicts Uanacaze imperial expansion and control of the surrounding territory. It is a visual trope of conquest. The second scene containing a map belongs to the ethnographic section of part 3 of the *Relación* (see fig. 22). In it, the captain general calls his audience to war while standing in front of a drawing of a town laid out on a circular grid. Small footprints among the rows of houses indicate the coming invasion. The right-hand side of the image shows the invasion itself, thus revealing that representations of land were often closely associated with their political consolidation.[60]

In his analysis of the *Relación*'s text, the historian Moisés Franco Men-

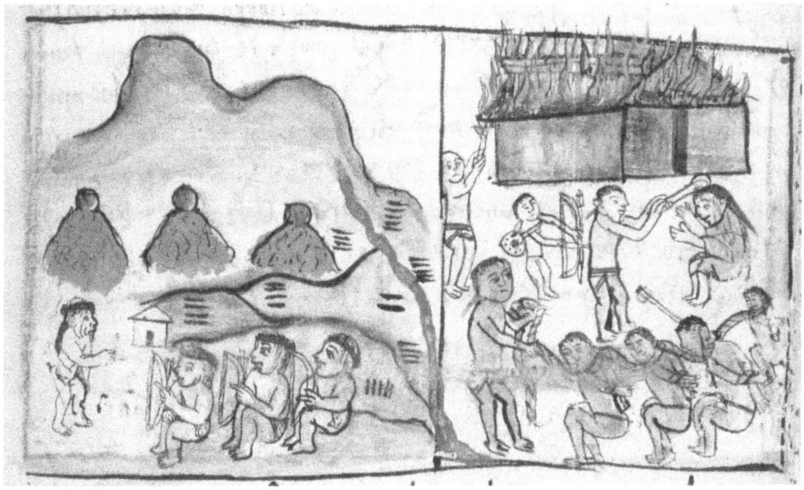

FIGURE 43. Artists 3 and 4. "Como Tariacuri mostró a sus sobrinos y hijo la manera que habían de tener en la guerra y como les señaló tres Señoríos y como destruyeron el pueblo [de] aquel señor llamado Hiuacha" (How Tariacuri showed his nephews and son the way to conduct war and how he appointed them three kingdoms and how they destroyed the town [of] that lord called Hiuacha). *Relación de Michoacán*, fol. 129r. Real Biblioteca del Monasterio de El Escorial, San Lorenzo de El Escorial, Spain, C IV 5. Photograph © Patrimonio Nacional, Spain.

doza has pointed out that the formal aspects and contents of the captain general's speech, which he is seen giving in the aforementioned image, parallel the formal aspects and contents of the petamuti's speech.[61] Both men call forth their divine mandates to justify the conquest of towns and the military and political control of the region. While the illustrations that show the petamuti giving his speech do not include a map per se, the intervening plates function as scenes in a cartographic history by illustrating events taking place in specific locations. Ultimately the text guides the reader from image to image, in the same way the ubiquitous footprints on Mesoamerican cartographic histories guide him or her from place to place. The narrative becomes an act of possession or of claiming territory.[62] Similar to other colonial migration stories, the *Relación* has its audience focus on a specific area by describing the migration to and consolidation of that land by the ancestors of those who participated in the making of the manuscript.

In her analysis of the *Relación*'s text, Stone has noticed that the narrators connect past actions to the present by anachronistically inserting colonial-era buildings into events that took place during pre-Columbian times.

While Stone is interested in a symbolic reading, logistically this connection between past and present offered the *Relación*'s collaborators a tactical opportunity to present the contemporary landscape as the end result of a particular pre-Columbian history.[63] For example, when the narrator explains how the Uanacaze sought an appropriate site for their temple in Pátzcuaro, he describes their reconnaissance in terms of first going to what had become the "fountain of the patio of the bishop," then walking down the hill past what had become the house of the governor, Don Pedro, and finally arriving at the site predestined for their temple, which the narrator then describes as the site where the cathedral was to be built.[64] These same landmarks were also cited in the court papers of the encomienda dispute with Infante and served as points of reference in the organization of the area.[65] In the process of reading the text and viewing the images of the *Relación*, the sixteenth-century reader/viewer would slowly become aware that the current geopolitical landscape was the result of the Uanacaze's history. Through the *Relación*, they claimed jurisdiction over the Lake Pátzcuaro basin.

Conclusion

The numerous emendations of this section of the *Relación* and the careful selection of images reveal what the editor and artists sought to highlight in its rather complex narrative. By illustrating some events in the narrative and omitting others, the artists depicted scenes that emphasized the Uanacaze and their allies' proprietorship of the Lake Pátzcuaro basin. In the absence of many toponyms and even many distinctive features, it is the lake basin that stands as an entity. By combining indigenous and European representational techniques, the *Relación*'s artists provided images readable to European eyes. The combined treatment of space allowed the artists to emphasize particular figures and events while framing them in a landscape that gave the illusion of reality to European eyes, which served to reinforce the indigenous claims to a *particular* landscape, the Lake Pátzcuaro basin.

In the end, the manuscript reveals tenuous and shifting alliances that often blur the distinction between colonizer and colonized. The disputes against Spanish encomenderos for the resources around the lake forced the Uanacaze and their allies to make unusual allies and fight for these lands, sometimes with bows and arrows, but mostly with the ferocity of their ink wells, quills, and brushes, producing thousands of folios and many paintings. Although these paintings do not survive, records about them reveal that they were of key importance, and much was done to control their content. The *Relación*, composed during these events, provided a unique opportunity to lay claim to this land before the Spanish viceroy without the intervention of opposing parties. Its significance must not be underestimated, for even though today, largely due to the *Relación*'s account, we may recognize the area as the heart of the Uanacaze domain in the sixteenth century, ownership of these lands was highly disputed. In the face of the encroachment of many Spaniards, indigenous nobles fought to keep control of as much of this area as possible.

The *Relación*'s migration story functions as a geography of action and, with its copious images, aims at focusing the viewer on the Uanacaze conquest of the Lake Pátzcuaro basin. This story reclaimed places that had been abandoned, recalled previous conquests, and rekindled a history of and through the land. It determined land boundaries throughout Michoacán. So geographical was the focus of this narrative that scholars such as Donald Brand and Dan Stanislawski in the 1940s, and more recently Claudia Espejel Carbajal, have based new territorial maps and cartographic representations of the Uanacaze travels on it.[66] Much like Spanish chronicles and maps of exploration that described and documented claims to possession of distant lands for the Spanish Crown, the *Relación*'s account and its images documented the exploration and possession of the Lake Pátzcuaro area, not by the Spaniards but by the Uanacaze and their allies.[67]

4

Creating Chichimec-Uanacaze Ethnic Identity

The previous chapter explored how the images illustrating the petamuti's speech about the migration of the Uanacaze into the Lake Pátzcuaro basin favored their and their Islander allies' claims to the area over those of their Spanish competitors during the early colonial period. However, this story does much more than determine territorial boundaries. The images provide a window into privilege. They focus on the attributes and deeds of the nobility, and the main, and often the sole, characters in the scenes are the Uanacaze leaders. Notoriously absent are workers, merchants, and even most women, probably because indigenous male nobles collaborated in the making of the manuscript. The *Relación* conveys a limited view of the past through the eyes of the male elite, as is the case for many early colonial manuscripts.[1] In its paintings, one can observe discussions among members of the noble family, meetings among dignitaries, and even a royal wife who cheats on her husband! In other words, one observes the machinations of the "inner circle."

In the course of depicting a particular view of the past, the *Relación* creates a Chichimec identity for the Uanacaze ruling family. In this process, it emphasizes their upstanding behavior to the detriment of other groups around the Lake Pátzcuaro area. These include the Islander ancestors of Don Pedro Cuiniarangari, the indigenous governor of the City of Michoacán. This chapter analyzes how, for a colonial audience, the artists represented the Uanacaze as an exceptional choice to rule this region. This was accomplished through the selection of particular weapons, costumes, and events that represent the Uanacaze's relationships with other ethnic groups. This recollection and depiction of the past sought to create an affinity between Uanacaze behavior and Christian values, as introduced by the Spaniards. It constructed a Chichimec-Uanacaze identity that they hoped Viceroy Antonio de Mendoza could have perceived as worthy of rulership.

The Uanacaze claim of a Chichimec ancestry and ethnicity has received attention from several scholars. The concept of ethnicity is a slippery one, and as other scholars have pointed out for other areas of the world and Mexico in particular, it is dynamic, has many connotations, and often varies from group to group and over time.[2] The difficulty in understanding ethnic classification among ancient cultures is exemplified in the many responses to the Uanacaze's claims in sixteenth-century Michoacán. To a few scholars, the uniqueness of some of Michoacán's cultural traits, such as its art, architecture, and language, supports the Uanacaze's claim to a Chichimec ancestry and a recent arrival from somewhere else.[3] Some archaeologists, however, have pointed to the discrepancies between the *Relación*'s text and the archaeological record. Helen P. Pollard, for example, has noted that Michoacán's rulers did not speak an Uto-Aztecan language, as did other Chichimec groups.[4] Basing their findings on field surveys in the Zacapu area, the archaeologists Marie-Charlotte Arnauld, Dominique Michelet, and Brigitte Faugère-Kalfon in turn have proposed that the formation of the Uanacaze state was a local development and not the result of a large migration into the region.[5] In other words, little archaeological evidence supports the Uanacaze's claim to be a Chichimec group that had recently migrated from another region. This is not to say that new research methods will not be more successful in identifying ethnic markers in the archaeological record.

Given the discrepancies between the *Relación* and the archaeological record as currently understood, scholars have wondered why the Uanacaze were so interested in asserting that their ancestors came from somewhere else. Arnauld and Michelet explain the Uanacaze story as an expression of a politically motivated desire to establish a connection with their powerful Aztec neighbors.[6] Nevertheless, one must point out that by the time the *Relación* was composed, such affiliations would have been detrimental. The Spanish armies and their allies had already defeated and humiliated the Aztecs, events known to and mentioned by the narrators of the *Relación*. The literary critic Cynthia Stone has attributed the story of the Uanacaze's migration to the friar's desire to present the Spanish invasion as only the most recent in a series of invasions in order to justify it and the Spanish right to rule.[7] However, as mentioned previously, migration stories were widespread among the indigenous peoples of Mexico during the early colonial period.

A concern with ethnic identity was not unique to the contributors of the *Relación*. The art historian Esther Pasztory has convincingly demonstrated that during the Classic period (ca. AD 150–650), indigenous cultures in central Mexico similarly articulated their ethnic identities by means of visual forms such as dress and architecture.[8] Michael Smith and James Lockhart, among others, have noted that, much as in the *Relación*, during the Postclassic and early colonial periods (fourteenth through sixteenth centuries) descent from a particular migrant group often determined one's belonging to that ethnic group, and consequently many indigenous people in Mexico depicted and narrated migration stories.[9]

Contemporary studies of social classification can help explain the need for the representation of ethnic distinctions in the *Relación*. Racial and ethnic classifications are powerful social tools. In stratified states, the governing group may define, justify, and reinforce racial and ethnic differences as a way of ordering social life. As a result, these can be fundamental to political power.[10] However, due to the inherent inequalities of a class system based on ethnic distinctions, its power is unstable.[11] It has to justify its very existence, and its rhetoric and privileges are always subject to potential challenges.

In their study of ethnic identity among Nahua peoples (Michoacán's neighbors to the east), the scholars Barbara L. Stark and John K. Chance have noted that groups in competition often stress ethnic distinctions.[12] In a similar manner, the Uanacaze, who had been ousted from power when the *Relación* was being written, would seek to reassert an ethnic identity that put them in a favorable light to the detriment of other ethnic groups, represented in the *Relación*'s images. The artists created utopian portrayals that allocated desirable attributes to the ethnicity of the Uanacaze, while representing other ethnic groups in less desirable terms.[13] This helped the Uanacaze construct and maintain social inequalities that they could exploit.

Viewed in this light, the *Relación*'s images are permanent records of the inequalities inherent in ethnic struggles in early colonial Michoacán.

As mentioned previously, initially the scribes of part 2 of the manuscript left room for only two images to illustrate the events narrated in the petamuti's speech (see figs. 36, 37), but the artists and editor carefully edited the manuscript and added many images, sometimes changing the emphasis of the text. Even though, in most cases, the editor made the decision to make room for the images, the artists did not always agree with him about the most significant events to depict.

The manuscript functions as a contested space in which the interests of the different contributors can still be traced. Michel de Certeau's work on modern-day consumer practices, text, and mass media can help unveil the intent and function of the many layers of the manuscript. Certeau explains that consumers of text and media use "tactics" to appropriate spaces produced by another and make them their own.[14] This can be extended to the process of production of the *Relación*. What were once indigenous accounts and narratives had been written down using alphabetic text in European book format. The process was mediated, edited, and supervised by the European friar, who lent his authority to the work and in turn gained cultural capital as he became the expert in the region. The book functioned as a new "space" that controlled knowledge about the region. But when the artists painted their images, they strategically interpreted the text, highlighting some elements of the narrative and sometimes altering the friar's intended message.[15] Sometimes the titles say one thing and the paintings depict another. Sometimes the artists depicted events not mentioned in the titles or events from previous chapters (see figs. 36, 45). In one instance, when faced with the liberties taken by an artist, the editor added text to one of the titles to make it match the artist's choice (fig. 44). In other words, within limits, the artists used painting as a tactic to make this space their own.

The artists often chose to illustrate the Uanacaze as morally upstanding, much to the detriment of other ethnic and elite groups. For example, in two images that according to the accompanying titles in the manuscript were supposed to show marital alliances between the Uanacaze and other groups, an artist decided instead to illustrate passages in the text that tell of a woman from one of these groups who cheated on her Uanacaze husband and cultural hero Tariacuri. These images become a driving theme in the life of Tariacuri, a pivotal character in the story. Under the title "How Tariacuri Got Married to a Daughter of the Lord of Curinguaro," an artist represented Tariacuri's marriage to a non-Uanacaze woman.[16] In this im-

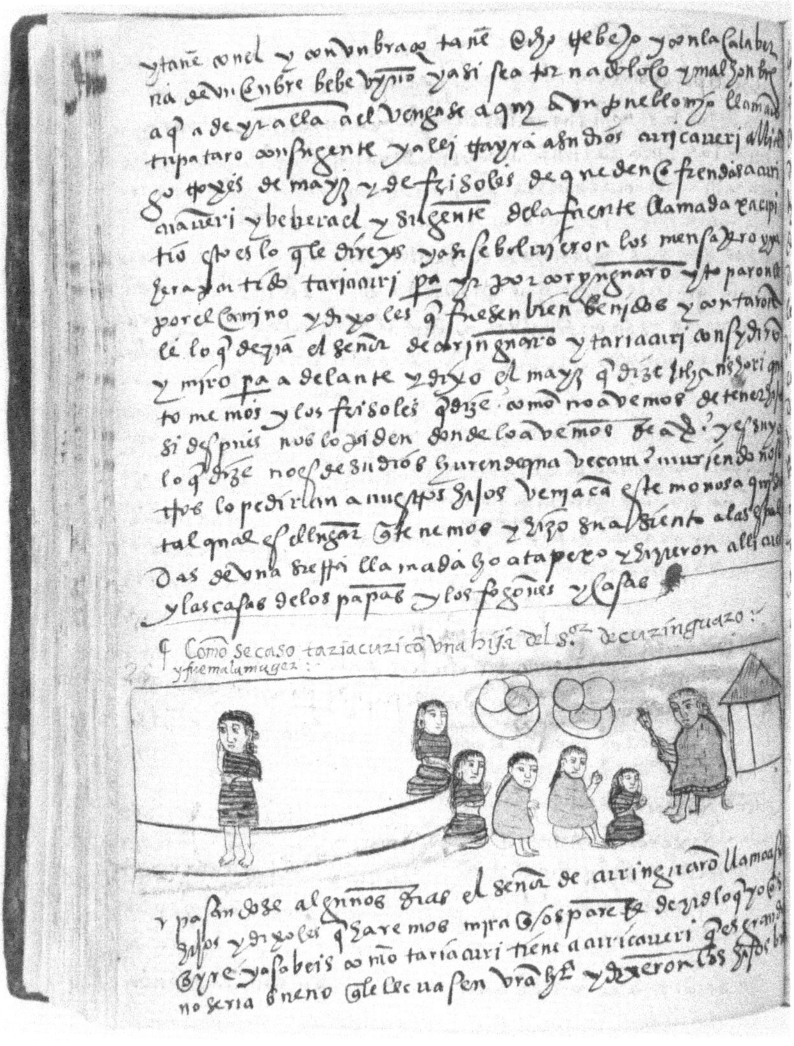

FIGURE 44. Artist 3. "Como se casó Tariacuri con una hija del señor de Curinguaro y fue mala muger" (How Tariacuri got married to a daughter of the lord of Curinguaro, and [she] was a bad woman). *Relación de Michoacán*, fol. 87v. Real Biblioteca del Monasterio de El Escorial, San Lorenzo de El Escorial, Spain, C IV 5. Photograph © Patrimonio Nacional, Spain.

age, Tariacuri sits in front of a party of two men and three women (fig. 44; see plate 19). Some dishes of food hover in the space above. In addition to the marriage scene taking place on the right, the artist included a woman walking on a path away from the wedding party, which scholars have interpreted as the same woman who later left her husband. It seems that the ed-

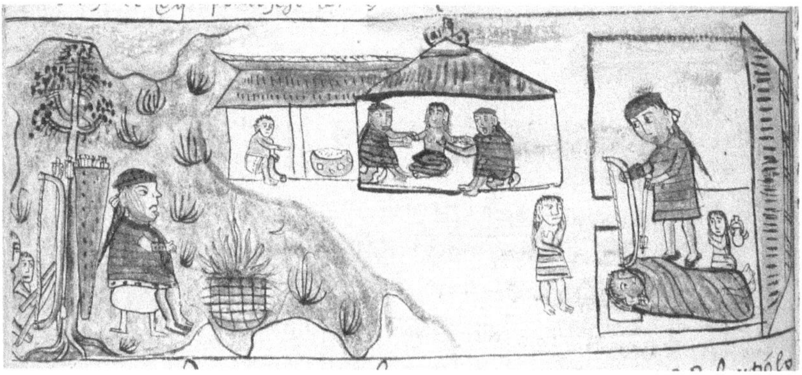

FIGURE 45. Artist 3. "Como Tariacuri sintió mucho como no le guardava lealtad su muger, y como se casó con otra por consejo de una su tía" (How Tariacuri felt a lot of sorrow because his wife was not loyal, and how he married another [woman] because one of his aunts advised him). *Relación de Michoacán*, fol. 92v. Real Biblioteca del Monasterio de El Escorial, San Lorenzo de El Escorial, Spain, C IV 5. Photograph © Patrimonio Nacional, Spain.

itor also understood it in this light, because after the image was completed, he wrote between its upper border and below the original title, "and [she] was a bad woman."[17]

The following image also highlights the misconduct of this non-Uanacaze woman. The title reads, "How Tariacuri Felt a Lot of Sorrow Because His Wife Was Not Loyal, and How He Married Another [Woman] Because One of His Aunts Advised Him."[18] Rather than portray Tariacuri's affliction, his aunt giving him advice, or his subsequent remarriage, the artist decided to illustrate the previous chapter's description of the first wife's infidelity (fig. 45; see plate 20).

In the center of the scene, we see his wife literally two-timing him, while on the left-hand side, Tariacuri—by marked contrast—is in the forest burning wood for his god. On the right-hand side of the illustration, he returns home and finds her smelling of wine and covered in the black body paint of her lovers. When analyzing the text, the historian James Krippner-Martínez has pointed out that Tariacuri's behavior follows Christian ideals.[19] This image does more than emphasize Tariacuri's Christian-like behavior; it creates a moral dichotomy between the Uanacaze rulers and their enemies.[20] Tariacuri's wife and her lovers are said to be nobles from another group. According to the text, her infidelity incited a war between the Uanacaze and her people. The tutelary god of the Uanacaze is said to have intervened in their favor, and in the next illustration in the *Relación*, the Uanacaze defeat and sacrifice the wife's people (see fig. 39).[21]

Tariacuri, the pious husband, on the other hand, goes on to become the mastermind behind the unification of most of Michoacán under Uanacaze rule. He gives directions to his two nephews and son on how to conquer the land (see fig. 43). The text also describes these young Uanacaze nobles as holding Christian-like values. They are said to be brave, austere, and temperate regarding sex and drink. In the only grisaille in the *Relación*, artist 2 painted Tariacuri giving a speech to his nephews and son on why the Uanacaze ought to conquer their enemies (fig. 46). Gray washes and lines represent volume and depth, resembling etchings in European printed sources. European prints during the early colonial period often served as models for paintings by indigenous artists. The grisaille in the *Relación* bears an uncanny resemblance to an image of Christ and his disciples from the *Book of Hours* that belonged to the Spanish king Charles V (fig. 47); and according to the nineteenth-century scholar Paul Durrieu, this book was copied from one or more books of hours printed in the late fifteenth and early sixteenth centuries.[22] Books of hours often traveled across the Atlantic among the belongings of clergy and laypeople and could have been used as models for the *Relación*'s images.

In the text accompanying the grisaille, Tariacuri bases the reasons for conquering the region on the deficiencies of his enemies. He says that some rulers are too old to rule; some quarrel, steal from each other, and never

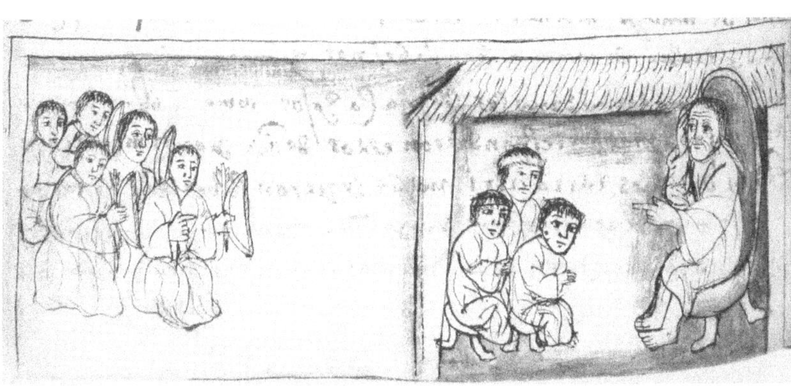

FIGURE 46. Artist 2. *Relación de Michoacán*, fol. 108v. Real Biblioteca del Monasterio de El Escorial, San Lorenzo de El Escorial, Spain, C IV 5. Photograph © Patrimonio Nacional, Spain.

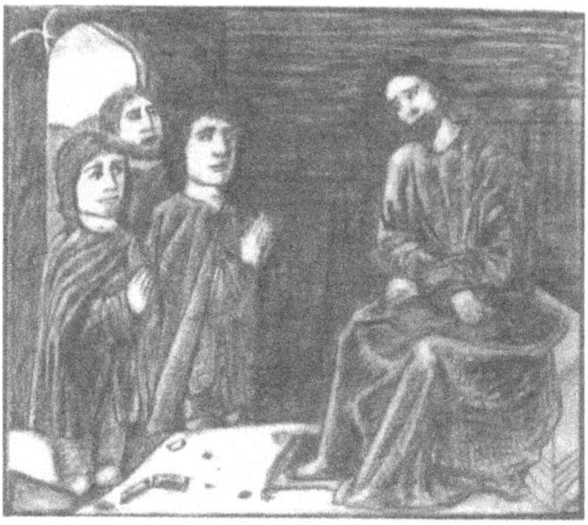

FIGURE 47. *Book of Hours* of Charles V. Biblioteca Nacional, Madrid, Spain. Drawing by Elizabeth Coughlin.

settle their differences; and others are impious and drink outside religious festivities, while some noblewomen are promiscuous.[23] The gods even sent pests to those who stopped worshipping and started drinking, as in biblical times. Because the flaws of the Uanacaze's enemies are represented as closely paralleling violations of the Christian code, they become justifications for their conquest and the necessity of Uanacaze rule over them.[24] Images illustrate this war as well as the misdeeds of the wife's son and his subsequent assassination (see figs. 39, 40, 41). The *Relación* also depicts the demise, either at the hands of enemies or righteous Uanacaze themselves, of those Uanacaze lords who gave in to vice (see fig. 21).

After the end of the Uanacaze priest's speech, the friar included two more chapters with related stories, at least one of which helps reinforce the parallels between the Uanacaze's behavior and proper Christian morals. In one chapter, a woman from one of the Uanacaze ruler's homes infiltrates an enemy's fiesta. There she seduces a nobleman away from his wife, only to decapitate him later. The accompanying image shows a female figure holding the head of an enemy in one hand and a knife in the other; the upper torso of her victim lies on the ground. This image has been compared to Catholic depictions of Judith and the beheading of Holofernes.[25] The viceroy would likely have easily recognized images based on European models; they represented the Uanacaze in ways he could understand.

Moralizing imagery and narratives like those found in the *Relación* also had counterparts in medieval and Renaissance European political treatises. From Saint Augustine's *De Civitate Dei* in the early fifth century, to Saint Thomas Aquinas's *De Regimine Principum* (ca. 1265–1266), then Marsiglio de Padua's *Defensor Pacis* (1342), up into the sixteenth century, these works stressed the personal moral virtues of rulers. Much as in the *Relación*, the princes were advised to refrain from vices and be self-restrained, chaste, humble, detached from worldly pleasures, and generous to their people. Their main functions were military and judicial, and they had to set good examples for their subjects.[26] These works derived their code of conduct from biblical precepts and set personal and moral virtues against the seven deadly sins: humility versus pride, kindness versus envy, measure versus wrath, and so on.[27] The literate population of Michoacán knew this genre. In his *Información de derecho*, bishop of Michoacán Vasco de Quiroga would cite works such as those of Saint Augustine. In addition, Jerónimo de Alcalá, alleged author of the *Relación*, reported that Mexico City's bishop Juan de Zumárraga had sent to Michoacán a book of "vices and virtues" in Latin.[28]

Colonial documents reveal that indigenous nobles understood the many advantages of representing themselves and their ancestors as fulfilling the ideals of European rulers and following the strictures of the Catholic Church. For example, Uanacaze heir Don Francisco Tariacuri would describe himself in 1542 as a "good Christian" when requesting grants from the Spanish Crown.[29] His brother Don Antonio Huitzimengari in his "Information of Merits and Services," a document requesting royal grants, had his witnesses attest that when the Spanish forces first arrived, the people of Michoacán were "brave men," excellent warriors, men of good qualities, strong, in fact the strongest in the colonies.[30] In addition, witnesses would describe him as a "good Christian" who performed many good deeds and, like the best of princes from European political treatises, set a good example for his subjects.[31] Just like his Uanacaze ancestors in the *Relación*, Don Antonio was described as having no vices and abstaining from alcohol.[32]

Rather than a way of life, the co-optation of Christian behavior seems to have been largely a rhetorical tool in colonial documents. In practice, Don Antonio had several children outside his Catholic marriage. The General Commissary of the Franciscans accused him of many excesses, including the corruption of indigenous women.[33] Likewise, the indigenous nobleman Juan Puruata—who married Don Antonio's widow and became governor of Michoacán—blamed excessive drinking and eating among indigenous people (not including himself) on the *relajamiento de las costumbres* (loosening of customs and mores) since the Spanish arrival. However, it seems that he in fact consumed or distributed vast quantities of alcohol and chocolate, because in 1581 he owed the exorbitant sum of 448 pesos for wine from Jerez, Spain, and cacao beans from Guatemala.[34]

In the *Relación*, the parallel between Uanacaze behavior and Christian morals is further reinforced through the accoutrements the Uanacaze carry and the activities they perform. In spite of the variations among the representations of clothing and accessories by the different artists, the ubiquitous feature marking the Uanacaze throughout the pages of the manuscript is the bow and arrow, which signifies their prowess in hunting and in war. Indeed, according to the text of the *Relación*, it is by this talent that the Uanacaze proudly distinguished themselves from the local populations.[35] Uanacaze rulers hold bows and arrows even when sitting in their palaces (see fig. 32). Eduard Seler has interpreted these weapons as diagnostic of groups from the northern part of Mexico known by the Nahuatl name Chichimec, and indeed, as we have seen, the *Relación* refers to the large migratory group led by the Uanacaze as Chichimec.[36]

Today, as noted previously, scholars have taken this claim of Chichimec ancestry to task because the Uanacaze did not speak a Uto-Aztecan language and the archaeological record does not seem to support their claim to have come from somewhere outside modern-day Michoacán. Nonetheless, questions remain: Why did the Uanacaze narrators of the *Relación* identify their ancestors as Chichimecs? What did they hope to achieve by representing themselves as Chichimecs to a colonial audience? In fact, the founding mother of their line belonged to a local group from the town of Naranjan, in northern Michoacán, but neither the text nor the images suggest that this had any impact on the Uanacaze sense of identity.

Other migration stories also tell us of Chichimec ancestors who would marry and create political alliances with local populations. Central Mexican manuscripts, such as the *Codex Xolotl*, show that migrant Chichimec ancestors, once settled in an area, forsook their animal-skin attire and adopted the clothing of local populations. This marked their adoption of new cultural practices and a sedentary lifestyle.[37]

After the arrival of the Spaniards in the sixteenth century, Chichimec identity in central Mexico often came to be associated with northern nomadic tribes lacking the Christian values of their already-converted sedentary neighbors to the south.[38] For example, the art historian Donna Pierce has interpreted the mural program at the Convent of Ixmiquilpan, Hidalgo, as a good-versus-evil battle representing the Otomí Eagle and Jaguar warriors, already converted to Christianity, as "good" and the Chichimec warriors as "evil."[39]

In marked contrast to central Mexican manuscripts, the artists of the *Relación* gave the same attire and accoutrements to the Uanacaze throughout the manuscript. Uanacaze rulers hold bows and arrows to identify their authority and martial prowess. Through these attributes they proudly distinguish themselves from other ethnic groups and even from their Aztec neighbors to the east.

The Uanacaze self-identification as Chichimecs may be partly explained in the particulars of the history of this region. Unlike the Aztecs, whose martial expertise was used against Spanish forces, Michoacanos would maintain that they had submitted peacefully and had in fact helped Spaniards conquer other groups. The Uanacaze heir, Don Francisco, and his troops had in fact accompanied Viceroy Mendoza to the Mixtón War. When the encomendero Juan Infante came to take possession of the lands belonging to the pueblo-hospital that Bishop Vasco de Quiroga had founded, Quiroga went to defend it accompanied by armed Chichimecs.[40] In turn, Bishop Quiroga, arguing that the Chichimecs in this region possessed many merits, asked the Spanish Crown's support for their conversion. Marking the difference between these Chichimecs and those of other regions was essential in receiving support from the Crown. In 1539, the Spanish king Charles V accepted Quiroga's request to support their conversion on the basis that Michoacán's Chichimecs, even though poor, "practiced no sacrifices, [had no] idols, . . . and were men of good nature."[41]

In addition to describing their prowess at war, the *Relación*'s text calls the Uanacaze superb hunters. Through the forests of Michoacán, they tracked and hunted deer with their bows and arrows. They offered the precious deer skins to their ancestral god Curicaueri, to whom they also performed many religious devotions. The emphasis on the Uanacaze as excellent hunters would have found a receptive European audience. Hunting enjoyed an enthusiastic following in medieval and Renaissance Europe as aristocrats, clergymen, and rulers cultivated a hunting culture. Aristocratic households spent great amounts of money maintaining large estates and the necessary accoutrements for hunting. Hunting scenes often decorated the walls and manuscripts of noble European households.[42]

While hunting practices varied from one side of the Atlantic to the other, the admiration of the hunting skills of the Uanacaze in the *Relación* had a strong correlation with those of European nobles. Holy Roman Emperor Maximilian I (1459–1519) was known for his skill with the crossbow. Like the Uanacaze ruler Tariacuri, who was said to be able to kill a hummingbird with an arrow, Maximilian was said to be able to kill ducks in flight with his crossbow.[43] Hunting was seen as part of a young nobleman's education, including the Mendozas'.[44] Theodore of Antioch, translator for Holy Roman Emperor Frederick II (thirteenth century), mentions that the "only amusement appropriate to kings is hunting."[45] In 1600, Alonso de Oñate, brother of the governor of New Mexico, took a Chichimec from New Mexico to the Spanish court so that this marksman would amuse the king by shooting arrows with his bow.[46]

Spanish conquistadors and officials continued their hunting practices in the Americas. Hernan Cortés received with his title of marquis two hunting estates in central Mexico, which he is said to have used avidly. Viceroy Mendoza is said to have loved hunting and carried out hunts for deer, rabbit, and coyote into Mexico's northern plains. According to Friar Toribio de Benavente (known as Motolinía), Mendoza did so using "Indian style" hunting practices with thousands of native beaters.[47] To commemorate the peace between the kings of France and Spain in 1538, Cortés and Mendoza organized a celebration that included a hunt in an artificial forest constructed specifically for this purpose in Mexico City's main plaza. In 1542, after the viceroy returned from the Mixtón War, an impressive hunt was held in his honor.[48]

According to the historian John Cummins, hunting in Europe was an expensive and self-indulgent entertainment often explained and justified in Christian terms: a vigorous pastime, it helped lessen temptations of the flesh and spirit. Pursuit of the hunt was often compared to a spiritual quest. For example, King John I of Portugal would describe the sight of bear hunting as "so splendid as to be comparable to experiencing the glory of God."[49]

Deer hunting in particular bore special symbolism among Christian audiences. The hart was often associated with longevity and consequently with the possibility of humankind's eternal life through the acceptance of Christ. Christ and his Passion were often associated with the deer hunt, and tracking prey was like tracking God's presence on earth.[50] This was epitomized in the vision of Saint Eustachio, a Roman nobleman of the second century, who converted to Christianity upon the miraculous sight of a crucifix among the antlers of a hart. European artists of the fifteenth and sixteenth centuries, such as Albrecht Dürer and Pisanello (also known as Antonio Pisano), depicted this theme.[51] Furthermore, the Archangel Gabriel was sometimes called the "heavenly hunter" and depicted with a spear, hunting horn, and hounds.

The makers of the *Relación* must have been well aware of hunting metaphors embodying the pursuit of Christian ideals, since Michoacán was evangelized early on. Hunting exercises, including target shooting and catching deer, were used in the conversion of neophytes according to Cristóbal Cabrera, the apostolic notary to Michoacán's first bishop, Vasco de Quiroga, between 1538 and 1545. These exercises were analogous to reaching Christ through personal effort and achieving spiritual perfection through practice. In Cabrera's words, children competed at shooting arrows so "that just as they directed their arrows at a given target, so too were the deeds of their life to converge towards a definite goal, Our Lord and Savior."[52] Cabrera went on to explain bows and arrows as means to an end: knowledge of the faith, a mightier weapon that would lead to spiritual salvation.

The association of hunting themes with Christianity also had a place within Franciscan and Augustinian conversion. Hunters and hunting scenes appear as graffiti on the stucco walls at the Augustinian convent in Tiripetío, Michoacán, and at the Franciscan convent in Tzintzuntzan. Indigenous labor built and decorated these convents, and the children of the indigenous nobility were often educated there.[53] Even though most of Tiripetío's sixteenth-century convent no longer exists, graffiti of a hunter holding a bow and arrow that was incised directly in the fresh stucco can be found on the wall that used to divide the church's choir from the second floor of the convent.[54]

The convent at Tzintzuntzan that survives today was not the first to be built, but it must have been near completion around 1618, since one of its walls on the second floor bears this date.[55] Some of its early paintings and graffiti can still be seen, and a few of these depict hunting scenes that both figuratively and literally join hunters and warriors with Christian themes.[56] On the second floor in the northeastern area of the convent, a small room that leads to the church's choir contains copious graffiti incised along its walls. On the northern wall, next to the door to the choir, hunters, prey, and warriors (some wearing deer antlers) rise from a musical notation incised near a graffito of a Christian insignia of a shield bearing a heart (figs. 48a, 48b).[57] It is possible that the scores and figures visually represent hymns used in the conversion of indigenous people. On the eastern wall of this room, Christ, in the guise of *Salvador Mundi*, is incised directly into the fresh stucco (fig. 48c). Other animals and figures accompany Christ, as well as the word *Acha*, meaning "lord" in P'urhépecha.[58] The coupling of these hunting figures with Christian imagery encodes indigenous practices within Christian doctrine.[59]

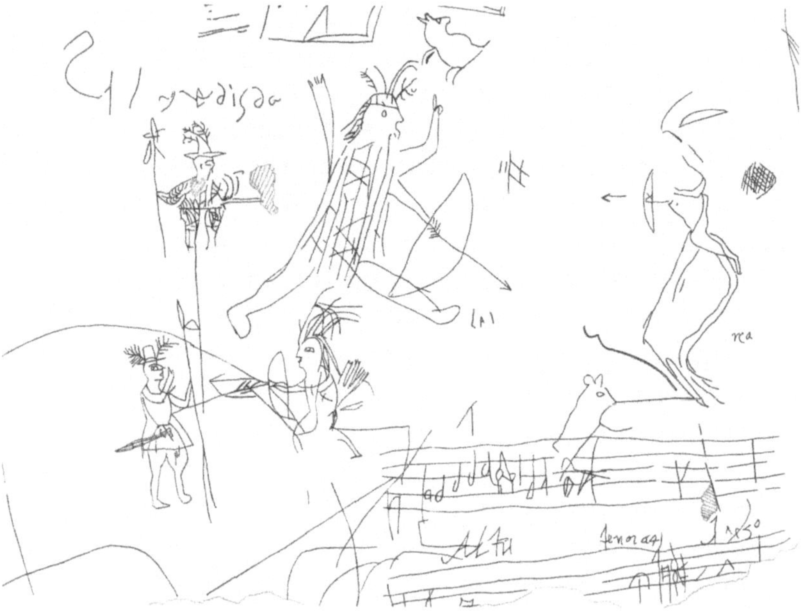

FIGURE 48A. Graffito of musical notation with hunters. Second floor, Convent of Tzintzuntzan, Michoacán. Possibly seventeenth century. Drawing by Viera Sairán Monfón based on original tracings by Viera Sairán Monfón and the author.

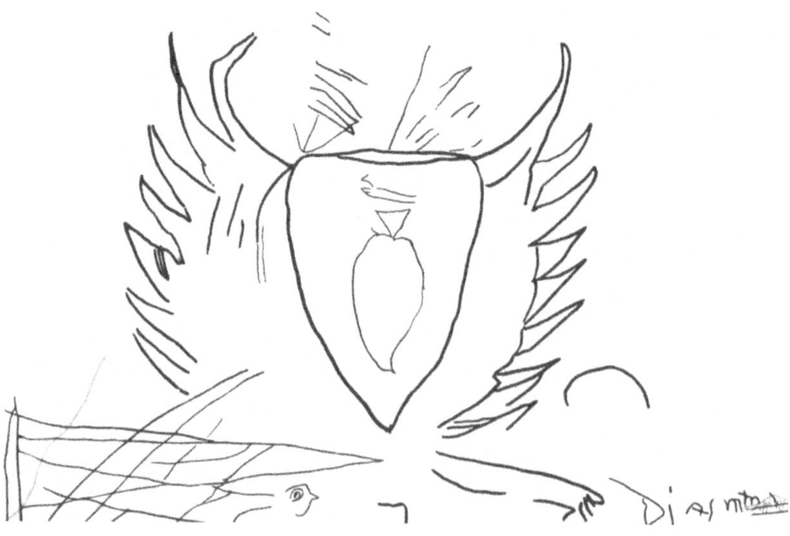

FIGURE 48B. Graffito of a Christian insignia of a shield bearing a heart. Second floor, Convent of Tzintzuntzan, Michoacán. Possibly seventeenth century. Tracing by Viera Sairán Monfón and the author.

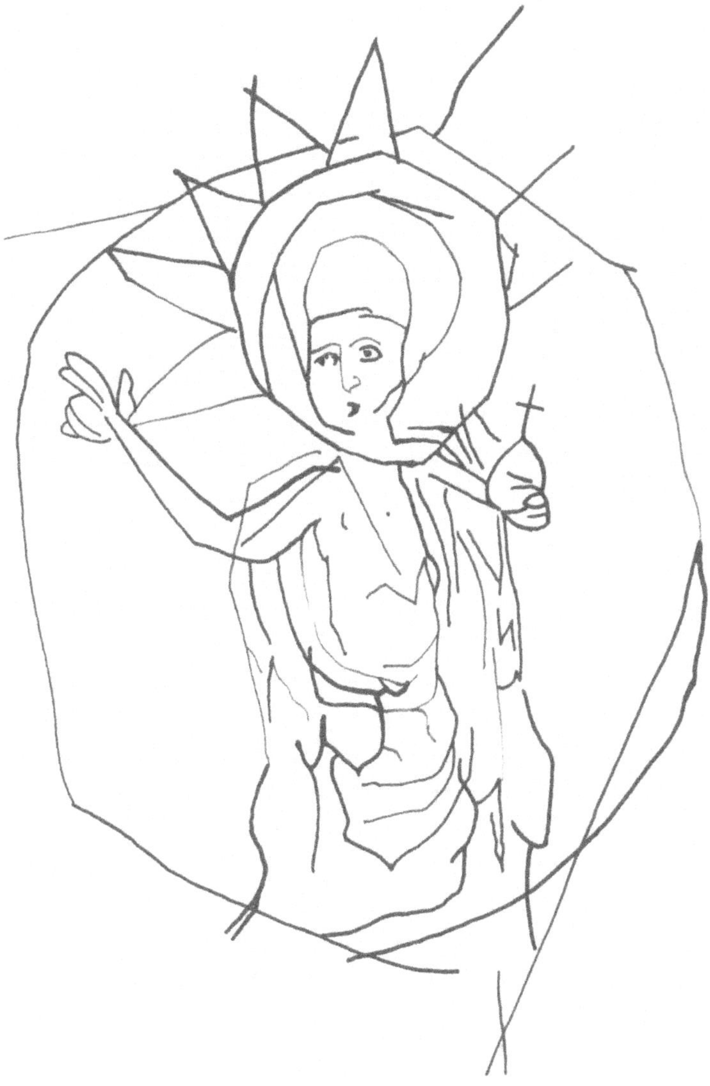

FIGURE 48C. Graffito of Christ as *Salvador Mundi*. Second floor, Convent of Tzintzuntzan, Michoacán. Possibly seventeenth century. Drawing by Viera Sairán Monfón based on original tracings by Viera Sairán Monfón and the author.

Outside the small room leading to the choir and along the second-floor balustrade overlooking the convent courtyard, complex graffiti depict a landscape with a large church, a town with a large cross in the center, and above them a small hunting scene. Hunting here is represented not as part of a pre-Columbian past but as taking place at the heart of a colonial town, overseen and accepted by Catholic authorities. Thus sanctioned by the clergy, and in all likelihood promoted by the indigenous nobility, hunters are depicted in close connection with Christian beliefs. This imagery would not only have assisted the clergy in the process of conversion but would also have preserved for the indigenous nobility a privileged place in colonial society. Defined and depicted as superb hunters in their spiritual quests, the Uanacaze nobility's Chichimec ancestors in the *Relación* bore in their very identity the values set by evangelization.

The text of the *Relación* casts the Uanacaze's Chichimec ancestors as upstanding Christians and serves to anchor the images pertinent to Chichimec identity within Christian rhetoric. The artists selected some elements from the narrative that are central to indigenous migration stories, yet they paired them with text that contextualizes those elements within a Christian value system. For example, in the *Relación*, artist 4 depicts three future rulers together at a cave. As mentioned previously, caves in Mesoamerican migration stories are often symbols of origin and transformation and can also represent the foundation of a polity. According to the text, this act solidified the relationship among these three men, who would subsequently conquer the region. The text also describes them as carrying out "penance." In Christian societies, caves were often recognized as symbols of penitence and an ascetic life. Saint Jerome, whom the friar mentions in the prologue of the *Relación*, is often depicted in a cave; and the mural *Allegory of the Eremitic Life* in the *sala de profundis* (friar's chapel) at the sixteenth-century convent of Actopan, Mexico, depicts Augustinian monks dwelling in caves. Thus, the image of the Uanacaze lords convening in a cave would have suggested that they lived a pious, proto-monastic life even before the arrival of the monastic orders in Mexico (see fig. 28).

Beyond its justification in Christian rhetoric, among European nobles, hunting was thought to prepare knights for war, both physically and mentally. Alfonso XI of Castile wrote about this preparation: "[O]ne must be vigorous, and do without sleep, suffer lack of good food and drink, rise early, sometimes have a poor bed, undergo cold and heat, and conceal one's fear."[60] The Uanacaze ancestors likewise are said not to have slept much or feared even death and to have endured many years of hardship. The result of this rigorous training was that the Uanacaze, like ideal European knights, possessed the four cardinal virtues of fortitude, justice, prudence, and temperance.[61] They are said to have been prudent in war; they defended their god Curicaueri against all odds; they brought justice to the region; they were moderate in food, sex, and drink; and they offered the material wealth acquired through war to their god.

In addition to portraying the Uanacaze as hunters and warriors, some of the artists of the *Relación* went so far as to clothe the Uanacaze ancestors in Christian-like attire, visually reinforcing the similarities between their and Christian practices. While artist 3 dressed the Uanacaze in shirts that come halfway down the thighs, artists 1, 2, and 4 often clothed them in long robes that come down to the ankles, much like those used by the mendicant Christian orders (compare fig. 49 to figs. 1, 46, and 28). José Tudela has noticed that these flowing ankle-length robes may not be direct representations of indigenous dress.[62] The *Relaciones geográficas*, produced in Michoacán at the end of the sixteenth century, describe the men's clothing as consisting of cotton or vegetable fiber shirts that reached halfway down the thighs or to the knees, loincloths, sandals, deer-leather garlands with feathers, and sometimes feathered capes, but the men might also go nude.[63] The shirts as described in the *Relaciones geográficas* probably come closest to the representations of artist 3 (see figs. 49, 56). The varying Christian and pre-Columbian clothing of the Uanacaze ancestors, as depicted by different artists, serves to blur the boundaries that separate pre-Columbian and Christian practices.

Blurring the lines of these dress codes is important because during the early colonial period, clothing served to identify indigenous lords in the eyes of the Spanish authorities as having accepted Spanish Christian customs and beliefs.[64] For instance, according to the corregidor of Taymeo, an Otomí settlement in Michoacán,

> they used to go about in the nude, and fight in war with their bows and arrows, and, thanks to the mercy of God, from many years back they [now] have our Christian ways and *policia*; and they go about dressed honestly with their shirts, long pants, and doublets and hats, and those who can have their cloaks with sleeves and cassocks like Spaniards.[65]

The Franciscan Juan de Torquemada states in his sixteenth-century *Monarquía indiana* that the lay brothers Lucas and Sebastián from Michoacán, who spent their lives preaching in P'urhépecha and Nahuatl, would live and dress as friars without taking vows.[66] And Don Juan, a nobleman from Tarecuato, Michoacán, imitated Saint Francis of Assisi by dressing in a long, coarse woolen cloth, and he pestered the friars to let him join them.[67]

These examples reveal that clothing served as a public symbol of conversion and adherence to Spanish ways.

The adoption of European religious and cultural practices was, needless to say, a source of great advantage to indigenous nobles. The Uanacaze descendants, aware of the social connotations of Spanish clothing, often pursued and fought for the right to wear it. Both of the Uanacaze heirs mentioned in the *Relación*, Don Francisco and Don Antonio, boasted about wearing Spanish clothing and used it as evidence of their social status, as well as their acceptance of Christian customs, when requesting royal grants.[68] These men's behavior indicates that indigenous people understood the symbolic value Spanish clothing held for Spanish audiences. To apply it to the Uanacaze ancestors in the *Relación*'s illustrations reinforced the Christian-like values and behavior of their lineage.

By depicting the Uanacaze lords with bows and arrows, the artists of the *Relación* represented them as Chichimecs. This classification served their descendants well, since an austere life, hunting prowess, and virtuous behavior had many parallels with Christian European beliefs and practices at the time. The exaltation of the Chichimec Uanacaze lords' moral virtues, as described in the text, depicted in the illustrations, and symbolized by Christian-like clothing, represented them as analogous to Christian princes and knights and thus worthy of rulership. This glorification of the Uanacaze ancestors came at the expense of the ancestors of the numerous other ethnic groups mentioned in the manuscript, whose descendants lived in Michoacán during the colonial period. From local populations, to Nahua groups, to Islanders from Lake Pátzcuaro's islands, and even other Chichimec factions, non-Uanacaze peoples often serve in the narrative as examples of how *not* to behave. They are not sufficiently pious, they drink too much, they are defeated in battle, and their women have sex outside marriage. Because of this, the petamuti reminds his audience at the end of his speech that the ancestors of the local nobles had been conquered and were forever obliged to serve the god Curicaueri and his representatives, the Uanacaze. The priest's speech resonates with some of the colonial measures taken by Viceroy Antonio de Mendoza, such as the prosecution of drunks and the mandate that they be turned into servants.[69]

Through this ethnic differentiation, the Uanacaze aimed to assert themselves over the other groups represented in the manuscript, a strategy not unlike that of other stratified states in which the governing elite uses ethnic differentiation to affirm its class status and legitimize its political power.

For the viceroy, this section of the *Relación* would have presented indigenous non-Uanacaze people as a social "other" within Michoacán's political system. It constructed a negative ethnic identity for the majority of Michoacán's population, which would have made it very difficult for anyone in it to reach the highest political posts.

The arrival of the Spaniards had altered power relations in Michoacán, allowing Don Pedro Cuiniarangari, a descendant of local non-Uanacaze nobles, to break ethnic boundaries by allying himself with the invading Spanish armies. Shortly after Spaniards killed the main Uanacaze ruler, Zinzicha Tangaxuan, Don Pedro occupied the governor's seat, the most important political post in the area during the early years of Spanish colonization. Given the predicament in which the Uanacaze found themselves—out of favor with the colonial government and subject to a lord who had once been subject to their rule—the narrative reveals itself as a strategy for ethnic differentiation and domination. The petamuti's account presents the Uanacaze's historical rise to power as the inevitable result of their enemies' "un-Christian" misconduct. This strategy would have affirmed the Uanacaze's status and legitimized their political power in the eyes of the viceroy.

The Islanders: A Slippery Relationship

Among all of the enemy groups mentioned in the *Relación*, the Islanders, the inhabitants of Lake Pátzcuaro's islands, receive the most attention. Their meeting with the Uanacaze first illustrates the historical narrative in part 2 of the *Relación* (see fig. 36). In the right-hand corner, the Uanacaze, standing at the shores of the lake, point to a fisherman, who in turn points to them to indicate that they are all speaking. According to the text, after four generations of wandering through northern Michoacán, the Uanacaze arrived at the shores of Lake Pátzcuaro, where they met this Islander fisherman and exchanged game for fish, requesting that he give them his young daughter.

Dominique Michelet suggests that this meeting serves as a cohesive narrative stratagem that unites the history of the Islanders with that of the Uanacaze. Michelet's intention is to distinguish so-called mythical versus historical elements in the narrative, but one can also see the meeting between the Uanacaze and the Islander as a pragmatic result of the manuscript's colonial context.[70] Furthermore, the images, having been inserted after the text was completed, show which aspects the artists sought to highlight, aspects that otherwise might have been lost in the complexity of the story being told.

The Islanders' strategic location within the Lake Pátzcuaro basin, an area in dispute with the Spanish encomendero Juan Infante, helps explain their importance in the manuscript. In addition, complex colonial interethnic disputes can also illuminate their significance and the way they are portrayed in the images. Don Pedro Cuiniarangari, the sole named collaborator in the making of the *Relación*, described himself as an Islander, not a Uanacaze noble. In part 3 of the *Relación*, Don Pedro explains how his collaboration with the Spanish forces upon their arrival in Michoacán earned him the post of governor.

Through an analysis of the text of the *Relación*, Cynthia L. Stone has pointed out how Don Pedro presents himself as an intermediary between the Uanacaze and the Spaniards. An initial analysis of the images seems to support this interpretation, yet the images dealing with the Islanders, and with Don Pedro in particular, further qualify the terms in which his role as intermediary and his position in relation to the Uanacaze were to be understood. After the death of the Uanacaze ruler, the position of governor was the most important post in the region and Don Pedro would have had to explain his position since he was not a Uanacaze noble. The images explain his relationship to the Uanacaze in terms that continued to present a united front among the indigenous nobility to the viceroy while simultaneously showing him as subservient to the Uanacaze and proposing them as the best choice to rule the region.

The complexity and delicate nature of representing Don Pedro as an intermediary can be best appreciated by the events that led to the Spanish conquest of Michoacán as described by him and recorded in the *Relación*. Upon the arrival of the Spaniards in the region, Tangaxuan, the Uanacaze ruler, sent out armies against them, some headed by Don Pedro. Don Pedro explains that he was captured by the Spaniards but subsequently set free and sent back to the Uanacaze palace to tell the ruler that the Spaniards had come in peace. On his way there, he told the ruler's armies to disperse, and once at the palace, he reported that the Spaniards had come to Michoacán in good faith. In the meantime, Tangaxuan was planning to drown himself in the lake, convinced to do so by other nobles. Eventually he listened to Don Pedro and gave up the idea. In this way, the text of the *Relación* presents a rather enthusiastic view of Don Pedro's intervention and the arrival of Europeans to Michoacán: thanks to Don Pedro's negotiations Tangaxuan survived and the region received the Spaniards peacefully.[71] Yet it also reveals Don Pedro's disregard for the Uanacaze ruler's orders at a critical moment in the Spanish conquest of the region.[72]

The process of creation of the scene that accompanies Don Pedro's account about the arrival of Spaniards reveals some of the tensions around this event and ultimately corroborates the significance of Don Pedro's role as intermediary between Spanish forces and the Uanacaze ruler (fig. 49; see plate 21). Originally the scene focused on the ruler's intention to drown himself. Several contour lines in a light wash allow one to see the original extent of the lake, which would have filled most of the left half of the image. The ruler in his palace would have faced that direction while being led to the lake by three nobles. In the final version, the artist reduced the side of the lake to include a hill with a path and three Spaniards on horses. Rather than look at the lake, the palace nobles look at the Spaniards on the hill at the other side of the lake. It is not possible to identify which of the men in the picture is Don Pedro, but one points to the Spaniards (with a hand that was added later) and the Uanacaze ruler, and it is possible that this figure represents Don Pedro, as he would be the one who would speak to both parties. By including the Spaniards, the artist has shifted the focus of the image to their arrival and consequently to Don Pedro's intervention.[73]

This visual and textual narrative, like many others in the *Relación*, reveals the perilous line the contributors of the manuscript walked when attempting to bring together their diverging interests and contradictory actions. Balancing his collaboration with Spaniards with the removal of the Uanacaze from power and his current position as governor was no simple act. Given the conflicts that the indigenous elite maintained with Spanish newcomers, Don Pedro needed to appear in the *Relación* as a governor who could at the very least represent the interests of the Uanacaze.

According to the *Relación*, the post of governor was the equivalent of the *angatacuri* of pre-Columbian times. Much like Don Pedro, the angatacuri played multiple roles and often acted as an intermediary between the ruler and others. The angatacuri sometimes served as captain general (as had Don Pedro), and in this role he often accompanied the petamuti when the latter imparted justice. In one of the justice scenes from the *Relación*, the angatacuri points to the criminals with an arrow and literally appears as the person standing between the audience of nobles, the Uanacaze priest, and the criminals (see fig. 30). He is looking at a point outside the picture frame.

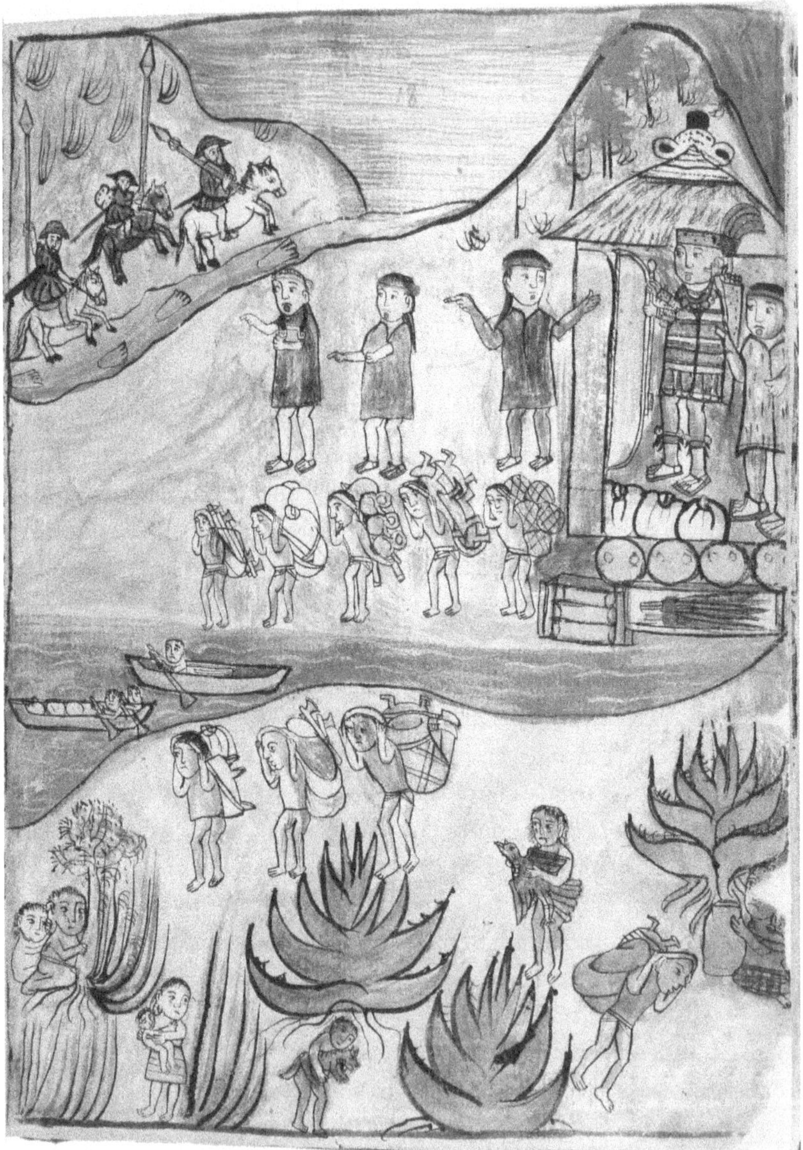

FIGURE 49. Artist 3. "Como el Cazonçi con otros señores se querían aogar en la laguna, de miedo de los españoles, por persuasión de unos prencipales, y se lo estorbó don Pedro" (How the cazonci and other nobles wanted to drown themselves in the lake, from fear of the Spaniards and persuasion of some nobles, and Don Pedro stopped it). *Relación de Michoacán*, fol. 46r. Real Biblioteca del Monasterio de El Escorial, San Lorenzo de El Escorial, Spain, C IV 5. Photograph © Patrimonio Nacional, Spain.

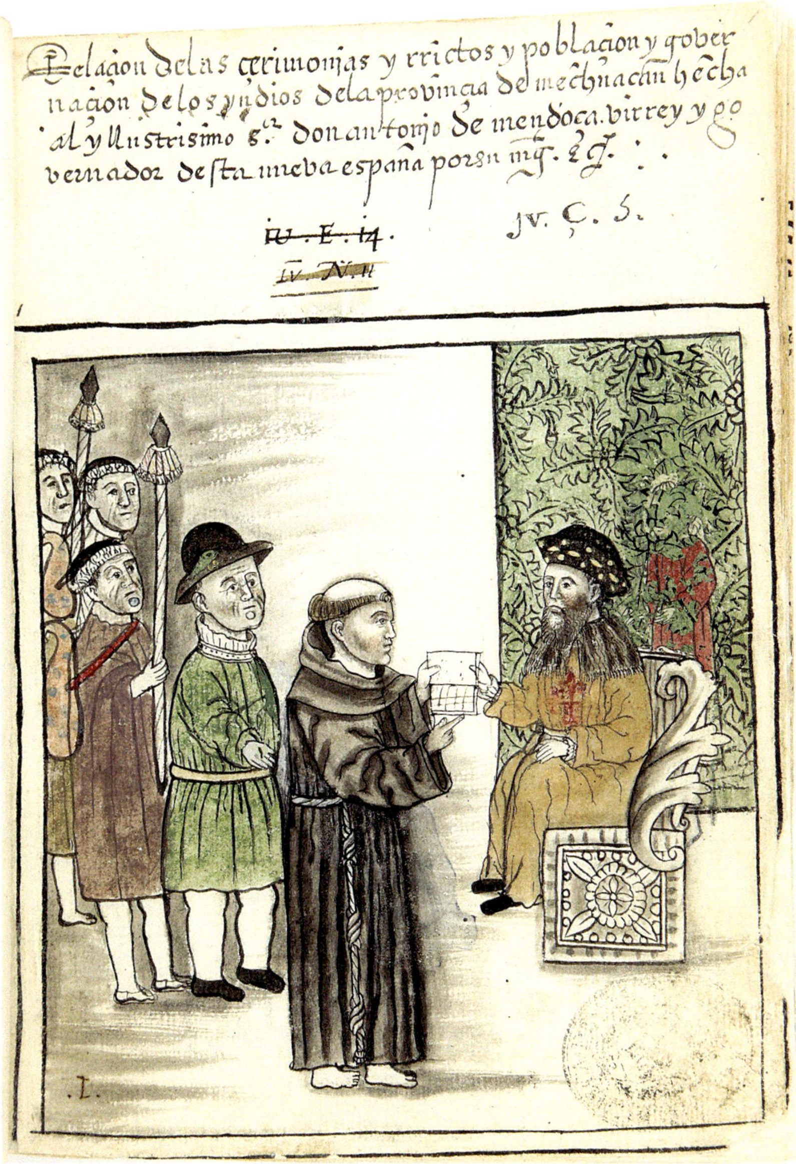

PLATE 1. Artist 1. *Relación de Michoacán*, fol. 1r, frontispiece. Real Biblioteca del Monasterio de El Escorial, San Lorenzo de El Escorial, Spain, C IV 5. Photograph © Patrimonio Nacional, Spain.

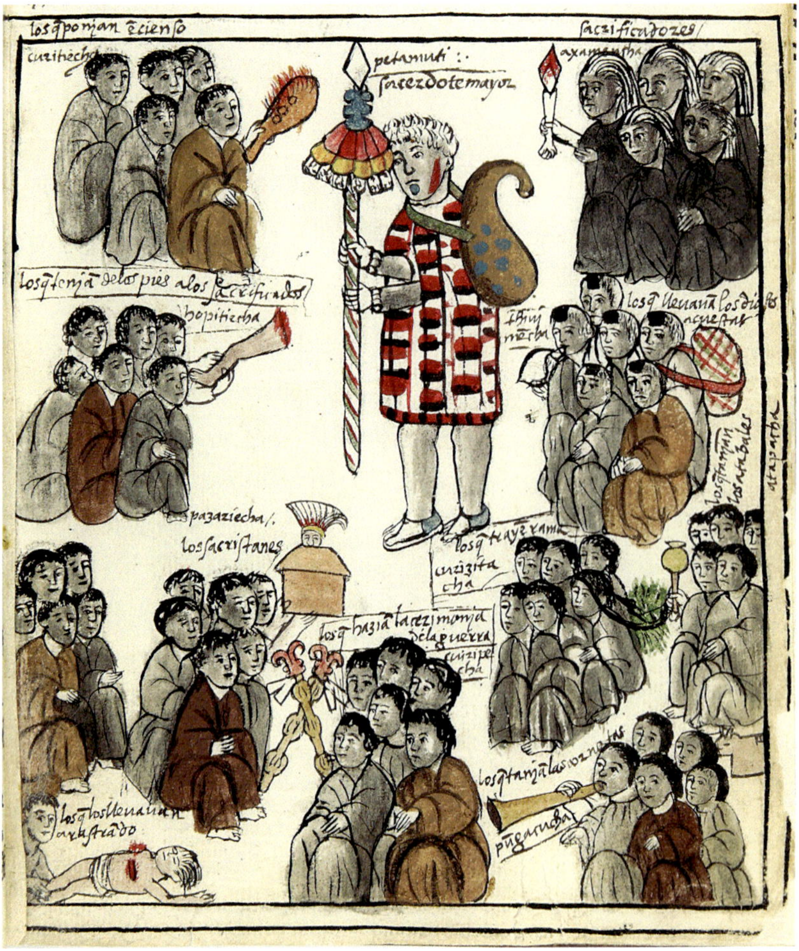

PLATE 2. Artist 1. "Estos son los sacerdotes officiales de los cúes" (These are the official priests of the temples). *Relación de Michoacán*, fol. 9r. Real Biblioteca del Monasterio de El Escorial, San Lorenzo de El Escorial, Spain, C IV 5. Photograph © Patrimonio Nacional, Spain.

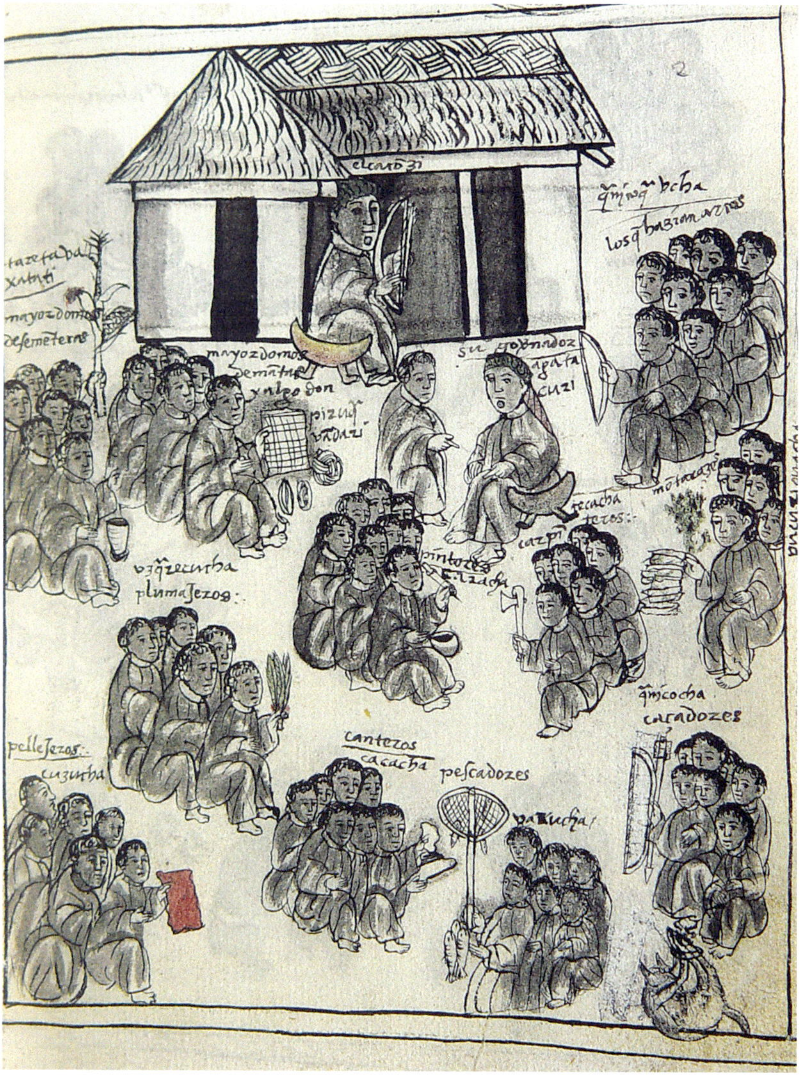

PLATE 3. Artist 1. *Relación de Michoacán*, fol. 5r. Real Biblioteca del Monasterio de El Escorial, San Lorenzo de El Escorial, Spain, C IV 5. Photograph © Patrimonio Nacional, Spain.

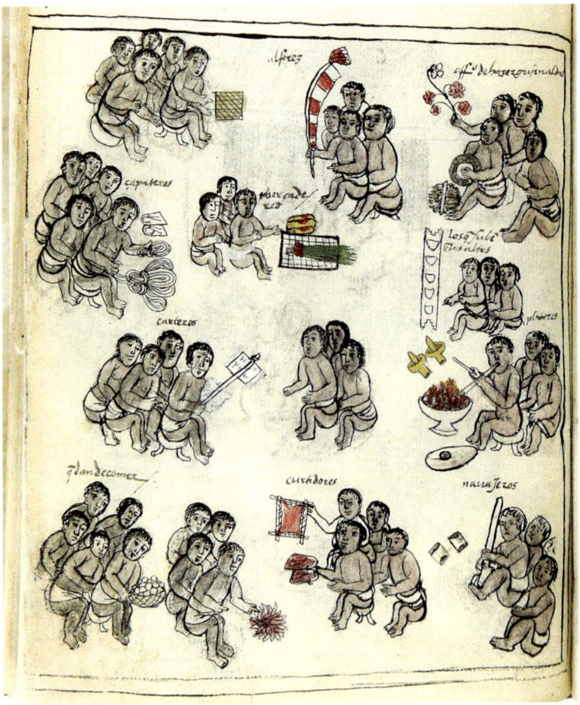

PLATE 4. Artist 2. *Relación de Michoacán*, fol. 5v. Real Biblioteca del Monasterio de El Escorial, San Lorenzo de El Escorial, Spain, C IV 5. Photograph © Patrimonio Nacional, Spain.

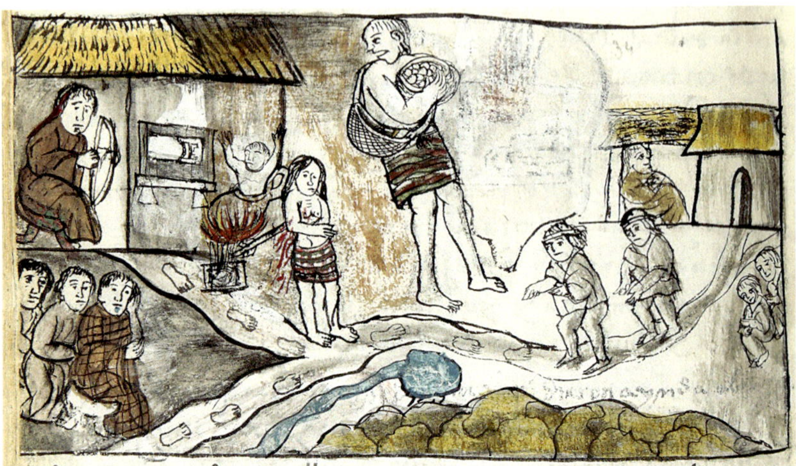

PLATE 5. Artists 2 and 4. "Como los del pueblo de Yziparamucu pidieron ayuda a los de Coringuaro y del agüero que tuvieron los de Yziparamucu" (How the [people] from the town of Yziparamucu asked those from Coringuaro for help, and of the omen those from Yziparamucu had). *Relación de Michoacán*, fol. 124v. Real Biblioteca del Monasterio de El Escorial, San Lorenzo de El Escorial, Spain, C IV 5. Photograph © Patrimonio Nacional, Spain.

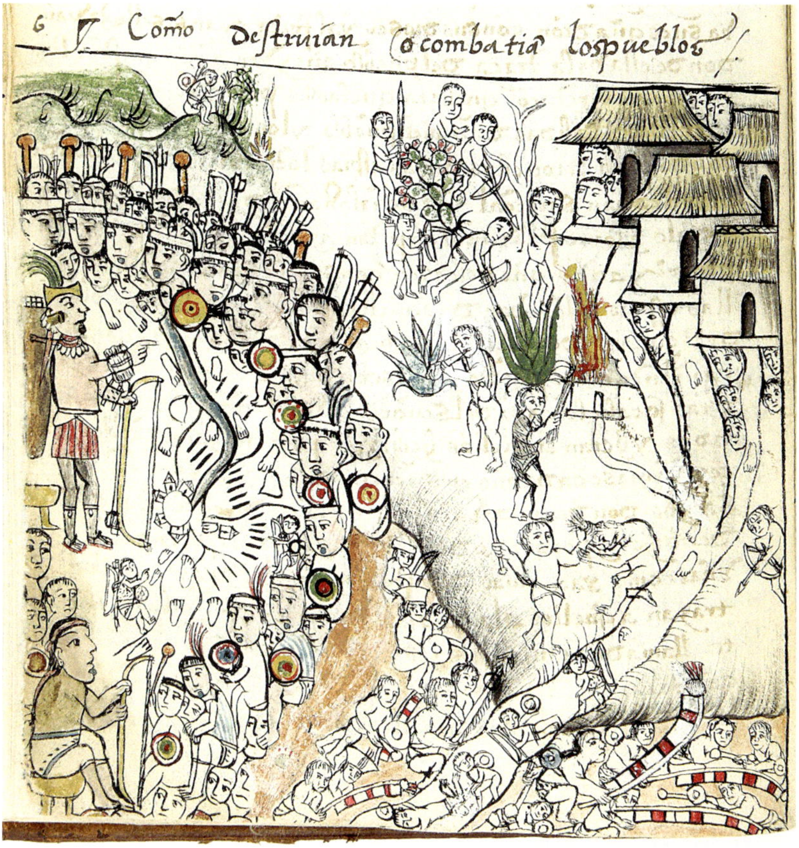

PLATE 6. Artists 3 and 4. "Como destruían o combatían los pueblos" (How they destroyed or fought the towns). *Relación de Michoacán*, fol. 15v. Real Biblioteca del Monasterio de El Escorial, San Lorenzo de El Escorial, Spain, C IV 5. Photograph © Patrimonio Nacional, Spain.

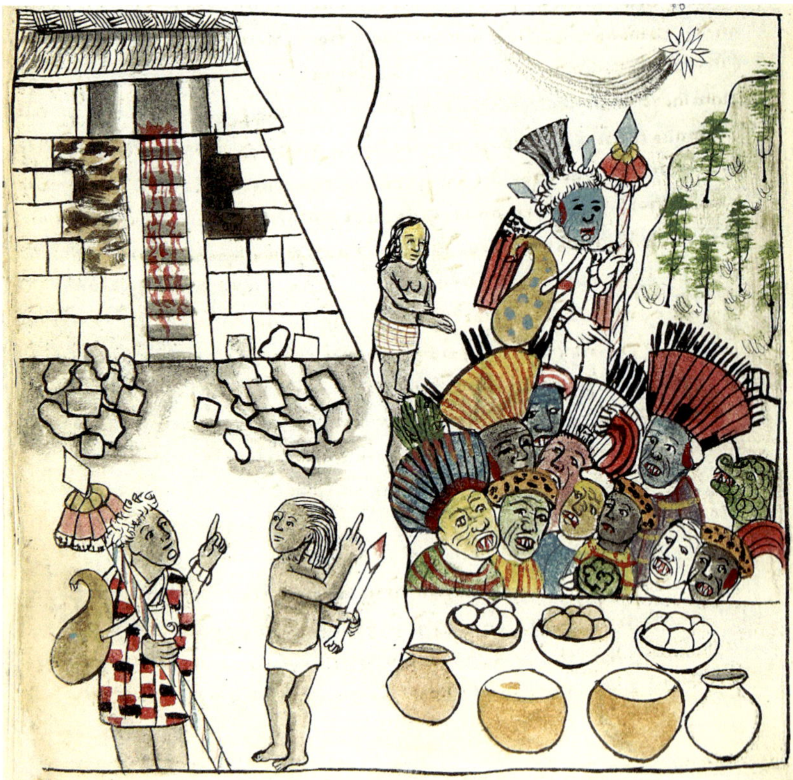

PLATE 7. Artist 1. "De los agüeros que tubo esta gente y sueños, antes que viniesen los españoles a esta Provincia" (Of the omens and dreams these people had before the Spaniards came to this province). *Relación de Michoacán*, fol. 35v. Real Biblioteca del Monasterio de El Escorial, San Lorenzo de El Escorial, Spain, C IV 5. Photograph © Patrimonio Nacional, Spain.

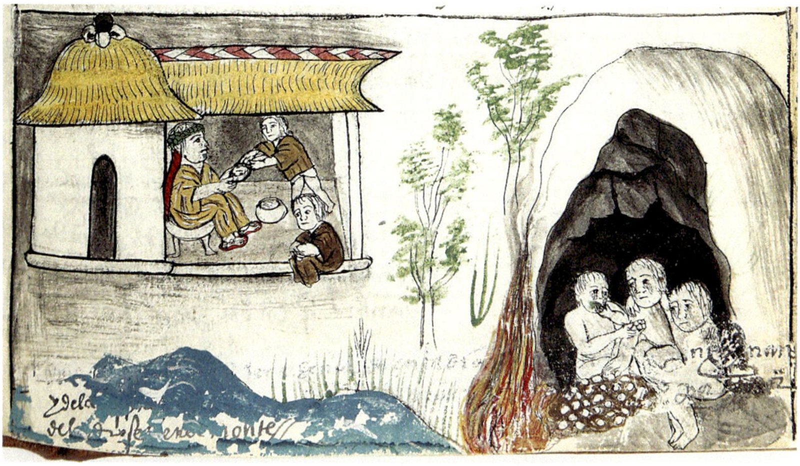

PLATE 8. Artist 4. "Como Curatame enbió por Hirepan y Tangaxoan que hazían penitencia en una cueva y de la respuesta que dieron" (How Curatame sent for Hirepan and Tangaxoan, who were doing penance in a cave, and the answer they gave). *Relación de Michoacán*, fol. 116r. Real Biblioteca del Monasterio de El Escorial, San Lorenzo de El Escorial, Spain, C IV 5. Photograph © Patrimonio Nacional, Spain.

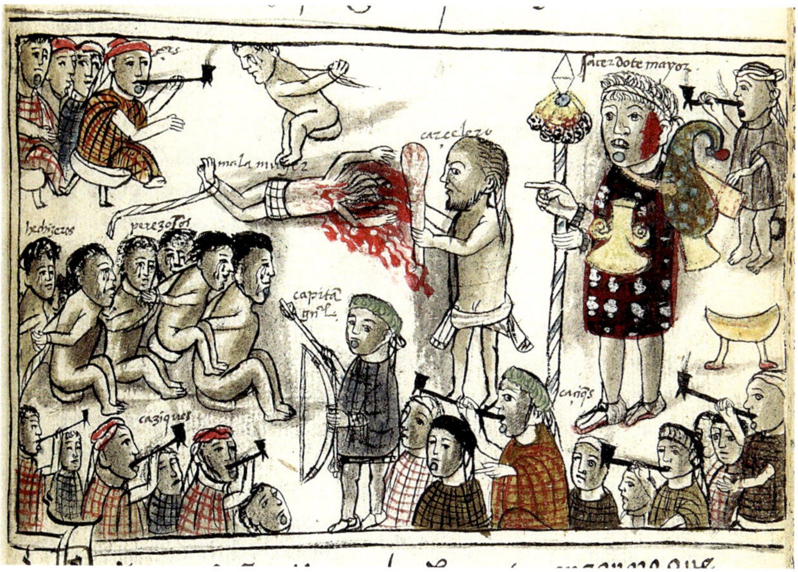

PLATE 9. Artist 1. "Síguese la historia, como fueron señores el Caçonçi y sus antepasados en esta Provincia de Mechuacan y de la justicia general que se hazía" (Here follows the history of how the cazonci and his ancestors were lords in this province of Mechuacan, and of the general justice carried out). *Relación de Michoacán*, fol. 61r. Real Biblioteca del Monasterio de El Escorial, San Lorenzo de El Escorial, Spain, C IV 5. Photograph © Patrimonio Nacional, Spain.

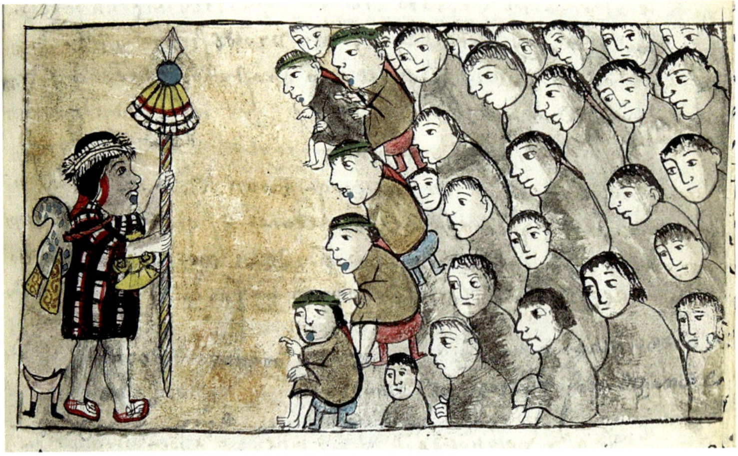

PLATE 10. Artists 3 and 4. "De la plática y razonamiento que hazía el Sacerdote Mayor a todos los Señores y gente de la provincia acabando esta historia pasada, diziendo la vida que avían tenido sus antepasados" (Of the speeches and reasoning that the main priest would give to all the nobles and people of the province upon finishing this past history, telling the life that their ancestors led). *Relación de Michoacán*, fol. 133r. Real Biblioteca del Monasterio de El Escorial, San Lorenzo de El Escorial, Spain, C IV 5. Photograph © Patrimonio Nacional, Spain.

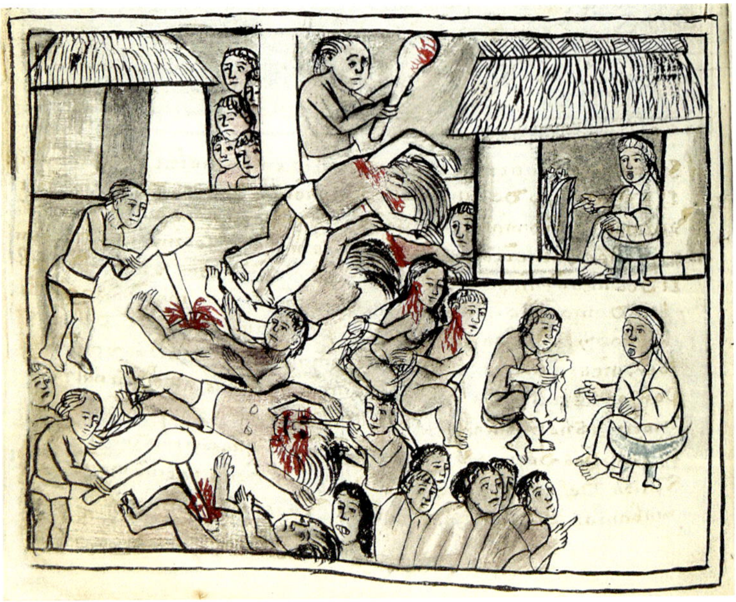

PLATE 11. Artist 1. "De la justicia que hazía el Cazonçi" (Of the justice done by the cazonci). *Relación de Michoacán*, fol. 20v. Real Biblioteca del Monasterio de El Escorial, San Lorenzo de El Escorial, Spain, C IV 5. Photograph © Patrimonio Nacional, Spain.

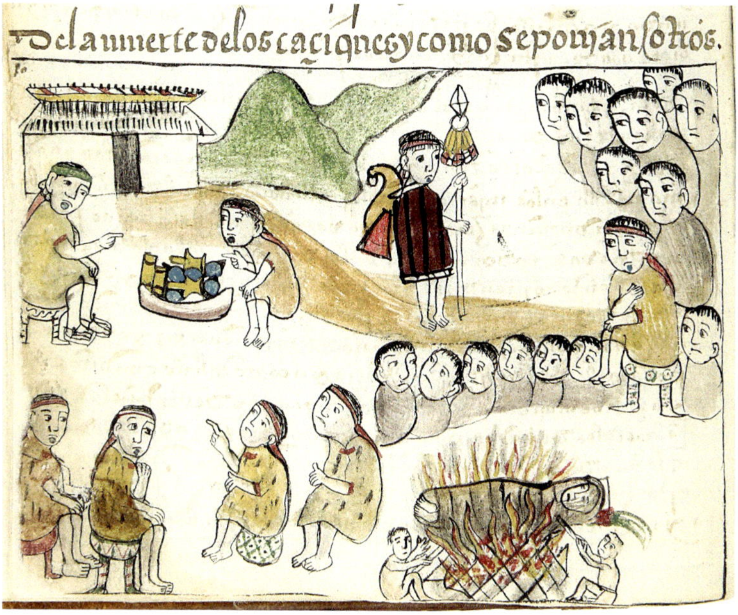

PLATE 12. Artist 3. "De la muerte de los caciques y como se ponían otros" (Of the deaths of the caciques and how they were replaced). *Relación de Michoacán*, fol. 21v. Real Biblioteca del Monasterio de El Escorial, San Lorenzo de El Escorial, Spain, C IV 5. Photograph © Patrimonio Nacional, Spain.

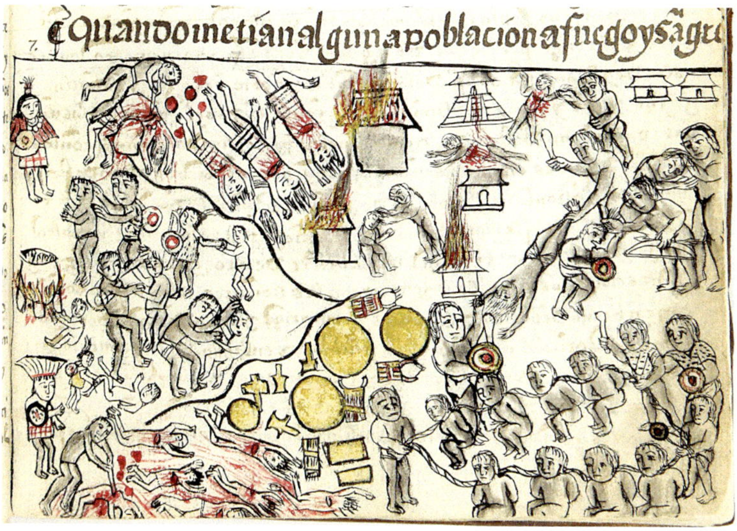

PLATE 13. Artists 3 and 4. "Quando metían alguna población a fuego y sangre" (How they destroyed a town through fire and blood). *Relación de Michoacán*, fol. 19r. Real Biblioteca del Monasterio de El Escorial, San Lorenzo de El Escorial, Spain, C IV 5. Photograph © Patrimonio Nacional, Spain.

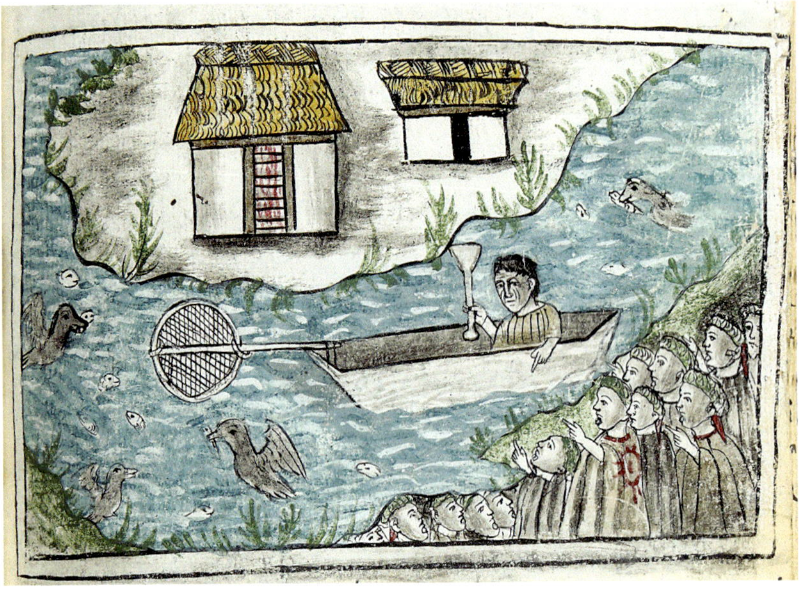

PLATE 14. Artist 1. "Como los señores de la laguna supieron de la muger que llevaron los chichimecas, y cómo les dieron sus hijas por mugeres" (How the lords of the lake found out about the woman the Chichimecs took, and how they gave them their daughters for wives). *Relación de Michoacán*, fol. 71r. Real Biblioteca del Monasterio de El Escorial, San Lorenzo de El Escorial, Spain, C IV 5. Photograph © Patrimonio Nacional, Spain.

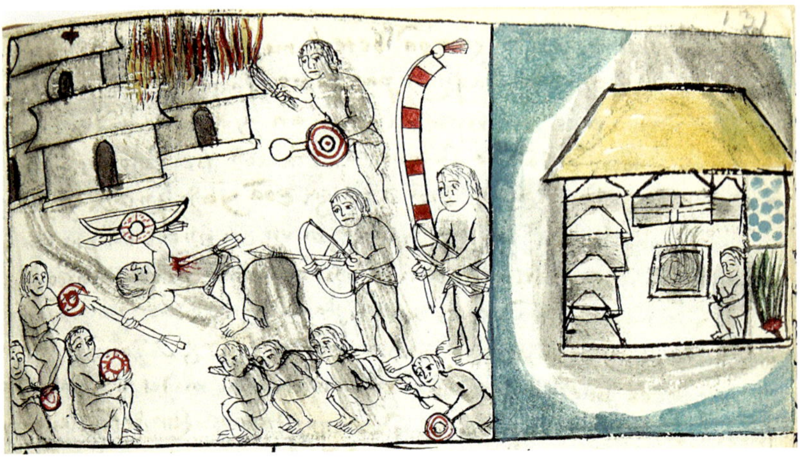

PLATE 15. Artist 4. "Como Hirepan y Tangaxoan y Hiquingaje conquistaron toda la provincia con los ysleños, y como la repartieron entre sí, y de lo que hordenaron" (How Hirepan and Tangaxoan and Hiquingaje conquered all the province with the Islanders, and how they divided it among themselves, and what they ordered). *Relación de Michoacán*, fol. 131r. Real Biblioteca del Monasterio de El Escorial, San Lorenzo de El Escorial, Spain, C IV 5. Photograph © Patrimonio Nacional, Spain.

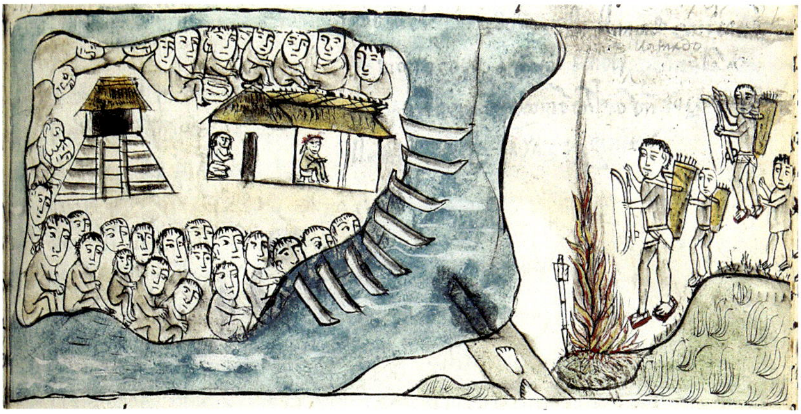

PLATE 16. Artist 3. "Como el señor de la ysla, llamado Caricaten, pidió socorro a otro Señor llamado Zurunban contra Tariacuri, que le tenía cercado en su ysla, y fue enbiado un sacerdote llamado Naca a hazer gente de guerra" (How the lord of the island, called Caricaten, asked for help of another lord, called Zurunban, against Tariacuri, who had him surrounded on his island, and a priest called Naca was sent to gather people for war). *Relación de Michoacán*, fol. 79r. Real Biblioteca del Monasterio de El Escorial, San Lorenzo de El Escorial, Spain, C IV 5. Photograph © Patrimonio Nacional, Spain.

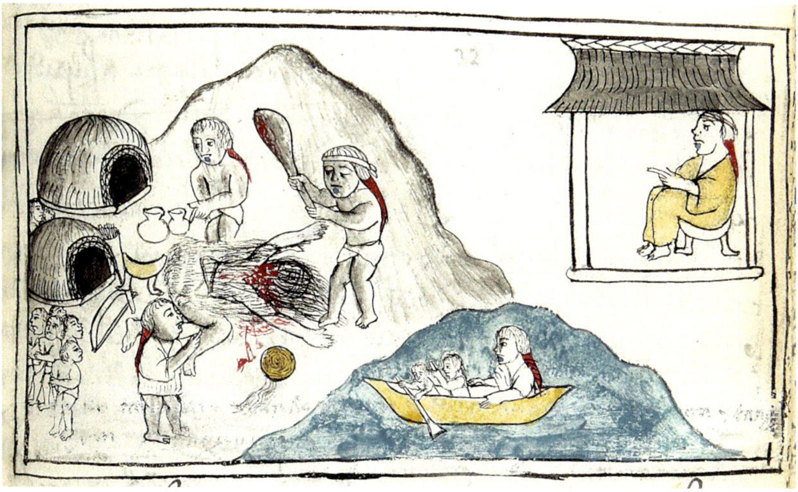

PLATE 17. Artist 4. "Como Tariacuri mandó matar su hijo Curatame; a Hirepan y Tangaxoan, porque se enborrachava: y le mataron después de borracho" (How Tariacuri ordered Hirepan and Tangaxoan to kill his son Curatame because he was a drunkard, and they killed him after he got drunk). *Relación de Michoacán*, fol. 121r. Real Biblioteca del Monasterio de El Escorial, San Lorenzo de El Escorial, Spain, C IV 5. Photograph © Patrimonio Nacional, Spain.

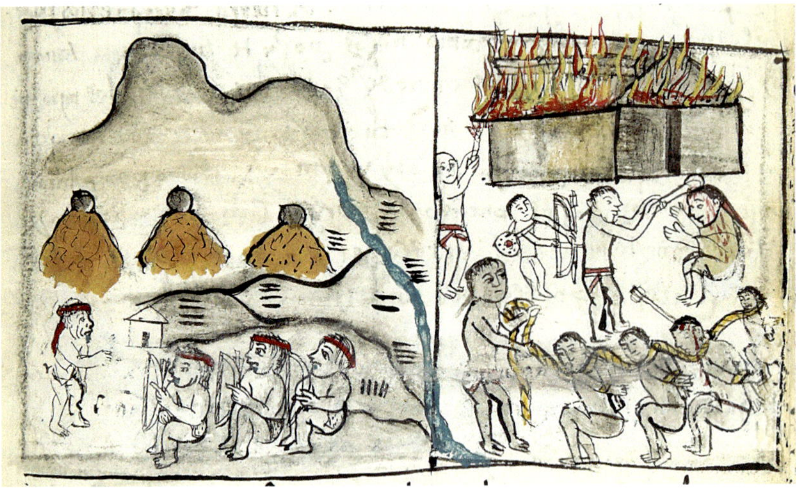

PLATE 18. Artists 3 and 4. "Como Tariacuri mostró a sus sobrinos y hijo la manera que habían de tener en la guerra y como les señaló tres Señoríos y como destruyeron el pueblo [de] aquel señor llamado Hiuacha" (How Tariacuri showed his nephews and son the way to conduct war and how he appointed them three kingdoms and how they destroyed the town [of] that lord called Hiuacha). *Relación de Michoacán*, fol. 129r. Real Biblioteca del Monasterio de El Escorial, San Lorenzo de El Escorial, Spain, C IV 5. Photograph © Patrimonio Nacional, Spain.

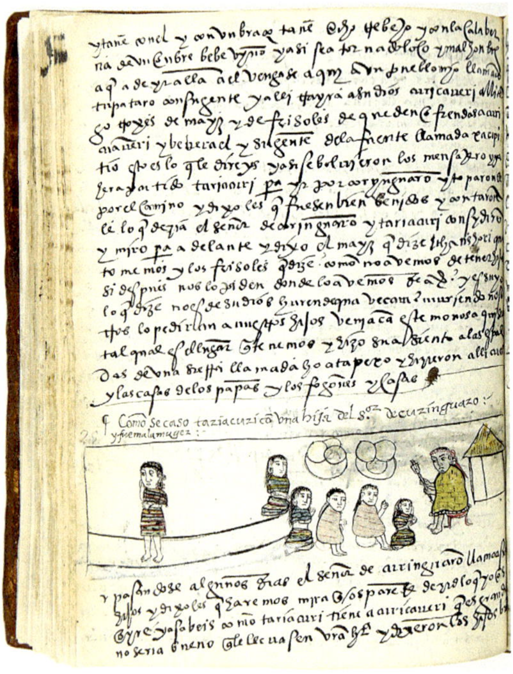

PLATE 19. Artist 3. "Como se casó Tariacuri con una hija del señor de Curinguaro y fue mala muger" (How Tariacuri got married to the daughter of the lord of Curinguaro, and [she] was a bad woman). *Relación de Michoacán*, fol. 87v. Real Biblioteca del Monasterio de El Escorial, San Lorenzo de El Escorial, Spain, C IV 5. Photograph © Patrimonio Nacional, Spain.

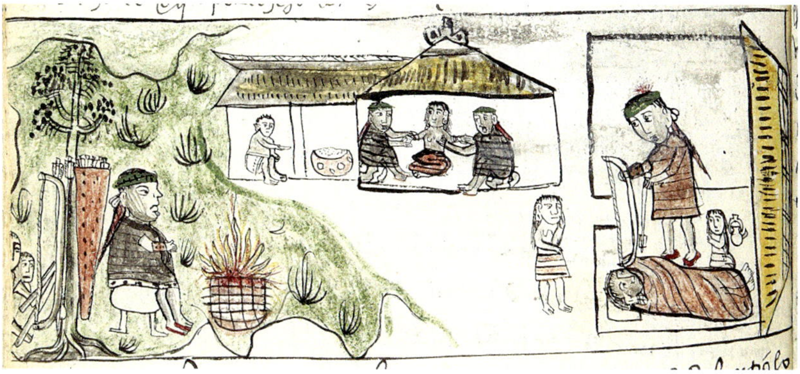

PLATE 20. Artist 3. "Como Tariacuri sintió mucho como no le guardava lealtad su muger, y como se casó con otra por consejo de una su tía" (How Tariacuri felt a lot of sorrow because his wife was not loyal, and how he married another [woman] because one of his aunts advised him). *Relación de Michoacán*, fol. 92v. Real Biblioteca del Monasterio de El Escorial, San Lorenzo de El Escorial, Spain, C IV 5. Photograph © Patrimonio Nacional, Spain.

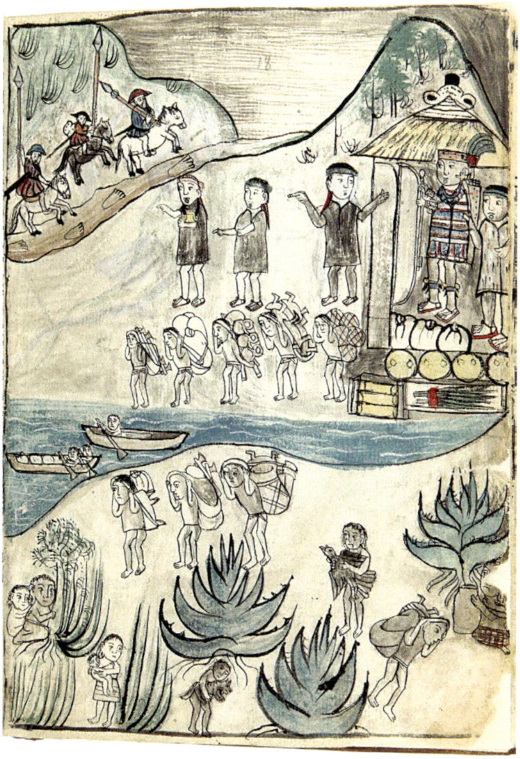

PLATE 21. Artist 3. "Como el Cazonçi con otros señores se querían aogar en la laguna, de miedo de los españoles, por persuasión de unos prencipales, y se lo estorbó don Pedro" (How the cazonci and other nobles wanted to drown themselves in the lake, from fear of the Spaniards and persuasion of some nobles, and Don Pedro stopped it). *Relación de Michoacán*, fol. 46r. Real Biblioteca del Monasterio de El Escorial, San Lorenzo de El Escorial, Spain, C IV 5. Photograph © Patrimonio Nacional, Spain.

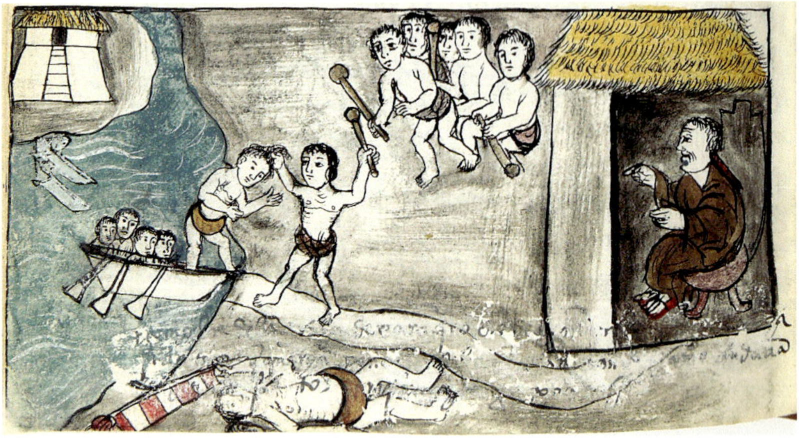

PLATE 22. Artist 2. "Como los ysleños enbiaron un principal llamado Zapiuatame a ponerse debaxo del mando de Tariacuri y ſue preso, y como andavan haziendo saltos Hirepan y Tangaxoan con su gente" (How the Islanders sent a noble called Zapiuatame to place himself under the orders of Tariacuri, and how he was imprisoned, and how Hirepan and Tangaxoan and their people were attacking [towns]). *Relación de Michoacán*, fol. 113v. Real Biblioteca del Monasterio de El Escorial, San Lorenzo de El Escorial, Spain, C IV 5. Photograph © Patrimonio Nacional, Spain.

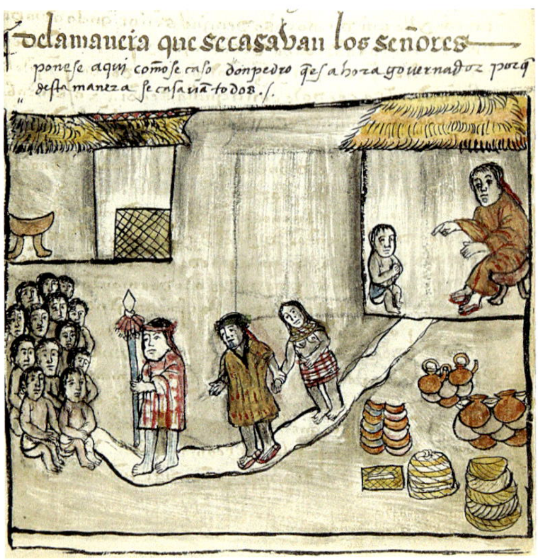

PLATE 23. Artist 2. "De la manera que se casavan los señores. Pónese aquí, como se casó don Pedro ques ahora Governador, porque desta manera se casavan todos" (Concerning how the nobles were married. Here it is written how Don Pedro, who now is governor, got married, because they all got married this way). *Relación de Michoacán*, fol. 24r. Real Biblioteca del Monasterio de El Escorial, San Lorenzo de El Escorial, Spain, C IV 5. Photograph © Patrimonio Nacional, Spain.

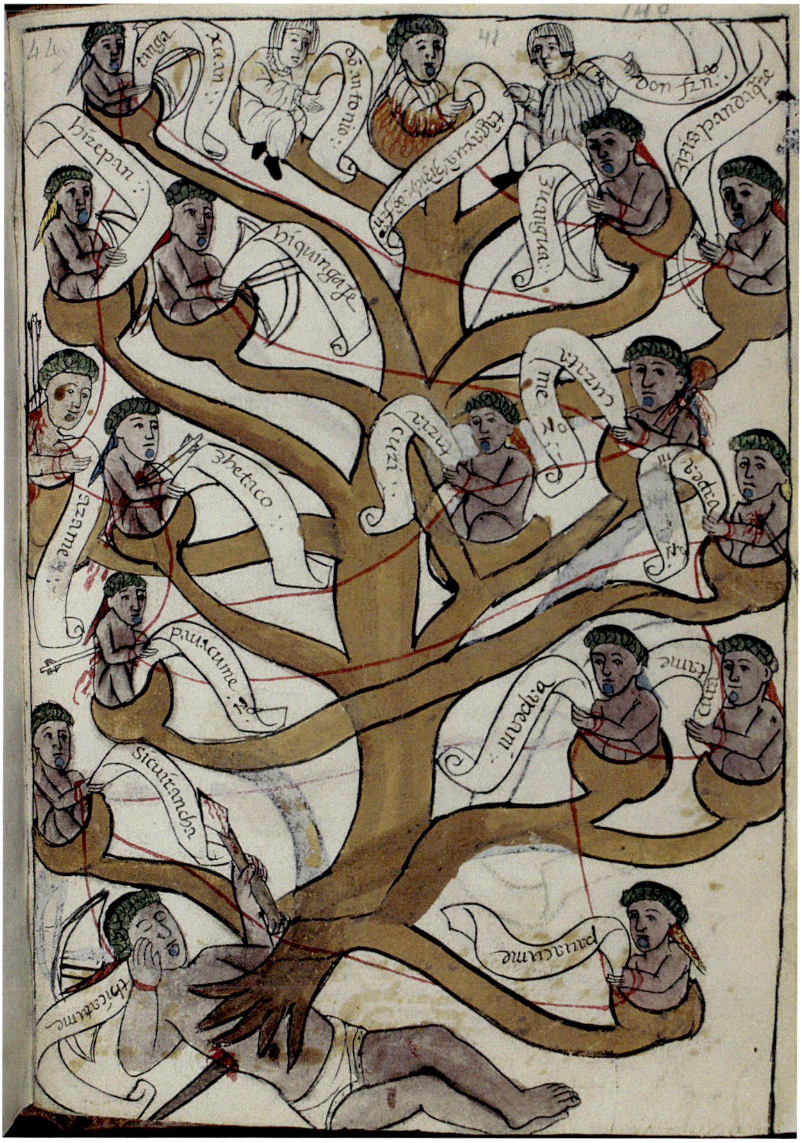

PLATE 24. Artist 1. "Genealogía de los Señores de Pazquaro y Cuyacan y Michuacan" (Genealogy of the lords of Pazquaro and Cuyacan and Michuacan). *Relación de Michoacán*, fol. 140r. Real Biblioteca del Monasterio de El Escorial, San Lorenzo de El Escorial, Spain, C IV 5. Photograph © Patrimonio Nacional, Spain.

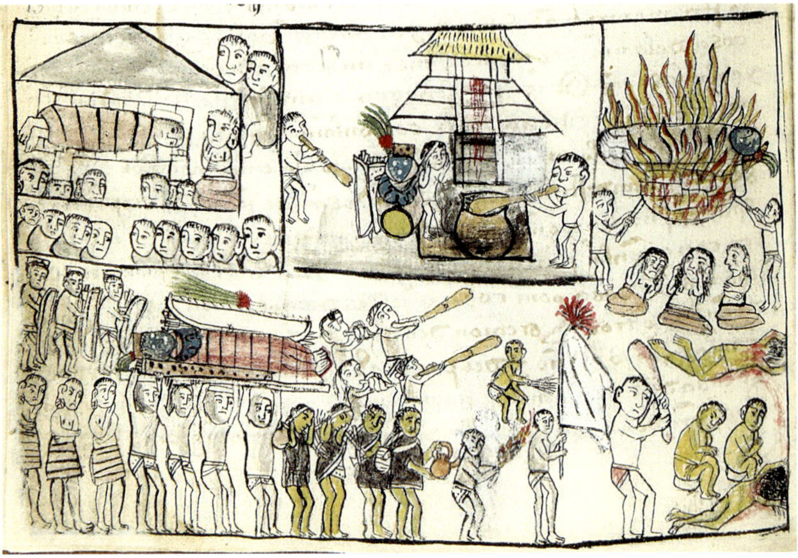

PLATE 25. Artist 3. "Como muría el Caçonci y las cirimonias con que le enterravan" (Of the way the cazonci died and the ceremonies with which they buried him). *Relación de Michoacán*, fol. 29v. Real Biblioteca del Monasterio de El Escorial, San Lorenzo de El Escorial, Spain, C IV 5. Photograph © Patrimonio Nacional, Spain.

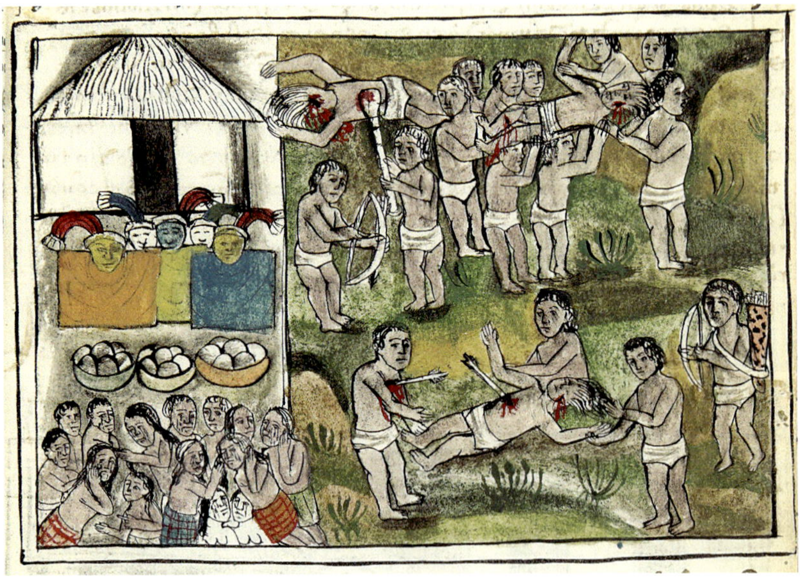

PLATE 26. Artist 1. "De los que murían en la guerra" (Of those who died at war). *Relación de Michoacán*, fol. 20r. Real Biblioteca del Monasterio de El Escorial, San Lorenzo de El Escorial, Spain, C IV 5. Photograph © Patrimonio Nacional, Spain.

His gaze meets that of the manuscript's audience, so he connects them (and today, us) to the administration of justice and the way of governing Michoacán. In other words, in this image he serves as an intermediary between the viceroy, as the intended audience, and the Uanacaze.

The contributors of the *Relación* characterized Don Pedro's role of intermediary and governor as subservient to the Uanacaze in the historic and ethnographic pages of the manuscript, rather than represent him in competition with the Uanacaze or as someone who had ousted them from the colonial government. The representation of the relationship between the Uanacaze and the Islanders in general, and Don Pedro's ancestors in particular, provides a foundation for justifying his role in the colonial government. The images portray the Islander nobles as a conquered people, the gods favoring the Uanacaze, and Don Pedro carrying out the necessary rituals to maintain this delicate relationship.

The first image that illustrates the relationship between the Uanacaze and the Islanders depicts not a marital allegiance among nobles, as suggested by its title, "How the Lords of the Lake Found Out about the Woman the Chichimecs Took, and How They Gave Them Their Daughters for Wives," but the meeting between the Uanacaze and the humble Islander fisherman from one of the islands described in the previous chapter of the narrative (see fig. 36). According to the text, the Uanacaze requested a daughter from the fisherman in marriage and in exchange for her promised him that they would rule the land together. In the lower right-hand corner of the image, the fisherman and the Uanacaze meet on the shores of the lake. Behind the fisherman, on the island, the stairs inside the entrance to the palace are covered with blood. The blood may foreshadow the future of the Islander nobles. Ultimately the arrival of the Uanacaze in this area would lead to the Islander nobility's defeat in war and removal from power.[74]

In the text, after the initial meeting between the Uanacaze and the fisherman, the Islander nobles married some of their daughters to the Uanacaze nobles. They even trained the Uanacaze in priestly practices. The marriage ceremony between the Uanacaze and noblewomen from the islands is never depicted in the *Relación*, and from this point forward, the relationship between the Islanders and the Uanacaze is never one of equals.

The alliance between the Uanacaze and the Islander nobles quickly came to an end when another Chichimec faction turned the Islander nobles against their Uanacaze in-laws. According to the text, in time Tariacuri, the son of the fisherman's daughter and the Uanacaze lord, grew up to lead the

Uanacaze. But this was in no small part due to his rejection of the "amoral" behavior of his enemies and even that of his Islander relatives. In spite of the political and marital union of the Uanacaze and the Islanders, Uanacaze political leadership followed the male line, and the custody of their patron god Curicaueri was passed along only to worthy Uanacaze men.

The second image illustrating the petamuti's speech shows the first of many military confrontations between the Islander noblemen and the Uanacaze (see fig. 38). The next few illustrations and their corresponding titles depict events in the continuing struggle between the Islander and Uanacaze nobles for control of the Lake Pátzcuaro area. First, the Uanacaze capture an Islander priest (see fig. 26). He is cooked and fed to the unsuspecting Islander noble Zurumban in the next scene (see fig. 19). On the left-hand side of the next image, Zurumban has the Uanacaze removed from his lands in retaliation, their houses dismantled, and their silos overturned (see fig. 11). On the right-hand side of the image, we see the Islanders sacrificing the Uanacaze and feeding their bodies to the fish in the lake, which are symbolic of the Islanders. Eventually, after the Uanacaze noble Tariacuri's marital alliance with a woman from another Chichimec group fails because of her philandering, he is said to take as wives women from Zurumban's household.

Since the relationship between the Uanacaze and the Islanders is complex, the text of the *Relación* tells us that Don Pedro's ancestors voluntarily made themselves subjects of the Uanacaze, thus distinguishing them from all other Islanders. Artist 2 marks this important event with an image depicting the Uanacaze hitting Don Pedro's Islander ancestors with a club (fig. 50; see plate 22). However, the text explains that when these Islanders arrived on the mainland, the Uanacaze first threatened to shoot them with arrows and then took them to Tariacuri, who accepted them as vassals. This discrepancy between text and image indicates that there is more to its meaning than meets the uninformed eye.

One may explore this scene not as a literal representation of events but as the visual expression of a concept, that is, as an ideogram. The sixteenth-century P'urhépecha words for hitting somebody with a club were *varicani* and *varihpeni*.[75] These words derive from the verb *varini*, "to die."[76] Given the cause-and-effect connection between being hit with a club and dying, the former could easily imply the latter. The root of *varini*, *vari-*, is also used in words meaning "captivity" or "slavery." For example, the sixteenth-century *Diccionario grande* translates *varingati* as "captive."[77] *Varingati*

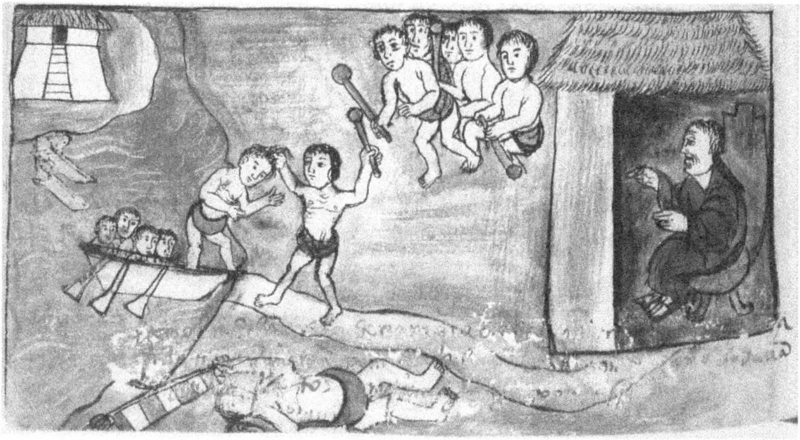

FIGURE 50. Artist 2. "Como los ysleños enbiaron un principal llamado Zapiuatame a ponerse debaxo del mando de Tariacuri y fue preso, y como andavan haziendo saltos Hirepan y Tangaxoan con su gente" (How the Islanders sent a noble called Zapiuatame to place himself under the orders of Tariacuri, and how he was imprisoned, and how Hirepan and Tangaxoan and their people were attacking [towns]). *Relación de Michoacán*, fol. 113v. Real Biblioteca del Monasterio de El Escorial, San Lorenzo de El Escorial, Spain, C IV 5. Photograph © Patrimonio Nacional, Spain.

comes from the root *vari-* and *-ngati*, a particle indicating compassion or incarceration. Its literal translation is "the poor person who is going to die" or "the one who is being held and will die."[78] Likewise, in the *Relación* the concepts of death, captivity, and slavery are quite close, since on several occasions it mentions that those people who were taken captive during wars were sacrificed, and those who were not sacrificed became slaves. In the text of the *Relación* accompanying the image of Don Pedro's ancestors being clubbed, the Islanders are not clubbed and do not die; instead, they offer themselves as vassals to the Uanacaze god Curicaueri, and by extension to the Uanacaze lords. To represent the Uanacaze clubbing Don Pedro's ancestors does not necessarily show an actual event but instead indicates the act of taking them captive or enslaving them. What the artist was representing by means of symbols was the subordination of the Islander ancestors of Don Pedro to the Uanacaze.

After this alliance between two powerful yet unequal partners is established, the gods intervened to ensure the conquest of the region. Although the gods never revealed themselves to Tariacuri, the god Curicaueri and the

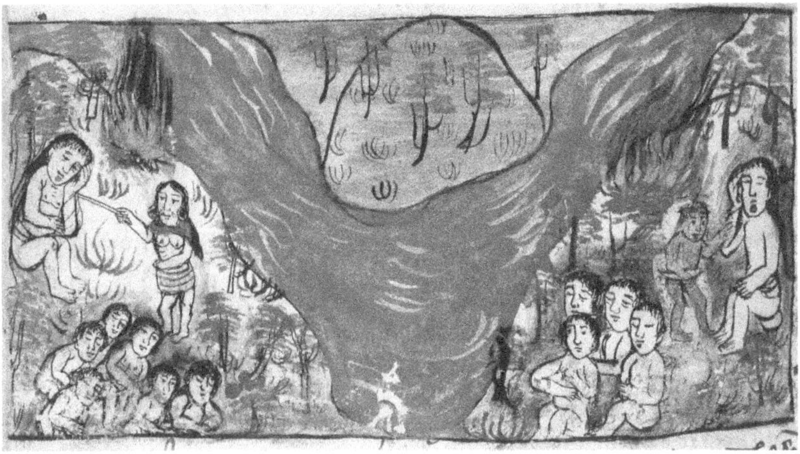

FIGURE 51. Artist 2. "Como aparescieron entre sueños el dios Curicaueri a Hirepan y la diosa Xaratanga a Tangaxoan y les dixeron que avían de ser señores" (How the god Curicaueri appeared in dreams to Hirepan and the goddess Xaratanga to Tangaxoan, and told them they would be lords). *Relación de Michoacán*, fol. 122v. Real Biblioteca del Monasterio de El Escorial, San Lorenzo de El Escorial, Spain, C IV 5. Photograph © Patrimonio Nacional, Spain.

local goddess Xaratanga appeared to Tariacuri's nephews on the Uanacaze side (fig. 51). While Curicaueri was already in the custody of the Uanacaze, Xaratanga was in the custody of Zurumban, the Islander priestly noble living on the mainland with whom the Uanacaze had already been in conflict. Xaratanga appeared to the young Uanacaze noble who would eventually father the Tzintzuntzan line and told him she was not getting appropriate worship. She requested that he take her from her present home to Tzintzuntzan, in exchange for which she promised riches and power.[79] Tariacuri's nephews, with Tariacuri's guidance and his son's assistance, then managed to unify the region.

The text of the *Relación* explains the complexity of the situation and eventually justifies the conquest of the Islanders who lived on the mainland, based on their leader's misconduct. The Uanacaze had initiated numerous scuffles as well as attempts at forming liaisons with this particular group of Islanders, including Tariacuri having taken as wives two women from the ruler's house. However, Hiuacha, this group's heir apparent and a priest versed in the use of calendars, is described in the text as a drunk.[80] First, Tariacuri sent his nephews and son to convince Hiuacha to stop drinking and join them in battle, but Hiuacha refused and even offended the young Uanacaze by not offering them the gifts due to them at the end of their visit. Instead, he gave the gifts to others who were also present. Afterward, the Uanacaze nobles went into the forest, where a tree fell down, a symbol signifying the splitting up of groups in other colonial codices (see fig. 27). Later, following Tariacuri's advice, they unleashed a war against Hiuacha, capturing and sacrificing him and his people (see fig. 43).[81] The murder of Hiuacha and the winning of this battle by the Uanacaze and their Islander allies are what propelled their conquest of the region.[82]

At the end of many battles, the Uanacaze and their Islander allies—Don Pedro's ancestors—emerged victorious. These Islanders were key players in the conquest of many towns in the Tierra Caliente region south of Lake Pátzcuaro, where they acquired land. They also wrested control of some towns in the highlands of Michoacán. However, the seat of power, first divided among Pátzcuaro, Ihuatzio-Cuyuacan, and Tzintzuntzan on the shores of Lake Pátzcuaro and then consolidated in Tzintzuntzan, remained in the Uanacaze's hands. Thus, the story highlights a common interest shared by Don Pedro's ancestors and the Uanacaze: the control of the Province of Michoacán. It distinguishes Don Pedro's ancestors from all other Islanders and local lords, and while it does not make them equal to the Uanacaze, it does make them worthy of high political posts.

The parameters of this vassalage are then further specified through the images and text of part 3 of the *Relación*. In an ethnographic manner, six chapters of part 3 describe marriage practices according to social class among the people of Michoacán. But rather than refer only to marriages of nobles in the abstract, the text specifically tells how Don Pedro married a woman from the Uanacaze ruler's house.[83] After the text was completed, an artist added an image depicting this wedding ceremony (fig. 52). The friar-editor, upon reviewing the original title, "Concerning How the Nobles Got Married," then added the following amendment: "Here Is Written How Don Pedro, Who Is Now Governor, Got Married Because They All Got Married This Way."[84] Stone proposes that the inclusion of this image was a mistake by the artists because she believes the image was meant to illustrate the *Relación*'s following chapter about the marriages of the indigenous elite.[85] However, the image in fact serves to highlight the marriage of Don Pedro. Its inclusion in the manuscript would have allowed Don Pedro to assert the benefits that his marriage entailed, his relationship to the Uanacaze ruler, and his own position as a nobleman.

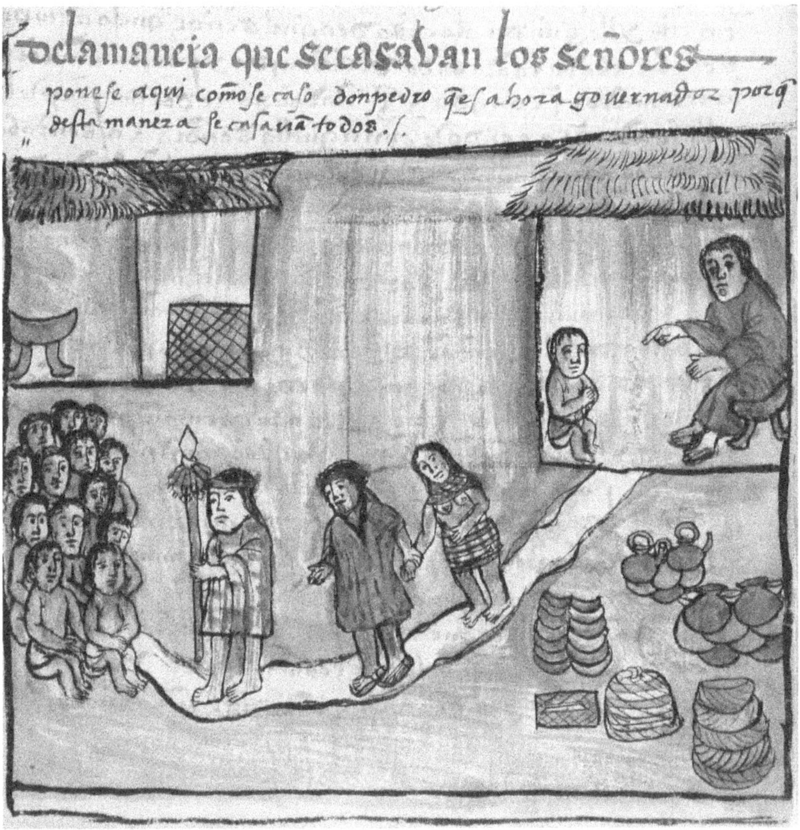

FIGURE 52. Artist 2. "De la manera que se casavan los señores. Pónese aquí, como se casó don Pedro ques ahora Governador, porque desta manera se casavan todos" (Concerning how the nobles were married. Here it is written how Don Pedro, who now is governor, got married, because they all got married this way). *Relación de Michoacán*, fol. 24r. Real Biblioteca del Monasterio de El Escorial, San Lorenzo de El Escorial, Spain, C IV 5. Photograph © Patrimonio Nacional, Spain.

According to colonial records, Don Pedro had married several women, including the widows of Zinzicha Tangaxuan.[86] This marriage scene and text would have forced the audience to focus on only one of those marriages. If the picture was meant to illustrate the text, it is noteworthy that in the upper right corner, Don Pedro and the ruler meet inside a palace. The ruler, dressed in his long robe, points directly to Don Pedro. Don Pedro's status is revealed as lower than that of the ruler, as he is dressed only in a loincloth and sits on the floor. However, his private audience with the ruler and marriage to a woman from the ruler's house place Don Pedro high up in the hierarchy of the indigenous nobility. After this original meeting, a procession leads the bride to meet the groom's party. The dowry is shown on the right-hand side of the image. In the upper left corner, and above the reception group, a palace awaits with an empty throne, like the one used by the Uanacaze ruler, and a woven mat. In other indigenous Mesoamerican codices, marriage ceremonies are often symbolized by a couple lying on woven mats.[87] Thus, the mat serves as a symbol of the impending marriage, and the small throne as a symbol of the even higher status that awaits Don Pedro.

Although not visually represented here, Don Pedro's wife would have brought lands with her. In fact, one of Don Pedro's wives, Doña Inés (who may be the woman pictured), testified in the encomienda dispute against the Spaniard Juan Infante that some of the lands in question had come to her as part of her "dowry and paraphernalia" (i.e., the possessions a woman brings to her marriage apart from her dowry).[88] Don Pedro had administered these lands and had given at least some of them to Bishop Vasco de Quiroga. In P'urhépecha, the verb *minguareni*, "to possess land," also means "to become a relative by marriage," so the marriage depicted here also implies possession of new lands.[89]

The relationship established through this marriage, however, is not one of equals. Implicit in it is a hierarchy created between Don Pedro and his Uanacaze in-laws. Several sixteenth-century P'urhépecha words indicate that filial bonds established hierarchical relationships and obligations. The verb *hapimbeni*, for example, means "to have lots of relatives or slaves."[90] The word *mimi* (pl. *mimiecha*) means "relative, sibling, and servant."[91] In the text accompanying the image of his marriage, Don Pedro further explains this inequality based on the Uanacaze conquest of the region. According to Don Pedro, those conquered (in his particular case the Islanders) and their descendants became the servants of the Uanacaze.[92] Don Pedro chose to recount this event in the passage describing his marriage and in this way reasserted P'urhépecha ways of establishing hierarchical relations through marriage. Don Pedro continues his speech by expressing that through their service to the Uanacaze, the Islanders developed a relationship with them, and the Uanacaze began to call them "brothers." At that point, he continues, some of the Islanders became governors under Uanacaze rulers. Thus, through the marriage image and accompanying text, Don Pedro explains his post of governor as subordinate. He presents himself as a relative of the ruler by marriage and a noble servant.

Don Pedro, assisted by the other contributors to the *Relación*, carefully crafted his role and identity, portraying himself as a mediator. His characterization as a servant to the Uanacaze, rather than being detrimental to his post as governor, helped justify it. In the historical section of the manuscript, the *Relación*'s contributors emphasize that Don Pedro's ancestors submitted to the Uanacaze and helped them conquer the region. In the ethnographic section, his own marriage proves his noble yet subservient status and demonstrates his right to administer Uanacaze lands. The text further states that he had served as the intermediary between the Uanacaze and the Spaniards. Don Pedro's life and post are explained in ways that help present a united indigenous front to the viceroy.

Conclusion

Even though the archaeological record for the pre-Columbian period shows a more or less homogeneous population in Michoacán, part 2 of the *Relación* reveals that ten to fifteen years after the Spanish conquest, the Uanacaze lords were not interested in effacing the differences that divided local ethnic groups. It is in this desire to differentiate themselves from others and how they accomplished it that the political intention to construct identity along ethnic lines during the colonial period is most clearly revealed. The *Relación*'s text and images serve to highlight the Uanacaze's upstanding moral behavior and superb skill as hunters and warriors. They claimed that their Chichimec ancestors, with the aid of a handful of dissenting Islanders, had successfully waged war against the independent cities in the region. Whereas the Islander allies were each rewarded with the governance of local towns, the Uanacaze gained control of the entire province. To maintain this social hierarchy, which was central to their authority, they had to codify ethnic differentiation in visual and tangible ways. Part 2 of the *Relación* provides an ideal past in which the Uanacaze, through impeccable behavior and worship of their god, are represented as the indisputable, deserving rulers of this area.

For Spanish viceroy Antonio de Mendoza, this section of the *Relación* would have presented the Uanacaze as morally upstanding, the natural choice to govern a specific land. Mendoza was a ruler, a knight of the Order of Santiago, and having been raised among chivalric narratives, could have easily recognized the merits and virtues of the Uanacaze as comparable to his own.[93] Much like the ancestors of the Uanacaze in the *Relación*, the Mendozas in Europe legitimized their positions and made their claims to political power through their own—as well as their ancestors'—military prowess.[94]

The historian Gabrielle Spiegel has pointed out that in medieval chronicles, representations of the past created stereotypes of good versus evil, provided guidance toward correct political action, and could legitimize contemporary practices as well as act as a vehicle for change.[95] The *Relación*, in its account of past events, would point out the appropriate rulers for Michoacán to Viceroy Mendoza. The strategy clearly worked. After receiving the *Relación*, the viceroy supported the Uanacaze heir Don Francisco's request for royal grants by sending the Crown a letter on his behalf, and upon the death of Don Pedro Cuiniarangari, returned the governorship to the Uanacaze heirs mentioned in the *Relación*, Don Francisco and Don Antonio. Both of these heirs would occupy their position as governor for life.

5

Mimicry, Identity, and the Tree of Jesse

At the end of the petamuti's speech in part 2 of the *Relación*, the contributors included an image of a family tree on a separate sheet of paper (fig. 53; see plate 24). This image not only summarizes the genealogy of rulers included in the petamuti's narration but is key to understanding how competing agendas played out through the manuscript. Genealogical and dynastic information was a common theme among indigenous elites throughout Mexico before and after the arrival of Europeans. Mixtec genealogies and dynastic lists from southern Mexico populate many of the surviving codices from pre-Columbian and colonial times.[1] Their pre-Columbian, Nahua counterparts from central Mexico do not survive, yet they are a common theme among documents from the colonial period.[2]

Among pre-Columbian sources, trees often play a significant role and in many cases serve as the origin place of ancestors.[3] These trees generally do not include an ancestor's progeny, so they do not serve the same purpose or follow the same format as European genealogical trees, which generally trace long genealogies among the branches of vegetation sprouting from a

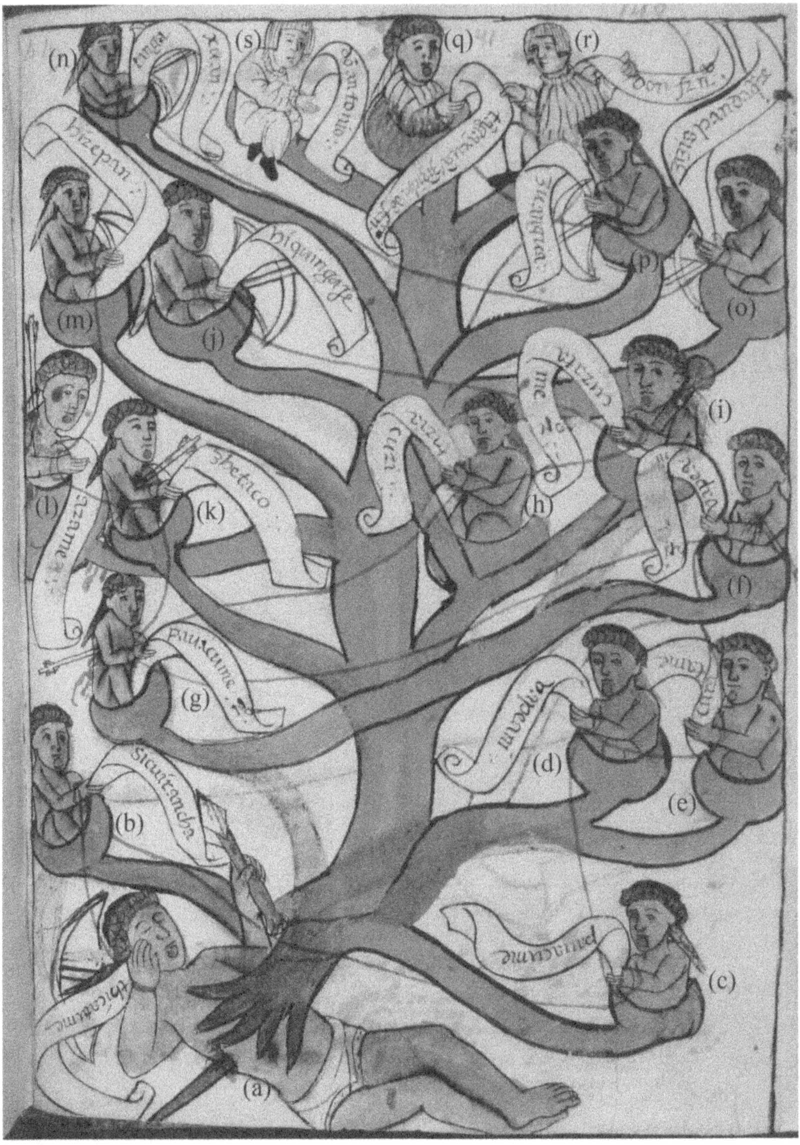

FIGURE 53. Artist 1. "Genealogía de los Señores de Pazquaro y Cuyacan y Michuacan" (Genealogy of the lords of Pazquaro and Cuyacan and Michuacan). *Relación de Michoacán*, fol. 140r. Real Biblioteca del Monasterio de El Escorial, San Lorenzo de El Escorial, Spain, C IV 5. Photograph © Patrimonio Nacional, Spain; alphabetic labeling of the figures by the author.

common ancestor at the bottom or root of the tree. Therefore, the *Relación*'s artist's use of the genealogical tree to represent the Uanacaze lineage speaks of his colonial context. Artist 1 adapted the European Tree of Jesse motif by substituting the Uanacaze royal family for the lineage of Christ. This genealogical tree is one of the earliest to survive, if not the earliest, depicting an indigenous lineage. Genealogical trees would become a common subject among indigenous elite families in the colonial period, and the *Relación*'s early example can provide insight into the ways nobles throughout New Spain articulated the European model to meet their local needs.[4]

The artistic choices the artist of the *Relación* made capitalized on what I call "visual mimicry" to picture the Uanacaze leaders as the rightful rulers. His aim was to help the Uanacaze overcome the claims of competing indigenous pretenders, including Don Pedro, as well as challenge contending claims by Spanish colonizers. In his analysis of mimicry in colonial contexts, Homi K. Bhabha has pointed out that disparities between the colonizers' models and those used by colonized people perpetuate the differences that maintain the boundaries necessary for colonial dominance. Although he acknowledges that this kind of mimicry poses a threat to colonizers by narrowing the gap between the racial and historical differences separating them from the colonized, Bhabha sees a slippage in the colonizers' desire to convert the colonized into subjects who are almost, "but not quite," the same as them.[5] Bhabha's argument therefore analyzes mimicry from the perspective of colonizers. Of equal interest is mimicry's value to colonial subjects in Michoacán, one of whom painted the Uanacaze family tree in the *Relación de Michoacán*.

Artist 1 first drew its contour lines with charcoal, revised them with black ink, and filled them in with rich brown, blue, green, red, beige, and gray pigments. Changing his mind several times in the process, he made corrections to the tree by applying white pigment over parts of it and reapplying color. He drew small cartouches in the hands of each nobleman, in which the editor—presumably Fray Jerónimo de Alcalá—dutifully inscribed their names. In its final form, the tree sprouts from the torso of a reclining man, named Thicatame, whose eighteen descendants perch on the branches above him. The first fifteen members of his lineage sit on small stools in the tree's branches and are connected to each other by a red line. They wear green garlands on their heads, a ribbon wrapped around their hair, and blue lip plugs, emblems of rulership and noble status. Several of them carry bows and arrows. The men connected to the red line are all nude, except the last one, seated at the top of the tree, who wears a white tunic and whose seat has burst into flames (fig. 53q). That man is Zinzicha Tangaxuan Don Francisco. His two sons, one also named Don Francisco (fig. 53r) and the other Don Antonio (fig. 53s), sit on the branches next to him and, like him, wear white garments. Unlike Zinzicha Tangaxuan, Don Francisco and Don Antonio are not connected to the red line, nor do they wear the green garland, and they sit directly on the branches of the tree. In a rare deviation from the Christian motif, the artist depicted many of the lords suffering from the wounds that killed them. This difference signals a breach between the meaning of the European sign and this new signifier.

Alessandra Russo, Hans Roskamp, Claudia Espejel Carbajal, and Cynthia L. Stone have separately analyzed the genealogical tree in the *Relación*. Stone sees a connection between the *Relación*'s tree and pre-Columbian beliefs, and even though she acknowledges its European prototype, she does not investigate its implications.[6] Russo, Roskamp, and Espejel Carbajal explore the *Relación*'s tree as an adaptation of the Christian Tree of Jesse (fig. 54). Espejel Carbajal suggests that the artist's adaptation of the motif is evidence that the friar intervened in the production of the manuscript. For Espejel Carbajal, the artist's visual mimicry of the Tree of Jesse was driven by European interests; she ignores the changes he made that transformed the European model into a unique colonial articulation that responded to its local Michoacán context.[7] Roskamp and Russo see the image as a delicate interweaving of indigenous and European traditions. They both emphasize the indigenous artist's appropriation and alteration of the European motif. Roskamp provides an iconographic reading of the image's pre-Columbian elements, while Russo proposes that the tree responds to its colonial moment by representing a rupture between pagan and Christian beliefs.[8] She interprets Tangaxuan's two sons, the last two men in the line, as the first members of the Uanacaze family to adhere to Christianity. Russo notes that Tangaxuan's sons are shown as separate from their pagan father and other pagan ancestors (see figs. 53q, 53a–53p), as they are not connected to the red line that begins at the bottom with Thicatame (see fig. 53a), the first ancestor, and ends at the top with Tangaxuan. Russo, however, ignores the cartouche bearing Tangaxuan's baptismal name, Don Francisco, and his white baptismal tunic, both of which connect him to his two sons and indicate that he, too, has accepted Catholicism. In fact, these visual elements point to continuity rather than rupture in the beliefs of the two generations. It will become clear that the tree reveals a more complex relationship between

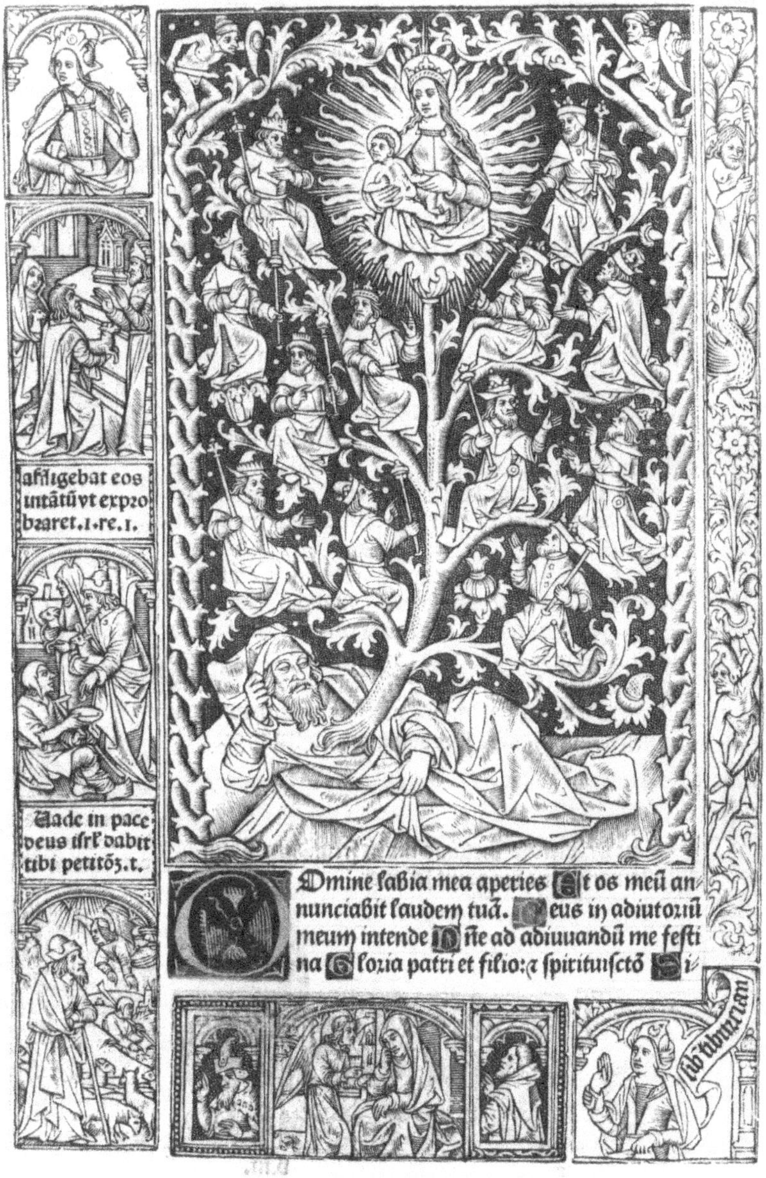

FIGURE 54. Master of Anne de Bretagne, Tree of Jesse, from the *Book of Hours* printed by Philippe Pigouchet for Simon Vostre, 1498, metal cut, 6.5 × 4.5 inches. The Pierpont Morgan Library, New York PML 125444 [ChL 1483], fol. b3v. Photograph provided by the Pierpont Morgan Library.

colonizers and colonized, one in which indigenous factions' interests and alliances shaped its final form.

The Tree of Jesse in the Relación de Michoacán *as a Political History*

The European Tree of Jesse is the pictorial interpretation of a biblical passage in Isaiah 11:1–3: "And there shall come forth a rod out of the stem of Jesse, and a Branch shall grow out of his roots: and the spirit of the Lord shall rest upon him, the spirit of wisdom and understanding, the spirit of counsel and might, the spirit of knowledge and of the fear of the Lord."[9] European artists generally illustrated these verses with a tree that traces Christ's genealogy from Jesse, the father of King David. The tree sprouts from Jesse, its branches bearing his descendants or, in some cases, prophets and sibyls who announce the coming of Christ. Christ crowns the tree, sometimes as an adult, sometimes crucified, and sometimes as a baby in the arms of his mother.[10] At the very top of the tree, he symbolizes wisdom, strength, and the spiritual promise of redemption. The power of the Uanacaze tree in the *Relación* to convey a family lineage to European audiences relies on its mimicry of this European model. At the same time, through its subtle alterations, it conveys a complex political history.

The selection of the Tree of Jesse as a vehicle for charting the genealogy of the Uanacaze lords points to artist 1's Franciscan training and reveals his knowledge of Catholicism and its iconography. The Franciscan order introduced the Tree of Jesse to indigenous populations in New Spain very early in the colonial period. Fray Toribio de Benavente, also known as Motolinía, mentioned that by 1539 the open-air chapel of the convent of San Francisco of Tlaxcala in central Mexico already had a Tree of Jesse painted on its wall.[11] In Michoacán, about 1540, indigenous artists used this motif to decorate two bishop's miters made with feathers.[12]

The *Relación*'s artists were not the first to adapt the Tree of Jesse to the needs of ruling houses. Thérèse McGuire has pointed out that medieval versions of the Tree of Jesse always depicted Jesus's descent from King David to exalt the ruling dynasties in Europe. This association was based on the claim that some kings were chosen by God and accountable only to him.[13] The practice continued into the sixteenth century, when European artists often adopted the format of the Tree of Jesse to represent European dynastic lines.[14]

Like its European counterparts, the tree of the *Relación* substitutes the genealogy of the Uanacaze lords for that of Christ and traces a political history to the benefit of a ruling house. The red line connecting the men in this genealogy, as it weaves back and forth from bottom to top, indicates their political order of succession, as described in the *Relación*'s text. There, the leadership of the group, like the red line, begins with Lord Thicatame, founder of the line, and passes upward from father to son, uncle to nephew, and brother to brother until it ends with Zinzicha Tangaxuan Don Francisco, also known by the title Cazonci, who was in power when the Spaniards arrived in Michoacán.[15] His two sons, who sit next to him, had not yet governed at the time the *Relación* was being compiled, which would explain why the red line does not connect to them.

According to the *Relación*, Thicatame commanded the Uanacaze when they migrated to Michoacán, introducing the worship of the Uanacaze tutelary god Curicaueri to the local inhabitants. In the image, Thicatame carries in his left hand a bloodstained blade identifying him as an *axamencha* (sacrificer), a role reserved for rulers.[16] Two bows and arrows lying beside his head further identify him as a Chichimec/Uacúsecha warrior and a hunter. The bow and arrow appear as accoutrements of rulers elsewhere in the *Relación*, as well as in other pictorial documents from colonial Michoacán (see fig. 3).[17]

Bows and arrows in the possession of some of the other members of the tree seem to endow them with a higher status than the other rulers. The ten lords who follow Thicatame do not carry bows and arrows, even though they were leaders of their people, because they ruled before the consolidation of Michoacán under Uanacaze leadership (see fig. 53b–i, k, l). The next three lords, who carry bows and arrows, are reported to have consolidated the territory (see fig. 53j, m, n). Their two successors, who also carry bows and arrows, governed as independent rulers before the Spanish arrival, fulfilling their tutelary god Curicaueri's mandate to conquer and govern the land (see fig. 53o, p). The last three lords at the top of the tree do not carry bows and arrows, probably because the man in the center had governed and the other two were in line to govern under Spanish colonial rule (see fig. 53q–s).

Yet artist 1's depiction of the Uanacaze's genealogy in the tree was selective. For the pre-Columbian period, he portrayed only those men who succeeded their fathers, uncles, or brothers on the throne, ignoring their numerous siblings. In this way, the tree functions as a dynastic list rather than a full-fledged genealogy of the Uanacaze family. For example, the *Relación* mentions that Tangaxuan had seven brothers and "numerous" sisters, but none of them is portrayed in the tree.[18] The heirs of the Uanacaze family living in Cuyuacan-Ihuatzio disappear after Hirepan, even though some of them are mentioned in the text of the *Relación*.[19] Interestingly, when representing the Uanacaze during the colonial period, the artist chooses to portray two of Tangaxuan's sons who had yet to rule, and none of the other surviving Uanacaze are shown. At least one archival document reveals the existence of another son of Tangaxuan who is not represented in the tree.[20]

One can only assume that the privileging of Don Francisco and Don Antonio in the tree was partly due to the influence they may have had in the compilation of the manuscript, the high social status of their mothers (Uanacaze rulers practiced polygamy), their own position in colonial society, and/or a combination of these factors. According to archival documents, Don Francisco was the elder, and given Spanish succession laws, his placement in the tree would indicate that he was the next in line to lead the colonial government. In a letter written sometime before 1542, Don Francisco's legal representative mentions that his deceased mother's name was Doña Beatriz; given the absence of a last name and the honorific title Doña, she was most likely an indigenous noblewoman who had been christened.[21] Michoacán's rulers practiced polygamy before the arrival of Europeans, so it is possible that she was his principal wife. Since Don Francisco was the first of the Uanacaze line to be approved by the colonial government, she may well have married Tangaxuan under the auspices of the Catholic Church.

The presence in the tree of the younger brother Don Antonio as a future successor is a bit more difficult to explain, because not only was he younger than Don Francisco but he was also his half brother. Scholars have often assumed that Don Francisco and Don Antonio were full brothers, but colonial documents show otherwise.[22] In the "Information of Merits and Services" (1553), which Don Antonio presented to request a grant from the Spanish Crown, he and his witnesses referred to his mother as Guatique Uacujane, which was not a Christian name. Had she had a Christian name, he and his witnesses would probably have used it (just as they used his father's Christian name), since they were trying to prove that Don Antonio was born of a Catholic marriage and had been raised Catholic. It may be presumed that Guatique Uacujane was a prominent woman in the early colonial period, for the name Uacujane would later survive as a last name among nobles in the Lake Pátzcuaro area, but that she did not marry Tangaxuan within the Catholic Church.[23]

Furthermore, at the time the *Relación* was being compiled, the Uanacaze did not rule Michoacán. Rather, the Islander Don Pedro Cuiniarangari occupied the governor's seat. Portraying Don Francisco and Don Antonio as future rulers optimistically projected these candidates into the uncertain future of the Uanacaze ruling house.

In this light, the role the brothers might have played in the making of the manuscript acquires significance, as their birth alone does not entirely explain their presence in the tree. As discussed previously, archival documents place the brothers in the same places and at the same times as Fray Jerónimo de Alcalá when the manuscript was being produced. The eldest had even accompanied Alcalá and Viceroy Mendoza to the Mixtón War, all of which could explain their privileged place in the manuscript's contents.

Interestingly enough, it is not they who occupy the focal point in the tree, but their father (see fig. 53q). If the tree had followed the Christian format or a biological one, the last in the line, Don Francisco and Don Antonio, would sit at the top center instead of their father. The artist has carefully adapted the Christian model to make Tangaxuan the visual focus of the image, in all likelihood because his death played a pivotal role in the politics of Michoacán, and particularly in the lives of his heirs.

The paraphernalia that Tangaxuan carries has been conscientiously selected to mark the continuity of the Uanacaze reign, even as it indicates his acceptance of the Catholic faith. Like his ancestors (see fig. 53a–p), he wears as signs of his rank a green wreath on his head, a blue lip plug on his lower lip, and a ribbon binding his hair at the nape of his neck. In addition, his seat resembles the ruler's throne seen elsewhere in the *Relación* (see fig. 3).[24] While his ancestors' torsos are nude and the ribbons in their hair are red, blue, or yellow, Tangaxuan wears a white robe and hair ribbon. His robe, like those of his sons, differentiates him from his ancestors and marks his acceptance of European norms by specifically referencing his baptismal status. According to Cristobal Cabrera, the apostolic notary to Michoacán's first bishop, Vasco de Quiroga, between 1538 and 1545, on the day of their baptism neophytes wore "white tunics" and sang hymns in their own language that compared them to "trees planted at the shore of a stream, that with time would bear fruit."[25] Their new robes represented their souls' "change of habit," their spiritual transformation.[26]

Corroborating that Tangaxuan has accepted the Catholic faith is the small cartouche he carries in his hand bearing his birth name followed by his baptismal name, Don Francisco. Among the indigenous population during this early period of evangelization, baptismal names distinguished Catholic converts from those yet to be converted. In the "Information of Merits and Services," Spanish witnesses referred to Tangaxuan as Don Francisco, emphasizing his baptismal status. They also referred to him as "he who in Christian [parlance] was called Don Francisco," stating that "he became Christian and received the waters of the holy baptism and was named Don Francisco."[27] In sum, by means of a visual and a verbal construction—that is, his robe and name—Zinzicha Tangaxuan Don Francisco is shown in the genealogical tree as a baptized Catholic. Interestingly, the painter conflated Tangaxuan's baptism and death by depicting flames rising from his throne, thus collapsing two separate events in space and time.

Tangaxuan's Death

Colonial documents containing information about Tangaxuan's death show it had a strong impact on the political life of the region.[28] It is known that Spanish forces executed him. Precisely how he died, though, was highly disputed. The Uanacaze version, as give in the *Relación*'s tree, pictures Tangaxuan staring at the viewer while his seat and lower body burst into flames; in other words, it shows Tangaxuan being burned alive, even though he was a baptized Catholic. The opposing version maintained that Tangaxuan died by suffocation, the approved form of execution for baptized Catholics, which allowed their souls to escape before their bodies were burned.

In addition to having arranged the order in which the Uanacaze nobles appear in the tree to focus on Tangaxuan, artist 1 used a bright red pigment representing blood to form a visual zigzag path leading upward from Thicatame to Tangaxuan, at the top of the tree. He painted those of Tangaxuan's ancestors who had died violent deaths as receiving their mortal wounds. At the bottom of the tree, the father of the line, Thicatame, who has been killed at the end of a lance, closes his eyes, a common convention in indigenous codices for death.[29] The rulers in the branches above Thicatame are shown at the precise moments of their deaths. We know we are witnessing the very moments of their deaths because their eyes are open. They are represented bleeding from their fatal wounds and looking at the viewer as if in that precise moment life is escaping them (see fig. 53f, g, i, k, l). Like Christian martyrs, they are represented with the weapons of their torment (in this case, a lance, arrows, and a club).[30] Only those Uanacaze nobles whom the *Relación*'s text describes as dying of natural causes are not matched with weapons.

The blood applied to the wounds and the weapons tell us that these Uanacaze lords died from arrow wounds, stabbing, and bludgeoning, except for Tangaxuan, who is being burned alive, which is clear from the yellow and red flames emanating from his thronelike seat. Since Tangaxuan is the only figure in the scene who burns in a fire and does not bleed to death from his wounds, his portrait is an anomaly. The flames emanating from his throne, which symbolizes his position as a ruler, imply that he was burned because of his political position as ruler.

This implication was not far from reality. The political sway Tangaxuan continued to hold over his people after the Spanish arrival, together with his opposition to the Spaniards, was in no small part the cause of his death.[31] In 1530, during an expedition to western Mexico, Nuño de Guzmán, president of the First Royal Audience, condemned Tangaxuan to death for obstructing the work of the Spaniards in the region and for having supposedly prepared an ambush against Guzmán's troops during the expedition, as well as for alleged idolatries and sodomy. Tangaxuan's sentencing in 1530 carried significant consequences for the political life of the region because it removed the Uanacaze from power and despoiled them of their riches.

The *Relación* and numerous reports, letters, Crown bills, witness declarations, memoirs, chronicles, and even paintings from this era attest to the importance of this event. They make clear that Crown officials discussed even the smallest details surrounding his captivity and death, which carried grave repercussions for those involved. The way Tangaxuan died became the subject of contradictory testimonies that varied according to the political affiliations of the testifiers.

The trial records that Guzmán sent to the Crown after examining the witnesses and evidence reveal that he had in fact condemned Tangaxuan to death by fire. However, Guzmán specified that since Tangaxuan had been baptized, he could die as a Christian:

> If the aforementioned Cazonci would want to die as a Christian, since he has received the waters of baptism, . . . I order that before burning him a garrote to his throat be given so that the aforementioned Cazonci die and from his vital spirit he be separated; and after, he be thrown in the fire and burned as I have said.[32]

The *Relación*'s image of Tangaxuan in the tree challenges Guzmán's testimony, showing Tangaxuan being burned alive. To Catholics of the time this would have implied that Tangaxuan's "vital spirit" had been prevented from leaving his body and was thus consigned directly to the flames of hell.

By portraying Tangaxuan as a Catholic who had been burned to death, the *Relación* painter joined the debate about the mode of Tangaxuan's death. The debate, motivated by several conflicting colonial interests, transpired as follows: Guzmán maintained in his letters to the Spanish monarchs in 1530 and 1532, in his legal correspondence, and years later in his memoir (1538–1539) that Tangaxuan had received a just trial in which he was found guilty.[33] Nevertheless, Spanish authorities evidently were not equally confident. They carefully examined indigenous witnesses as early as 1531, scrutinizing details that had grave implications for Guzmán and his collaborators. They questioned witnesses about the gold and silver Tangaxuan had given and to whom, about his treatment while in Guzmán's custody, and about why and how he had died.[34] Witnesses contradicted one another and even themselves. Indigenous noblemen Gonzalo Xuarez and one known only as Sebastián attested on February 14, 1531, that Guzmán had ordered that Tangaxuan be tied to a pole at the neck, suffocated, and then burned only after his death.[35] But in the following month, testifying on behalf of Hernán Cortés, a bitter enemy of Guzmán, in a lawsuit against two of the latter's allies, Xuarez recanted his testimony, stating that Zinzicha Tangaxuan had been "very cruelly dragged and burned."[36] Later, on June 15, 1531, Xuarez repeated his claim that Tangaxuan had been burned alive and added that Guzmán had threatened to burn other noblemen if the Spaniards found out that Tangaxuan had paid Guzmán in hopes of reclaiming his freedom.[37] Thus, it seems that only a year after Tangaxuan's death, confusion, perhaps fomented intentionally, plagued memory of the events.

Soon the discrepancies in the witnesses' accounts gave way to reinterpretation, and the death of Tangaxuan became an emblem of Guzmán's cruelty. In the incriminating expedition report known as the "Fourth Anonymous Relation," whose narrator accuses Guzmán of multiple abuses, Tangaxuan is again said to have been burned alive: "Then he [Guzmán] sentenced Don Francisco for being a traitor, and he ordered he be dragged by the tail of a horse, like we all saw; and after, tied to a pole they burned him, they say alive. I, because of compassion, did not want to see it."[38] After having had a falling out with Guzmán, García del Pilar, his translator, wrote his condemnation of the events, based almost literally on the "Fourth Anonymous Relation," likewise indicating that Tangaxuan had been "burned alive."[39] When the Second Royal Audience asked him to expand on his account on January 24, 1532, Pilar declared that after Tangaxuan had given Guzmán many valuable gifts, he was tied to a pole surrounded by wood, whereupon Guzmán's men "started the wood on fire and he [Tangaxuan] started to burn; this is how the aforementioned Cazonci burned until he naturally lost his life."[40] Later, in 1553, Francisco López de Gómara, in his chronicle *Historia general de las indias*, which takes the side of Cortés, retold the events of Zinzicha Tangaxuan's death in the same manner and described him as a "friend of Cortés, a servant of Spaniards, and a vassal of the emperor."[41]

Accusing one another of burning an indigenous noble was not uncommon among conquistadors, friars, and Spanish officials, who sought to dim the luster of their enemies by claiming that they had abused their authority.[42] For example, Guzmán himself accused the Franciscans of burning indigenous people.[43] In his memoir, Guzmán wrote against his old enemy Cortés that "Sandoval, under the orders of the Marquis [Cortés], came with one hundred and fifty men on horse to the province of Panuco and in one day he burned three hundred lords from this province."[44] Likewise, Fray Bartolomé de Las Casas accused one of Guzmán's stewards of killing "many Indians, hanging and burning them alive and throwing them to mad dogs, and cutting off their feet, and hands, and heads, and tongues, while the Indians were in peace; without an excuse other than to frighten them into serving him and giving him gold and tribute."[45] It is not surprising, then, that the Uanacaze nobles and their supporters would adopt this version of the events and claim Tangaxuan as a Catholic who had been burned alive.[46] In the aforementioned "Information of Merits and Services," Spanish witnesses do not say how Tangaxuan died, but five of seven indigenous witnesses testify that Guzmán had ordered him burned.[47] In years and even centuries to come, the Spanish chroniclers who sided with the indigenous nobility often mentioned Tangaxuan's death by fire.[48]

In sum, the contextualization of the Tree of Jesse reveals that it formed part of a heated political debate in which the clear-cut division between European colonizer and indigenous colonized does not adequately reflect the political associations that crossed these boundaries. While Guzmán maintained that Tangaxuan had received a just trial and was suffocated, his Spanish enemies, the Uanacaze, and the Uanacaze's indigenous and Spanish allies reported the events surrounding Tangaxuan's death to match his depiction in the tree in the *Relación de Michoacán*: that Zinzicha Tangaxuan Don Francisco, although a baptized Christian, had been burned alive.

The *Relación*'s tree, then, rather than a passive copy in which the colonized artist mimicked a Christian model, represented an active appropriation of the European motif. The art historian Robert Nelson defines *appropriation* as a distortion that builds on the previous meaning of a sign to create yet a new sign.[49] In the *Relación*'s case, the artist transformed the Christian Tree of Jesse into a new signifier that communicated a genealogy as well as the Uanacaze's interests by picturing the injustices committed against Tangaxuan. By understanding the tree not merely as an act of mimicry but as a careful appropriation of a Christian model, one can recognize its artist as what Nelson calls an "active agent of signification," a painter who has infused an old sign with new meaning.[50]

The Political and Economic Implications of Representing Tangaxuan's Death

For artist 1, the *Relación*'s family tree constituted more than a historiographic exercise. By portraying the Uanacaze's version of the events, the image became a means of seeking justice and the return of the Uanacaze to power. It contained a political message that would be delivered directly into the hands of Viceroy Mendoza, who had commissioned the *Relación* and would decide who should govern Michoacán. Within the new colonial context, the manner of Tangaxuan's death had had economic and political repercussions for the people of Michoacán, especially for Tangaxuan's heirs. According to Spanish custom, whether a person died as a Catholic or an idolater determined the future of his or her material possessions. Having found Zinzicha Tangaxuan guilty of idolatry, Guzmán wrote in the trial record, "And I condemn the aforementioned Cazonci to lose all his possessions, which I apply to the Chamber and Treasury of his Majesty and to the costs of this trial."[51] The image denies that Tangaxuan died in a state of sinful idolatry, for it not only shows Tangaxuan wearing his baptismal robe but also conflates his baptism (which took place about 1525) with his death in 1530, making it a single event in time and space.[52] In Catholic belief at the time, the soul of a person who died immediately after being baptized was considered pure, and thus the image connoted Tangaxuan as a pure soul.[53]

To picture the ruler as a Catholic who had been burned alive—that is, unjustly killed—implied that his social position, possessions, and right to rule should be reinstated to his descendants, Don Francisco and Don Antonio.[54]

Yet the text of the *Relación* affirms that Guzmán's men first suffocated Tangaxuan with a garrote and then burned his body only after his death.[55] This discrepancy, which suggests a division between the interests represented in the image and those of the narrator of this part of the *Relación*, bears investigation. According to the friar who compiled the *Relación*, the indigenous governor Don Pedro Cuiniarangari narrated the events surrounding Tangaxuan's death. With Tangaxuan's execution, Don Pedro became governor. It must be remembered that Don Pedro described himself not as a member of the conquering Uanacaze family but as a local Islander, which means that his appointment challenged the ethnic barriers that predated the arrival of the Spaniards. Very likely, Don Pedro's role as an intermediary between Tangaxuan and the Spanish conquistadors had earned him this important post. As mentioned previously, he even told the compiler of the *Relación* that it was he who had peacefully surrendered Michoacán to the Spaniards. In the text, he swiftly moves from his status as a slave of the Uanacaze ruler to become governor and administrator of his domains. He explains:

> In the beginning, we were conquered by his [Tangaxuan's] ancestors, and we the Islanders are his slaves. We used to carry the food of the kings on our backs, and the axes to go to the forest for wood, and we carried their drinking jars, and that is why they began to call us brothers, because we used to do what the kings ordered us, like governors.[56]

In such an ethnically stratified state, this difficult trajectory would have required Don Pedro's constant strategic planning.

In the *Relación*, Don Pedro uses his account of Tangaxuan's trial and sentencing to reinforce his newly acquired right to rule. He accuses the former indigenous leader of crimes that would have invalidated his claim, as well as those of his descendants, to rulership in the new colonial order. In Don Pedro's account of Tangaxuan's death, Cynthia L. Stone sees an apology on the part of Don Pedro for not having sufficiently protected his lord from the Spaniards.[57] In fact, Don Pedro reveals numerous charges the Spaniards had brought against Tangaxuan and provides no defense for several of them. Tangaxuan remains accused of having had lords who served him secretly, of robbing towns, of idolatries, of dancing in the skins of dead Spaniards, even of possibly having killed several of them. Furthermore, Don Pedro testifies that Tangaxuan was executed by suffocation for these crimes, which implies that Tangaxuan's death was lawful and Christian. It is noteworthy that the artists of the *Relación* did not include any images to illustrate Don Pedro's narration. Thus, the tree becomes the only visual record in the *Relación* of this important event.

This was not the first time Don Pedro had turned against his lord. In Tangaxuan's trial in 1530, Don Pedro gave the most incriminating testimony.[58] And in 1532, he testified in Guzmán's defense, stating that during Tangaxuan's trial several indigenous noblemen had told him that Tangaxuan confessed to killing and skinning Spaniards, declaring that he knew Tangaxuan had hidden much gold and silver from them.[59] In 1539, just before the *Relación* was compiled, Guzmán had to defend himself against accusations that he had received much gold from Tangaxuan. Don Pedro again testified on Guzmán's behalf, adding that in fact it had been Guzmán who had given valuable presents to Tangaxuan.[60] Don Pedro's account in the *Relación* was therefore one of many strategic moves in his effort to legitimize his position in the new colonial order.

If Don Pedro had completely vindicated Tangaxuan and verified the injustices visited upon him (that is, that Tangaxuan, even though a Catholic, had been burned alive, as represented in the tree), he not only would have had to explain his previous accusations but also would have had to defend his position as governor and the privileges that came with it. At the time the *Relación* was being compiled (1539–1541), he had to watch his every move.[61] As noted earlier, the eldest son of Tangaxuan, Don Francisco, was at or nearing his age of majority and thus was most likely eligible to serve as governor (see fig. 53r).[62] In 1543, Don Francisco accused Don Pedro of having "usurped" lands that belonged to his father while Don Pedro was governor and submitted a petition (including a painting) to Viceroy Mendoza to recover those lands, revealing the tensions that existed between the Uanacaze heirs and Don Pedro.[63] In response, the viceroy inquired whether the land had belonged to Don Francisco's father and if he had owned it "due to inheritance and governance."[64] That is, he asked whether Don Francisco's alleged noble privileges derived from his Uanacaze lineage and especially from his relationship to Tangaxuan. Thus, to portray Don Francisco as an heir of the Uanacaze lineage in the tree was to advocate for his noble privileges.

Don Francisco knew Spanish legal traditions and used them effectively. A key element of his arguments was his direct descent from the Uanacaze line. From a letter written in 1542 by the viceroy, we know that Don Francisco had previously instigated litigation for land and jewels that was resolved in his favor because he had successfully made the case that they belonged to him as the "son of the aforementioned Cazonci," meaning Tangaxuan.[65]

Besides attempting to reclaim his family's property and position from Don Pedro, Don Francisco sought his lost privileges from the Spanish Crown. The probanza he wrote to the Crown before April 20, 1542, is now lost, but a cover letter explaining the internal logic of the document survives. It states that due to his father's death, the entire province was granted to his majesty, leaving Don Francisco without any means of support. It continues that since he was a good Christian and lived like a Spaniard, Don Francisco was worthy of a grant.[66]

Verifying that Don Francisco and his legal advisers understood and met the criteria of the Spanish legal system, Viceroy Mendoza sent a missive on April 20, 1542, to the Spanish Crown supporting Don Francisco's probanza. In his letter to the Crown, the viceroy expresses the same concerns as those detailed in Don Francisco's letter. He mentions that Don Francisco was the son of Tangaxuan, lord of the province; that he had been educated in the Christian doctrine; that he always dressed "in Spanish clothes"; and that he always "dealt like a Spaniard."[67] The artist of the *Relación*'s genealogical tree accordingly painted Don Francisco and his younger brother wearing baptismal gowns and black shoes, with short, ear-length hair rather than long hair tied in a ribbon, as their ancestors wore it. That is, they dressed and presented themselves like Spaniards and followed Christian doctrine. In the "Information of Merits and Services," indigenous witness Don Marcos Quaniguata attested that Don Antonio had cut his hair to show his acceptance of Catholicism.[68] The *Relación*'s tree, then, by portraying Don Francisco and Don Antonio as the sons of Tangaxuan and as Catholic converts, reveals a visual and political strategy aimed at proving them to be the deserving heirs to Uanacaze privileges.

Don Antonio's "Information of Merits and Services" demonstrates this strategy in even greater detail. The document contains a series of elaborate questions that cleverly lead the witnesses to answer to Don Antonio's benefit.[69] Don Antonio identifies himself as the eldest son of Tangaxuan in this questionnaire because by this time his older brother had passed away.

First, he established his claim based on his descent from the Uanacaze on his father's side by including questions such as, "Item, [ask them] if they know that the aforementioned Cazonci was lord of the aforementioned land by natural legitimate succession of more than seven hundred years, [and] that his ancestors had succeeded the eldest son to the father on the father's male line following the natural laws, and that it was not based on a people's election."[70] In the fifth question, Don Antonio asserts that his father had handed over his kingdom peacefully, received baptism, and cooperated in the conversion of his subjects:

> Item, [ask them] if they know that . . . [Tangaxuan] received the Spaniards in peace and turned himself in and his children and his land with everything he had to his majesty; and he received the Christian faith, and ordered all his subjects to receive it, which they received and once received they kept and keep it to this day. Say so.[71]

In the eighth question, Don Antonio maintains that in spite of his father's collaboration with the Spaniards, Guzmán had him killed unjustly: "Item, [ask them] if they know that the aforementioned Cazonci gave great treasure to those who governed in the name of his majesty, especially to Nuño de Guzmán, who paid him with his death, without guilt, in order to cover up, so it would not be known what he had received or any information of it. Say so."[72] Questions eleven to sixteen declare that Don Antonio was the son of a Catholic marriage, raised as a Spaniard and a Christian, benefited from Spanish customs and education, and was "very much a friend of Spaniards."[73] The questionnaire, by citing Don Antonio's lineage and the deeds and death of Tangaxuan, establishes Don Antonio's rights. It also demonstrates that because of his Spanish comportment and connections he was worthy of royal grants.

This document, as well as Don Francisco's request for royal grants (now lost), like the artist's use of the *Relación*'s genealogical tree to show the brothers' noble indigenous lineage, the unjust and cruel death of Tangaxuan, and their acceptance of Spanish customs and religion, was a savvy way to legitimize the indigenous nobility's privileges in the early colonial period. This representational strategy responded to competing claims that sought to discredit first Tangaxuan and later his heirs. One might say that the painter of the tree narrowed the gap between colonizer and colonized by presenting Don Francisco and Don Antonio as Catholics who behaved and dressed according to Spanish custom. In representing them *like* Spaniards, the image asserted their eligibility for positions of power in the colonial government. At the same time, artist 1 made it clear that their claim as legitimate rulers of the indigenous population derived from their Uanacaze descent. Thus, in this visual mimicry of a genealogical model, the difference between the Uanacaze's tree and the colonizer's prototype not only reveals the political boundaries established by Spanish colonizers but also works in the interest of the colonized by marking Don Francisco and Don Antonio as the rightful heirs to the indigenous government. While Spanish colonial authorities may have given them *permission* to rule, their *ability* to govern the area relied on the fact that they were *not* Spaniards but native sons.

The Tree and Indigenous Traditions

We have seen that the artist of the *Relación*'s tree image most clearly expressed the interests of the indigenous nobility in his alterations to—or distortions of—the European model. By changing the European model, artist 1 appropriated it, made it his own, and in the process provided a vision of current and past events to promote the interests of the Uanacaze family. In this transformation, the tree ceased to be a European model and became an indigenous sign. The choices artist 1 made by illustrating the genealogy in a tree, as well as the particular species of tree he used, resonated with local traditions. These choices allowed the artist to present an image with multiple possible readings. While Spaniards would have recognized the tree's value as a genealogical chart, the artist and other indigenous collaborators of the *Relación* would have seen it as affirming the Uanacaze as the legitimate regional rulers.

In his study of the *Relación*'s family tree, Roskamp has pointed out that trees played an important role in indigenous Mesoamerican cosmovisions, where they represented, among other things, the well-being of ruling lineages and their connection to the land.[74] In Michoacán, as Roskamp has mentioned, the P'urhépecha term for lineage is *sirukua*, whose root means "to be born, to root, and to put out branches," a clear analogy to a tree. Furthermore, Espejel Carbajal has noted that the text of the *Relación* associates the wood used to build fires in the temples with the indigenous god Curicaueri.[75] Stone has observed that this wood serves in the *Relación* as a metaphoric link between gods and mortals, and specifically between the gods and the Uanacaze.[76] According to the *Relación*, Uanacaze lords themselves spent days collecting wood for the temples, and they ordered people from all other social classes to do so as well. Curicaueri, in addition to being the tutelary god of the Uanacaze, was the founder of their lineage.[77] His destiny was to conquer and govern the land, and in the second part of the *Relación*, the Uanacaze lords follow this destiny as his representatives.[78] Thus, wood serves as a symbolic link between the god Curicaueri and the Uanacaze's destiny to govern.

But not all wood or all trees have the same symbolic value in the *Relación*. Even though the prophet Isaiah in the Bible does not specify the kind of tree that sprouts from Jesse, European artists generally attached Jesse's descendants to the blossoms of rosebushes or placed them on the branches of a grapevine or a fruit tree. In the tree of the *Relación*, the Uanacaze do not emerge from flowers or from branches but sit inside the inverted crowns of little acorns, where their bodies replace the kernel or nut. The scholars José Corona Núñez and Stone have commented that the acorns may indicate that the genealogical tree in the *Relación* is an oak, a species of tree that proliferates in Michoacán.[79] The central region of Michoacán is home to a specific variety of oak called *tocuz*, which has an erect trunk and numerous branches that, like those of rosebushes and grapevines, can easily accommodate multiple members of a fertile ancestry (fig. 55).[80]

In the text of the *Relación*, oaks are significant. The wood burned at the temples came from oaks, and live oak trees provided protection to humans and facilitated communication between humans and gods.[81] For example, one of the Uanacaze lords runs away from his enemies and resettles next to an oak. Another Uanacaze lord, mortally wounded, lies down under an oak. When the gods announce the arrival of new gods to a woman, she wakes up from her trance beside an oak.[82]

More important, in the text of the *Relación* two oak trees serve as heralds of the divine message that the Uanacaze will unify the region. The gods Curicaueri and Xaratanga appear before two Uanacaze lords sleeping beside oak trees to implore them to conquer the region. These lords relate the events to their uncle, who replies that "because of the virtue of that tree, that is why you had the dream you had," and orders them to fell the oaks and offer them as incense to the gods.[83]

Interestingly, the P'urhépecha word *vapatzequa*, used in sixteenth-century documents to mean "pueblo," "barrio/collación," and/or "sujeto," also means "oak gall" (sometimes known as "oak apple," a growth on oak

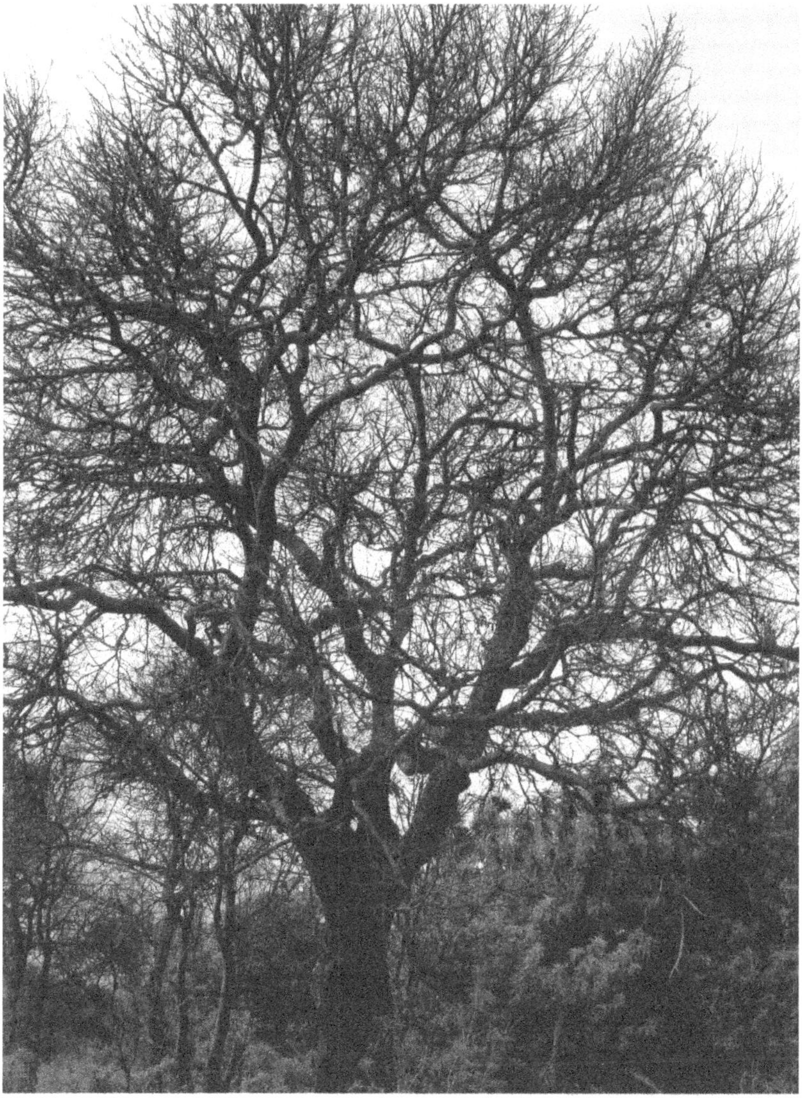

FIGURE 55. Tocuz oak near the town of Tiripetío, Michoacán. Photograph by the author.

trees that resembles small apples).[84] The parallel between oak apples and barrios/collaciones/sujetos kindles the idea that the artist's choice of an oak tree responded to the oak as a symbol of an orderly society where the rulers and their people were connected through the branches and tree trunk to the gods and a common ancestor.[85]

Conclusion

Artist 1 mimicked the European motif of the Tree of Jesse in order to communicate with the manuscript's colonial audience. His use of mimicry in this case was not a passive act but an active appropriation and transformation of a European sign into a new signifier. It registered the lineage of the Uanacaze royal family and served as a call for political changes in favor of Tangaxuan's sons, Don Francisco and Don Antonio, during the tumultuous early colonial period. The representation of Uanacaze lords dying as they look at the manuscript's audience from their thrones has no precedent in the European iconography of the Tree of Jesse. The dying lords lead the viewer's eyes upward to the dying Zinzicha Tangaxuan Don Francisco, wearing his baptismal robe as he is consumed by flames.

Documents containing information about Tangaxuan's death show that this painting responded to a heated political debate. Early sixteenth-century Michoacán was not a society neatly divided into colonizer versus colonized but was populated by members of different indigenous ethnic groups that allied themselves with different colonizers, who were likewise divided by economic interests and loyalties. Nuño de Guzmán, Tangaxuan's executioner, maintained that Tangaxuan had received a just trial, and that because he had been baptized, he had been garroted and then burned only after death. However, in the political debate that emerged from this event and continued for many years, the Uanacaze and their supporters were adamant that he had been burned alive, and they accordingly protested his unjust death and emphasized his role in bringing Catholicism to the region.

Calling attention to Tangaxuan's unjust death benefited Tangaxuan's sons because they were the immediate heirs who had lost their privileges and possessions following their father's death. The documents Don Francisco and Don Antonio filed asking for royal grants, as well as the positive responses they received, reveal that the painter of the Uanacaze royal lineage in the *Relación* successfully conveyed the message, using mimicry as a way of communicating that the Uanacaze were the legitimate rulers of the area and, through the differences between their tree and the colonizer's model, presented Don Francisco and Don Antonio as the rightful heirs to the local government. Perched on the branches of a tocuz oak, the brothers appear as members of the Uanacaze lineage, Catholic converts, and future rulers of Michoacán. In its visual form, this tree allowed them to settle conflicting agendas, outshine competing ethnic groups, and carve out for themselves a place in the new colonial society.

6

Memories of an Ethnographic Funeral

In 1530, civil unrest in Michoacán followed the untimely execution of the Uanacaze ruler Zinzicha Tangaxuan by order of Nuño de Guzmán, Mendoza's predecessor as president of the Royal Audience. While Guzmán continued in his expedition to western Mexico, the *Relación* mentions that people in Michoacán were jailed to prevent them from deserting their towns. Eighteenth-century chroniclers later reported that indigenous people renounced the Spanish government and Michoacán was temporarily lost "to God and to the King."[1]

In much of colonial Mexico, Spanish authorities depended on the leadership of the indigenous nobility to administer the indigenous population at large. After the death of Tangaxuan, the Islander Don Pedro Cuiniarangari returned to Michoacán from Guzmán's expedition and became governor. By 1539, Guzmán had been removed from his post as president of the Royal Audience and was having to answer for his actions. The eldest of Tangaxuan's children was already, or almost, old enough to rule, and it was up to the recently appointed viceroy Antonio de Mendoza to decide which indigenous nobles should govern and how future successors should be chosen.

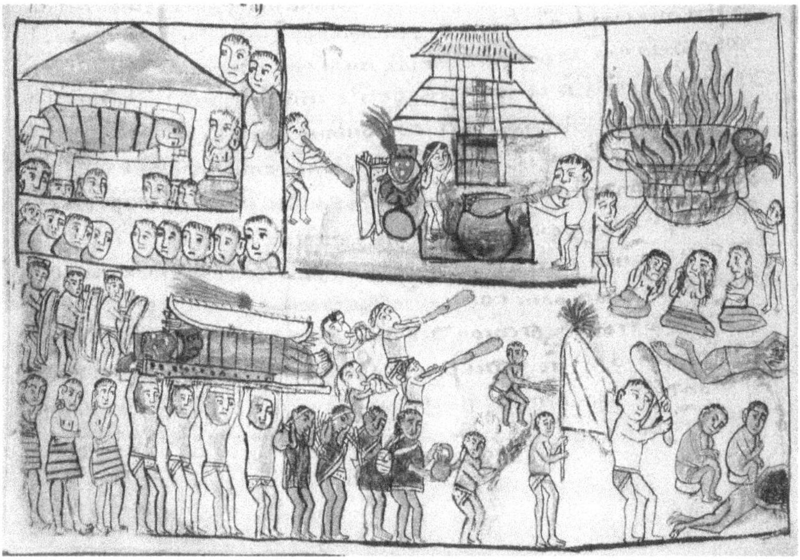

FIGURE 56. Artist 3. "Como muría el Caçonci y las cirimonias con que le enterravan" (Of the way the cazonci died and the ceremonies with which they buried him). *Relación de Michoacán*, fol. 29v. Real Biblioteca del Monasterio de El Escorial, San Lorenzo de El Escorial, Spain, C IV 5. Photograph © Patrimonio Nacional, Spain.

Contributors to the *Relación* sought not only to present the Uanacaze lineage as the rightful rulers of this region but also to answer the question of how successors should be selected.

Artist 3 painted a scene to accompany the chapter titled "Of the Way the Cazonci Died and the Ceremonies with Which They Buried Him," included in the ethnographic section of the *Relación*.[2] It depicts a liminal moment—the death of a ruler and his funeral—that would have resulted in the transfer of power to the next generation (fig. 56; see plate 25). This image and its accompanying text projected into the past a formula for understanding royal funerals, and at the same time it expressed the Uanacaze legitimacy to the viceroy while seeking to reestablish their succession. According to the text, when a cazonci was old, his son and successor would have ruled by his side.[3] Upon his death, elaborate funerals would have followed. In the scene representing such an event, the artist used the body paint and accoutrements of the Uanacaze party, the sacrificial victims, and the dead ruler to differentiate the Uanacaze ethnically and politically from their competitors, the Islanders, and represent the Uanacaze as the legitimate successors.

In ways typical of ethnographic records, the funeral scene and accompanying text consolidate diverse memories of funerals past and convert them into a single event, a formula for royal funerals. While the text purports that this is *the* way in which royal funerals were conducted, this ethnographic account is the last of three very distinct references to pre-Columbian royal funeral ceremonies documented in the *Relación*. The other two ceremonies (not illustrated) are part of the historical section of the *Relación*.

Comparing the accounts of the three funeral ceremonies reveals their differences, as well as the ways in which they symbolize the rise of Uanacaze political power in the region. They vary in their elaborate nature and descriptions of burial furnishings, differences that mark the Uanacaze's increasingly firm political hold over the region. The first funeral required only jewels for the burials of two lords who died when the Uanacaze's ancestors were still a wandering people; the second planned for the sacrifice of enemies to be entombed with Tariacuri, a savvy political leader whose rule had led to the unification of the region. The third funeral ceremony, the ethnographic account discussed here, describes a funeral ceremony as the product of unmatched effort from all the nobility of Michoacán.

Indigenous funerals had not been performed with this kind of pomp and decorum since the arrival of the Spaniards nearly twenty years before. The contributors of the *Relación* had to re-create on paper, either from memory or imagination, funeral practices that were no longer part of their recent lived experience. They meticulously described and painted the participants of the funeral. One could say they restored on paper a ceremony that could no longer be performed.

The work of the philosopher Svetlana Boym and the historian Eric Hobsbawn on restored or invented traditions provides some thought-provoking ideas, although less than a perfect framework, for understanding some of the dimensions of how this image and its accompanying text functioned. According to Boym, restored and invented traditions often have a higher degree of symbolism and formalization than the actual forms after which they were patterned.[4] According to Hobsbawn, these traditions seek to inculcate specific norms of behavior among practicing populations by implying continuity with the past.[5] In the case of the *Relación*, we can explore the symbolism embodied in the ceremony, yet the funeral scene portrays events that could not be performed under colonial rule by this P'urhépecha community. The ceremony was reconstructed for Viceroy Antonio de Mendoza, the audience of the manuscript, so we must investigate what response such representation sought to generate not in the people performing it but in the receiving audience.

One must remember that the viceroy had the power to decide who should rule and how this official should be chosen in the colonial period. The funeral scene depicted a transitional moment when a ruler had died and the possibility of a new one had arisen. It presented the smooth transition of power at the funeral of a ruler. By creating the formula for a funeral, it also created a formula for succession for the eyes of the viceroy. In this way, the contributors of the *Relación* hoped to shape the future of the region.

In the image "Of the Way the Cazonci Died and the Ceremonies with Which They Buried Him," the artist divided the picture into sections to show the successive stages of the funeral much as we see today in comic strips, where a single character may appear more than once in order to indicate a sequence of events and actions. In the top left section, the artist has partially removed the walls and roof of the ruler's home so that the viewer can see events taking place within its quarters. Inside this rectangular structure, the ruler, wrapped in a red-striped blanket, lies on a small bed of boards. Kneeling next to the head of the bed, a woman dressed in a red skirt holds her right hand to the side of her face, a hand gesture used in another funerary scene to represent grieving (see fig. 57). The artist has portrayed five people by the side of the bed. Only their heads are visible. In all likelihood, three of them are women, since he represents them with long, stretched ears with small bars across their lobes, a convention artist 3 uses for other women in this and other pictures in the manuscript (see figs. 19, 44). Outside the house, eleven people sit in waiting.

In the illustration, the artist devotes most of the space to the funeral procession, a public event full of pomp, mourners, music, and hand-carried torches that involved human sacrifice. In an L-shaped frame starting at the bottom left corner and ending at the top right corner of the scene, the ruler's corpse appears twice, once carried on a litter in the procession and once being cremated, indicating that we are witnessing at least two different events.

In the first part of the procession, the funeral party accompanies the ruler's remains. Three figures march at the front of the procession: one carries a parasol, one carries a torch, and another sweeps the road. Close observation of the original manuscript reveals that the artist first started to paint the torchbearer facing the procession but changed his mind and painted him facing the other way.[6] Behind these three figures, two people play long, trumpetlike instruments, while another two blow conch shells. Below them, four men with their bodies painted yellow march in a single file. One holds a small round jar with a pouring spout. The other three figures carry objects on their backs held by tumplines, including axes, a bundle of wood, and a large yellow jug. Directly behind them, four bearers carry the ruler on a litter, and a small group of people follow closely behind.

Of the four bearers carrying the ruler's body three wear loincloths and one wears a loincloth and a headband. The ruler's remains receive a great deal of attention. A red mantle covers his body. He wears matching red sandals, a blue moon-shaped pectoral, a blue mask with a brownish-yellow headband, and a plume of green feathers attached to the top of a mask with a small red band. Next to his body lies a jaguar pelt quiver. On top of his body lie a bow, three arrows, and a plume of long green feathers bound to a red base with a short white handle.

Behind the ruler's litter, six figures march in two rows. In the bottom row, three women follow the catafalque. They wear striped red skirts and thin bars on their stretched earlobes. Across from the women walk three men. They each carry a bow and arrow and wear loincloths and small headbands.

In the second scene contained in the L-shaped frame, a large figure wearing a red loincloth dispatches with a bloody club the people whose bodies are covered in yellow pigment. Two of them lie on their stomachs while blood covers their necks and upper backs and drips onto the ground around them. Two other yellow-painted figures await their fate as they sit on small stools. Above them, in the upper right corner, the ruler's body burns on the funeral pyre. Two men, one at each end of the pyre, stretch out their arms with small sticks in their hands, presumably lighting the fire. Between these two men, three women in red skirts kneel while crying, and two of them hold their hands to their faces in a mourning pose.

In the last scene, depicted within its own frame at the top center of the illustration, three figures stand before a temple and next to a large urn in a grave. Two of them play the trumpetlike instruments and the other carries a bundle on his back, presumably the cremated remains of the ruler. Attached to the outside of the bundle are a golden plate, the ruler's blue pectoral and mask, a jaguar pelt headband, and a plume of green feathers with a red base. Next to the bundle are a quiver, bows, and arrows.

The text of the accompanying chapter provides some clarifying information to help interpret this image. It mentions that when the ruler's doctors determined that he was nearing death, governors, town leaders, and warriors paid him a visit and brought him presents. Once the ruler died, a private mourning ceremony took place. The nobles who had come to see him cried for him (presumably those represented in the top left box of the image). They prepared his body and the people to be sacrificed at his funeral. Nobles and elders bathed and then dressed his corpse in all his finery. They put a fine thin shirt and leather sandals on him, as well as his sumptuous jewelry, which included large gold earspools, a feather "braid," a turquoise lip plug, several necklaces made of turquoise and another one made of highly valued white fish bones, turquoise and gold bracelets, and gold rattles on his legs—and this was only the innermost layer! Next, they made for him a bed of colorful blankets on a wooden platform, and once they had placed him on it, they covered him with many more blankets, finally dressing the bundle yet again with similar jewelry plus precious long green feathers, and his bow, arrows, and quiver. They also bathed and dressed the more than forty sacrificial victims. About seven of them were women, and the rest were men, part of his private staff, including silversmiths, doctors, a cook, feather workers, arrow makers, and wood collectors. Some had such specific duties as to care for his jewels, hold his urinal, and pour his drinks.[7]

The text continues to explain that at midnight a carefully orchestrated public procession transferred his body from his home to a funeral pyre, as seen in the image. People with torches led the procession; after them trumpet players followed; and then the sacrificial victims walked, cleaning the road for the ruler to follow. They all carried with them the tools of their trade. The ruler's children and nobles carried his body directly behind the sacrificial victims. All of the ruler's relatives also attended the ceremony. They sang and marched—presumably behind his remains—toward the pyre. The text describes them as carrying their "insignias of brave men," which in the case of these men we can safely assume refers to the bows and arrows they hold. All of the nobles from Michoacán and great numbers of other people also followed the procession.[8]

The procession ended at the plaza before the temples, where a great pinewood pyre awaited. The people walked around the pyre four times while some played trumpets. Then they placed the ruler's body on top of the pyre, and his relatives sang and lit it. Last, they clubbed the sacrificial victims and placed them with the jewels in a grave behind the temple of the god Curicaueri. At dawn, the nobles collected the ashes and the melted gold and silver from the ruler's pyre. They took them to the entrance of the priests' house, where they wrapped them in a mantle, creating a bundle. Then they proceeded to arrange on the bundle jewels, feathers, and the ruler's turquoise mask. Next to the bundle, they placed his bow and arrows.

They then proceeded to prepare the grave for the ruler's remains. They dug it (presumably the one depicted in the picture) at the bottom of the steps leading to Curicaueri's temple. They covered the grave in new *petates* (woven mats) and silver and gold plates. They set a wooden bed with a large urn on top at the bottom of the grave. Around the bed they placed offerings of food, drink, and arrows. One of the priests in charge of carrying the gods' bundles then brought the ruler's bundled ashes on his back and deposited them inside the urn with the mask facing east. The bundle was covered with more mantles, *petacas* (trunks), feather arrangements, and silver and gold plates, among other things. At this point, the tomb was sealed with wooden beams and mud. Last, they covered the sacrificial victims they had previously placed in a grave behind the temple with soil.

After the funeral ceremony, everybody bathed (to avoid disease) and went to the cazonci's homes, where they cleaned themselves once more with white cotton and were fed white corn in the patios or in front of the houses. For the next five days all the fires of the city were put out, nobody ground corn, all markets were closed, and people stayed home. Then all the political leaders in the province, along with other nobility, gathered at the priests' houses, where they prayed and mourned.

Comparison of the text with the image's figures, composition, and use of color yields information about the choices the artist made to give meaning to this event, its participants, and even the placement of the final remains of the ruler. For example, the text mentions that the ruler's sons and lords carried his body in the public procession while his relatives and noble allies marched close behind. We can thus safely assume that the four figures carrying his body are his sons and noblemen, and the figures directly behind them are their relatives and other nobles who were allies. Artist 3 marks the ethnicity of the men by dressing them not as lords and governors, who usually wore long shirtlike garments, but as Chichimec warriors wearing only small loincloths. Moreover, the men marching directly behind the catafalque carry bows and arrows, the preferred weapons of the Chichimecs. Throughout the *Relación*, these weapons also serve to identify the Uanacaze rulers, who carried a bow and arrows as emblems of their ethnicity (see figs. 3, 38). Their use by the ruler's family helps mark their social rank as well.

The text also identifies other people depicted in the procession. It mentions that sacrificial victims were chosen from among the servants to the cazonci and marched at the front of the procession.[9] The artist differentiates the sacrificial victims at the front of the procession by the yellow color of their skins, their aristocratic raiment, and the items they carry.[10] According to the text, these individuals were dressed in the same manner as the cazonci's corpse, and indeed, in the image they do wear long shirtlike garments. In the bottom right corner of the procession, a man sacrifices these yellow-painted men, who are now dispossessed of their accoutrements, presumably so that they can accompany the ruler into the afterworld.

While the text helps identify some of the participants depicted and explain the sequence of events taking place, its near absence of punctuation, the discrepancies between text and image, and some of the information the text omits have been cause for controversy. For example, because there is so little punctuation in the *Relación*'s original text, scholars have often ignored or erroneously described the differences in body pigments among the procession's participants in the image.[11] José Tudela, in his well-known edition of the *Relación*, describes the servants as being *tiznados de negro* (covered in black ash), and Leoncio Cabrero, in his 1989 edition, describes *all* of the participants as having faces painted yellow.[12] However, around 1543, when Friar Toribio de Benavente (known as Motolinía) transcribed the funeral chapter from the *Relación* into his own manuscript titled *Memoriales*, he correctly described only the sacrificial victims as having faces painted yellow.[13] Seventeenth- through eighteenth-century writers copied Motolinía's transcription and accurately reported that only the sacrificial victims were painted yellow, thus matching the *Relación*'s image.[14]

Confusion around which of the figures represented the sacrificial victims has also resulted from apparent contradictions between the text and the picture. The text mentions nearly forty sacrificial victims, seven of whom were women, yet the artist painted only three men. Considering he had limited space, these three figures stand for all those mentioned in the text. Perhaps trying to account for the absence of women among the sacrificial victims, scholars have often interpreted the women depicted at the back of the procession as sacrificial victims.[15] These women, however, not only are apart from the sacrificial victims but are not portrayed with yellow pigment, nor do they carry the utensils that would identify them as servants of the ruler. Unlike the sacrificial victims, they march behind the ruler's remains together with the other nobles and members of the royal family. In the scene in the upper right quadrant of the image, which depicts events that took place after the yellow-painted sacrificial victims had been executed, these same women mourn beside the funeral pyre.

The artist's use of yellow pigment to distinguish the sacrificial victims from others in the procession bears investigation. The use of yellow body paint identifies them with the local non-Uanacaze nobility.[16] In the historical section of the *Relación*, the color yellow is associated with the goddess Cuerahuaperi and her priestly elite. Lord Zurumban, originally from the island city of Xarácuaro in Lake Pátzcuaro, is said to have covered himself in yellow paint to carry out ritual sacrifices for the goddess Cuerahuaperi.[17] Zurumban had left the island at a time of severe drought to relocate to the mainland city of Taríaran. Thanks to his devotion to the local goddess Xaratanga, daughter of Cuerahuaperi, his fortunes improved and he became Xaratanga's main priest and the ruler of Taríaran.[18]

The fact that this Islander priest covered himself in yellow pigment is no insignificant matter. According to the *Relación*, only after the Uanacaze defeated Zurumban and his heir were the Uanacaze able to unify the area.[19] Theirs was a conflict of cosmic proportions that required careful planning, battles, strategic marriages, and even the participation of local deities.[20] One of the Uanacaze nobles claimed that Xaratanga, the patron deity of Zurumban, had appeared to him to request that he remove her from Zurumban's custody and place her in the care of the Uanacaze nobles (see fig. 51).[21] The Uanacaze proceeded to defeat Xaratanga's priests and incorporated the goddess into their own ceremonies.[22] Thus, the use of the color yellow in the *Relación* was associated with the Islander noble lineage defeated by the Uanacaze.

In spite of the Uanacaze having co-opted the goddess's cult into their own religious practices, the nobility associated with Xaratanga and her mother continued to use the color yellow for ritual practices throughout the *Relación*.[23] In their account of the events leading up to the arrival of the Spanish army, the contributors of the *Relación* describe how Xaratanga's mother possessed a woman from a noble house and revealed to her the coming of new people. Even though the text does not mention it, the accompanying illustration shows the woman's face painted yellow (see fig. 25).

The identification of the sacrificial victims in "Of the Way the Cazonci Died . . ." with the enemies of the Uanacaze is supported by comparing this funeral with the second of two funerals mentioned in the historical section of the *Relación*. In the latter, Lord Tariacuri, one of the Uanacaze nobles credited with unification of the region, needed sacrificial victims for a new temple. In order to justify this high-stakes need, he pretended to require victims for his own funeral and called for a war against an Islander lord. In sending envoys to this lord, Tariacuri is reported to have said,

> Tell him that we are both already old and tired, and that we already want to go to the god of hell. Thus where will we get a group of people to take with us for our dais? Ask him to point where the fight will be, in a field of green corn, at the lakeshore? If I kill his people there, those who die will be my bed and dais in death. And if he kills my people, they also will be the dais for his death.[24]

This statement corroborates that the sacrifices in the illustration re-create earlier sacrifices of enemies at royal funerals.

In the *Relación*, Uanacaze nobles and their Chichimec ancestors, however, generally covered themselves in black ash from the fires dedicated to their divine ancestor Curicaueri.[25] This can be seen in the illustration of the ruler's funeral procession, where a light black wash covers the skin of the ruler's sons and nobles who carry his corpse. Color differentiation therefore visually reinforces the ethnic categorization of these two groups of individuals: black body paint appears only on the ruling Uanacaze, and yellow body paint is reserved for the sacrificial victims who stood for members of the indigenous priesthood and nobility conquered by the Uanacaze's ancestors. In spite of the depiction of sacrificial victims, as conquered nobles, the text accompanying the image identifies them as servants of the ruler. It bears mentioning that, according to the *Relación*, palace servants were nobles, and conquered Islander nobility occupied both roles simultaneously.[26]

The governor Don Pedro, as previously noted, mentions in the *Relación* that the Uanacaze had conquered his Islander ancestors and the latter had become the Uanacaze's servants. Their fate was in accordance with that of other conquered groups in the *Relación*. In the *Relación*, conquered peoples who were not sacrificed (*teruparaqua euaecha*) became servants of their new lords. According to the sixteenth-century *Diccionario grande*, *teruparaqua* refers to a servant (*criado*), and it can be translated literally as "those whose backs have been taken from them."[27] In other words, it refers to people whose backs are not their own but who carry things for others.[28] In a similar manner, in explaining how the Islanders served the Uanacaze, Don Pedro says that they used "to carry the food of the kings on our backs, and the axes to go to the forest for wood, and we carried their drinking jars."[29] In the funeral scene, the yellow-painted sacrificial victims accordingly carry the three items Don Pedro names: axes, drinking jars, and food vessels.[30] Furthermore, by showing them carrying these tools, the artist identifies them as servants to the royal palace and thus reasserts their submission to the deceased ruler and the heir apparent—who was the man responsible for their impending fate.

In sum, the artist identifies the sacrificial victims as conquered enemies in his use of yellow pigment for their skin, by the tools they carry, and by their noble garments. He further identifies the Uanacaze nobles as Chichimec warriors by their black body pigment, the bows and arrows they carry, and their warrior garments. In this way, artist 3 differentiated the Uanacaze elite from the local elites, thereby revealing the local ethnic and political hierarchy.

In addition to the sacrificial victims, the remains of the ruler, to which the artist devotes a great deal of attention, deserve some consideration. Like his family members at the rear of the procession, the ruler carries a bow, arrows, and a quiver, which identify him as Chichimec. The artist also includes other elements in the scene that help identify his remains as an embodiment of their divine Chichimec ancestor, the god Curicaueri.

Not mentioned anywhere in the passage of the text describing the procession, but present in several places in the illustration, is the turquoise mask that tops the cazonci's funeral bundle. The mask appears again on the bundle as it is cremated, and yet again on its remains as they are about to be buried. Only at this point of the narration does the text identify it as a turquoise mask.[31] The text does not explain the meaning of this mask, but it probably served to strengthen the ruler's association with the god Curicaueri. Only two other illustrations in the *Relación* show individuals wearing a blue mask: one depicts the masked funerary bundles of nobles who died in war and who, like the ruler, carried out the mandates of Curicaueri and were cremated after death (left side of figure 57; see plate 26); and the other, masked supernaturals who appeared to a noblewoman in a vision (see also fig. 25).[32] In a similar manner, deceased Aztec rulers of central Mexico, who also represented a deity, likewise donned the insignia of the patron deity of their hometown or temple prior to cremation.[33] Thus, the mask on the ruler's remains reinforced his association with Curicaueri.

Other people in the description and depiction of the funeral ceremony also established the ruler's connection to the god Curicaueri. Tudela has identified two individuals playing conch shells marching in front of the procession as the priests who used to carry the gods on their backs (compare

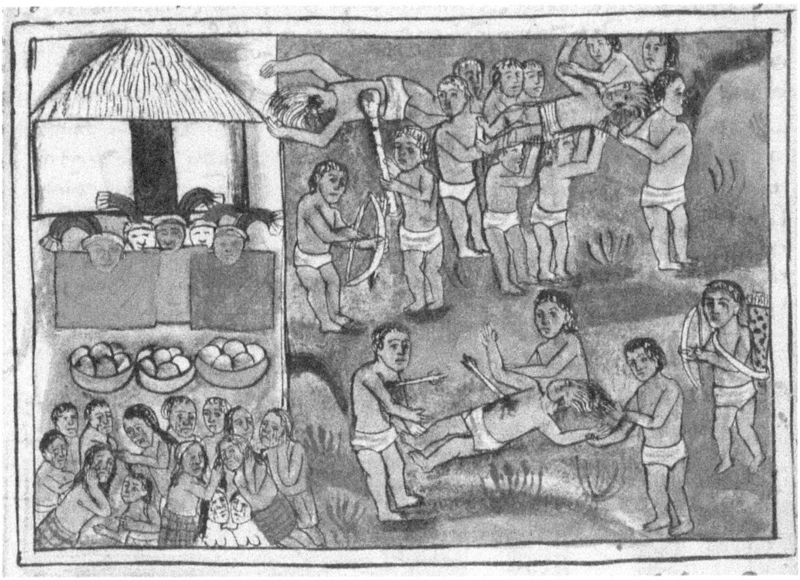

FIGURE 57. Artist 1. "De los que murían en la guerra" (Of those who died at war). *Relación de Michoacán*, fol. 20r. Real Biblioteca del Monasterio de El Escorial, San Lorenzo de El Escorial, Spain, C IV 5. Photograph © Patrimonio Nacional, Spain.

figs. 2 and 56).[34] The text mentions that one of the priests who used to carry the gods on their backs would bury the ruler's remains next to Curicaueri's temple after the cremation.[35] The artist depicts this at the top center frame, in which we see an individual carrying the ruler's remains in a bundle on his back and walking toward an urn in front of a temple while two other individuals play trumpetlike instruments.

Connecting the ruler to his powerful deified ancestor was a strategic political move. The *Relación*'s contributors do not limit the connection to the images; the text actually states "the one who was the cazonci, was in [the] place of Curicaueri."[36] This connection reinforced the Uanacaze family's link to the god as well as to their right to rule over Michoacán. According to the *Relación*, Curicaueri, the founder of the Uanacaze lineage and source of their Chichimec ethnicity, had been destined to conquer the region.[37]

By associating the ruler with his deified ancestor in "Of the Way the Cazonci Died . . . ," the artist further connected the sacrificial victims in the procession to the defeat and sacrifice of powerful enemies. According to the text, the funeral procession took place at the propitious hour of midnight. In the *Relación*, several other kinds of ceremonies invoking deities took place at midnight. These ceremonies included the burning of incense as part of elaborate war ceremonies and the sounding of trumpets in anticipation of the sacrifice of enemies, such as that of the quintessential enemy, the son of the Islander Zurumban, who, significantly, was sacrificed to the god Curicaueri.[38] Like the victims in the funeral procession, Zurumban's son was depicted being clubbed by the Uanacaze as well, a symbol also used to represent the taking of enemy captives (see fig. 43).

Finally, in "Of the Way the Cazonci Died . . ." an individual sweeps the road before the group carrying the deceased ruler. José Tudela has noticed that the metaphor of sweeping the ground also appears in the goddess Xaratanga's command to a Uanacaze lord to take her away from Zurumba's custody, "clean the road" before her, and lead her to the Uanacaze capital.[39] This was, in other words, a gesture made for a divinity and a command of war that, like the funeral scene, resulted in the defeat and sacrifice of enemies.

The funeral scene depicts the liminal moment when power would have been transferred from father to son in a public spectacle that would have recreated the defeat of Uanacaze enemies. At the beginning of the chapter describing the funeral, the text explicitly mentions that when the cazonci was old, he would choose the heir apparent to govern by his side and succeed him on the throne. Most likely, artist 3 represented the heir in the scene, as one figure carrying the body of the cazonci wears a headband, distinguishing him from the other lords and children of the cazonci that the text mentions carried the body. In all likelihood, in the sacrificial scene he is the figure clubbing the sacrificial victims, since sacrifice was the prerogative of the nobility and he would have been the highest-ranking noble.

The *Relación*'s ethnographic representation of royal burial practices would have benefited the Uanacaze heirs by depicting an apparently smooth and unquestionable transition of power from father to son. It distinguishes him from other members of the nobility, reaffirms the hereditary nature of the ruler's post, and reminds the manuscript's audience that the successor would have been chosen by the previous ruler. In particular, this would have benefited Don Francisco Tariacuri, son of Zinzicha Tangaxuan, who was either old enough to govern or close to that age and who in all likelihood contributed to the making of the *Relación*.[40] The artist leaves no question as to the role of the Islander nobility, as the yellow-painted sacrificial victims. Their job is to serve the Uanacaze ruler in this life and the next (not to govern the region as Don Pedro was doing at this time).

The tensions between what may have been the desires of the Uanacaze heir, changing cultural practices, and the interests of other contributors to the *Relación* become apparent in the discrepancies between the claims made in this chapter of the *Relación* and the practices represented in others. For example, rather than a father-son succession formula, the historical section of the *Relación* describes how brothers and even cousins succeeded a dead ruler. Furthermore, the chapter after the funeral ceremony documents how a council of elders elected the ruler from eligible candidates.[41] Rather than a set formula of succession, the *Relación* contains multiple and often contradictory narratives, which help reveal the interests of the different contributors.

The Uanacaze royal burial of Zinzicha Tangaxuan took place after the arrival of Spaniards in Michoacán. Analysis of the different accounts of Tangaxuan's funeral and a comparison with the ethnographic account included in the *Relación* can provide some insight into the sympathies of the different colonial interlocutors. For example, in the eighteenth century, Friar Joseph Moreno, who emphasized the innocence of Tangaxuan and the injustice of his death, said that when Tangaxuan was about to be burned alive, he pointed out to his son-in-law that this was how the Spaniards had repaid him for his collaboration and urged his son-in-law to take his ashes to his parents' grave.[42] In this account, Tangaxuan's stoicism and request for an almost Christian-like burial presented him in a good light, to the detriment of his executioners, who had betrayed Tangaxuan's allegiance and unjustly burned him at the stake.

Moreno's version was not the only way in which Tangaxuan's burial would be remembered. The *Relación* also contains the account of these events as told by the Islander Don Pedro. As mentioned previously, at the time the *Relación* was being produced, Don Pedro had to justify his post to colonial authorities. His narration of Tangaxuan's burial is significant because it helped him consolidate his position. His account, in contrast to Moreno's, implicates the members of the Uanacaze royal palace in acts condemned by Spanish authorities during the colonial period. Don Pedro relates that, once Tangaxuan had died, his *criados*—a word used in sixteenth-century Spanish to refer both to one's servants and to those raised under one's roof—had gathered his ashes and secretly sacrificed a woman to be buried with him.[43] In the *Relación*'s ethnographic description of the royal funeral, the successor to the Uanacaze throne was in charge of the funerary ceremonies for the deceased ruler; consequently Don Pedro's account implies that his main competitor for the governor's seat (as well as other nobles from the palace) continued to practice idolatry. Since, as Don Pedro reminds us, he was Guzmán's captive at the time, he was not present at Tangaxuan's funeral. The differences between Don Pedro's account, Moreno's, and the practices recorded in the ethnographic chapter point to the pivotal role funeral ceremonies played in the transfer of power during the early colonial period, as well as the competing agendas that shaped these narratives and accompanying illustrations in the *Relación*.

Conclusion

By re-creating a funeral ceremony for the Spanish viceroy, the artist was able to imbue the ceremony with symbolism at every step of the way. In "Of the Way the Cazonci Died . . ." his depiction of body paint and attire re-creates ethnic categories determining the social order. First, the visual treatment of the ruler's remains in this image allies him with the divine Chichimec ancestor Curicaueri. Second, the ruler's descendants, dressed as Chichimec warriors, appear as the rightful heirs to power, since they had come to rule through war. Third, by means of yellow body paint and aristocratic raiment, the artist identifies the sacrificial victims as representatives of the formerly defeated Islander indigenous nobles, thereby making visible ethnic differences that sought to reinstate a political hierarchy in favor of the Uanacaze. Rather than represent the funeral of all Uanacaze rulers through time, the artist portrayed a synthetic image of pre-Columbian events from a colonial present.

The question of who should succeed a deceased ruler or how this person should be chosen in the first fifty years of Spanish rule was of utmost importance. Ethnographic documentation collected during this early period sought to set the precedent of how things should be carried out during the colonial period. Through political alliances, court litigation, and the careful crafting of the contents of the *Relación*, the Uanacaze sought to regain lost privileges and position themselves in the new colonial government. While the ceremonies that would have assured the transference of power among Uanacaze nobles could no longer be performed, this ethnographic representation of a funeral sought to root in the past the transference of rulership within the ruler's lineage. Apparently, they successfully argued their case to colonial authorities, for even though the Spanish crown established in the mid-sixteenth century that all indigenous officers should be elected yearly, in Michoacán the Uanacaze ruler Zinzicha Tangaxuan's sons inherited their posts and became lifetime governors.[44]

Conclusion

About 1539, the newly appointed Spanish viceroy to Mexico, Antonio de Mendoza, commissioned a Franciscan friar in the City of Michoacán to record the customs of the region so that he could govern it more effectively. The friar, who has been identified as Jerónimo de Alcalá, employed indigenous informants who were members of the local P'urhépecha-speaking nobility. Their testimony was recorded in the manuscript's text, which was divided into three parts preceded by a prologue. Alcalá also engaged four anonymous native artists to create the forty-four small paintings that illustrate what is now known as the *Relación de Michoacán*.

The *Relación de Michoacán* presented an optimal opportunity for its contributors. It gave the anonymous Franciscan the opportunity to present himself and his order as necessary in the process of evangelization. It also gave him the opportunity to work with the indigenous nobility, who still controlled many of the resources and administered the labor during the early colonial period. For the manuscript's indigenous contributors, the *Relación* presented a unique opportunity to shape the viceroy's views about past and current events in hopes of carving out for themselves a place in the new colonial society.

The agendas of the indigenous contributors were not, however, uniform. The friar presumably worked with members of the Uanacaze ruling family and their allies, and with the current indigenous governor of the City of Michoacán, Don Pedro Cuiniarangari, a descendant of Islander priests. The Uanacaze were the leaders of a group referred to in the *Relación* sometimes as Chichimecs and sometimes as Uacúsecha. They had allegedly migrated to Michoacán and conquered its local population. In the pages of the *Relación*, they seek to present themselves as the legitimate rulers of the region. Don Pedro Cuiniarangari, a non-Uanacaze noble who had come to occupy the post of governor after his collaboration with Spanish armies and provided testimony against the Uanacaze ruler, had to explain how he had managed to acquire that post. In spite of their diverging interests, both of these indigenous groups also had to fight several Spanish newcomers in the region, requiring that they present, at one level, a united front. Since the differing testimonies of both parties can be seen in the *Relación de Michoacán*, the manuscript provides an excellent opportunity to examine the roles played by visual images in political disputes among colonized peoples and their colonizers.

The process of creating the *Relación* reveals complex working relationships among its various contributors. After the scribes had copied the manuscript, leaving spaces for illustrations, the artists and friar collaborated to alter the text to accommodate additional images that highlighted significant events while ignoring others. The friar rewrote the titles of the chapters of part 2 of the *Relación* so that there would be more room for images and the titles would serve as both chapter and image headings. For the most part, the artists illustrated the events mentioned in the titles. However, in some cases, their illustrations did not match their associated titles. And in part 3, the artists left blank several spaces reserved for images. Through their selective use of imagery, the artists were able to alter the course of the narrative. Scholars have often assumed that through these alterations either the process of creating the manuscript had been streamlined or the emendations were only a matter of practical necessity. Where the images have disagreed with the text, scholars have seen the discrepancies as mistakes on the part of the artists. However, these emendations and discrepancies reflect a careful editorial process on the part of the manuscript's contributors because they often respond either to elements the artists were seeking to highlight in the narrative or to the indigenous concepts they sought to represent.

When illustrating the *Relación*, the artists faced the difficult task of representing indigenous concepts and histories to their colonial audience. They carefully selected from a range of Mesoamerican and European motifs and visual techniques. As they blended them, the artists managed to create images that conveyed a sense of knowledge about the pre-Columbian past but which a European audience could understand and accept as "true" depictions of events. These acts of visual mimicry altered the original models and created new signs to serve the artists' current needs.

The success of the images in communicating to colonial (and modern) audiences is partly a result of their relationship to the alphabetic text. The script, in the form of glosses in the images, the titles, and the accompanying text, transforms indigenous thoughts into concepts understandable to the Spanish-speaking audience. It allows indigenous concepts to be anchored within a European logic. Furthermore, when the friar-editor added captions to some of the images after they were completed, he demonstrated his ultimate control of the project by translating P'urhépecha concepts into a Spanish way of thinking. He, as interpreter, converted the images into subjects that the viceroy could relate to and understand, while at the same time accruing cultural capital to himself.

Though most of the *Relación*'s images seek to represent events or practices that predated the arrival of Europeans in the region, they do so by responding to their colonial context. The indigenous peoples of Michoacán faced many challenges during the first twenty years of colonization. Diseases and war took a toll on Michoacán's population. Secular and ecclesiastical authorities promoted new educational systems, ways of living, and an unrelenting conversion to Catholicism. Indigenous labor and resources were distributed among the Spanish newcomers in the form of encomienda grants, which promptly undermined the political power of the indigenous nobility in the region.

In the late 1520s, the president of the First Royal Audience, Nuño de Guzmán, imprisoned the Uanacaze ruler Zinzicha Tangaxuan and other nobles in his court. In their absence, Spanish encomenderos encroached on resources around Lake Pátzcuaro that were well beyond their original grants. In 1530, Nuño de Guzmán tried and sentenced Tangaxuan to death. In the trial, the Uanacaze ruler was accused of interfering with the work of encomenderos, sodomy, and idolatry. Because he was accused of idolatry, his lands and possessions were seized to pay for his trial and to go to the Spanish Crown, thus leaving a much discredited and relatively impoverished ruling family. After Tangaxuan's death, Michoacán no longer had an indigenous ruler, and the post of governor became the highest political position. Don Pedro, who under torture had provided the most incriminating evidence against Tangaxuan, returned from his ordeal to occupy that post.

In the pages of the *Relación*, the tensions of the political situation of the time are revealed in some of the discrepancies between the text and the images, as well as in the ways each faction sought to represent itself. For example, in the tree portraying the Uanacaze lineage, Tangaxuan is represented being burned alive. But in the account that Don Pedro provides, Tangaxuan is described as dying by suffocation and being burned only after death. Documentary evidence reveals that the charges against Tangaxuan, as well as the way in which he had died, were highly debated. On the one hand, the Uanacaze and their supporters were adamant that he had been burned alive, emphasizing the injustices committed against him and consequently against his heirs. On the other hand, Nuño de Guzmán and his supporters stated that Tangaxuan had received a just death, that he had died by suffocation and been burned only afterward. Don Pedro, who testified against Tangaxuan, and many times in favor of Nuño de Guzmán later on, described events in the same way in the *Relación*. In listing the accusations against Tangaxuan, he does not provide evidence to the contrary because he could not completely vindicate Tangaxuan, since that would have challenged his post as governor and his role in the events that led to the ruler's death. Furthermore, at the time the *Relación* was being compiled, the eldest of Tangaxuan's sons, Don Francisco Tariacuri, was at or nearing the age at which he could begin to rule. In 1543, a year or two after the *Relación* was completed, Don Francisco accused Don Pedro of usurping his father's lands. On the branches of the tree, Don Francisco and his younger brother, Don Antonio, sit next to their father, dressed in baptismal gowns, with their hair cut in Spanish style and bearing their baptismal names. In other words, they are represented as part of the Uanacaze lineage, Catholic converts, and future rulers of Michoacán.

In the ethnographic section of the *Relación*, royal burial practices further seek to confirm the Uanacaze as the rightful successors to the government in this region. The text and image describing the funeral of a Uanacaze ruler not only express the wealth and might of the Uanacaze but carefully reconstruct the public spectacle when power would have been transferred from father to son. In this scene, the artist uses body paints and accoutrements to equate the sacrificial victims with the Islander enemies, while the Uanacaze appear as the heirs of the deceased ruler and destined to carry out the mandate of their deified ancestor, who was also destined to rule the land.

The legitimacy of the Uanacaze lineage is also reinforced through the pages of the manuscript; the images and text justify Uanacaze rule by describing their ancestors as exhibiting impeccable Christian-like behavior. Even their hunting and war prowess became signs of their Christian-like conduct. These activities, also practiced by European nobles, sought to generate a sympathetic response in the viceroy. However, the Uanacaze enemies from other ethnic groups are described as lacking the very morals the Uanacaze ancestors purport to have.

The Uanacaze conquest of those groups and dominion over the area are justified through the images and text as the Uanacaze become the bearers of good conduct and justice to the region. In the images depicting the Uanacaze justice system, the glosses explain crimes and punishments in ways that parallel the Spanish legal system. The accompanying text in the chapters also serves to explain the crimes and present the Uanacaze as the judges of a centralized judicial system, a key requisite for their return as part of the colonial government.

In spite of the latent tensions between the Uanacaze and Don Pedro, given the European nobility's emphasis on lineage and the viceroy's own aristocratic history, Don Pedro had to justify his position as the new governor via his relationship to the Uanacaze. Through the images and text of the *Relación*, he represents himself as an intermediary between the Uanacaze and the Spanish authorities, and as the humble subject of both. In the ethnographic section of the manuscript, when representing a marriage among nobles, the contributors decided instead to insert Don Pedro's marriage to a woman from the Uanacaze ruler's house, thus justifying his position and asserting his aristocratic connection.

While at first it may seem puzzling that the contributors of the *Relación* would qualify the relationship between Don Pedro and the Uanacaze in those terms, one must remember that they were also having to deal with the encroachment of Spanish encomenderos in the region. In court cases, these two indigenous factions had to present a united front. While Spanish encomenderos sought to fragment the lake basin and exploit it for their own benefit, indigenous nobles (including the Uanacaze, Don Pedro, and other significant players in the region) sought to keep the basin together, claiming that it was the City of Michoacán, had once been Tangaxuan's kingdom, and now was under the jurisprudence of the Spanish Crown and administered by its indigenous governor Don Pedro. This would have allowed these indigenous parties to maintain a sense of autonomy, collect tribute, and, in the case of the Uanacaze heirs, demand royal grants from the profits of these lands because the lands had belonged to their family "since time immemorial."

Accordingly, in part 2 of the *Relación*, the artists and friar carefully emended the text to make room for images that emphasized that the Uanacaze, aided by a handful of Islanders—ancestors of no other than Don Pedro—had conquered and unified the Lake Pátzcuaro basin. The artists of the *Relación* represented the Lake Pátzcuaro basin as a single territory. Its sociopolitical divisions (town, cities, etc.) were downplayed. The lake became the one constant geographical feature, and with the Uanacaze ruler in his palace on its shores, the adjoining land was presented as his kingdom.

While several paintings of lands involved in court disputes were produced, these were often contested. Opposing parties would have a chance to emend them and present witnesses to read them. However, the *Relación*'s contributors had a chance to send Viceroy Antonio de Mendoza an unedited message. The text would act as the only reading of the paintings, and text and images together would demonstrate Uanacaze possession of the basin since long before the arrival of Europeans.

Given their competing agendas, the *Relación* presents different strategies and conflicting reports, and its images do not always match the text. The emendations of the manuscript reveal what the different contributors sought to highlight in the text, and sometimes the ways in which they disagreed. While the Uanacaze would argue for their legitimacy as rulers of the region, Don Pedro sought to justify his post as governor and his role in the new colonial order. Together they would fight to keep the Lake Pátzcuaro basin under indigenous rule. Although the viceroy did not ultimately decide in their favor in the disputes over the basin, after receiving the *Relación*, he did support the eldest of the Uanacaze heirs' request for royal grants by sending the Crown a letter on his behalf. Upon the death of Don Pedro Cuiniarangari, the viceroy gave the governorship of the area to the Uanacaze heirs.

Notes

INTRODUCTION

1. The English-language literature often refers to the people of Michoacán as Tarascans, but according to the *Relación* and some of their modern-day descendants (who call themselves P'urhépecha), this term had pejorative connotations. The term "P'urhépecha" during the sixteenth century seems to have been reserved for the working classes (like the Nahuatl *macehualli*). Neither term recognizes the diversity of ethnic groups living in Michoacán in the sixteenth century. In this book, I call the different groups living in the region by the names used for them in the *Relación*. Uanacaze refers to the ruling family, and Uacúsecha and Chichimec, to the larger ethnic group to which they belonged. I call the language P'urhépecha to honor the cultural and linguistic connections that exist between the indigenous people of Michoacán today and their sixteenth-century ancestors. For a detailed discussion of and the latest points of view about the meaning and uses of these terms, see Pedro Márquez Joaquín, ed., *¿Tarascos o p'urhépecha? Voces sobre antiguas y nuevas discusiones en torno al gentilicio michoacano* (Morelia, Mexico: Universidad Michoacana de San Nicolás de Hidalgo, El Colegio de Michoacán, Universidad Intercultural Indígena de Michoacán, and Fondo Editorial Morevallado, 2007).

2. When quoting sixteenth-century Spanish, I have preserved the spelling used

in the editions consulted. The chapters in the *Relación* are not numbered, but following the practice of other scholars, I have numbered them here for the purpose of this analysis. All translations in this book are mine unless noted otherwise.

3. Donald Robertson, *Mexican Manuscript Painting of the Early Colonial Period: The Metropolitan Schools* (Norman: University of Oklahoma Press, 1994), 45–46; and H. B. Nicholson, "The History of the *Codex Mendoza*," in *The* Codex Mendoza, ed. Frances Berdan and Patricia Anawalt, 1–11 (Los Angeles: University of California Press, 1996). In addition, the indigenous authors of the botanical and medicinal treatise *Codex Badianus* called the viceroy "Maecenas," indicating that he was key in its compilation as well. See Serge Gruzinski, *Painting the Conquest: The Mexican Indians and the European Renaissance*, trans. Deke Dusinberre (Paris: Flammarion, 1992), 156.

4. For the dating of Sahagún's books, see H. B. Nicholson, "Introduction," in *Primeros memoriales*, by Bernardino de Sahagún, paleography of Nahuatl text and English translation by Thelma Sullivan, ed. H. B. Nicholson et al., 3–5 (Norman: University of Oklahoma Press, 1997).

5. For the date of arrival of the *Relación* to the Escorial and for the kind of paper used in the manuscript, see María del Carmen Hidalgo Brinquis, "Descripción material," in *Relación de Michoacán*, ed. Armando Escobar Olmedo, 44, 53, 58 (Morelia, Mexico: Patrimonio Nacional, H. Ayuntamiento de Morelia; Madrid: Testimonio Compañía Editorial, 2001). All the sheets bear one of four different watermarks representing a hand with a star. Based on the watermarks, as well as the manufacturing techniques, Hidalgo Brinquis has determined that the paper was produced during the first half of the sixteenth century, possibly in Italy. Paper with the watermark of a hand and a star was often imported to the Americas and used in other colonial documents, including the *Codex Tudela* and the *Codex Magliabechiano*. See Elizabeth Boone, Codex Magliabechiano *and the Lost Prototype of the Magliabechiano Group* (Berkeley: University of California Press, 1983), 1:19–21. In addition, paper with the same watermarks of a hand and a star was used in the court documents of the labor and land dispute the viceroy traveled to Michoacán hoping to settle (Archivo General de Indias [AGI], Justicia, Legajo 130).

6. The tight binding of the latest restoration makes it very difficult to see the signatures of paper, so I am using Hidalgo Brinquis's study for this. Hidalgo Brinquis, "Descripción material," 41–74.

7. The manuscript may have been bound at the monastery before 1671. See ibid., 48.

8. In the upper right-hand corner on the recto leaves, someone inserted Arabic numerals in ink every ten pages (10, 20, 30, 40, 50, etc.), ending with page 157. This count includes an extra leaf between pages 80 and 90, and between pages 30 and 40 there are only nine leaves. Another numbering system, in pencil and using Arabic numerals, counts the pages with text and images in them. Following the practice of previous scholars, I use this numbering system when referring to the original manuscript. Hidalgo Brinquis uses this system and numbers the pages with no content by creating a subcount based on the last page with content (e.g., 60.1, 60.2, etc.).

9. For information about the restorations, see Hidalgo Brinquis, "Descripción material." After Hidalgo Brinquis's work was published, the manuscript underwent one more restoration in 2005, when the binding was refurbished, the pages cleaned, and the insect holes patched. José Luis del Valle Merino, director of the Royal Library of the Monasterio de El Escorial, pers. comm., July 2007.

10. See also Hans Roskamp, "El carari indígena y las láminas de la *Relación de Michoacán*: Un acercamiento," in *Relación de las cerimonias y rictos y población y gobernación de los indios de la provincia de Michoacán* [*Relación de Michoacán*], ed. Moisés Franco Mendoza, 235–264 (Zamora, Mexico: El Colegio de Michoacán; Morelia, Mexico: Gobierno del Estado de Michoacán, 2000).

11. Herón Pérez Martínez, "El arte literario de la *Relación de Michoacán*," in Franco Mendoza, *Relación de Michoacán*, 82–84.

12. The literature on documents produced by indigenous nobles is extensive. For an introduction as well as some recent approaches, see Robertson, *Mexican Manuscript Painting*, 34–58; Eduardo de Jesús Douglas, *In the Palace of Nezahualcoyotl: Painting Manuscripts, Writing the Pre-Hispanic Past in Early Colonial Period Tetzcoco, Mexico* (Austin: University of Texas Press, 2010), 1–16; Tom Cummins, "The Madonna and the Horse: Becoming Colonial in New Spain and Peru," in *Phoebus: A Journal of Art History* 7 (1995): *Native Artists and Patrons in Colonial Spanish America*, ed. Emily Umberger and Tom Cummins, 52–83; Elizabeth Boone, *Stories in Red and Black: Pictorial Histories of the Aztecs and Mixtecs* (Austin: University of Texas Press, 2000); and Barbara Mundy, *The Mapping of New Spain: Indigenous Cartography and the Maps of the* Relaciones geográficas (Chicago: University of Chicago Press, 2000).

13. Carolyn Dean and Dana Leibsohn, "Hybridity and Its Discontents: Considering Visual Culture in Colonial Spanish America," *Colonial Latin American Review* 12, no. 1 (2003): 5–35.

14. Kevin Terraciano, "Competing Memories of the Conquest of Mexico," in *Contested Visions in the Spanish Colonial World*, ed. Ilona Katzew, 55–77 (Los Angeles: Los Angeles County Museum of Art; New Haven, CT: Yale University Press, 2011).

15. For the study of ethnic/race differentiation as a way to affirm class hierarchies, see, for example, Fredrik Barth, *Ethnic Groups and Boundaries: The Social Organization of Culture Difference* (Bergen-Oslo, Norway: Universitets Forlaget; London: George Allen and Unwin, 1969), 27–28; Michel Foucault, *The History of Sexuality*, vol. 1, *An Introduction*, trans. Robert Hurley (New York: Vintage, 1978), 135–159; Elizabeth Brumfiel, "Ethnic Groups and Political Development in Ancient Mexico," in *Factional Competition and Political Development in the New World*, ed. Elizabeth Brumfiel and John Fox, 89–102 (Cambridge: Cambridge University Press, 1994); Arjun Appadurai, *Modernity at Large: Cultural Dimensions of Globalization* (Minneapolis: University of Minnesota Press, 2000), 14, 139–157; and Ann Stoler, *Carnal Knowledge and Imperial Power: Race and the Intimate in Colonial Rule* (Berkeley: University of California Press, 2002), 140–161.

16. For a review of the editions of the *Relación*, see Moisés Franco Mendoza,

"Ediciones de la *Relación de Michoacán*," in Franco Mendoza, *Relación de Michoacán*, 17–36; Gerardo Sánchez Díaz, "Las ediciones de la *Relación de Michoacán* y su impacto historiográfico," in Escobar Olmedo, *Relación de Michoacán*, 205–238; and Gerardo Sánchez Díaz, "Los manuscritos y las ediciones de la *Relación de Michoacán*: Su impacto historiográfico," *Tzintzun: Revista de Estudios Históricos* 40 (2004): 11–50. English-speaking readers should be aware that the *Relación* has been translated into English by Eugene R. Craine and Reginald C. Reindrop under the title *The Chronicles of Michoacán* (Norman: University of Oklahoma Press, 1970).

17. See, for example, Eduard Seler, "Los antiguos habitantes de Michoacán," in Franco Mendoza, *Relación de Michoacán*, 139–234; Shirley Gorenstein and Helen P. Pollard, *The Tarascan Civilization: A Late Prehispanic Cultural System*, Publications in Anthropology, vol. 28 (Nashville, TN: Vanderbilt University, 1983); Helen P. Pollard, *Taríacuri's Legacy: The Prehispanic Tarascan State* (Norman: University of Oklahoma Press, 1993); Claudia Espejel Carbajal, "Voces, lugares y tiempos: Claves para comprender la *Relación de Michoacán*" (PhD diss., El Colegio de Michoacán, 2004); and David Haskell, "History and the Construction of Hierarchy and Ethnicity in the Prehispanic Tarascan State: A Syntagmatic Analysis of the *Relación de Michoacán*" (Master's thesis, University of Florida, 2003).

18. Seler, "Los antiguos habitantes de Michoacán," 139.

19. Paul Kirchhoff, "Estudio preliminar: La *Relación de Michoacán* como fuente para la historia de la sociedad y cultura tarascas," in *Relación de las ceremonias y ritos y población y gobierno de los indios de la provincia de Michoacán (1541)*, ed. and ann. José Tudela, with revisions of Tarascan words by José Corona Núñez, xix–xxxii (Madrid: Aguilar, 1956).

20. See, for example, Gorenstein and Pollard, *The Tarascan Civilization*; Pollard, *Taríacuri's Legacy*; Helen P. Pollard, "Ethnicity and Political Control in a Complex Society: The Tarascan State of Prehispanic Mexico," in *Factional Competition and Political Development in the New World*, ed. Elizabeth Brumfield and John Fox, 79–88 (Cambridge: Cambridge University Press, 1994); and Helen P. Pollard, "Central Places and Cities in the Core of the Tarascan State," in *El urbanismo en Mesoamérica/Urbanism in Mesoamerica*, ed. William Sanders et al., 345–390 (Mexico City: Instituto Nacional de Antropología e Historia; University Park: Pennsylvania State University, 2003).

21. Dominique Michelet, "Histoire, mythe et apologue: Note de lecture sur la seconde partie de la *Relación [...] de Michoacán*," in *Enquêtes sur l'Amérique moyenne: Mélanges offerts à Guy Stresser-Péan*, ed. Guy Stresser-Péan and Dominique Michelet, 105–112 (Mexico City: Instituto Nacional de Antropología e Historia, Consejo Nacional para la Cultura y las Artes, and Centre d' Études Mexicaines et Centraméricaines, 1989).

22. Ibid.

23. For a critique of the distinction between "history" and "myth," see Elizabeth Boone, "History and Historians," in *Stories in Red and Black*, 15–16.

24. See, for example, Cynthia L. Stone, "Rewriting Indigenous Traditions: The Burial Ceremony of the Cazonci," *Colonial Latin American Review* 3, no. 1–2 (1994):

87–114; Roskamp, "El carari indígena y las láminas de la *Relación de Michoacán*," 235–264; Miguel León-Portilla, "Jerónimo de Alcalá y los primeros frailes etnógrafos en Mesoamérica, siglo XVI," in Franco Mendoza, *Relación de Michoacán*, 57–78; Pérez Martínez, "El arte literario de la *Relación de Michoacán*," 79–105; and Cynthia Stone, *In Place of Gods and Kings: Authorship and Identity in the* Relación de Michoacán (Norman: University of Oklahoma Press, 2004).

25. J. Benedict Warren, "Fray Jerónimo de Alcalá: Author of the *Relación de Michoacán*?," *The Americas* 27, no. 3 (1971): 307–326; and J. Benedict Warren, "Fray Jerónimo de Alcalá, autor de la *Relación de Michoacán*," in Franco Mendoza, *Relación de Michoacán*, 37–56.

26. Moisés Franco Mendoza, "El discurso del petámuti en la estructura de la lengua p'urhépecha," in Franco Mendoza, *Relación de Michoacán*, 265–284; Pérez Martínez, "El arte literario de la *Relación de Michoacán*," 79–105; Jean Marie Le Clézio, "Universalidad de la *Relación de Michoacán*," in Franco Mendoza, *Relación de Michoacán*, 107–119; and Stone, *In Place of Gods and Kings.*

27. James Krippner-Martínez, "The Politics of Conquest: An Interpretation of the *Relación de Michoacán*," *The Americas* 47, no. 2 (1990): 177–197; James Krippner-Martínez, *Rereading the Conquest: Power, Politics, and the History of Early Colonial Michoacán, Mexico, 1521–1565* (University Park: Pennsylvania State University Press, 2001), 47–69; Espejel Carbajal, "Voces, lugares y tiempos"; and Claudia Espejel Carbajal, "La voz del interprete," in *La justicia y el fuego: Dos claves para leer la* Relación de Michoacán (Zamora, Mexico: El Colegio de Michoacán, 2008), 1:237–297.

28. Carlos Paredes Martínez, "La estratificación social de los tarascos," *Arqueología Mexicana* 4, no. 19 (1996): 34–39; and Otto Schöndube, "Los tarascos," *Arqueología Mexicana* 4, no. 19 (1996): 14–21. See also Hans Roskamp, *La historiografía indígena de Michoacán: El lienzo de jucutácato y los títulos de Carapan* (Leiden, Netherlands: Research School CNWS, Leiden University, 1998), 12.

29. *Relación de las ceremonias y ritos y población y gobierno de los indios de la provincia de Michoacán (1541)*, edited and annotated by José Tudela, with revisions of Tarascan words by José Corona Núñez (Madrid: Aguilar, 1956).

30. See, for example, Patricia Anawalt, *Indian Clothing before Cortés: Mesoamerican Costumes from the Codices* (Norman: University of Oklahoma Press, 1981), 83–94; and Pollard, "Central Places and Cities in the Core of the Tarascan State," 345–390.

31. Boone, *Stories in Red and Black*, 3–5.

32. Tudela is one of the scholars who denies the existence of pre-Columbian books in the area. José Tudela, "Prólogo," in *Relación de Michoacán (1541)*, edited and annotated by José Tudela, with revisions of Tarascan words by José Corona Núñez, xi (Madrid: Aguilar, 1956). For discussions on preconquest writing systems in Michoacán, see Roskamp, *La historiografía indígena de Michoacán*; Roskamp, "El carari indígena y las láminas de la *Relación de Michoacán*," 235–264; and Juan José Batalla Rosado, "Una aproximación a la iconografía tarasca a través de las ilustraciones de la *Relación de Michoacán*," in Escobar Olmedo, *Relación de Michoacán*, 143–172.

33. "Estas pinturas del códice de El Escorial tienen más relación con el arte infantil que con el arte primitivo, siendo esto lo que les presta su principal encanto. . . .

El estilo de estas pinturas de la *Relación* entra dentro del ámbito infantil, no hecho por los niños precisamente, pero sí por los indios con alma de tales, con los encantos de su pureza visual, sin trucos ni convencionalismos ya formados o heredados, creando los suyos propios." Tudela, "Prólogo," xiv.

34. "[L]o que parece claro, sobre todo a la vista de la propia *Relación de Michoacán*, es que no usaron ningún sistema de escritura." Batalla Rosado, "Una aproximación a la iconografía tarasca," 149.

35. Nora Jiménez, "Indígenas michoacanos y escritura fonética: Tres datos del siglo XVI," *Historias* 60 (2005): 37–41. The belief that the images are straightforward illustrations of the text has been expressed most recently in Claudia Espejel Carbajal's study of the *Relación*. See Espejel Carbajal, "La voz del interprete," 293.

36. Boone, "History and Historians," 28–31.

37. Boone, *Stories in Red and Black*, 31–33. For an analysis of the phonetic contents of Nahuatl writing, see Alfonso Lacadena, "Vowel Length and Glottalization in Nahuatl Hieroglyphic Writing," *Revista Española de Antropología Americana* 38, no. 2 (2008): 121–150.

38. See, for example, AGI, Justicia, Legajo 188, No. 3, Year 1535; Archivo General de la Nación (AGN), Mercedes 2, Exp. 485, fol. 199v, October 27, 1543; AGN, Mercedes 2, Exp. 490; Archivo Histórico de la Ciudad de Pátzcuaro (AHCP), Caja 131, Legajo 4, Exp. 12, fol. 7, Year 1573; AHCP, Caja 131, Legajo 5, Year 1584. For a review of the surviving pictorial documents from colonial Michoacán, see Roskamp, *La historiografía indígena de Michoacán*, 29–78.

39. Even though fifteenth- and sixteenth-century sources discussing the Uanacaze and their enemies, the Mexica, give the impression that they had little to do with each other, these accounts, as Michael Smith points out, are mostly about royal and state activities. As such they reflect the ideology of the ruling elite and are full of propaganda. The archaeological evidence points to merchants crossing imperial borders and people on both sides importing metal and obsidian goods from enemy territories. Featherwork and lacquered vessels from Michoacán were highly valued in Tenochtitlan. Sculptures such as Chac-mools, coyotes, and sacrificial stones at ceremonial centers in Michoacán were also common in other areas of Mesoamerica. See Michael Smith, *The Aztecs* (Cambridge: Blackwell Publishers, 1996), 127; Tricia Gabany-Guerrero, "Deciphering the Symbolic Heritage of the Tarascan Empire: Interpreting the Political Economy of the Pueblo-Hospital of Parangaricutiro, Michoacán" (PhD diss., University at Albany, State University of New York, 1999), 60–75; Dorothy Hosler, *Los sonidos y colores del poder: La tecnología metalúrgica sagrada del occidente de México*, trans. Eduardo Williams et al. (Zinacantepec, Mexico: El Colegio Mexiquense, 2005); Dorothy Hosler and Andrew Macfarlane, "Copper Sources, Metal Production, and Metals Trade in Late Postclassic Mesoamerica," *Science* 273 (1996): 1819–1824; Helen P. Pollard, "Ecological Variation and Economic Exchange in the Tarascan State," *American Ethnologist* 9, no. 2 (1982): 250–268; Pollard, *Taríacuri's Legacy*; Helen P. Pollard, "The Political Economy of Prehispanic Tarascan Metallurgy," *American Antiquity* 52, no. 4 (1987): 741–752; Helen P. Pollard et al., "Las élites, el intercambio de bienes y el surgimiento del área nuclear tarasca,"

in *Estudios cerámicos en el occidente y norte de México*, ed. Eduardo Williams and Phil Weigand, 289–309 (Zamora, Mexico: El Colegio de Michoacán; Morelia, Mexico: Instituto Michoacano de Cultura, 2001); Roskamp, *La historiografía indígena de Michoacán*; and J. Benedict Warren, *The Conquest of Michoacán: The Spanish Domination of the Tarascan Kingdom in Western Mexico, 1521–1530* (Norman: University of Oklahoma Press, 1985), 21.

40. Hans Roskamp, "Las 44 láminas de la *Relación de Michoacán*: Una propuesta de lectura," in Franco Mendoza, *Relación de Michoacán*, 323–691.

41. Stone, *In Place of Gods and Kings*, 74–110.

42. Espejel Carbajal, "Voces, lugares y tiempos," 67–68.

43. AGI, Patronato Real 182, No. 44, Year 1573, "Relación de los pueblos de indios que en aquel año tenían a su cargo los religiosos de San Agustín en Nueva España. Por Juan Adriano, provincial." This document states that Tarascan was spoken in Ucareo, Tiripetío, Tecámbaro, Cuiseo, and Hiurirapundaro; Matlalzinca and Tarascan in Matlalcingo; Tlalzinga in Undameo; and five different languages in Xacona, even though almost everybody there understood Tarascan. I am grateful to Carlos Paredes Martínez from the Centro de Investigaciones y Estudios Superiores en Antropología Social, Michoacán, for providing me with this information.

44. According to Felipe Castro Gutiérrez, Cuanajo in all likelihood had been part of the Curinguaro chiefdom during pre-Columbian times, but during colonial times it became a barrio of Pátzcuaro. Felipe Castro Gutiérrez, *Los tarascos y el imperio español 1600–1740* (Mexico City: Universidad Nacional Autónoma de México; Morelia, Mexico: Universidad Michoacana de San Nicolás de Hidalgo, 2004), 112.

45. See *Relaciones geográficas de la diócesis de Michoacán, 1579–1580*, ed. José Corona Núñez, vol. 2 (Guadalajara, Mexico: Colección Siglo XVI, 1958). According to the *Relación geográfica* from Cuseo, Matlatzinga people lived near Cuseo as a subject town to this Tarascan town (2:48); the *Relación geográfica* from Acámbaro also tells us that people who spoke Chichimec, Otomí, Mazagua, and Tarascan lived within its confines (2:57). The *Relaciones geográficas* of Tuxpa (2:86), Tamazula (2:100), Jiquilpan (1:9), and Zapotlan (2:93) mention that three different languages were spoken in the first three towns, and five in Zapotlan. Mexican/Nahuatl was the lingua franca of all four towns. The *Relaciones geográficas* of Taymeo and Necotlan mention that these towns were Otomí settlements (1:38, 42). See also Hans Roskamp, *Los códices de Cutzio y Huetamo: Encomienda y tributo en la tierra caliente de Michoacán, siglo XVI* (Zamora, Mexico: El Colegio de Michoacán; Zinacantepec, Mexico: El Colegio Mexiquense, 2003).

46. For example, a nobleman by the Nahuatl name of Axayacatl was cacique of the town of Xirosto when the Spaniards first arrived in the area. Among the sculptors we find Pablo Coyote, official of Pátzcuaro, who testified he had been a lapidary of the lord of Ihuatzio during pre-Columbian times. Francisco Quezpal was a Nahuatl interpreter whose task was to send youth to the convent at Tzintzuntzan to be indoctrinated; he testified against the Spanish official Pedro de Arellano. Gabany-Guerrero, "Deciphering the Symbolic Heritage of the Tarascan Empire," 113; Delfina López Sarrelangue, *La nobleza indígena de Pátzcuaro en la época virreinal*

(Morelia, Mexico: Morevallado Editores, 1999), 165; AHCP, Caja 1, Exp. 31, fol. 8, 1556 (I thank Carlos Paredes Martínez for lending me a transcription of this document); and "El Fiscal con don Pedro de Arellano estante en esta corte sobre cierta acusación que contra él le puso," AGI, Justicia, Legajo 187, No. 1, Ramo 2, published in *El Michoacán antiguo*, ed. Brigitte Boehm de Lameiras, 375 (Zamora, Mexico: El Colegio de Michoacán; Morelia: Gobierno del Estado de Michoacán, 1994).

47. The Nahua groups in Tzintzuntzan seem to have been especially powerful and economically solvent. The *Relación* mentions they lived in the area before the arrival of the Spaniards, and it is also possible that their numbers increased as they came into the area as allies of the Spanish forces. Don Domingo, a Nahua nobleman, argued in 1540 that he had paid for the organ of the convent of Tzintzuntzan—not a low-priced item—and refused to let it be moved to Pátzcuaro, where the Uanacaze and Spanish authorities were moving (AGI, Justicia, Legajo 157, No. 1, Pieza 2). When the Uanacaze heir, Don Antonio Huitzimengari, raised tribute contributions, the Nahua group in Tzintzuntzan refused to pay (AGI, Justicia, Legajo 96; AGI, Justicia, Legajo 278, Nos. 1 and 2). The tensions between Don Antonio and the Nahua people of Tzintzuntzan became such that one of his envoys was attacked when carrying one of his decrees to the town of Taximaroa (AHCP, Caja 2, Exp. 6). Huitzimengari dealt with the challenges by establishing allegiances through polygamy (in this way continuing pre-Columbian practices). In 1540, he fathered a child out of wedlock with Doña Ana Ocelo, niece of Don Antonio Jimenez Acatli, who was councilman of the Nahua population of Pátzcuaro. AGN, Ramo Indios 5, Exp. 802, fol. 213v, 1591, published in *"Y por mi visto . . ."*: *Mandamientos, ordenanzas, licencias y otras disposiciones virreinales del siglo XVI*, ed. Carlos Paredes Martínez et al., 369 (Mexico City: Centro de Investigaciones y Estudios Superiores en Antropología Social; Morelia, Mexico: Universidad Michoacana de San Nicolás de Hidalgo, 1994). See also López Sarrelangue, *La nobleza indígena de Pátzcuaro*, 210–215.

48. Rafael Diego Fernández, *Antonio de Mendoza*, Colección Grandes Protagonistas de la Historia Mexicana (Barcelona: Cayfosa-Quebecor, 2002), 123.

49. See, for example, AHCP, Caja 131, Legajo 3, Exp. 1.

50. Fintan [J. Benedict] Warren, *Vasco de Quiroga and His Pueblo-Hospitales of Santa Fe* (Washington, DC: Academy of American Franciscan History, 1963), 99; and J. Benedict Warren, "Fray Jerónimo de Alcalá, autor de la *Relación de Michoacán*," in *Estudios sobre el Michoacán colonial: Los inicios* (Morelia, Mexico: Universidad Michoacana de San Nicolás de Hidalgo and Fimax Publicistas, 2005), 157. This is corroborated by the fact that the *Relación* mentions the building of the house of Governor Don Pedro Cuiniarangari and the fountain of Bishop Vasco de Quiroga, which according to colonial records came under construction after January 1540. AGI, Justicia, Legajo 130, fols. 20r–21r.

51. AGI, Justicia, Legajo 130, fol. 30r. See also Warren, *Vasco de Quiroga and His Pueblo-Hospitales*, 90–91; J. Benedict Warren, "Vasco de Quiroga y la fundación de Pátzcuaro colonial," in *Estudios sobre el Michoacán colonial: Los inicios* (Morelia,

Mexico: Universidad Michoacana de San Nicolás de Hidalgo and Fimax Publicistas, 2005), 79–94.

52. See, for example, "El presidente de la Real Audiencia Nuño de Guzmán y los oydores Ortiz y Delgadillo ... el 14 de mayo de 1529," AGI, Justicia, Legajo 188, No. 3; and AGI, Justicia, Legajo 130.

53. Ethelia Ruiz Medrano, *Gobierno y sociedad en Nueva España: Segunda Audiencia y Antonio de Mendoza* (Zamora, Mexico: El Colegio de Michoacán; Morelia, Mexico: Gobierno del Estado de Michoacán, 1991), 53.

54. France Scholes and Eleanor Adams, *Proceso contra Tzintzicha Tangaxoan, el Caltzontzin, formado por Nuño de Guzmán, año de 1530* (Mexico City: Porrúa y Obregón, 1952); and Warren, *Conquest of Michoacán*, 211–236.

CHAPTER 1

1. For readings of this image, see Roskamp, "Las 44 láminas de la *Relación de Michoacán*," 323–325; Stone, *In Place of Gods and Kings*, 61–62, 117; and Rodrigo Martínez Baracs, *Convivencia y utopía: El gobierno indio y español de la "Ciudad de Mechuacan," 1521–1580* (Mexico City: Instituto Nacional de Antropología e Historia and Fondo de Cultura Económica, 2005), 297–305.

2. Sometime after the manuscript had been bound in its present form, somebody wrote Sahagún down as the possible author opposite the frontispiece on the back of a blank page. For the identification of the friar as Maturino Gilberti, see Tudela, "Prologo." For a review of the literature on the identity of the friar, see Stone, *In Place of Gods and Kings*, 43–73.

3. J. Benedict Warren first published his work about the friar in 1971 under the title "Fray Jerónimo de Alcalá: Author of the *Relación de Michoacán*?" He has most recently republished the work in Spanish, with some changes, "Fray Jerónimo de Alcalá, autor de la *Relación de Michoacán*," in Franco Mendoza, *Relación de Michoacán* (2000); and "Fray Jerónimo de Alcalá, autor de la *Relación de Michoacán*," in *Estudios sobre el Michoacán colonial: Los inicios* (Morelia, Mexico: Fimax Publicistas, 2005), 155–186. In the 2000 edition of his essay, Warren brought to light a document from the Archivo Histórico de la Ciudad de Pátzcuaro (AHCP, Protocolos 103, fol. 371r) in which in 1576, Diego Hurtado testified that Jerónimo de Alcalá "wrote the antiquities of this province [of Michoacán]" (escribió la antigüedad de esta provincia). I thank Carlos Paredes Martínez for giving me a copy of a transcription of this document.

4. Warren, "Fray Jerónimo de Alcalá" (2000), 40–44. For an analysis of Alcalá and his ethnographic work, see León-Portilla, "Jerónimo de Alcalá y los primeros frailes etnógrafos en Mesoamérica," 57–78.

5. See also Stone, *In Place of Gods and Kings*, 25–42.

6. Diego Fernández, *Antonio de Mendoza*, 72, 104, 129. Michoacán's economic resources in particular were central to his interests. Don Antonio financed many ex-

peditions that departed from the Puerto de la Navidad, a port in Colima, just west of Michoacán, and many of the supplies for these had to come from Michoacán.

7. Francisco J. Escudero Buendía, *Antonio de Mendoza: Comendador de la villa de Socuéllamos y primer virrey de la Nueva España* (Pedro Muñoz, Spain: Perea, 2003), 43–60.

8. Diego Fernández, *Antonio de Mendoza*, 20–22; and Guillermo Tovar de Teresa, "La utopía del virrey de Mendoza," in *La utopía mexicana del siglo XVI: Lo bello, lo verdadero y lo bueno*, ed. Guillermo Tovar de Teresa, Miguel León-Portilla, and Silvio Zavala, 27 (Mexico City: Grupo Azabache, 1992).

9. Stone, *In Place of Gods and Kings*, 48.

10. The historian James Krippner-Martínez points out that Nuño de Guzmán had well-known disputes with almost the entire Franciscan Order, including the first bishop, Juan de Zumárraga. Krippner-Martínez, *Rereading the Conquest*, 14, 56–58.

11. For a suggestion about how the friar may have collected the information and produced the *Relación*, see Stone, *In Place of Gods and Kings*, 16–42.

12. "[E]ste papa, todas las guerras y hechos atribuía a su dios *Curicaueri* que lo hazía, y no va contando más de los Señores." Escobar Olmedo, *Relación de Michoacán*, 367. All direct quotes from the *Relación* in this book come from Escobar Olmedo's edition, unless otherwise noted. Here, as in all quotes in this book, I have kept the spelling and punctuation given in the edition used.

13. Mary Ann Hedberg, "Conflicts and Continuities: Chapters in the History of Tuzuntla, a Town in Colonial Mexico" (PhD diss., University of Minnesota, 1994), 46.

14. Don Pedro had donated lands to the first bishop of Michoacán, Vasco de Quiroga, for his pueblo-hospital project in Santa Fe de la Laguna.

15. AGI, Justicia, Legajo 130, fols. 686r–807v.

16. René Becerril Patlán and Igor Cerda Farías, "Recatón, casquillo y dardo: La lanza del petámuti y los nuncios sinodales cristianos," in *Catálogo de documentos históricos coloniales de Michoacán. Expedientes microfilmados y reproducidos* (Morelia, Mexico: Universidad Michoacana de San Nicolás de Hidalgo, 2005), 147–153.

17. Scholes and Adams, *Proceso contra Tzintzicha Tangaxoan, el Caltzontzin, formado por Nuño de Guzmán, año de 1530* (Mexico City: Porrúa y Obregón, 1952). For a summary of this trial, see Warren, *Conquest of Michoacán*, 211–236; and Martínez Baracs, *Convivencia y utopía*, 151–157. In Don Pedro's defense, Stone has pointed out that his testimony was obtained under torture. Nevertheless, of all the indigenous witnesses questioned under torture in the trial, Don Pedro's testimony was the most incriminating. Stone, *In Place of Gods and Kings*, 154–187.

18. Over the course of the first twenty years of colonization, Spanish officials would struggle to determine who should become the indigenous governor and what kind of jurisdiction or benefits would be attached to his or her post. Even the viceroy would acknowledge to his own successor the confusion about how the person in this post should be chosen, whether by inheritance, election, or appointment. Diego Fernández, *Antonio de Mendoza*, 125.

19. In 1532, Don Pedro declared himself to be thirty-eight years old (AGI, Justicia 229). By the time the *Relación* was compiled (1539–1541), he would have been between forty-five and forty-seven years old. However, in 1539, Don Pedro claimed he was forty years old (AGI, Justicia, Legajo 187, No. 1, Ramo 2, Segunda Parte). Even while the Uanacaze ruler was still alive, Spaniards often perceived Don Pedro as having a key role in the region. See Warren, *Conquest of Michoacán*, 240.

20. AGI, Justicia 229, fol. 5v.

21. AGI, Justicia, Legajo 130, fol. 477r.

22. Nuño de Guzmán, *Memoria de los servicios que había hecho Nuño de Guzmán, desde que fue nombrado gobernador de Panuco en 1525*, ed. Manuel Carrera Stampa, 32–33 (Mexico City: José Porrúa e Hijos, 1955).

23. See, for example, Krippner-Martínez, "Politics of Conquest," 188.

24. AGN, Mercedes, Vol. 1, Exp. 33, fol. 18.

25. Ibid.

26. AGN, Mercedes, Vol. 2, Exp. 490.

27. According to bishop and Franciscan friar Juan de Zumárraga, indigenous children were not educated at the convents but in houses attached to them: "[C]ada convento de los nuestros tiene otra casa junto para enseñar a los niños, donde hay escuela, dormitorios, refectorio y una devota capilla." From "Carta de Zumárraga al capítulo general de Tolosa . . . ," cited in Miguel León-Portilla, "Fray Juan de Zumárraga y las lenguas indígenas en México," in *La utopía mexicana del siglo XVI: Lo bello, lo verdadero y lo bueno*, ed. Guillermo Tovar de Teresa, Miguel León-Portilla, and Silvio Zavala, Colección Arte Novohispano, 53–54 (Mexico City: Grupo Azabache, 1992).

28. For the information on Don Francisco, see AGN, Mercedes, Vol. 1, Exp. 33. I am grateful to René Becerril Patlán at the Ex-Convento de Tiripetío for sharing his unpublished transcription of this document with me.

29. The Augustinian Matías de Escobar would write in the eighteenth century that Don Antonio had studied at the Augustinian Colegio de Estudios Mayores de Tiripetío. In addition, an eighteenth-century painting shows Don Antonio being schooled by Augustinians. These late sources reveal an interest on the part of Augustinians to link themselves to the indigenous nobility and claim him as one of their own. However, no sixteenth-century document found to date corroborates that Don Antonio studied and lived in Tiripetío, as Fray Matías mentions. Nevertheless, modern-day scholars have continued to make that claim. Instead, in the 1546–1547 *Residencia* (a document attesting to and justifying a person's actions) of Viceroy Mendoza, twenty-one witnesses mention that Don Antonio was educated at the Colegio in Pátzcuaro. In his account, Juan de Alvarado specifies that Don Antonio used to pay extended visits to the convent in Tiripetío; perhaps this led to later pro-Augustinian interpretations that Don Antonio went to school there instead of in Pátzcuaro. Matías de Escobar, *Americana Thebaida* (Morelia, Mexico: Balsal Editores, 1970), 121–126; Delfina Esmeralda López Sarrelangue, *La nobleza indígena de Pátzcuaro* (Mexico City: Universidad Nacional Autónoma de México, Instituto de Investigaciones Históricas, 1965), 173–174; José Corona Núñez, "Anto-

nio Uitziméngari, primer humanista tarasco," in *Humanistas novohispanos de Michoacán* (Morelia, Mexico: Universidad Michoacana de San Nicolás de Hidalgo, 1982), 50–52; and AGI, Justicia, Legajo 263, Pieza 3.

30. Warren, "Fray Jerónimo de Alcalá" (2005), 156.

31. For a discussion of some of the Nahuatl terminology in the *Relación*, see Stone, *In Place of Gods and Kings*, 27–30.

32. Rodrigo Martínez Baracs has identified two other governors before 1540 based on Pablo Beaumount's *Crónica de la provincia de los santos apóstoles San Pedro y San Pablo de Michoacán* (Morelia, Mexico: Balsal Editores, 1969), but this document dates to the end of the eighteenth century and no other documents from the sixteenth century found to date seem to corroborate this information. Martínez Baracs, *Convivencia y utopía*, 258–259.

33. Scholes and Adams, *Proceso contra Tzintzicha Tangaxoan*, 61–63.

34. Ibid., 54.

35. AGI, Justicia, Legajo 130, fols. 571v–574r, 614r.

36. AGI, Justicia, Legajo 187, No. 1, Ramo 2.

37. Ibid.

38. This physical analysis comes from personal observation of the surviving pages as well as from Stone's study of the manuscript. See Stone, *In Place of Gods and Kings*, 25–42.

39. For a study of some of the corrections the friar made to the text, see ibid., 62–73.

40. Perla Valle, "Códices coloniales: Memorias en imágenes de los pueblos indios," *Arqueología Mexicana* 7, no. 38 (1999): 9; Michael Coe and Justin Kerr, *The Art of the Maya Scribe* (New York: Harry N. Abrams, 1998), 160, 173; and Eloise Quiñones Keber, "An Introduction to the Images, Artists, and Physical Features of the *Primeros memoriales*," in *Primeros memoriales by Fray Bernardino de Sahagún*, edited by H. B. Nicholson et al., 34 (Norman: University of Oklahoma Press, 1997).

41. *Popol Vuh: The Mayan Book of the Dawn of Life*, trans. Dennis Tedlock (New York: Simon and Schuster, 1996), 25; Coe and Kerr, *Art of the Maya Scribe*, 25, 36, 89–110; Jeanette F. Peterson, "The *Florentine Codex* Imagery and the Colonial Tlacuilo," in *The Work of Bernardino de Sahagún, Pioneer Ethnographer of Sixteenth-Century Aztec Mexico*, ed. J. Jorge Klor de Alva, H. B. Nicholson, and E. Quiñones Keber, 285 (Albany: Institute for Mesoamerican Studies, University at Albany, State University of New York, 1988); and Gruzinski, *Painting the Conquest*, 14.

42. AGN, Mercedes, Vol. 4, November 18, 1555, fol. 264; AHCP, Caja 10, Carpeta 8, 1633; AHCP, Caja 131, Legajo 6, Exp. 11, fol. 4. See also María Concepción Castro Gómez, "Arte popular indígena colonial en Michoacán" (undergraduate thesis, Universidad Nacional Autónoma de México, 1984), 87.

43. *Relaciones geográficas*, 2:115. See also Castro Gutiérrez, *Los tarascos y el imperio español*, 44–45.

44. Castro Gutiérrez, *Los tarascos y el imperio español*, 220. See also AGN, Mercedes, Vol. 4, November 18, 1555, fol. 264, in which Viceroy Luís de Velasco sought

to limit to four the number of painters and scribes at the convent of Ucareo because he thought the system whereby painters and scribes were excused from performing mandatory labor was being abused.

45. In P'urhépecha documents of 1564 from Tuzantla, Michoacán, the only office to be referred to in P'urhépecha is the office of *carari*, in this instance used as "scribe." All other offices (i.e., *gobernador*, *alcalde*, etc.) appear by their Spanish titles at the bottom of the documents together with the signatures, but in the document they are referred as *achaecha* (lords). Hedberg, "Conflicts and Continuities," 126–130.

46. Castro Gutiérrez, *Los tarascos y el imperio español*, 128.

47. For example, Don Juan de la Cerda, a nobleman, scribe, and translator in Pátzcuaro, was also named judge-governor of Tancítaro in 1581; Francisco de la Cerda was scribe in 1588, interpreter and judge-governor of Taximaroa in 1593, and mayor of Pátzcuaro in 1606; and Diego Tzitziqui, a principal from Ajuno, a town subject to Pátzcuaro, was elected mayor and scribe in 1590. María de Lourdes Kuthy-Saenger, "Strategies of Survival, Accommodation and Innovation: The Tarascan Indigenous Elite in Sixteenth Century Michoacan" (PhD diss., Michigan State University, 1996), 155, 159, 184.

48. Don Antonio Huitzimengari was a royal scribe, and his son Don Pedro Pablo Huitzimengari was a scribe and translator, as was Don Antonio's grandson, Alonso de Cáceres. Nicolás León, "Testimonio de mercedes y tierras concedidas a la frontera de Guachichil, y el pueblo de San Francisco de Penjamo," in *Anales del Museo michoacano*, ed. Edmundo Aviña Levy (Guadalajara, Mexico: Biblioteca de Facsímiles Mexicanos, 1968), 251–255; José Bravo Ugarte, "*La Relación de Michoacán*," *Historia Mexicana* 12, no. 45 (1962): 22; and López Sarrelangue, *La nobleza indígena de Pátzcuaro*, 222–224.

49. Don Juan de Arrue was the son of Martha Cazonci (daughter of Zinzicha Tangaxuan). He was born in the province of Ávalos. López Sarrelangue, *La nobleza indígena de Pátzcuaro*, 201.

50. In 1555, Viceroy Luis de Velasco would grant the right to have a small horse to both Lorenzo and Francisco, *principales* of the painters of the City of Michoacán, a privilege generally reserved for the indigenous nobility. AGN, Mercedes, Vol. 4, December 3, 1555, fols. 291v, 292.

51. AGI, Justicia 96, July 5, 1547, fols. 64r–65r.

52. See AGN, Mercedes, Vol. 4, Exp. 257, Exp. 186.

53. AGI, Justicia, Legajo 278, Nos. 1–2.

54. AGN, Ramo Indios, Vol. 4, Exp. 856, fols. 221v–222r, published in *"Y por mi visto . . ."*

55. See, for example, AGI, Justicia, Legajo 188, No. 3, May 14, 1529; and AHCP, Caja 131, Legajo 4, Exp. 12, Year 1573.

56. AHCP, Caja 4, Exp. 55.

57. Ibid., fol. 7v.

58. Ibid., fols. 3v–4r.

59. AHCP, Caja 10, Carpeta 8, fols. 860–863.

60. Tudela, "Prólogo," xiv; Batalla Rosado, "Una aproximación a la iconografía tarasca," 159–160.

61. Nuria Salazar Simarro, "Relación de las ceremonias y ritos y población y gobierno de los Indios de la provincia de Michoacán," in *Los siglos de oro en los virreinatos de América 1550–1700*, ed. Sociedad Estatal para la Conmemoración de los Centenarios de Felipe II y Carlos V, 210 (Madrid: Brizzolis, 1999); and Espejel Carbajal, *La justicia y el fuego*, 1:76–82.

62. Espejel Carbajal, "Voces, lugares y tiempos," 67–68; and Espejel Carbajal, *La justicia y el fuego*, 1:292–293.

63. See, for example, Sandro Botticelli's *The Annunciation*, 1489–1490, and Raphael's *The Miraculous Draught of Fish*, 1515.

64. For a review of Renaissance painting techniques, see Erwin Panofsky, "Painting in Italy and the Lowlands during the Fifteenth Century," in *Readings in Art History*, ed. Harold Spencer, 25–34 (New York: Scribner, 1969).

65. Robertson, *Mexican Manuscript Painting*, 12–24; and Donald Robertson, "Tulum Murals: The International Style of the Late Post-Classic," in *Proceedings of the 38th International Congress of Americanists (Stuttgart and Munich, 1968)*, 77–88 (Munich: Kommissionverlag K. Renner, 1970). This style has also been referred to as the Mixteca-Puebla style, first proposed by George C. Vaillant and later refined by H. B. Nicholson. For a review of the literature, contributions, and tensions between Robertson and Nicholson, see Pablo Escalante Gonzalbo, "The Mixteca-Puebla Tradition and H. B. Nicholson," in *Fanning the Sacred Flame: Mesoamerican Studies in Honor of H. B. Nicholson*, ed. Matthew A. Boxt and Brian Dervin Dillon, 293–307 (Boulder: University Press of Colorado, 2012).

66. Robertson, *Mexican Manuscript Painting*, 12–24.

67. See, for example, Ellen Baird, *The Drawings of Sahagún's* Primeros memoriales*: Structure and Style* (Norman: University of Oklahoma Press, 1993), 21–29; Boone, *Stories in Red and Black*, 28–44; Douglas, *In the Palace of Nezahualcoyotl*, 26–35; and Karl Taube, "At Dawn's Edge: Tulúm, Santa Rita, and Floral Symbolism in the International Style of Late Postclassic Mesoamerica," in *Astronomers, Scribes, and Priests: Intellectual Interchange between the Northern Maya Lowlands and Highland Mexico in the Late Postclassic Period*, ed. Gabrielle Vail and Christine Hernández, 145–191 (Washington, DC: Dumbarton Oaks, 2010).

68. Elizabeth H. Boone and Michael E. Smith, "Postclassic International Styles and Symbol Sets," in *The Postclassic Mesoamerican World*, ed. Michael E. Smith and Frances F. Berdan, 186–193 (Salt Lake City: University of Utah Press, 2003).

69. Douglas, *In the Palace of Nezahualcoyotl*, 34.

70. For examples of European presentation scenes, see Espejel Carbajal, "Voces, lugares y tiempos," 79.

71. The viceroy in the frontispiece originally was depicted with only a left leg, but artist 1 later added the right leg and foot.

72. Pedro Marquéz Joaquín defines Yzí Parámuco as "charco de agua en la orilla o en la entrada." Pedro Márquez Joaquín, "El significado de las palabras p'urhépecha

en la *Relación de Michoacán*: Glosario de voces p'urhépecha," in *Relación de las ceri-monias y rictos y población y gobernación de los indios de la provincia de Michoacán*, ed. Moisés Franco Mendoza, 725 (Zamora, Mexico: Colegio de Michoacán; Morelia, Mexico: Gobierno del Estado de Michoacán, 2000).

73. Even though artist 3 knew the pre-Columbian way of representing vegetation (i.e., including its roots), as seen in figures 18 and 49 of part 3 of the *Relación*, in part 2 he represents it that way only when it is important to the story. For example, in figure 45, the tree represented in the image and mentioned in the text is an oak, which served as a conduit of communication with the gods. For examples of pre-Columbian depictions of trees, see *The* Codex Nuttall*: A Picture Manuscript from Ancient Mexico*, ed. Zelia Nuttall (New York: Dover Publications, 1975), 71.

74. Espejel Carbajal, "Voces, lugares y tiempos," 83. She also compares the illustration on page 192 of the *Leyenda dorada* to figure 56 in this book. Although interesting, it seems more loosely based.

75. I thank Benjamin Lucas for this information. Pers. comm., December 2006. The use of European iconography by indigenous artists during the colonial period was widespread. For an introduction to the different meanings and functions this iconography could take at the hands of indigenous artists, see T. Cummins, "The Madonna and the Horse," 52–83.

76. James Lockhart, *The Nahuas after the Conquest: A Social and Cultural History of the Indians of Central Mexico, Sixteenth through Eighteenth Centuries* (Stanford, CA: Stanford University Press, 1992), 326–373; and Boone, *Stories in Red and Black*, 28–44.

77. Even Tudela, who tries to find direct correlations between the elements represented in the *Relación* and Michoacán's material culture, recognizes that they cannot be taken at face value and that the pyramids in the *Relación* more closely resemble pyramids in other areas of Mexico, such as those of the Maya, Mixtec-Zapotec, Totonac, and Aztec, than those in Michoacán. Tudela, "Prologo," xi.

78. We do not know today what the temples on top looked like.

79. See, for example, *The* Codex Mendoza, ed. Frances Berdan and Patricia Anawalt (Berkeley: University of California Press, 1992), 3:14.

80. Seler, "Los antiguos habitantes de Michoacán," 201. See also *Diccionario grande de la lengua de Michoacán*, ed. J. Benedict Warren (Morelia, Mexico: Fimax Publicistas, 1991), 2:293.

81. Alfonso Caso, "Comentario al Códice Baranda," *Miscellanea Paul Rivet, octogenario dicata* 1 (1958): 373–389.

82. "Advertir y considerar." *Diccionario Grande*, 2:465.

83. Patrick Johansson, "*Tira de la peregrinación* (*Códice Boturini*): Análisis de láminas, paleografía y traducción de textos en náhuatl," in "Edición especial: Códices," *Arqueología Mexicana* 26 (2008): 21.

84. Batalla Rosado, "Una aproximación a la iconografía tarasca," 153–154.

85. Federico Navarrete has pointed out that representations of footprints in other sixteenth-century manuscripts have a long history in Mesoamerican visual culture, from the Olmecs at La Venta to the Tetitla murals of Teotihuacan in cen-

tral Mexico, and should be understood as metonyms representing movement and migrations rather than as natural representations. Federico Navarrete, "The Path from Aztlan to Mexico: On Visual Narration in Mesoamerican Codices," *Res* 37 (2000): 37.

86. *Diccionario grande*, 2:35, 1:56. Benjamín Lucas, pers. comm., December 2006.

87. "[Y] tú pisaríes, por la parte la tierra, y por la otra parte el agua, y nosotros tanbién, por una parte pisaremos el agua, y por la otra la tierra." Escobar Olmedo, *Relación de Michoacán*, pt. 2, chap. 5, p. 381.

88. See, for example, AGI, Audiencia de México, Legajo 68, Ramo 3, No. 11, 2–4, fol. 1r; and AGI, Audiencia de México, Legajo 96. See also Ethelia Ruiz Medrano, "Códices y justicia: Los caminos de la dominación," *Arqueología Mexicana* 7, no. 38 (1999): 44–50.

89. Diego Fernández, *Antonio de Mendoza*, 122. See also Robertson, *Mexican Manuscript Painting*, 50–51. Although Robertson maintains that no such journal survives, AGI, Audiencia de México, Legajo 96, shows such an example.

90. Jeannette F. Peterson, "Synthesis and Survival: The Native Presence in Sixteenth-Century Murals of New Spain," in *Native Artists and Patrons in Colonial Latin America*, ed. Emily Umberger and Tom Cummins, *Phoebus: A Journal of Art History* 7, Arizona State University (1995): 14–35.

91. See, for example, the description of Juan Infante walking over his newly acquired encomienda in order to take possession of it, in Warren, *Vasco de Quiroga and His Pueblo-Hospitales of Santa Fe*, 92. For Nahuatl foundation rituals, see María Elena Bernal García and Ángel Július García Zambrano, "El Altepetl colonial y sus antecedents prehispánicos: Contexto teórico-historiográfico," in *Territorialidad y paisaje en el Altepetl del siglo XVI*, ed. Federico Fernández Christlieb and Ángel García Zambrano, 57–67 (Mexico City: Universidad Nacional Autónoma de México and Fondo de Cultura Económica, 2006).

92. The *Tira de la peregrinación*, for example, includes a broken tree to indicate the split of allies. Patrick Johansson, "*Tira de la peregrinación*," 29.

93. For the meaning of caves among Texcocan manuscripts, see Boone, *Stories in Red and Black*, 187.

94. Helen Nader, "The Mendoza in the Fifteenth-Century Renaissance," in *The Mendoza Family in the Spanish Renaissance 1350–1550*, 77 (New Brunswick, NJ: Rutgers University Press, 1979); and Gruzinski, *Painting the Conquest*, 156.

CHAPTER 2

The original idea for this chapter arose during the seminar "Body Matters," cotaught by Cecelia F. Klein and Charlene Villaseñor Black at the University of California, Los Angeles, in the winter and spring of 2003. A portion of this chapter was presented at the Association for Latin American Art "Open Session for Emerging Scholars," College Art Association 94th annual conference, Boston, February 22–25, 2006.

1. Foucault, *A History of Sexuality*, 1:86–87.

2. Francisco Tomás y Valiente, "El derecho penal de la monarquía absoluta (siglos XVI, XVII y XVII)," in *Obras completas* (Madrid: Centro de Estudios Políticos y Constitucionales, 1997), 201–246; Javier Barrientos Grandon, *La cultura jurídica en la Nueva España* (Mexico City: Universidad Nacional Autónoma de México, 1993), 11–21; and Espejel Carbajal, "La voz del interprete," 250n41.

3. Douglas, *In the Palace of Nezahualcoyotl*, 150–159.

4. "Síguese la historia, cómo fueron Señores el Caçonçi y sus antepasados en esta Provincia de Mechuacan y de la justicia general que se hazía." Escobar Olmedo, *Relación de Michoacán*, 503–508. All citations from the *Relación de Michoacán* in this chapter refer to Armando Escobar Olmedo's 2001 edition, unless otherwise noted.

5. For the act of smoking as marker of nobility, see Seler, "Los antiguos habitantes de Michoacán."

6. One could, however, as easily argue for the relevance of this ceremony to part 3 of the *Relación de Michoacán*, "Of the Government These People Had among Themselves," which deals with the administration of justice by the main ruler, the subject of the third image discussed in this chapter. For José Tudela's commentary, see *Relación de Michoacán*, 11n1, 14n5.

7. *Diccionario grande*, 1:424.

8. I am grateful to Benjamín Lucas for the many hours we spent together going over these definitions in December 2006. This chapter has benefited from his wealth of knowledge and his infinite patience in helping me translate these terms.

9. According to Benjamín Lucas, the literal translation of *justicia himbo curanditahpeni* is "hacerse obedecer con justicia." Pers. comm., December 2006. Other related terms include *justicia hacer* (to do justice), which the *Diccionario grande* (1:424) translates as "cez atsipeni justicia" and "niyatatspeni justicia," literally meaning "to do justice well" and "to grant justice," respectively (Alicia Mateo, pers. comm., July 2008).

10. "Curandini: entender lenguaje" and "curandini: ser de vida pacífica, no hazer mal a nadie." Maturino Gilberti, *Vocabulario en lengua de Mechuacán*, ed. Agustín Jacinto Zavala, Clotilde Martínez, and J. Benedict Warren (Zamora, Mexico: Colegio de Michoacán; Mexico City: Fideicomiso Teixidor, 1997), 73. In addition, modern-day speakers define *curandini* as *ser obediente* (to be obedient) (Alicia Mateo, pers. comm., July 2008).

11. *Diccionario grande*, 2:114, 1:592.

12. According to Francisco Hurtado Mendoza, the word *petamuti* derives from the verb *petamoni* (to pronounce), plus the agentive suffix *-ti*. Thus, Hurtado Mendoza translates *petamuti* as "the one who pronounces/speaks, dictates or determines with authority." José Corona Núñez translates it as "announcer," and Pedro Márquez Joaquín reads it as "the one who utters or pronounces words." See Francisco Hurtado Mendoza, *La religión prehispánica de los purhépechas: Un testimonio del pueblo tarasco* (Morelia, Mexico: Linotipográfica "Omega," 1986), 104; Tudela, *Relación de Michoacán*, 13n2; and Márquez Joaquín, "El significado de las palabras p'urhépecha en la *Relación de Michoacán*", 714.

13. Castro Gutiérrez, *Los tarascos y el imperio español*, 126.

14. Francisco Cervantes de Salazar, "Crónica de la Nueva España," MS 2011, Biblioteca Nacional de Madrid, chap. 25. Microfilm copy viewed at the Ex-Convento de Tiripetío. According to Francisco Cervantes de Salazar, these "brave men" became *alguaciles* (constables) during the colonial period.

15. Pierre Bourdieu, *Distinction: A Social Critique of the Judgment of Taste*, trans. Richard Nice (Cambridge, MA: Harvard University Press, 1979), 3.

16. This would not be the only time the contributors of the *Relación* would try to equate pre-Columbian and European practices. The historian Claudia Espejel Carbajal has shown that in its discussions of pre-Columbian political posts, part 3 contains much of the same language used in Alfonso X's *Siete Partidas*. Espejel Carbajal, "La voz del interprete," 237–259.

17. Roland Barthes, "Rhetoric of the Image," in *Image, Music, Text*, trans. Stephen Heath (New York: Hill and Wang, 1977), 37–41.

18. For the adaptation of the *Siete Partidas* to the colonies and the implementation of the Spanish judicial system in New Spain, see Woodrow Borah, *Justice by Insurance: The General Indian Court of Colonial Mexico and the Legal Aides of the Half-Real* (Berkeley: University of California Press, 1983), 6–78; Barrientos Grandon, *La cultura jurídica en la Nueva España*, 29–30; Ethelia Ruiz Medrano and Perla Valle, "Los colores de la justicia, códices jurídicios del siglo XVI en la Bibliothèque nationale de France," *Journal de la Société des Américanistes de Paris* 84, no. 2 (1998): 227–241; and Ruiz Medrano, "Códices y justicia," 44–50. For the similarities between the crimes prosecuted in the *Relación* and those in *Siete Partidas*, see Espejel Carbajal, "La voz del interprete," 250–251.

19. Louise Mirrer, "The 'Unfaithful Wife' in Medieval Spanish Literature and Law," in *Medieval Crime and Social Control*, ed. Barbara A. Hanawalt and David Wallace, 143–155 (Minneapolis: University of Minnesota Press, 1999).

20. For the punishment of sorcery and adultery, see Alfonso X, "Partida 7," in *Las Siete Partidas del Rey Don Alfonso el Sabio*, 568–569, 667–668, 647–658 (Madrid: Imprenta Real, 1807).

21. As early as 1536 Bishop Juan de Zumarraga began to prosecute indigenous people accused of adultery and sorcery. For the punishment of sorcery in Michoacán, see also Érika Jiménez Martínez, "Sobre una sentencia de 200 azotes, 100 en Michoacán y 100 en México, a un indio de Michoacán que decía era Dios y venía del cielo y además afirmaba que era el ánima del Caltzontzin, 1536," *Boletín del Archivo General de la Nación* 12, 6ª época (2006): 15.

22. See, for example, AHCP, Caja 2 bis, Exp. 82, Year 1569, fols. 670–672; AHCP, Caja 3 bis, Exp. 54, Year 1578; AHCP, Caja 4, Exp. 33, Year 1587; AHCP, Caja 4, Exp. 39, Year 1588; AHCP, Caja 4, Exp. 55; AHCP, Caja 5 bis, Exp. 73, fols. 1–6; AHCP, Caja 131, Legajo 4, Exp. 21, Year 1578; AHCP, Caja 3, Exp. 78 (cited in Rodrigo Martínez Baracs and Lydia Espinosa Morales, *La vida michoacana en el siglo XVI: Catálogo de los documentos del siglo XVI del archivo histórico de la ciudad de Pátzcuaro*, Serie Fuentes [Mexico City: Instituto Nacional de Antropología e Historia, 1999], 138); AGN, Ramo Indios 2, Exp. 727, fol. 166r, in *"Y por mi visto*

. . . ," 214–215; "Ordenanzas reales sobre los indios (Las leyes de 1512–1513)," in *Anuario de Estudios Americanos* 13, no. 9 (1956): 434; "Ordenanza para el gobierno de Indios, 1546," *Boletín del Archivo General de la Nación* 11, no. 2 (1940): 185–186; and Zeb Tortorici, "'Heran todos putos': Sodomitical Subcultures and Disordered Desire in Early Colonial Mexico," *Ethnohistory* 54, no. 1 (2007): 35–67.

23. "Ay entre los naturales algunas yndias y yndios enbaydores que se hasen medicos de curar sin ser sabidores de nada, antes entiendo que son hechiseros" (Among the indigenous people there are some deceptive female and male Indians who say they are curing doctors without knowing a thing; much to the contrary, I understand they are sorcerers). *Relaciones geográficas*, 2:24.

24. The early seventeenth-century *Tesoro de la lengua castellana o española* mentions that *hechizar* (a verb derived from the word *hechicero* [sorcerer]) was done "con pacto del demonio expresso o tácito." Sebastián de Covarrubias Orozco, *Tesoro de la lengua castellana o española*, ed. Martín de Riquer, 4th ed. (Barcelona: Alta Fulla, 1998), 680. See also Gabany-Guerrero, "Deciphering the Symbolic Heritage of the Tarascan Empire," 178–179. Spaniards equally distrusted and condemned soothsayers in Nahua and Maya regions. See Elizabeth Boone, *Cycles of Time and Meaning in the Mexican Books of Fate* (Austin: University of Texas Press, 2007), 20–28.

25. In spite of the royal prohibitions, indigenous doctors continued to practice medicine throughout the sixteenth century. Shortages in certified doctors and the many epidemics that swept through Mexico in the sixteenth century made such edicts impossible to enforce. In 1545, Mexico City had only four certified doctors, and not until 1578 was a chair of medicine established at the university there. Guenter B. Risse, "Medicine in New Spain," in *Medicine in the New World: New Spain, New France, and New England*, ed. Ronald L. Numbers, 30, 33, 51 (Knoxville: University of Tennessee Press, 1987); and Gabany-Guerrero, "Deciphering the Symbolic Heritage," 179.

26. See Castro Gutiérrez, *Los tarascos y el imperio español*, 218, 250–263.

27. The implication of the *Relación*'s text is that the "natural" outcome would have been for the Uanacaze to have killed the indigenous nobles' ancestors, but since they had not been sacrificed, they were indebted to the Uanacaze god and rulers as the god's earthly representatives. One of the Uanacaze lords who had been captured in battle by enemies and his life spared was then sacrificed by his own father. See *Relación de Michoacán*, 503–508.

28. "Gente baxa de Michuacan." Ibid., 504. The Jesuit Francisco Ramírez in 1585 states that in pre-Columbian times those who did not work the fields of the ruler or who committed adultery were sentenced to death. Francisco Ramírez, "Relación sobre la residencia de Michoacán (Pátzcuaro) hecha por el padre Francisco Ramírez," in *Monumenta mexicana 1581–1585*, ed. Félix Zubillaga and Miguel Angel Rodríguez, 2:495 (Rome: Apud "Monumenta Historica Soc. Iesu," 1959).

29. "¿Por qué no myráys a las espaldas, al tiempo pasado, quando érades esclavos?; por qué os conquistaron? Ahora no guardáys lo que prometistes. . . . Ahora *Curicaueri* ha lástima de sí en este año presente en que estamos, por eso os tiene aquí para hacer de vosotros justicia." *Relación de Michoacán*, 504.

30. Douglas, *In the Palace of Nezahualcoyotl*, 150–159.

31. This is also confirmed in the *Codex Plancarte* in a speech quoted from one of the Uanacaze lords, in which he announces the bringing of justice to the town of Carapan to rationalize turning it into a subject city: "[A]nd he announced to them how soon there would be a new law and in that law no lazy people, nor adulterers, nor deceitful people, nor liars, nor sorcerers would be allowed" ([Y] les avisó como presto había de haber nueva ley y en aquella ley no consentieran flojos ni adulteros ni embusteros ni mentirosos ni hechiseros). José Corona Núñez, *Tres códices michoacanos* (Morelia, Mexico: Universidad Michoacana de San Nicolás de Hidalgo, 1986), 56.

32. See, for example, AHCP, Caja 3 bis, Exp. 54; and Castro Gutiérrez, *Los tarascos y el imperio español*, 115, 21–22.

33. "[C]on lo qual se les quita toda la auoridad [*sic*] de los oficios." AGN, Indios, Vol. 4, Exp. 148, fols. 47v–48r, in "*Y por mi visto . . .*," 279. See also Castro Gutiérrez, *Los tarascos y el imperio español*, 126.

34. "De la justicia que hazía el Cazonçi." *Relación de Michoacán*, 281.

35. Michell B. Merback, *The Thief, the Cross and the Wheel: Pain and the Spectacle of Punishment in Medieval and Renaissance Europe* (Chicago: University of Chicago Press, 1998), 129–131.

36. For a general description of the kinds of punishments imposed, see Alfonso X, "Partida 7," 707–714.

37. *Codex Mendoza*, fols. 70r–71r. See *The* Codex Mendoza, ed. Frances F. Berdan and Patricia Rieff Anawalt (Berkeley: University of California Press, 1992), 3:147–149. For a review of the dating and production of the *Codex Mendoza*, see Nicholson, "History of the *Codex Mendoza*," 1–11.

38. See Douglas, *In the Palace of Nezahualcoyotl*, 151–159.

39. "Ordenanza para el gobierno de Indios," 185–186.

40. "[A]quello que induce mucho miedo en el cuerpo." Castro Gutiérrez, *Los tarascos y el imperio español*, 26. Castro Gutiérrez also cites the word *chemazqua*, meaning "authority and majesty" (*autoridad, majestad*). Its root is *cheni-*, which he translates as "to fear and to scare" (*tener miedo, espantar*).

41. Paul de Wolf, "El cuerpo humano en la sufijación verbal del Tarasco," in *Seis estudios lingüísticos sobre la lengua Phorhé*, 47–110 (Zamora, Mexico: El Colegio de Michoacán, 1989). See also Gabany-Guerrero, "Deciphering the Symbolic Heritage," 142–143, citing Swadesh and Friedrich.

42. Gabany-Guerrero, "Deciphering the Symbolic Heritage," 142–143.

43. Ibid., 34–35.

44. For parallels with the Nahuas of central Mexico, see Alfredo López Austin, *Cuerpo humano e ideología: Las concepciones de los antiguos nahuas* (Mexico City: Universidad Nacional Autónoma de México, 1980).

45. "Salud: Varaquan piquareraqua." *Diccionario grande*, 1:639. *Vraquan* comes from the noun *vraqua-* and the suffix *-ni*, which transforms it into a verb. *Vraqua* means "franqueza, magnanimidad y valentia"; and *piquareraqua*, "sentido intelectual." *Diccionario grande*, 2:746, 432.

46. Other terms include *cesi pajperakua* and *cesi arhijperani*, meaning "to get along well with everybody," "to accept everybody," and "to try to live well with everybody." This information was collected by the author while attending the Universidad Intercultural Indígena de Michoacán, December 2006.

47. *Relación de Michoacán*, 281–283, 363–365.

48. "[L]a cura que hasen es henchir vna xicara de agua, y alli soplan y myran al cielo, y andan soplando por la casa, y disen algunas palabras que no se entienden, y aprietan las carnes del enfermo y disen que le sacan gusanos." *Relaciones geográficas*, 2:24.

49. *Relación de Michoacán*, 332.

50. Ibid., 297–298. See also María Teresa Sepúlveda y Herrera, *La medicina entre los purépecha prehispánicos* (Mexico City: Universidad Nacional Autónoma de México, Instituto de Investigaciones Antropológicas, 1988), 101–102.

51. "Ytsi eramnastani: Adivinar en el agua como hechizero" and "Hechizero que mira en agüeros: eramansri." *Eramansri* comes from the verb *eramani*, meaning "to look into the water" (*mirar en el agua*). *Diccionario grande*, 1:406, 2:188, 298; and Benjamín Lucas, pers. comm., December 2006.

52. "Y el marido que tomaba a su muger con otro, les hendía las orejas a entranbos, a ella y al adúltero, en señal que los avía tomado en adulterio y les quitava las mantas y se venían a quexar, y las mostrava al que tenía cargo de hazer justicia, y era creído con aquella señal que traíe." *Relación de Michoacán*, 365.

53. Ibid., 297.

54. Ibid., 291–295.

55. Although polygamy was supposedly not accepted by the colonial system, Uanacaze lords seem to have continued the practice. Don Antonio Huitzimengari, governor of Michoacán between 1545 and 1562, for example, had many children outside his Catholic marriage. See López Sarrelangue, *La nobleza indígena de Pátzcuaro*, 207–228.

56. "Mirad que muy altamente [h]a sido engendrado *Curicaueri* y con gran poder [h]a de conquistar la tierra." *Relación de Michoacán*, 368.

57. Ibid., 281.

58. See Kevin Terraciano, "Crime and Culture in Colonial Mexico: The Case of the Mixtec Murder Note," *Ethnohistory* 45, no. 4 (1998): 720–721.

59. AHCP, Caja 5 bis, Doc. 73, Year 1597.

60. AHCP, Caja 4, Exp. 55.

61. See Mirrer, "The 'Unfaithful Wife,'" 146; Alfonso X, "Partida 7," 647–658; "Ordenanza para el gobierno de indios," 185; and AGN, Ramo Indios 2, Exp. 727, fol. 166r, in *"Y por mi visto . . . ,"* 214–215. For punishment in Michoacán, see, for example, AHCP, Caja 4, Exp. 39.

62. "[L]a sangre que están [*sic*] en el dicho ídolo es de sangre de las orejas de indios que se sacrificaron." Scholes and Adams, *Proceso contra Tzintzicha Tangaxoan*, 66.

63. *Relación de Michoacán*, 396.

64. That ruler is described as letting blood from his ears as an adult in a cere-

mony dedicated to the gods Curicaueri and Punguarancha, a war deity. In this ceremony, he stands in stark contrast to two men from the noble house of Itxiparámuco who had sex with his wife. In a complex lie, the men from Itxiparámucu deny having had sex with the ruler's wife and charge him with having wrongly punished them by cutting their ears. Thus, not only does the ear serve to mark the ruler's devotion but it helps differentiate him from other nobles whose behavior is deemed inappropriate. *Relación de Michoacán*, 422–426. For bloodletting during war ceremonies, see ibid., 499. For other examples of ear sacrifice in the *Relación* and other colonial documents, see Véronique Darras, "La obsidiana en la *Relación de Michoacán* y en la realidad arqueológica: Del símbolo al uso o del uso de un símbolo," in *Génesis, culturas y espacios en Michoacán*, ed. Veronique Darras, 68–70 (Mexico City: Centre Français d'Études Mexicaines et Centraméricaines, 1998).

65. "[D]ava yo de comer al dios." *Relación de Michoacán*, 405.

66. "[T]ienen las horejas gordas y hinchadas de los sacrificios que abían hecho y de la sangre quc avían sacado dellas." Ibid., 471. For parallels with the Aztec nobility of central Mexico, see Cecelia F. Klein, "The Ideology of Autosacrifice at the Templo Mayor," in *The Aztec Templo Mayor: A Symposium at Dumbarton Oaks, 8th and 9th October 1983*, ed. Elizabeth Boone, 293–370 (Washington, DC: Dumbarton Oaks Research Library and Collection, 1987).

67. See Ramírez, "Relación sobre la residencia de Michoacán," 2:492–494.

68. Alonso de la Rea, *Crónica de la orden de N. seráfico P.S. Francisco, provincia de S. Pedro y S. Pablo de Mechoacán en la Nueva España*, ed. Patricia Escandón, 83 (Zamora, Mexico: Colegio de Michoacán and Fideicomiso Teixidor, 1996).

69. *Relación de Michoacán*, 493.

70. Ibid., 487.

71. Isidro Félix de Espinosa, *Crónica de la provincia franciscana de los apóstoles San Pedro y San Pablo de Michoacán*, ed. Nicolás León and José Ignacio Paulino Dávila Garibi, 2nd ed. (Mexico City: Editorial Santiago, 1945), 45.

72. *Relación de Michoacán*, 283–285.

73. AGI Justicia, Legajo 229, May 4, 1532, fols. 2v, 6r. For a list of exchange items between Guzmán and the Uanacaze ruler Tangaxuan, including golden earspools, see also AGI, Justicia, Legajo 226, No. 2, Ramo 2, "Relacion sacada una probanza hecha por pedimento de Guzmán. . . ."

74. "Quando metían alguna población a fuego y sangre." *Relación de Michoacán*, 278.

75. According to the text, after capturing the enemy nobles, the army took them to the capital for an audience with the Uanacaze ruler. There, the defeated nobles gave him presents and swore allegiance to him. Ibid., 278–279.

CHAPTER 3

Portions of this chapter were presented at the Interdisciplinary Methods in Colonial Studies: Nature and Society in the Americas, Third Annual Colloquium, University of New Mexico in Albuquerque, March 7–8, 2008; and at the symposium "The Image of Peru: History and Art, 1550–1880," Getty Research Institute, Los Angeles, October 17–18, 2008. An abbreviated version of this chapter was published in *New World Manuscripts*, edited by Emily Engel, Barbara Anderson, and Tom Cummins (Los Angeles: Getty Research Institute, 2014).

1. Luz María Mohar Betancourt, *Códice Mapa Quinatzin: Justicia y derechos humanos en el México antiguo* (Mexico City: Consejo Nacional de Derechos Humanos México, CIESAS, and Miguel Angel Porrúa, 2004); *Códice Xolotl*, ed. Charles Dibble (Mexico City: Universidad Nacional Autónoma de México, 1951); and Douglas, *In the Palace of Nezahualcoyotl*.

2. Michel de Certeau, *The Practice of Everyday Life* (Berkeley: University of California Press, 1984), 115–130. The literary scholar Cynthia Stone uses Certeau's work for her symbolic reading of the narrative, but here I take a more historical approach.

3. Cecelia F. Klein, "Editor's Statement: Depictions of the Dispossessed," *Art Journal* 49, no. 2 (1990): 107.

4. Mundy has claimed that colonial functionaries did not see the need for maps outside the Valley of Mexico and stayed away from them because they were the province of indigenous people, except when land disputes were at stake. Mundy, *Mapping of New Spain*, 57–59. This was precisely the case in Michoacán between 1528 and 1553.

5. See, for example, Batalla Rosado, "Una aproximación a la iconografía tarasca," 151; and Francisco Miranda Godínez, *La* Relación de Michoacán*: Estudio preliminar y notas* (Mexico City: Secretaría de Educación Pública, 1988), 15–16.

6. Stone, *In Place of Gods and Kings*, 21–25, 54.

7. Roskamp, "El carari indígena y las láminas de la *Relación de Michoacán*," 250.

8. In folio 71r, below the title and under the white wash, one can still read "pesco con la red asentado en mi canoa a popa y pongo a mi hija en la canoa pa que reme y de dia pesco con anzuelo unos pececillos" (I fish with a net while sitting on the stern of my canoe, and I bring my daughter in the canoe so she can paddle, and during the day I fish with a hook for some small fish). It is hard to see the rest of the text, although it continues. Underneath the small boat in the scene a few more words can still be read: "[escla]va esto solo les diras" ([sla]ve, this you will tell them).

9. Stone, *In Place of Gods and Kings*, 114–115; and Marie-Chalotte Arnauld and Dominique Michelet, "Les migrations postclassiques au Michoacán et au Guatemala: Problèmes et perspectives," in *Vingt études sur le Mexique et le Guatemala réunies à la mémoire de Nichole Percheron*, ed. Alain Breton et al., 67–92 (Toulouse, France: Presses Universitaires du Mirail, 1991).

10. See, for example, *Historia tolteca-chichimeca*, ed. Paul Kirchhoff, Lina Odena Guémes, and Luís Reyes García (Mexico City: Fondo de Cultura Económica, 1989); *Códice Xolotl*; and Johansson, "*Tira de la peregrinación*," 17–73. Federico Navarrete has proposed that the Mexican migration stories constitute a genre of their own that includes annals, maps, and event-oriented stories. While he separates the Mexican migration from other migrations, such as that of the Acolhua of Texcoco, there are in fact many commonalities among these and other Mesoamerican migra-

tion stories. Navarrete, "The Path from Aztlan to Mexico," 42–44. For more information about cartographic histories, see Mundy, *Mapping of New Spain*, 107–112; and Boone, *Stories in Red and Black*, 162–196.

11. Roskamp, *La historiografía indígena de Michoacán*, 81–195.

12. For her reading on this speech, see Stone, *In Place of Gods and Kings*, 111–153. Bishop Vasco de Quiroga was a complex and litigious character to say the least. He left a long court record from the many fights he took on.

13. Boone, *Stories in Red and Black*, chaps. 2, 7, esp. 162–164. See also Dana Leibsohn, "Mapping Metaphors: Figuring the Ground of Sixteenth-Century New Spain," *Journal of Medieval and Early Modern Studies* 26, no. 3 (1996): 505; and Navarrete, "The Path from Aztlan to Mexico," 31–48.

14. Mundy, *Mapping of New Spain*, 107; and Boone, *Stories in Red and Black*, 127–128. Many of these stories in the shape of cartographic histories and painted on *lienzos* continued to be used well into the nineteenth and twentieth centuries.

15. Michelet, "Histoire, mythe et apologue," 105–112. While the first four generations are summarized in chapters 2–9, the Uanacaze leader Tariacuri and his successors, who went on to form a triumvirate, are featured in some twenty-two of the thirty-two chapters in which the main priest narrates the history of the Uanacaze.

16. James Krippner-Martínez, "Alterity, Alliance, and the *Relación de Michoacán* [1541]," in *Rereading the Conquest*, 59–61.

17. "Cómo los Señores de la laguna supieron de la muger que llevaron los chichimecas, y cómo les dieron sus hijas por mugeres." Escobar Olmedo, *Relación de Michoacán*, 383. All citations from the *Relación* in this chapter come from Escobar Olmedo's edition, unless otherwise noted.

18. "Como Hirepan y Tangaxoan y Hiquingaje conquistaron toda la Provincia con los ysleños, y como la repartieron entre sí, y de lo que hordenaron." *Relación de Michoacán*, 498.

19. For similar strategies among indigenous painters in central Mexico, see Douglas, *In the Palace of Nezahualcoyotl*, 41–93.

20. "Como el Señor de la ysla, llamado Caricaten, pidió socorro a otro Señor llamado Zurunban contra Tariacuri, que le tenía cercado en su ysla, y fue enbiado un sacerdote llamado Naca a hazer gente de guerra." *Relación de Michoacán*, 399.

21. Cited in Denis Cosgrove, "Introduction: Iconography and Landscape," in *The Iconography of Landscape: Essays on the Symbolic Representation, Design and Use of Past Environments*, ed. Denis Cosgrove and Stephen Daniels, 3 (Cambridge: Cambridge University Press, 1988).

22. See, for example, *Codex Nuttall*, 80.

23. Robertson, *Mexican Manuscript Painting*, 12–24; and Baird, *Drawings of Sahagún's* Primeros memoriales, 21–29.

24. For an overview of European depictions of space, see Mundy, *Mapping of New Spain*, 1–9.

25. "Charco de agua en la orilla o en la entrada." Márquez Joaquín, "El significado de las palabras p'urhépecha en la *Relación de Michoacán*," 725.

26. Other famous origin and transformative caves in Mesoamerican literatures include Chicomoztoc, or Seven Caves, in migration stories such as the *Codex Mexicanus*, the *Historia tolteca-chichimeca* from Cuauhtinchan, and Uucub Pec (also meaning Seven Caves) mentioned in the Maya Quiché *Popul Vuh*. See Navarrete, "The Path from Aztlan to Mexico," 40.

27. Denis Cosgrove, "Introduction," in *Social Formation and Symbolic Landscapes*, 20 (Totowa, NJ: Barnes and Noble, 1985).

28. Viceroy Mendoza actually owned and annotated Alberti's treatise *De Re Aedificatoria* on Renaissance-style architecture and urban planning. If not directly known to the viceroy, Alberti's work on painting would have influenced much of the art of his time. Tovar de Teresa, "La utopia del Virrey de Mendoza," 19, 27, 29, 95–96.

29. Cosgrove, "Introduction," in *Social Formation*, 26.

30. Panofsky, "Painting in Italy and the Lowlands," 23–34.

31. Mundy, *Mapping of New Spain*, 1–3.

32. Warren, *Conquest of Michoacán*, 81–82, 95–101.

33. Bravo Ugarte, "*La Relación de Michoacán*," 13–25; and Martínez Baracs, *Convivencia y utopía*, 252–296.

34. See, for example, the account of Alonso de Ávalos on September 9, 1538, in AGI, Justicia, Legajo 173, No. 1, Ramo 2; and Don Antonio Huitzimengari in AHCP, Caja 1, Exp. 11, Doc. 36, 1551.

35. Warren, *Conquest of Michoacán*, 160.

36. Bernal García and García Zambrano, as well as Lori Diel, have similarly noted that Spanish and indigenous geopolitical divisions in central Mexico were never a perfect match and generated much confusion. Bernal García and García Zambrano, "El Altepetl colonial y sus antecedents prehispánicos," 31–56; and Lori B. Diel, *The Tira de Tepechpan: Negotiating Place under Aztec and Spanish Rule* (Austin: University of Texas Press, 2008), 2–5.

37. In 1528, for example, the Spanish royal treasurer, Alonso de Estrada, tried to take the barrio of Pátzcuaro for his personal benefit but was not able to do so because it belonged to Tzintzuntzan. AGI, Justicia, Legajo 130. See also Warren, *Conquest of Michoacán*, 160–161.

38. Sixteenth-century documents use the word *vapatzequa* to refer to pueblos, sujetos, and barrios of large cities such as Tzintzuntzan and to the sujetos of Tuzuntla. For example, AGI, Audiencia de México, Legajo 96, Ramo 1, fol. 1r; AGI, Justicia, Legajo 278, No. 1, fol. 8v; AHCP, Caja 2, Exp. 6, fols. 18v, 19r; and *P'urhépecha documents 1564, Michoacán Manuscript Collection*, from the James Ford Bell Library, vol. 1, cited in Hedberg, "Conflicts and Continuities," 131, 137. For the P'urhépecha/Spanish translation of *vapatzequa*, see *Diccionario grande*, 2:678.

39. Covarrubias, *Tesoro de la lengua castellana o española*, 335.

40. For the subdivisions of the archaeological site of Tzintzuntzan, see Pollard, *Taríacuri's Legacy*, 29–62.

41. Warren, *Conquest of Michoacán*, 200–203.

42. For summaries of these disputes, see Warren, *Vasco de Quiroga and His*

Pueblo-Hospitales, 88–103; Warren, *Conquest of Michoacán*, 157–71; and Martínez Baracs, *Convivencia y utopía*, 143–146, 285–287.

43. AGI, Justicia, Legajo 188, No. 3.

44. Scholes and Adams, *Proceso contra Tzintzicha Tangaxoan*, 211–236.

45. Warren, *Vasco de Quiroga and His Pueblo-Hospitales*, 90; and J. Benedict Warren and Cristina Monzón, "Carta de los principales de Pátzcuaro al obispo Vasco de Quiroga. 10 de marzo de 1549," *Relaciones: Estudios de Historia y Sociedad* 25, no. 99 (2004): 194n15.

46. AGI, Justicia, Legajo 130, fols. 16r–21r. This legajo has several numbering systems. I am using the numbers penciled in the upper right-hand corner.

47. AGI, Justicia, Legajo 130, fol. 30r. See also Warren, *Vasco de Quiroga and His Pueblo-Hospitales of Santa Fe*, 90–91; and Warren, "Vasco de Quiroga y la fundación de Pátzcuaro colonial," 79–94.

48. AGI, Justicia, Legajo 130, fols. 20r–21r; Warren, "Fray Jerónimo de Alcalá" (2005), 157; and Warren, *Vasco de Quiroga and His Pueblo-Hospitales*, 99.

49. AGI, Justicia, Legajo 130, fols. 20r–25r; Warren, "Fray Jerónimo de Alcalá" (2005), 157; and Warren, *Vasco de Quiroga and His Pueblo-Hospitales*, 99.

50. "Las Leyes Nuevas, 1542–1543," transcribed by Antonio Muro Orejón, *Anuario de Estudios Americanos* 2 (1945): 811–835.

51. Warren, *Vasco de Quiroga and His Pueblo-Hospitales*, 97–102; and Warren, "Fray Jerónimo de Alcalá" (2005), 157.

52. AGI, Justicia, Legajo 188, No. 3.

53. AGI, Justicia, Legajo 130, fol. 16r.

54. "[L]a dicha pintura que ha presentado es muy mal hecha y no está verdadera ni cierta" (The aforementioned painting is poorly made, and it is neither true nor right). Ibid., fol. 91r.

55. See, for example, ibid., questions 7, 29, 30–38 in fols. 179v–211r.

56. See, for example, ibid., fols. 272v, 464r, 469r–v, 470r–v.

57. "[E]sta tierra se ha de repartir ahora entre los cristianos y cada uno ha de tener su parte y yo me quedaré con esta dicha ciudad y con todos los pueblos de alrededor de la laguna y esto será para mi señorío." Ibid., fol. 534r.

58. See, for example, ibid., fols. 500r, 507v–508r, 520v, 561v, 572v–573r, 576r, 589v–590r, 600r–600v.

59. The 1579 map of Santa María Magdalena, Cuitlahuaca, also uses lines to depict agricultural fields. See Alessandra Russo, *El realismo circular: Tierras, espacios y paisajes de la cartografía indígena novohispana, siglos XVI y XVII* (Mexico City: Universidad Nacional Autónoma de México, Instituto de Investigaciones Estéticas, 2005), 148.

60. Similarly, the artists of the *Florentine Codex* would represent a ruler and his main captains reviewing a map of a town they would later invade. As in the *Relación*, on the right-hand side of the image, the artist has depicted the actual town. *Florentine Codex*, vol. 2, fol. 283v; see also Gruzinski, *Painting the Conquest*, 125.

61. Franco Mendoza, "El discurso del petámuti," 265–284.

62. One could argue that, by extension, the viceroy's reading of this story would

have claimed this land for the Spanish Crown. Given the politics of the area, this was not entirely undesirable. If the land had been returned to the Crown, the Uanacaze could have requested grants, goods, and labor from it.

63. Stone, *In Place of Gods and Kings*, 111–153.

64. *Relación de Michoacán*, pt. 2, chap. 7, p. 387.

65. AGI, Justicia, Legajo 130, fol. 131r.

66. See, for example, Donald Brand, "An Historical Sketch of Geography and Anthropology in the Tarascan Region," *New Mexico Anthropologist* 6–7, no. 2 (1943): 37–108; Dan Stanislawski, "Tarascan Political Geography," *American Anthropologist* 49, no. 1 (1947): 46–55; Claudia Espejel Carbajal, *Caminos de Michoacán . . . y pueblos que voy pasando* (Mexico City: Instituto Nacional de Antropología e Historia, 1992), 35–39; Claudia Espejel Carbajal, "Guía arqueológica y geográfica para la *Relación de Michoacán*," in *Relación de las cerimonias y rictos y población y gobernación de los indios de la provincia de Michoacán*, ed. Moisés Franco Mendoza, 301–314 (Zamora, Mexico: El Colegio de Michoacán; Morelia, Mexico: Gobierno del Estado, 2000); Espejel Carbajal, "Voces, lugares y tiempos," 85–157; and Claudia Espejel Carbajal, "Tarascan Ethnohistory and Archaeology," Foundation for the Advancement of Mesoamerican Studies, http://www.famsi.org/reports/06041/06041EspejelCarbajal01.pdf.

67. For a discussion of Spanish mapping traditions, see Mundy, *Mapping of New Spain*, 11–27.

CHAPTER 4

A section of this chapter was presented at the fortieth annual meeting of the American Society for Eighteenth-Century Studies, Richmond, Virginia, March 26–29, 2009.

1. For the role of gender in manuscripts from central Mexico, see Betty Ann Brown, "Seen but Not Heard: Women in Aztec Ritual—the Sahagún Texts," in *Text and Image in Pre-Columbian Art: Essays on the Interrelationship of the Verbal and Visual Arts*, ed. Janet Berlo, 119–153 (Oxford: BAR International Series, 1983); and Margaret Arvey, "Women of Ill-Repute in the Florentine Codex," in *The Role of Gender in Precolumbian Art and Architecture*, ed. Virginia E. Miller, 179–204 (Lanham, MD: University Press of America, 1988).

2. Barbara L. Stark and John K. Chance, "Diachronic and Multidisciplinary Perspectives on Mesoamerican Ethnicity," in *Ethnic Identity in Nahua Mesoamerica: The View from Archaeology, Art History, Ethnohistory, and Contemporary Ethnography*, ed. Frances F. Berdan et al., 1–37 (Salt Lake City: University of Utah Press, 2008).

3. See, for example, Warren, *Conquest of Michoacán*; and Brigitte Faugère-Kalfon, "Venados y hogares sagrados en la *Relación de Michoacán*: Reivindicación nórdica y construcción del estado en los pueblos tarascos," in *Génesis, culturas y espacios en Michoacán*, ed. Véronique Darras, 89–99 (Mexico City: Centre Français d'Études Mexicaines et Centraméricaines, 1998).

4. Pollard, *Taríacuri's Legacy*, 13. In her work, Pollard has proposed that the Uacúsecha ethnic group based their state within Michoacán on assimilation and segregation policies. According to Pollard, power was consolidated between 1350 and 1525, with the ethnic identity of the ruling elite replacing independent and varied ethnic identities as the basis for political domination. In Pollard's view, the core of the state (the Pátzcuaro Lake basin and surrounding areas) consisted of a largely homogeneous population, which assured the elite a loyal and exploitable constituency surrounded by a mixed area of assimilated and unassimilated peoples. On the frontiers, independent but allied ethnic groups served as buffers against possible attacks from the Mexica of central Mexico. Pollard acknowledges that her model does not explain the presence in the archaeological record of a non-Uacúsecha (possibly Otomí) enclave in Tzintzuntzan, the Uanacaze capital.

5. Arnauld and Michelet, "Les migrations postclassiques au Michoacán et au Guatemala," 67–92; and Marie-Charlotte Arnauld and Brigitte Faugère-Kalfon, "Evolución de la ocupación humana en el centro-norte de Michoacán (Proyecto Michoacán, CEMCA) y la emergencia del estado tarasco," in *Génesis, culturas y espacios en Michoacán*, ed. Véronique Darras, 13–34 (Mexico City: Centre Français d'Études Mexicaines et Centraméricaines, 1998).

6. Arnauld and Michelet, "Les migrations postclassiques au Michoacán et au Guatemala," 67–92.

7. Stone, *In Place of Gods and Kings*, 113–114.

8. Esther Pasztory, "Identity and Difference: The Uses and Meanings of Ethnic Styles," in *Cultural Differentiation and Cultural Identity in the Visual Arts*, ed. Susan Barnes and Walter Melion, 15–38 (London: National Gallery of Art; Hanover, NH: University Press of New England, 1989). For the complexities of identity in the fifteenth and sixteenth centuries in central Mexico, see Emily Umberger, "Ethnicity and Other Identities in the Sculptures of Tenochtitlan," in *Ethnic Identity in Nahua Mesoamerica: The View from Archaeology, Art History, Ethnohistory, and Contemporary Ethnography*, ed. Frances F. Berdan et al., 64–104 (Salt Lake City: University of Utah Press, 2008).

9. For discussion of migration stories and ethnic identities in central Mexico, see, for example, Michael E. Smith, "The Aztlan Migrations of the Nahuatl Chronicles: Myth or History?," *Ethnohistory* 31, no. 3 (1984): 153–186; and Lockhart, *Nahuas after the Conquest*, 15–16.

10. For the study of ethnic/race differentiation as a way to affirm class hierarchies, see, for example, Barth, *Ethnic Groups and Boundaries*, 27–28; Foucault, *History of Sexuality*, 1:135–159; Klein, "Editor's Statement," 106–109; Elizabeth Brumfiel, "Ethnic Groups and Political Development in Ancient Mexico," in *Factional Competition and Political Development in the New World*, ed. Elizabeth Brumfiel and John Fox, 27–28, New Directions in Archaeology (Cambridge: Cambridge University Press, 1994); Appadurai, *Modernity at Large*, 14, 139–157; Stoler, *Carnal Knowledge and Imperial Power*, 140–161; and Stark and Chance, "Diachronic and Multidisciplinary Perspectives," 1–37.

11. Foucault, *History of Sexuality*, 1:92–98; and Stark and Chance, "Diachronic and Multidisciplinary Perspectives," 6.

12. Stark and Chance, "Diachronic and Multidisciplinary Perspectives," 11.

13. The Mexica of central Mexico are also known for having glorified their own ethnicity to the detriment of subject groups. See ibid., 28.

14. Certeau, *Practice of Everyday Life*, xviii–xx, 29–42.

15. I thank Miranda Brady from Carleton University, Ontario, Canada, for this observation (pers. comm., March 2009).

16. "Como se caso Tariacuri con una hija del señor de Curinguaro." Escobar Olmedo, *Relación de Michoacán*, 417. All citations from the *Relación* in this chapter come from Escobar Olmedo's edition, unless otherwise noted.

17. "[Y] fue mala mujer." Ibid.

18. "Como Tariacuri sintió mucho como no le guardaba lealtad su muger y como se casó con otra por consejo de una su tía." Ibid., 427.

19. Krippner-Martínez, "Politics of Conquest," 186; and Krippner-Martínez, *Rereading the Conquest*, 59.

20. For an interpretation of this vignette on infidelity as aiming to emphasize male dominance in the text, see Krippner-Martínez, "Politics of Conquest," 193–194.

21. Likewise, part 3 of the *Relación* tells us that the Uanacaze ruler Zuangua justified the Spanish conquest of central Mexico by citing central Mexicans' inappropriate worship of their gods by means of only songs and no fires: "¿Qué aprobecha los cantares solos?, ¿cómo los dioses los [h]an de faborecer con sólos cantares?" *Relación de Michoacán*, 326.

22. Paul Durrieu, *Manuscrits d'Espagne remarquable par leurs peintures* (Paris, 1893). Cited in the Biblioteca Nacional, Spain, general catalogue, http://catalogo.bne.es/uhtbin/cgisirsi/De5X2gs4DX/BNMADRID/22380003/9.

23. *Relación de Michoacán*, 456–464.

24. Dominique Michelet has noted the moralizing nature of the *Relación*'s narrative, in which excess and drunkenness are constant themes. However, because his work focuses on the *Relación* as a source for understanding pre-Columbian events, he does not explain how this narrative strategy might have worked in a colonial society where upstanding Christian moral behavior is a criterion of rulership. Michelet, "Histoire, mythe et apologue," 105–112.

25. Francisco Miranda Godínez, "Las láminas de la *Relación de Michoacán*: Una descripción," in *Relación de Michoacán*, ed. Armando Escobar Olmedo, 202 (Morelia, Mexico: Patrimonio Nacional, H. Ayuntamiento de Morelia; Madrid: Testimonio Compañía Editorial, 2001).

26. See Lester Born, "The Perfect Prince: A Study in Thirteenth- and Fourteenth-Century Ideals," *Speculum* 3, no. 4 (1928): 470–504.

27. See Richard Osberg, "The Jesse Tree in the 1432 London Entry of Henry VI: Messianic Kingship and the Rule of Justice," *Journal of Medieval and Renaissance Studies* 16, no. 2 (1986): 227; and Born, "The Perfect Prince," 470–504.

28. Silvio Zavala, "La 'utopía' de Tomás Moro en la Nueva España," in *La utopía mexicana del siglo XVI: Lo bello, lo verdadero y lo bueno*, ed. Guillermo Tovar de Teresa, 72–73, Colección Arte Novohispano (Mexico City: Grupo Azabache, 1992); and Warren, "Fray Jerónimo de Alcalá" (2005), 165–166. Another book that came to Michoacán slightly later but that would also give advice to the aristocracy against vices is *Espejo de la consolación* by the Franciscan Juan de Dueñas. It was first published in 1548 and must have arrived in Michoacán shortly after, because by 1563 it was being sold in a public auction in Pátzcuaro, Michoacán, after the death of its owner in that city. AHCP, Caja 131, Legajo 3, Exp. 17, Year 1564.

29. AGI, Indiferente, Legajo 1382b, Year 1542.

30. AGI, Patronato Real, Legajo 60, Ramo 3, No. 2, "Información de méritos y servicios de don Antonio Huitzimengari, hijo del último Cazonci de Michoacán, 1553–1554." See question seven and its answers.

31. See, for example, the testimony by Jorge Carrillo: "A las catorce preguntas dijo, que este testigo sabe, que el dicho don Antonio es muy buen cristiano, porque le ha visto hacer obras de tal, y le parece a este testigo y es notorio que los naturales de la dicha provincia de Michoacán toman ejemplo en él, porque hacen obras de cristianos y andan vestidos los más de ellos en hábitos de españoles, etc." (To the fourteenth question he said that this witness knows that the aforementioned Don Antonio is a good Christian, because he has seen him carry out deeds as such, and it seems to this witness, and it is noteworthy that the natives of the aforementioned Province of Michoacán take example in him, because they carry out deeds of Christians and the majority of them dress in Spanish clothing, etc.). Ibid., fol. 40r.

32. Ibid. See the answers to question sixteen.

33. Many of Don Antonio's illegitimate children eventually occupied important posts in the colonial government, including the governor's seat. For a review of their lives and activities, see López Sarrelangue, *La nobleza indígena de Pátzcuaro*, 207–228.

34. Castro Gutiérrez, *Los tarascos y el imperio español*, 52; and Kuthy-Saenger, "Strategies of Survival," 270.

35. See, for example, *Relación de Michoacán*, 367–371.

36. Seler, "Los antiguos habitantes de Michoacán," 192.

37. For a detailed study of the *Codex Xolotl*, see Douglas, *In the Palace of Nezahualcoyotl.*

38. For the meaning of Chichimec identity in pre-Columbian central Mexico, see Umberger, "Ethnicity and Other Identities," 73–78.

39. Donna Pierce, "Identification of the Warriors in the Frescoes of Ixmiquilpan," *Research Center for the Arts Review* 4, no. 4 (1981): 1–8. See also Margaret Greer, "La caza sacro-política: De *El bosque divino* de González de Eslava a Calderón," in *El teatro en la Hispanoamérica colonial*, ed. Ignacio Arellano and José Antonio Rodríguez Garrido, 75–98 (Pamplona: Universidad de Navarra; Madrid: Editorial Iberoamericana, 2008). See also *Códice Xolotl*; and Umberger, "Ethnicity and Other Identities," 74–75.

40. AGI, Justicia, Legajo 129, No. 3. See also Warren, *Vasco de Quiroga and His Pueblo-Hospitales*, 104–105.

41. AGI, Justicia, Legajo 173, No. 1, Ramo 2, fol. 5v. Nicolás León published a section of this document in *Documentos inéditos referentes al ilustrísimo señor don Vasco de Quiroga* (Mexico City: Antigua Librería Robredo, de José Porrúa e Hijos, 1940), 39.

42. John Cummins, *The Hound and the Hawk: The Art of Medieval Hunting* (New York: St. Martin's Press, 1988); and Greer, "La caza sacro-política," 75.

43. *Relación de Michoacán*, 428–429; and J. Cummins, *The Hound and the Hawk*, 95.

44. Nader, "The Mendoza in the Fifteenth-Century Renaissance," 77–78.

45. J. Cummins, *The Hound and the Hawk*, 5.

46. AGI, Audiencia de México, Legajo 95.

47. Cited in Gruzinski, *Painting the Conquest*, 149.

48. Luis Weckmann, *La herencia medieval de México* (Mexico City: El Colegio de México and Fondo de Cultura Económica, 1994), 135; Bernal Díaz del Castillo, *Historia verdadera de la conquista de la Nueva España, II*, ed. Miguel León-Portilla, 397–398 (Madrid: Dastin, 2000); and Greer, "La caza sacro-política," 79–80.

49. J. Cummins, *The Hound and the Hawk*, 5–6.

50. Ibid., 68–74.

51. Ibid., 68–69, plate 31.

52. Ernest Burrus, "Cristobal Cabrera on the Missionary Methods of Vasco de Quiroga," *Manuscripta* 5, no. 1 (1961): 24. See also Warren, *Vasco de Quiroga and His Pueblo-Hospitales*, 104.

53. Tiripetío was known for its academic and artistic training of indigenous children. Igor Cerda Farías, *En el pueblo de Tiripetío, en la Provincia de Michoacán. La edad dorada. El siglo XVI* (Morelia, Mexico: Universidad Michoacana de San Nicolás de Hidalgo, 2005). Uanacaze heir Don Antonio Huitzimengari spent retreats in Tiripetío and corresponded with one of the convent's most renowned educators, Friar Alonso de la Veracruz. AGI, Justicia, Legajo 263, Pieza 3.

54. I would like to thank Igor Cerda Farías for sharing this information with me during the spring of 2006.

55. I am grateful to Héctor Álvarez Contreras from the Secretaría de Cultura, Michoacán, for introducing me to these graffiti in January 2006. I also thank Viera Sairán Monfon for helping record them, and Igor Cerda Farías and his research team for allowing me to accompany them to document this and other convents in Michoacán during the spring of 2006.

56. Even though the convent enjoyed continuous use until the nineteenth century and its walls were often repainted, changing the pictorial program of its interior, some of its early layers can be seen where later painting has chipped off.

57. Indigenous people in Michoacán were often associated with the church's choirs. One might recall that the person who purchased Tzintzuntzan's first convent's organ was a Nahua nobleman, and the *Relación geográfica* from Chilchota,

Michoacán, mentions that the organ players of its church were two indigenous men. See *Relaciones geográficas*, 2:20.

58. Christ in the guise of *Salvador Mundi* holds up the index and middle fingers of his right hand in a gesture of blessing, and his left hand holds a globe with a cross on top.

59. In addition, in the northeastern corner of the building, in a small room above the convent's *portería* (entrance), fragments of a mural depicting a map and a large painted figure wearing a feather headdress and carrying an arrow and long feathers still survives. The long, stylized feathers in all likelihood represent eagle feathers and, together with the arrow, identify the figure as a *Uacus* (eagle, pl. *Uacusecha*), a warrior and hunter. The word *Uacus* was used to identify the large ethnic group to which the Uanacaze belonged. The map west of the figure, surrounded by a decorative border in black pigment, illustrates several colonial buildings, a river or a road, and a small anthropomorphic figure. The map, in juxtaposition with the Uacusecha figure, marks the landscape as Uacusecha territory.

60. J. Cummins, *The Hound and the Hawk*, 4.

61. In a sermon, the English master Rypon in the fourteenth century characterizes the cardinal virtues as the steps by which knights may ascend into heaven: "First there is the virtue of Fortitude, to be exhibited in bold and strenuous defense of Church and State. Secondly, there is Justice—'that they fight in a just cause, and do no injury or insult to any man'; thirdly, Prudence in action; fourthly, Moderation, not only in food, indeed, but also in a rational appetite for wealth." G. R. Owst, *Literature and Pulpit in Medieval England: A Neglected Chapter in the History of English Letters and of the English People* (New York: Barnes and Noble, 1961), 552.

62. Tudela, "Prólogo." Even though some scholars have argued that these robes are the same sitting or standing, in fact, in the frontispiece (plate 1) where the Spanish friar was first shown sitting, which later on was emended to represent him standing, the robe is depicted reaching the ground both as he sits and as he stands.

63. In *Relaciones geográficas*, see "Chilchota," 2:22; "Acámbaro," 2:61; " Yuririapundaro," 2:68; "Jiquilpan," 1:12; "Chocandiran," 1:19; "Tarecuato," 1:25; "Perivan," 1:33; and "Sirandaro, Huayameo y Cuseo," 1:42.

64. Maria-Lourdes Kuthy-Saenger has also noted that Spanish clothing on indigenous people meant to Spaniards that they had become "civilized" and accepted Spanish disciplinary customs, or had *policia*. Kuthy-Saenger, "Strategies of Survival," 104.

65. "[S]olían andar a su modo desnudos, y hazer la Guerra con sus arcos y flechas, y, por la bondad de Dios, de muchos años a esta parte que an sido dotrinados, tienen nuestro modo cristiano y mucha puliçia; y andan vestidos honestamente con sus camisas y saragueles y jubones y sonbreros, y los que pueden traen sus capotes y sayos como españoles." *Relaciones geográficas*, 1:39.

66. See Torquemada, 5:350–351, 6:436–439, 441, cited in Castro Gutiérrez, *Los tarascos y el imperio español*, 247.

67. "Se revistió de sayal y hasta su muerte estuvo importunando a los francis-

canos para que lo aceptaran en sus filas." Torquemada, 5:352–353, cited in Castro Gutiérrez, *Los tarascos y el imperio español*, 247.

68. For example, in "Información de méritos y servicios de don Antonio Huitzimengari," fol. 59v, one of Don Antonio's witnesses would attest that "y en lo que toca al hábito de español, es notorio que nunca el dicho don Antonio se ha vestido manta ni traído cabello largo ni barba pelada como suelen los indios, sino traje de puro español, y así lo ha visto con él este testigo trayendo luto y otras veces no lo trayendo, etc." (as far as the Spanish costume is concerned, it is noteworthy that never has the aforementioned Don Antonio dressed in *manta* [i.e., indigenous clothing] nor had long hair nor shaven beard as it is customary among the Indians, but only Spanish clothing, and in this way has this witness seen him wearing his mourning clothes and sometimes not, etc.). The *Relación geográfica* from Tingüindín, Michoacán, also mentions that indigenous people *se precian* (flaunt) their Castilian clothing. *Relaciones geográficas*, 2:76. See also López Sarrelangue, *La nobleza indígena de Pátzcuaro*, 114–116.

69. Diego Fernández, *Antonio de Mendoza*, 127–128.

70. For a critique of the distinction between history and myth, see Elizabeth Boone, "History and Historians," in *Stories in Red and Black*, 15–16.

71. *Relación de Michoacán*, pt. 3, chap. 10, p. 290. Tangaxuan's children, however, would argue in years to come that it was their father who had initially submitted willingly to the Spanish conquistadors.

72. For the many interpretations of Don Pedro's role, see Stone, *In Place of Gods and Kings*, 154–166.

73. For a different reading of this image, see ibid., 154.

74. Even though Roskamp sees the existence of these stairs within the palace as a mistake on the artist's part, it should be noted that the entrance to the palace in figure 3 also has stairs (see fig. 3). The stairs are painted black and do not reproduce well, so they have been missed by most scholars. In the original, they can be clearly discerned. Roskamp, "El carari indígena y las láminas de la *Relación de Michoacán*," 250.

75. "Varicani, varihpeni. Aporrearlos." *Diccionario grande*, 2:682.

76. "Varini. Morir." The root of the word is *vari-*, and the suffix *-ni*, which marks it as a verb. Ibid., 684.

77. Ibid.

78. Benjamín Lucas, pers. comm., December 2006.

79. *Relación de Michoacán*, 482–485.

80. Hiuacha is depicted reading a piece of paper, presumably a codex, in figure 27.

81. *Relación de Michoacán*, 490–498. The *Relación* also mentions that Don Pedro had in fact built his house in Pátzcuaro on the site where Hiuacha and his people were sacrificed.

82. According to Boone, the format of the "Aztec annals . . . links the polity to the year count and thereby implies that the polity will continue as long as the year

count does." Boone, *Stories in Red and Black*, 241. In the *Relación*, the death of Hiuacha, who kept the year count, might symbolize the end of the year count and therefore the end of his independent polity.

83. For a different reading of the meaning of this marriage ceremony, see Krippner-Martínez, *Rereading the Conquest*, 61–63.

84. "De la manera que se casavan los señores. Pónese aquí, como se casó don Pedro ques ahora Governador, porque desta manera se casavan todos." *Relación de Michoacán*, 288.

85. Stone, *In Place of Gods and Kings*, 24–25.

86. See "El fiscal contra Arellano, 1532," AGI, Justicia, Legajo 187, No. 1, Ramo 2; and Warren, *Conquest of Michoacán*, 241–242.

87. See, for example, *Codex Mendoza*, 61r; Berdan and Anawalt, *Codex Mendoza*, 3:129.

88. "[B]ienes dotales y parafernales." AGI, Justicia, Legajo 130, fol. 150r.

89. "[Minguareni,] poseer la tierra era a la vez contraer un parentesco." Castro Gutiérrez, *Los tarascos y el imperio español*, 27.

90. "Tener mucha familia, o esclavos." *Hapimberaqua*, a noun derived from the verb *hapimbeni*, means "slavery or subjection." See *Diccionario grande*, 2:214.

91. See Gilberti, *Vocabulario en lengua de Mechuacán*, 108; and *Diccionario grande*, 2:331.

92. *Relación de Michoacán*, pt. 3, chap. 10, p. 290.

93. Nader, "The Mendoza in the Fifteenth-Century Renaissance," 77–78.

94. Tovar de Teresa, "La utopía del Virrey de Mendoza," 24; and Nader, "The Mendoza in the Fifteenth-Century Renaissance," 77.

95. Gabrielle M. Spiegel, "Political Utility in Medieval Historiography: A Sketch," *History and Theory* 14, no. 3 (1975): 314–325. Michel de Certeau has also noticed that "tales and legends" create a "utopian space" outside daily competition and thus can be used to subvert established powers. See Certeau, *Practice of Everyday Life*, 23. I believe this is also the case with "histories" and can be a useful perspective from which to analyze such narratives.

CHAPTER 5

The original idea for this chapter arose during the seminar "'We See and Hear': Constructing Identity in the Pictorial Histories of the Sixteenth-Century Americas," co-taught by Cecelia F. Klein and Jeanette F. Peterson at the Getty Center, Los Angeles, in the spring of 2004. Portions of this paper were presented at the May 2006 meeting of the Grupo Kw'anískuyarhani de estudiosos del pueblo purépecha in Pátzcuaro, Michoacán, Mexico, and at the April 2008 annual meeting of the Renaissance Society of America, Chicago, which contributed valuable feedback. An earlier version of this chapter was published by the College Art Association as "The Tree of Jesse and the 'Relación de Michoacán': Mimicry and Identity in Colonial Mexico," in the December 2010 issue of the *Art Bulletin*.

1. The literature on Mixtec codices and their genealogical information is extensive. For an overview, see Boone, *Stories in Red and Black*, 87–124; see also Bruce E. Byland and John M. D. Pohl, *In the Realm of Eight Deer: The Archaeology of the Mixtec Codices* (Norman: University of Oklahoma Press, 1994); and Joyce Marcus, *Mesoamerican Writing Systems: Propaganda, Myth, and History in Four Ancient Civilizations* (Princeton, NJ: Princeton University Press, 1992), 272–278.

2. Nahua and Mixtec genealogies and dynastic lists present many differences in their formats. Some of these differences are based on their function and the descent and succession practices that guided these groups. For a discussion of Nahua genealogies and dynastic lists, see H. B. Nicholson, "Pre-Hispanic Central Mexican Historiography," in *Investigaciones contemporáneas sobre historia de México: Memorias de la tercera reunión de historiadores mexicanos y norteamericanos (1969)*, 38–81 (Austin: University of Texas Press, 1971); Elizabeth H. Boone, "The Aztec Pictorial History of the *Codex Mendoza*," in *The* Codex Mendoza, ed. Frances F. Berdan and Patricia R. Anawalt, 42–43 (Berkeley: University of California Press, 1992); Delia Cosentino, "Genealogías pictóricas en Tlaxcala colonial: Nobles afirmaciones del orden social," *Relaciones* 27, no. 105 (2006): 205–236; and Eduardo de Jesús Douglas, "Our Fathers, Our Mothers: Painting an Indian Genealogy in New Spain," in *Contested Visions in the Spanish Colonial World*, ed. Ilona Katzew, 117–131 (Los Angeles: Los Angeles County Museum of Art, 2011). For a discussion of the differences between Nahua and Mixtec genealogies and dynastic lists, see Douglas, *In the Palace of Nezahualcoyotl*, 95–98.

3. See, for example, the ancestors of Maya ruler Pakal represented in his sarcophagus and the Mixtec ancestors represented in *Codex Vindobonensis Mexicanus*, fol. 37 (http://www.famsi.org/research/graz/vindobonensis/img_page37.html); *Codex Selden*, fol. 2 (http://www.famsi.org/research/pohl/jpcodices/selden/selden02.jpg). See also Boone, *Stories in Red and Black*, 94–100; and Marcus, *Mesoamerican Writing Systems*, 274–276, 290–296.

4. Other well-known examples of colonial genealogical trees that used the Tree of Jesse as a model include the Yucatecan Xiu family tree (1558–1560) and the family tree included in the *Códice de Tepotzotlán*, 6r (also known as the *Fragment d'histoire chichimèque* dating to the end of the seventeenth century or beginning of the eighteenth). See Constance Cortez, "Gaspar Antonio Chi and the Xiu Family Tree" (PhD diss., University of California, Los Angeles, 1995), 67–109; Raquel Crespo Chiapa, "Fondo Mexicano de la Biblioteca Nacional de Francia, documento No. 081, El Códice de Tepotzotlán," http://www.amoxcalli.org.mx/presentaCodice.php?id=081. In addition, in the second half of the sixteenth century and beginning of the seventeenth, religious orders in Michoacán would use the Tree of Jesse format to represent their own members, as can be seen in the trees in the convents of Copándaro de Galeana (seventeenth century) and Charo (1578).

5. Homi K. Bhabha, "Of Mimicry and Man: The Ambivalence of Colonial Discourse," in *The Location of Culture* (London: Routledge, 2006), 121–131.

6. Stone, *In Place of Gods and Kings*, 83–85.

7. Espejel Carbajal, "Voces, lugares y tiempos," 64–67, 81.

8. Roskamp, "Las 44 láminas de la *Relación de Michoacán*," 547; and Alessandra Russo, "El renacimiento vegetal: Árboles de Jesé entre el viejo mundo y el nuevo," *Anales del Instituto de Investigaciones Estéticas* 73 (1998): 28–30.

9. Arthur Watson, *The Early Iconography of the Tree of Jesse* (London: Oxford University Press, 1934), 2; and *The Holy Bible Containing the Old and New Testaments* (London: George Eyre and Andrew Strahan, 1817), 575.

10. Watson, *Early Iconography of the Tree of Jesse*, 77–141.

11. Toribio de Benavente, *Historia de los indios de la Nueva España*, ed. Claudio Esteva Fabregat (Madrid: Dastin, 2001), 135. See also George Kubler, *Mexican Architecture of the Sixteenth Century* (New Haven, CT: Yale University Press; London: Oxford University Press, 1948), 2:374; Delia Cosentino, "Zinacantepec's *Tree of Saint Francis*: Cross Cultural Roots and Colonial Blossoms in a Sixteenth-Century Mexican Mural" (master's thesis, University of California, Los Angeles, 1996), 22; and Russo, "El renacimiento vegetal," 5–23.

12. Russo, "El renacimiento vegetal," 19–23.

13. Thérèse B. McGuire, "The Symbol of Power in Suger's *Tree of Jesse*," in *The Propagation of Power in the Medieval West*, ed. Martin Gosman, Arjo Vanderjagt, and Jan Veenstra, 301–311 (Groningen, Netherlands: Egbert Forsten, 1997); see also Osberg, "The Jesse Tree," 213–232.

14. See, for example, the dynastic trees by artists Simon Bening and António de Holanda in "Leaves from the Genealogy of the Royal Houses of Spain and Portugal, 1530–4," in *Illuminating the Renaissance: The Triumph of Flemish Manuscript Painting in Europe*, ed. Thomas Kren and Scot McKendrick, 460–463 (Los Angeles: J. Paul Getty Museum, 2003).

15. For the etymology of the term *cazonci*, see Martínez Baracs, *Convivencia y utopía*, 48–55. The art historian Constance Cortez and Roskamp have separately indicated that this line possibly represents a cord expressing the Nahuatl concept of *mecayotl* (lineage), which is derived from the root *mecatl*, meaning "cord." Cortez, "Gaspar Antonio Chi and the Xiu Family Tree," 130–131; and Roskamp, "Las 44 láminas de la *Relación de Michoacán*," 547.

16. Roskamp, "Las 44 láminas de la *Relación de Michoacán*," 547.

17. See, for example, Hans Roskamp's analysis of the *Lienzo de Jucutacato* in *La historiografía indígena de Michoacán*, 153.

18. "De los Señores que ubo después de muertos Hirepan y Tangaxoan y Hiquingaje." Escobar Olmedo, *Relación de Michoacán*, 512. All citations from the *Relación* in this chapter come from Escobar Olmedo's edition, unless otherwise noted.

19. Ibid., 513.

20. AHCP, Caja 131, Legajo 5, Exp. 21, 1588, fol. 3r. In this document, several *vecinos* (residents) of Pátzcuaro, while attempting to remove Don Constantino Huitzimengari, Don Antonio Huitzimengari's son, from the gubernatorial seat, mention that he was able to stay in power thanks to the assistance of Don Juan Paqui, his cousin. While the document does not mention the names of Paqui's parents, it does state that he was the son of one of Don Antonio's bothers: "[E]s publico

y notorio que el dicho don Juan Paqui es primo del dicho don Constantino, hijo del hermano del padre don Juan Paqui" ([I]t is public and well known that the aforementioned Don Juan Paqui is cousin of the aforementioned Don Constantino, son of the brother of the father of Don Juan Paqui). Given that Don Francisco (Don Antonio's brother portrayed in the tree) did not bear children, we can safely assume they are referring to a different brother.

21. AGI, Indiferente, Legajo 1382b, Year 1542.

22. See, for example, Delfina López Sarrelangue, *La nobleza indígena*, 167–178; and Corona Núñez, "Antonio Uitziméngari," 49–61.

23. Although little is understood of the naming customs of the people of Michoacán prior to the arrival of Spaniards, during the colonial period the names of prominent people during the first years of colonization often became the family names of their descendants. The name Uacujane survived as a family name (variously spelled Uacuxan, Guacuja, and Huacujane) among noblemen of Pátzcuaro in the archival documents from the sixteenth and seventeenth centuries, indicating that she or someone with her name possibly played an important role around the time of the conquest. See Centro de Documentación Histórica de Chapultepec, Instituto Nacional de Antropología e Historia, Serie Michoacán 114, 116, 118, cited in Kuthy-Saenger, "Strategies of Survival," 214–215.

24. Stone, *In Place of Gods and Kings*, 83.

25. "[C]omo arbolitos plantados a la vera del arroyo, que darán a su tiempo sus frutos." Leopoldo Campos, "Métodos misionales y rasgos biográficos de don Vasco de Quiroga según Cristobal Cabrera, Pbro," in *Don Vasco de Quiroga y arzobispado de Morelia*, ed. Manuel Ponce, 144 (Mexico City: Editorial Jus, 1965).

26. "[E]n tanto que por el sacramento del bautismo sus almas se vistieran de Jesucristo." Ibid., 149.

27. "[E]n cristiano se llamaba don Francisco" and "tornó cristiano y recibió el agua del santo bautismo y se llamo don Francisco." "Información de méritos y servicios de don Antonio Huitzimengari, hijo del último Cazonci de Michoacán, 1553–1554," AGI, Patronato Real, Legajo 60, Ramo 3, No. 2, fols. 27v, 28v.

28. Several historians have pointed out the significance of the death of Tangaxuan for colonial-period Michoacán. J. Benedict Warren, "The Death of the Cazonci," in *Conquest of Michoacán*, 211–236; Krippner-Martínez, "Politics of Conquest," 177–197; and Martínez Baracs, *Convivencia y utopía*, 151–157. The section that follows has benefited greatly from Warren's and Martínez Baracs's previous archival research.

29. In these same codices, trees often sprout from the inert bodies of sacrificial victims, as in the *Codex Borgia*, fol. 52. See *The Codex Borgia: A Full-Color Restoration of the Ancient Mexican Manuscript*, ed. Gisele Díaz and Alan Rodgers (New York: Dover, 1993), 26. See also Delia Cosentino, *Las joyas de Zinacantepec: Arte colonial en el monasterio de San Miguel* (Mexico City: El Colegio Mexiquense and Instituto Mexiquense de Cultura, 2003), 68–72. Although the European trees usually represent Jesse sleeping, a dead Jesse is not without precedent (as in the British Mu-

seum manuscript Harl. 2889, *Lectionary*, fol. 4r). Watson, *Early Iconography of the Tree of Jesse*, 85, plate 2. See also María Jesús Sanz, "Algunas representaciones del árbol de Jessé, durante el siglo XVI, en Sevilla y su antiguo reino," *Cuadernos de Arte e Iconografía* 2, no. 4 (1989): 123–124.

30. In her insightful analysis of the Tree of Saint Francis at the convent of San Miguel in Zinacantepec, Mexico, Delia Cosentino has pointed out that the artist showed the saints with swords piercing their chests or palm fronds to represent their martyrdom. See Cosentino, *Las joyas de Zinacantepec*, 63–64.

31. Other scholars have pointed out that Spaniards in the area were often weary of the political power Tangaxuan continued to exert during the early colonial period and saw him as interfering with their own interests. See, for example, Warren, "Death of the Cazonci," 211–236; and Martínez Baracs, *Convivencia y utopía*, 151–157.

32. "Y si el dicho Caçonçi quisiese morir como cristiano, pues ha recibido agua del bautismo, . . . mando que antes que sea quemado le sea dado un garrote a la garganta en manera que el dicho Caçonçi muera y del espíritu vital sea apartado y después sea echado en el fuego y quemado como dicho es." Scholes and Adams, *Proceso contra Tzintzicha Tangaxoan*, 66–67. For an analysis of this document, see Warren, *Conquest of Michoacán*, 222–236.

33. For his letters to the Spanish monarchs, see Nuño de Guzmán, "Carta a S.M. del presidente de la Audienzia de Mexico Nuño de Guzmán, en que refiere la jornada que hizo a Mechoacan a conquistar la provincia de los Tebles Chichimecas, que confinan con Nueva España. A ocho de julio de 1530" and "Carta a la emperatriz, de Nuño de Guzmán, dando cuenta del estado en que se hallaba la conquista y población de la Nueva Galicia y quejándose de los daños que le hacían la Audiencia y el marqués del Valle. De la ciudad de Compostela, a 12 de junio, 1532," in *Guadalajara y el Nuevo Mundo Nuño Beltrán de Guzmán: Semblanza de un conquistador*, ed. Adrián Blázquez and Thomas Calvo, 205–225, 237–262 (Guadalajara, Mexico: Institución Provincial de Cultura "Marqués de Santillana," 1992); for additional legal correspondence, see AGI, Justicia, Legajo 229; and for his memoir, see Nuño de Guzmán, *Memoria de los servicios que había hecho Nuño de Guzmán, desde que fue nombrado gobernador de Panuco en 1525*, ed. Manuel Carrera Stampa, 63–66 (Mexico City: José Porrúa e Hijos, 1955). The date for this memoir comes from the analysis done by Blázquez and Calvo, *Guadalajara y el Nuevo Mundo*, 51.

34. The treasure Tangaxuan relinquished varied from "stuff of very little price and value" to substantial sums of silver and gold, depending on the witness. For the former, see "Relación sacada de la probanza hecha por parte de Nuño de Guzmán . . . ," AGI, Justicia, Legajo 226, No. 2, Ramo 2; and for the latter, see "Información hecha pedida a Pedro de Arellano corregidor de Michuacán cerca de lo que dieron a Nuño de Guzmán, 15 de junio, 1531," AGI, Justicia, Legajo 226. According to some, Tangaxuan gave treasures only to Nuño de Guzmán, while others reported that García del Pilar, the translator for Guzmán, received a substantial portion. For example, compare "Información hecha pedida a Pedro de Arellano . . . , 15 de junio de 1531" to "Información tomada a los indios de Michuacán cerca de la plata y oro que el

Cazonci dio a Nuño de Guzmán, de febrero 14, 1531," AGI, Justicia, Legajo 226; and "Juicio seguido por Hernan Cortes contra los lics. Matienzo y Delgadillo, año 1531," *Boletín del Archivo General de la Nación* 9, no. 3 (1938): 339–407.

35. Each of these witnesses had even submitted a painting of the events (now lost) in evidence. "Información tomada a los indios de Michuacán . . . de febrero 14, 1531," AGI, Justicia, Legajo 226. Only Gonzalo had been present at the death of Tangaxuan, but Sebastián assured the authorities he had heard reports from eyewitnesses.

36. "Le arrastraron y quemaron muy cruelmente." "Juicio seguido por Hernan Cortes," 362. In this lawsuit, six witnesses say that Zinzicha Tangaxuan died by fire, one that he died by garrote, and five that they do not know how or do not specify it.

37. "Información hecha pedida a Pedro de Arellano . . . , 15 de junio, 1531," AGI, Justicia, Legajo 226.

38. "Luego sentenció por traidor a D. Francisco, y le mandó arrastrar á cola de un caballo, como todos vimos, y despues atado á un palo, y allí le quemaron, dicen que vivo: yo de compasion no le quise ver." "Cuarta Relación anónima de la jornada que hizo Nuño de Guzmán á la Nueva Galicia," in *Memoria de los servicios que había hecho Nuño de Guzmán, desde que fue nombrado gobernador de Panuco en 1525*, ed. Manuel Carrera Stampa, 100 (Mexico City: José Porrúa e Hijos, 1955).

39. "[Q]uemaron vivo." García del Pilar, "Relacion de la entrada de Nuño de Guzmán, que dió García del Pilar, su intérprete," in *Memoria de los servicios que había hecho Nuño de Guzmán, desde que fue nombrado gobernador de Panuco en 1525*, ed. Manuel Carrera Stampa, 181 (Mexico City: José Porrúa e Hijos, 1955). Warren has noticed the dependency of Pilar's account on the "Cuarta Relación anónima." Warren, *Conquest of Michoacán*, 319.

40. "[L]e pusieron fuego a la leña y comenzó a arder, así se quemó el dicho Cazonci hasta que naturalmente perdió la vida." "Averiguación de la plata del Cazonci. El dicho de García del Pilar y otros testigos," AGI, Justicia, Legajo 226, fol. 414v. I thank J. Benedict Warren for sharing with me his transcription of this document.

41. "[A]migo de Cortés, servidor de los españoles y vasallo del emperador, y que estaba en paz." Francisco López de Gómara, *Historia general de las indias: "Hispania Vitrix,"* ed. Pilar Guibelalde and Emiliano M. Aguilera (Barcelona: Editorial Iberia, 1965), 2:363–364. Not all of Guzmán's enemies remembered the events in this way. Bartolomé de Las Casas in 1542 accused Guzmán of having killed Tangaxuan by torture; and Bernal Díaz del Castillo charged Guzmán of having strangled him. However, both writers emphasized Guzmán's cruelty. See Bartolomé de Las Casas, *Brevísima relación de la destrucción de las indias*, ed. Isacio Pérez Fernández (Bayamón, Puerto Rico: Universidad Central de Bayamón, Centro de Estudios de los Dominicos del Caribe, Instituto de Estudios Históricos Juan Alejo de Arizmendi, 2000), 449–450; and Bernal Díaz del Castillo, *Historia verdadera de la conquista de la Nueva España*, ed. Joaquín Ramírez Cabañas (Mexico City: Editorial Porrúa, 1999), 534.

42. James Krippner-Martínez, writing about Nuño de Guzmán and his multi-

ple enemies, has pointed out that accusing a rival of extreme violence was a way to discredit him in sixteenth-century Mexico. James Krippner-Martínez, *Rereading the Conquest*, 38–39.

43. Guzmán, "Carta a la emperatriz," 247.

44. "[V]ino Sandoval por mandato del marqués a la provincia de Panuco con ciento y cincuenta de a caballo y quemó en un día trecientos señores della." Guzmán, *Memoria de los servicios*, 42.

45. "Un mayordomo suyo mató muchos indios ahorcándolos y quemándolos vivos y echándolos a perros bravos y cortándoles pies y manos y cabezas y lenguas, estando los indios de paz, sin otra causa más de por amedrentallos para que le sirviesen y diesen oro y tributos." De Las Casas, *Brevísima relación*, 452. Also, the "Cuarta Relación anónima" accused Nuño de Guzmán's field commander, Gonzalo López, of capturing the most important lord of Jalisco and burning him alive. And Pilar declared that in the town of Nochistlan, Guzmán's expedition had killed three indigenous men from Toluca by burning them and commented that in the province of Piastla, when indigenous allies wanted to abandon Guzmán's expedition, he and his associates had burned one alive and hanged another one. See "Cuarta Relación anónima," 113; and García del Pilar, "Relacion de la entrada de Nuño de Guzmán," 183, 190.

46. Felipe Castro Gutiérrez sees the version of Zinzicha Tangaxuan being burned alive as an invention by the indigenous nobility. Castro Gutiérrez, *Los tarascos y el imperio español*, 20–22. I do not seek to establish *how* Tangaxuan died but instead to demonstrate that the image in the *Relación* was part of a highly political debate.

47. "Información de méritos y servicios de don Antonio Huitzimengari," fols. 67r–79v. One of the indigenous witnesses, Don Marcos Quaniguata, even mentions that he saw it happen; ibid., fol. 69r. Indigenous witnesses also testified in 1541 that Tangaxuan had been burned. See AGI, Justicia, Legajo 130, fols. 507v, 572v, 581r, 589v, 600v, 602v.

48. See Francisco Ramírez, *El antiguo colegio de Pátzcuaro*, ed. Germán Viveros (Zamora, Mexico: El Colegio de Michoacán; Morelia, Mexico: Gobierno del Estado de Michoacán, 1987), 69; Beaumont, *Crónica de la provincia de los santos apóstoles San Pedro y San Pablo de Michoacán*, 2:193–211; and Moreno, *Vida de don Vasco de Quiroga*, 12, 30–31.

49. Robert Nelson, "Appropriation," in *Critical Terms for Art History*, ed. Robert Nelson and Richard Shiff, 116–128 (Chicago: University of Chicago Press, 1996).

50. Ibid., 127.

51. "Y más le condeno al dicho Caçonçi en perdimiento de todos sus bienes, los cuales aplico a cámara y fisco de su Majestad y en las costas de este proceso juntamente hechas." Guzmán, quoted in Scholes and Adams, *Proceso contra Tzintzicha Tangaxoan*, 67.

52. For the dating of Tangaxuan's baptism, see Warren, *Conquest of Michoacán*, 83–84.

53. See, for example, Ludolf von Sachsen, "De como el que muere ë acabado de

batizar se va derecho a parayso," in *Vita Cristi cartuxano romanaçado por fray Ambrosio* (Seville: J. Croberger, 1551), vol. 1, chap. 5, fol. rj. Fray Alcalá, who compiled the *Relación*, mentioned this book in a court deposition for a suit between Bishops Vasco de Quiroga and Juan de Zumarraga in 1541. See AGI, Justicia, Legajo 140, No. 2, Pieza 4; and Warren, "Fray Jerónimo de Alcalá" (2000), 42–43.

54. According to Delia Cosentino, during the colonial period genealogical trees from central Mexico were often included in court documents about land and political disputes. Delia Cosentino, "Drawing Out the Truth in Colonial Nahua Courtrooms," paper presented at the College Art Association annual conference, Seattle, 2004. In Michoacán, the *Codex Chilchota*, containing a genealogy from the seventeenth century, served the same purpose. Roskamp, *La historiografía indígena de Michoacán*, 284.

55. Roskamp has noted the discrepancy between the text and the image but has provided no explanation. Roskamp, "Las 44 láminas de la *Relación de Michoacán*," 547.

56. "Que nosotros en el principio fuímos conquistados de sus antepasados, y sus esclabos somos los ysleños. Y llevávamos sus comidas a los reys a cuestas, y achas para yr al monte por leña, y les llebábamos los jarros con que bebían, y por esto nos enpezaron a dezir hermanos, por ser sus Governadores, y entendíamos en lo que los reys nos mandaban." Don Pedro Cuiniarangari, quoted in *Relación de Michoacán*, 290.

57. Stone, *In Place of Gods and Kings*, 183–184.

58. Don Pedro was questioned under torture, and as Stone has pointed out, these were hardly normal circumstances. But of all the indigenous witnesses questioned under torture in the trial, he provided the most incriminating testimony.

59. See AGI, Justicia 229, May 4, 1532, where Guzmán's legal defense is presented by Antonio de Terán, especially Don Pedro's answers numbers eight and fifteen.

60. See "Relación sacada de la probanza hecha por parte de Nuño de Guzmán . . . ," AGI, Justicia, Legajo 226, No. 2, Ramo 2. This document does not have a date, but Don Pedro mentions he is forty-five years old, and in 1532, he had said he was thirty-eight (AGI, Justicia, Legajo 229, May 4, 1532). The seven-year difference gives us a date of 1539.

61. Don Pedro governed until his death in 1543.

62. By April 20, 1542, Don Francisco Tariacuri, eldest son of Zinzicha Tangaxuan, was married and owned land, the two prerequisites for reaching the majority of age. AGN, Mercedes, Vol. 1, Exp. 33, fol. 18.

63. AGN, Mercedes, Vol. 2, Exp. 490. I thank René Becerril Patlán of the Ex-Convento de Tiripetío for sharing his transcription of this document with me.

64. "[L]as tenya por herençia y por gobernación." Ibid. The dispute between the Uanacaze heirs and Don Pedro's descendants continued for many years. Once the capital was moved from Tzintzuntzan to Pátzcuaro, the son of Don Pedro led numerous suits against Don Antonio, when the latter became governor, accusing him of abusing his power and charging too much tribute. See, for example, AGI, Au-

diencia de México, Legajo 96; and AGI, Justicia, Legajo 155, No. 2; Legajo 157, No. 1; and Legajo 278, Nos. 1–2.

65. AGN, Mercedes, Vol. 1, Exp. 33, fol. 18, Year 1542. During the sixteenth century, other noblemen from Michoacán also sought to defend their lands from Spaniards by arguing that the lands belonged to them based on their lineage and inheritance rights. See, for example, AGN, Mercedes, Vol. 8, fol. 72.

66. AGI, Indiferente, Legajo 1382b, Year 1542.

67. "Ha andado siempre en hábito de español" and "siempre se ha tratado como español." AGN, Mercedes, Vol. 1, Exp. 33. For sumptuary laws during the colonial period, see López Sarrelangue, *La nobleza indígena de Pátzcuaro*, 114–116.

68. "Información de méritos y servicios de don Antonio Huitziméngari," AGI, Patronato Real, Legajo 60, Ramo 3, No. 2, fol. 69r. An official account of the geography and culture of Cuitzeo, Michoacán, solicited by the Spanish king, also mentions that short hair was the style of Spaniards. "Cuitzeo," in *Relaciones geográficas*, 1:53.

69. "Información de méritos y servicios de don Antonio Huitziméngari." For a brief analysis of this document, see Martínez Baracs, *Convivencia y utopía*, 321–325.

70. "Ítem, si saben que al dicho Cazonci pertenecía el señorío de la tierra de suso contenida por natura de sucesión legítima de más de setecientos años atrás que sus pasados habían sucedido el hijo mayor al padre por línea de varón conforme a ley de natura y que no le pertenecía por elección de gentes." "Información de méritos y servicios de don Antonio Huitziméngari," fol. 2v.

71. "Ítem, si saben que . . . [Tangaxuan] recibió de paz a los españoles y se entregó a sí y a sus hijos y tierra con todo lo que tenía a su Majestad, y recibió la fe de Cristo y mandó que todos sus súbditos la recibiesen la cual recibieron y recibida la conservaron y conservan hasta el día de hoy. Digan." Ibid., fol. 3r.

72. "Ítem, si saben que el dicho Cazonci dio grandísimo tesoro a los que gobernaban en nombre de su Majestad, en especial a Nuño de Guzmán, el cual en pago de ello le dio la muerte sin culpa por encubrir que no se supiese lo que de él había recibido ni de ello hubiese noticias. Digan." Ibid., fol. 3v.

73. "[M]uy amigo de españoles." Ibid., fol. 4r.

74. Roskamp, "Las 44 láminas de la *Relación de Michoacán*," 548. For more on the meaning of trees in Mesoamerica in the early colonial period, see Cortez, "Gaspar Antonio Chi and the Xiu Family Tree," esp. chap. 4. For a comparison of the *Relación*'s genealogical tree with other Mesoamerican beliefs, see Russo, "El renacimiento vegetal," 5–39.

75. Espejel Carbajal, "Voces, lugares y tiempos," 269–278.

76. Stone, *In Place of Gods and Kings*, 83–85.

77. *Relación de Michoacán*, 367.

78. Ibid., 250.

79. Corona Núñez, *Tres códices michoacanos*, 123; and Stone, *In Place of Gods and Kings*, 83.

80. I thank archaeologist Igor Cerda Farías for the information he provided me in the spring of 2006 about the tocuz oak.

81. *Relación de Michoacán*, 267. The judicial case of Juan Infante against Bishop Vasco de Quiroga and indigenous nobles in 1540 mentions that indigenous people burned oak wood at the temples. AGI, Justicia, Legajo 130, fols. 474v–475. I thank Igor Cerda Farías for this reference.

82. *Relación de Michoacán*, 315.

83. Ibid., 483–484. Today, oak trees continue to play an important role among the peoples of Michoacán. Many P'urhépecha communities appreciate the oak for its strength, and it is seen as a protector. Among its many functions the wood is utilized to make a highly valued charcoal, its branches to make verandas for the different celebrations of patron saints, and its acorns to use as food and to make dyes for cloth. I thank Nana Josefina Chávez from Cherán, Tata Pompeyo Cervantes from Sicuicho, and Alicia Mateo from Tarecuato for this information.

84. Gilberti defines *vapatzequa* as "barrio," and it is defined in the *Diccionario grande* as "barrio" and "collación." Gilberti, *Vocabulario en lengua de Mechuacan*, 182; and *Diccionario grande*, 2:678. For documents containing this term, see, for example, AGI, Audiencia de México, Legajo 96, Ramo 1, fol. 1r; AGI, Justicia, Legajo 278, No. 1, fol. 8v; AHCP, Caja 2, Exp. 6, fols. 18v, 19r; and P'urhépecha documents 1564, vol. 1, Michoacán Manuscript Collection, the James Ford Bell Library, University of Minnesota, Minneapolis, cited in Hedberg, "Conflicts and Continuities," 131, 137. I thank Benjamín Lucas for the information about oak galls, shared in the spring of 2006.

85. The compatibility of Michoacán's oaks with Christian beliefs did not go unnoticed by ecclesiastical authorities. In spite of biblical associations between the oak and the enemies of Yahweh (Russo, "El renacimiento vegetal," 9), the oak as a carrier of divine messages in Michoacán was adapted to transmit the Christian faith. A crucifix from the Church of the Capuchinas in Morelia, Michoacán, was finely carved from the trunk of an oak at the end of the sixteenth or beginning of the seventeenth century (today at the Museo Regional Michoacano in Morelia). In this way, oaks continued to be conductors of divine messages, though at that point they brought the message of a new god.

CHAPTER 6

An earlier version of this chapter was presented at the panel "Beyond Style: Fashioning Cultural Identity in Ancient Mesoamerican Art and Architecture," College Art Association 92nd annual conference, Seattle, February 2004.

1. "Con esto quedaba la provincia perdida para Dios y para el Rey." Joseph Moreno, *Vida de don Vasco de Quiroga, ordenanzas, testamento* (Morelia, Mexico: Balsal Editores, 1989), 31. See also Escobar Olmedo, *Relación de Michoacán*, 362; Beaumont, *Crónica de la provincia de los santos apóstoles San Pedro y San Pablo de Michoacán*, 2:137, 208–209; Scholes and Adams, *Proceso contra Tzintzicha Tangaxoan*, 7; Vasco de Puga, *Provisiones, cédulas, instrucciones de su magestad* (Mexico City: J. M. Sandoval, 1878), 1:289–290; and Warren, *Conquest of Michoacán*, 222. All cita-

tions from the *Relación* in this chapter come from Escobar Olmedo's edition, unless otherwise noted.

2. "Cómo muría el Caçonci y las cirimonias con que le enterravan," in *Relación de Michoacán*, 299.

3. Ibid., 299.

4. Svetlana Boym, "Restorative Nostalgia: Conspiracies and Return to Origins," in *The Future of Nostalgia* (New York: Basic Books, 2001), 41–42.

5. Eric Hobsbawm, "Introduction: Inventing Traditions," in *The Invention of Tradition*, ed. Eric Hobsbawm and Terence Ranger, 1 (Cambridge: Cambridge University Press, 1984). I find the relationship between tradition, custom, and convention more complex than Hobsbawm allows for in his work, but his discussion of traditions at times of change and their significance among practioners is thought provoking.

6. Personal observation of the original manuscript, summer 2007.

7. *Relación de Michoacán*, 301.

8. "Y todos llebaban sus ynsignias de balientes honbres." Ibid., 302.

9. "Yvan delante toda aquella gente que llebaban consigo para matar." Ibid.

10. According to Helen P. Pollard, the jar is of a type associated with the elite housing districts of Tzintzuntzan. Pollard, *Taríacuri's Legacy*, 35–38.

11. An exception is Cynthia L. Stone, who in her 1994 article describes the servants as having faces painted yellow. Stone, "Rewriting Indigenous Traditions," 96.

12. Tudela, *Relación de Michoacán*, 218; and *Relación de Michoacán*, ed. Leoncio Cabrero, Crónicas de América (Madrid, Spain: Historia 16, 1989), 16.

13. "And many other of his servants would volunteer to go to serve him . . . they would not let them go because they would say that the other officials were enough, for them they would put garlands on their heads, and paint their faces with a yellow color" (Y otros muchos criados suyos se ofrecian para le yr a servir . . . no los dexavan yr porque dezian que bastauan aquellos otros ofiçiales, a los quales ponian guirnaldas en las cabeças, y theñianles los rrostros de color amarillo). See "Capitulo de donde tuvo principio la ydolatria y delas causas porque los ydolos fueron adorados en el mundo. De la muerte y cerimonias muy estrañas con que enterraban al calçonçin, señor de mchuacan [*sic*] y como mataban a otros muchos para que fuesen a servir al otro mundo." Toribio de Benavente, *Memoriales*, in the *Libro de oro*, Benson Latin American Collection, JGI 31, fol. 85r, University of Texas at Austin. I am grateful to Michael Hironymous of Rare Books and Manuscripts, Benson Latin American Collection, University of Texas at Austin, for sending me copies of this chapter.

14. See Warren, "Fray Jerónimo de Alcalá" (1971), 317; and Stone, "Rewriting Indigenous Traditions," 87–114. In his *Monarquía indiana*, Torquemada describes the procession in the following way: "It was an unbreakable law that at this time many had to die with the king; because they said (falsely and untruthfully) that they were going with him, to serve him in the other world. These were men and women, and the caççontzin left in [charge of] the kingdom and government would choose them. . . . They would wash and bathe them very carefully, and then they would

daub their entire bodies with a yellow ink, that they used to use, and they would put garlands on their heads; and organized in a line, one behind the other, they would go in procession in front of the catafalque of the body of the deceased, which they would take outside the palace at midnight sharp. And certain musicians would accompany him while playing cayman bones on turtle shells. The catafalque was carried on the shoulders of his sons and of the main nobles of the kingdom, and the nobles of the peoples of Eneani, Zacapu, Hireti, Uanacaye" (Era lei inviolable, que en esta ocasion havian de morir muchos, con el Rei; porque decian [falsa, y mentirosamente] que iban con èl, à servirle al otro Mundo. Estos eran Hombres, y Mugeres, y los havia de señalar el Cacçontzin, que quedaba en el Señorìo, y Gobierno. . . . A todos estos lababan, y bañaban, con gran cuidado, y luego los embadurnaban todo el cuerpo, con vna tinta amarilla, de que ellos vsaban, y les ponían Guirnaldas, en sus cabeças, y puestos, en renglera, vnos tras otros, hacian vna larga Procesión delante de las andas, del Cuerpo del Difunto, el qual sacaban al punto de la media noche de Palacio, y le acompañaban ciertos Musicos, tañendo con vnos huesos de Caimanes, en vnas rodelas de Tortugas. Iban las Andas en hombros de sus Hijos, y de los Señores mas Principales de el Reino, y los Señores de los Pueblos de Eneani, Zacapu, Hireti, Vanacaye). Juan de Torquemada, "De la solemnidad, con que se hacian los entierros, y obsequias de los reies de Mechoacan, que es capitulo de notar," in *Monarquía indiana*, 524–525 (Mexico City: Salvador Chavez Hayhoe, 1943). See also Pablo Beaumont, *Crónica de Michoacán*, 2:56; de la Rea, *Crónica de la orden de N. seráfico P.S. Francisco*, 86; and Isidro Felix de Espinosa, *Crónica franciscana de Michoacán*, ed. Nicolás León (Morelia, Mexico: Instituto de Investigaciones Históricas de la Universidad Michoacana de San Nicolás de Hidalgo and Morevallado Editores, 2003), 37.

15. Tudela, *Relación de Michoacán*, 218; *Relación de las ceremonias y ritos y población y gobierno de los indios de la provincia de Michoacán (1541)*, ed. José Corona Núñez (Mexico City: Balsal Editores, 1977), 218; and Roskamp, "Las 44 láminas de la *Relación de Michoacán*," 623.

16. Pablo Beaumont mentions in his eighteenth-century *Crónica de Michoacán* that the yellow substance came from something called *sacatlatlale*. I have not been able to locate the modern equivalent of sacatlatlale. Tudela mentions that the yellow substance was made from the cuscuta plant (*tiripu*). Beaumont, "Solemnidad en los entierros," 2:56; and Tudela, *Relación de Michoacán*, 221n10.

17. *Relación de Michoacán*, 428–430.

18. Ibid., 400. Corona Núñez has equated the goddess Cuerahuaperi with her daughter Xaratanga. José Corona Núñez, "Estudio preliminar," in *Relación de Michoacán (1541)*, ed. José Corona Núñez (Mexico City: Balsal Editores, 1977), xii; and José Corona Núñez, *Tres códices michoacanos* (Morelia, Mexico: Universidad Michoacana de San Nicolás de Hidalgo, 1986), 108.

19. For the defeat of Zurumban's son, Hiuacha, and the Uanacaze's subsequent conquest of the region, see *Relación de Michoacán*, 490–502.

20. Within the *Relación*, elites and cities maintained such intricate relationships with their deities that wars and events were often attributed to the latter. On the al-

location of supernaturals to individual towns and their elites, see ibid., pt. 2, chap. 2, p. 367, and chap. 4, pp. 375–378. Helen P. Pollard also notes this in her book *Tariacuri's Legacy*, 175.

21. *Relación de Michoacán*, 483–484.

22. Ibid., 500.

23. The conquered status of the local nobility was not lost on the contributors to the *Relación*. After the Uanacaze had co-opted the worship of the goddess mother of Xarantanga, the Uanacaze ruler addressed as "Mothers" the priests who had replaced their ruler, Zurumban, thereby marking their conquered status by means of gender reversal. According to James Krippner-Martínez, power struggles in the *Relación* are often expressed in gendered terms. Conquered people, and those about to be conquered, are often referred to in terms of gender reversals. For example, when Cortes's army defeated the Aztecs of central Mexico, Aztec men lamented their defeat by saying, "They have dressed us all in women's skirts" (A todos nos [h]an puesto nagüas de mugeres). Ibid., 343. Uanacaze rulers are often said to have taunted their about-to-be-defeated enemies by addressing them either as women acting and dressing as men, or as men acting as women. See ibid., pt. 2, chaps. 15, 18, 22; and Krippner-Martínez, "Politics of Conquest," 191–194. For a similar use of gender metaphors among the Aztecs, see Cecelia F. Klein, "Fighting with Femininity: Gender and War in Aztec Mexico," *Estudios de Cultura Náhuatl* 24 (1994): 219–253.

24. *Relación de Michoacán*, 476: "[D]ile que ya somos biejos y cansados, y que queremos ya yr al dios del ynfierno. Pues que ¿dónde tomaremos a la partida gente que llevemos con nosotros para nuestro estrado? Y dirásle que te señale dónde [h]a de ser la pelea, ¿en una sementera de maíz verde, a la ribera? Y que sy yo matare allí a los suyos, que aquellos que murieren será[n] mi cama y estrado para mi muerte. Y que sy él matare de los míos, que tanbién será estrado para su muerte."

25. The *Relación*, for example mentions, "[A]nd [Zurumban] took a bit of yellow pigment, and he had it in his hand and he came to Tariacuri and said to him: 'Sir, would you not put on a bit of this color?' Tariacuri answered: 'Brother, what do you say? How could I put on that color? I already have this black color; that color belongs to my god Curicaueri'" ([Y] [Zurumban] tomó de un color amarillo, y traíalo en la mano y llegó a Tariacuri y díxole: "Señor, ¿cómo no te pondrás un poco desta color?" Respondiole Tariacuri: "¿Qué dizes hermano? ¿Cómo me tengo de poner este color? Que ya yo tengo este color negro, que es de mi dios Curicaueri? [*sic*]"). *Relación de Michoacán*, 429. See also ibid., 431.

26. "There were others called *achaecha*, who were nobles, who continuously accompanied the cazonci and kept the palace for him" (Avía otros llamados *achaecha* que heran principales, que de contino acompañavan al Caçonçi, y le tenían palacio). Ibid., 251–252. In the sixteenth century, the friar and linguist Maturino Gilberti translated *achaecha* as *señores* (lords). Gilberti, *Arte de la lengua de Michuacán*, 100. See also Tudela, *Relación de Michoacán*, 173n17; Márquez Joaquín, "El significado de las palabras p'urhépecha en la *Relación de Michoacán*," 701.

27. *Diccionario grande*, 2:589; and Alicia Mateo, pers. comm., August 2008.

28. The term *manaratspeti*, also used in the sixteenth century for *criado*, corroborates this reading, as it literally means "the one who moves things." *Diccionario grande*, 1:179, 648; Gilberti, *Vocabulario en lengua de Mechuacán*, 332; and Benjamín Lucas, pers. comm., December 2006.

29. "Y llevávamos sus comidas a los reys a cuestas, y achas para yr al monte por leña, y les llebábamos los jarros con que bebían." *Relación de Michoacán*, 290.

30. The text describing the sacrificial victims also mentions that "all of them carried the tools of the service they used to do for the deceased cazonci" (llebaban todos estos consigo, todo aquello de sus oficios de que serbían al Cazonçi muerto). Ibid., 301.

31. Ibid., 303.

32. Some of the deceased lords in figure 57 carry a turquoise mask; and others, a yellow mask. It is likely that the yellow represents gold because in the *Relación*'s mention of the first Uanacaze royal funeral, the deceased (two Uanacaze lords) don gold masks. Ibid., 395.

33. Cecelia F. Klein, "Masking Empire: The Material Effects of Masks in Aztec Mexico," *Art History* 9, no. 2 (1986): 154–157.

34. Tudela, "Prólogo," xii.

35. *Relación de Michoacán*, 302–303.

36. "[E]l que hera, Caçonçi estava en lugar de Curicaueri." Ibid., 250.

37. Ibid.

38. The nephews and son of the Uanacaze leader Tariacuri defeat Hiuacha, son of Zurumban, in chapter 30 of part 2 of the *Relación* and sacrifice him at midnight to their god Curicaueri. Ibid., 495–498.

39. Tudela, *Relación de Michoacán*, 136n9.

40. According to Claudia Espejel Carbajal, *La información del derecho* by Vasco de Quiroga includes an almost identical description of succession practices (from father to son) dating to the 1530s. See also "Recaudos y títulos de las tierras del catzontzi," 1597, AGN, *Tierras*, Vol. 942, Exp. 2 (cited in Castro Gutiérrez, *Los tarascos y el imperio español*, 107).

41. *Relación de Michoacán*, 304–306.

42. "[A]tado a un palo y ya cercado de leña para ser quemado dijo a su Yerno D. Alonso Ecuánguri, que mirase cuál era el pago que le daban los Españoles por los servicios tan considerables que les había hecho; le encargó que recogiese sus cenizas y las llevase al sepulcro de sus Padres." Moreno, *Vida de don Vasco de Quiroga*, 31.

43. Indigenous lords often boasted of being the ruler's criados. See, for example, the testimonies of Hernand Cana, governor of Cuanaxo, in AGI, Justicia, Legajo 130, fol. 490v; and of Don Juan Chichique in "Información de méritos y servicios de don Antonio," AGI, Patronato Real, Legajo 60, Ramo 3, No. 2, fol. 70v. Interestingly, the P'urhépecha word for *criados* is *mimiecha*, which sixteenth-century dictionaries translate as "brothers or servants." For example, see Gilberti, *Vocabulario en lengua de Mechuacán*, 108; and *Diccionario grande*, 2:331. See also Kuthy-Saenger, "Strategies of Survival," 264.

44. See also Felipe Castro, *Los tarascos y el imperio español*, 29–31.

Bibliography

ARCHIVAL DOCUMENTS

Archivo General de Indias (AGI)

Audiencia de México

Legajo 25, No. 48
Legajo 27, No. 43
Legajo 68, Ramo 3, No. 11, 2–4
Legajo 94
Legajo 95
Legajo 96
Legajo 96, Ramo IV
Legajo 374
Legajo 374, Legajo 60, Ramo 3, No. 40

Indiferente

Legajo 1382a
Legajo 1382b, Year 1542
Legajo 1961, L3, fol. 178v, May 12, 1534

Justicia

Legajo 96
Legajo 108, No. 6
Legajo 112, No. 4
Legajo 116, No. 4
Legajo 129, No. 3
Legajo 130
Legajo 135, No. 3
Legajo 139, No. 1
Legajo 140, No. 2
Legajo 155, No. 2
Legajo 157, No. 1
Legajo 163
Legajo 173, No. 1, Ramo 2
Legajo 187, No. 1, Ramo 2
Legajo 188, No. 3, May 14, 1529
Legajo 188, No. 3, Year 1535
Legajo 189, No. 1, Ramo 2
Legajo 203
Legajo 226, fols. 409v–416v, "Averiguación de la plata del Cazonci. El dicho de García del Pilar y otros testigos"
Legajo 226, "Información hecha pedida a Pedro de Arellano Corregidor de Michuacán cerca de lo que dieron a Nuño de Guzmán, 15 de junio, 1531"
Legajo 226, "Información tomada a los indios de Michuacán cerca de la plata y oro que el Cazonci dio a Nuño de Guzmán, 14 de febrero, 1531"
Legajo 226, No. 2, Ramo 2, "Relación sacada de la probanza hecha por parte de Nuño de Guzmán . . ."
Legajo 227
Legajo 229
Legajo 263, Pieza 3, "Residencia del Virey Antonio de Mendoza de 1546 a 1547"
Legajo 278, No. 1
Legajo 278, No. 2
Legajo 1009, No. 1

Patronato Real

Legajo 21, No. 2, Ramo 3
Legajo 60, Ramo 3, No. 2, "Información de méritos y servicios de don Antonio Huitzimengari, hijo del último Cazonci de Michoacán, 1553–1554"
Legajo 182, No. 44, Year 1573, "Relación de los pueblos de indios que en aquel año tenían a su cargo los religiosos de San Agustín en Nueva España. Por Juan Adriano, provincial"

Archivo General de la Nación, Mexico (AGN)

Mercedes, Vol. 1, Exp. 33, Year 1542
Mercedes, Vol. 2, Exp. 258
Mercedes, Vol. 2, Exp. 485, fol. 199v, October 27, 1543
Mercedes, Vol. 2, Exp. 490
Mercedes, Vol. 4, Exp. 186, fol. 56v, August 23, 1554
Mercedes, Vol. 4, fol. 257, November 5, 1555
Mercedes, Vol. 4, fols. 264–264v, November 18, 1555
Mercedes, Vol. 4, fol. 291v, December 3, 1555
Mercedes, Vol. 4, fol. 292, December 3, 1555
Mercedes, Vol. 8, fol. 72
Mercedes, Vol. 17

Archivo Histórico de la Ciudad de Pátzcuaro (AHCP)

Caja 1, Exp. 11
Caja 1, Exp. 31, fol. 8, 1556
Caja 2, Exp. 6
Caja 2 bis, Exp. 55, Year 1566
Caja 2 bis, Exp. 82, fols. 670–672, Year 1569
Caja 3, Exp. 78
Caja 3 bis, Exp. 54, Year 1578
Caja 4, Exp. 33
Caja 4, Exp. 39, Year 1588
Caja 4, Exp. 55
Caja 4, Exp. 63
Caja 5 bis, Exp. 73
Caja 10, Carpeta 8, fol. 3
Caja 131, Legajo 3, Exp. 1
Caja 131, Legajo 3, Exp. 17, Year 1564
Caja 131, Legajo 4, Exp. 12, Year 1573
Caja 131, Legajo 5, Exp. 21
Caja 131, Legajo 5, Year 1584
Caja 131, Legajo 6, Exp. 11
Caja 131, Legajo 6, Exp. 20
Protocolos, No. 103

PUBLISHED MATERIALS

Adje Both, Arnd. "La música prehispánica: Sonidos rituales a lo largo de la historia." *Arqueología Mexicana* 16, no. 94 (2008): 28–37.

Alfonso X. "Partida 7." In *Las Siete Partidas del Rey Don Alfonso el Sabio*, 517–728. Madrid: Imprenta Real, 1807.

Anawalt, Patricia. *Indian Clothing before Cortés: Mesoamerican Costumes from the Codices*. Norman: University of Oklahoma Press, 1981.

———. "Pan-Mesoamerican Costume Repertory at the Time of Spanish Contact." PhD diss., University of California, Los Angeles, 1975.

Appadurai, Arjun. *Modernity at Large: Cultural Dimensions of Globalization*. Minneapolis: University of Minnesota Press, 2000.

Arnauld, Marie-Charlotte, and Brigitte Faugère-Kalfon. "Evolución de la ocupación humana en el centro-norte de Michoacán (Proyecto Michoacán, CEMCA) y la emergencia del estado tarasco." In *Génesis, culturas y espacios en Michoacán*, edited by Véronique Darras, 13–34. Mexico City: Centre Français d'Études Mexicaines et Centraméricaines, 1998.

Arnauld, Marie-Charlotte, and Dominique Michelet. "Les migrations postclassiques au Michoacán et au Guatemala: Problèmes et perspectives." In *Vingt études sur le Mexique et le Guatemala réunies à la mémoire de Nichole Percheron*, edited by Alain Breton, Jean-Pierre Berthe, and Sylvie Lecoin, 67–92. Toulouse, France: Presses Universitaires du Mirail, 1991.

Arvey, Margaret. "Women of Ill-Repute in the Florentine Codex." In *The Role of Gender in Precolumbian Art and Architecture*, edited by Virginia E. Miller, 179–204. Lanham, MD: University Press of America, 1988.

Baird, Ellen. *The Drawings of Sahagún's* Primeros memoriales*: Structure and Style*. Norman: University of Oklahoma Press, 1993.

Barrett, Elinore. *La cuenca del Tepalcatepec*. Translated by Roberto Gómez Ciriza. Mexico City: SepSetentas, 1975.

———. "Encomiendas, mercedes and haciendas in the Tierra Caliente of Michoacán." *Jahrbuch für Geschichte von Staat, Wirtschaft und Gesellschaft Lateinamerikas* 10 (1973): 71–112.

———. "Indian Community Hospitals in Colonial Michoacán." In *Historical Geography of Latin America, Papers in Honor of Robert C. West*, 63–73. Baton Rouge: Louisiana State University Printing Office, 1980.

———. "Indian Community Lands in the Tierra Caliente of Michoacán." *Jahrbuch für Geschichte von Staat, Wirtschaft und Gesellschaft Lateinamerikas* 11 (1974): 78–120.

———. "The King's Copper Mine: Inguarán in New Spain." *The Americas* 37, no. 1 (1981): 1–29.

———. "Land Tenure and Settlement in the Tepalcatepec Lowland, Michoacán, Mexico." PhD diss., University of California, Berkeley, 1970.

———. *The Mexican Colonial Copper Industry*. Albuquerque: University of New Mexico Press, 1987.

Barrientos Grandon, Javier. *La cultura jurídica en la Nueva España*. Mexico City: Universidad Nacional Autónoma de México, 1993.

Barth, Fredrik. *Ethnic Groups and Boundaries: The Social Organization of Culture*

Difference. Bergen-Oslo, Norway: Universitets Forlaget; London: George Allen and Unwin, 1969.

Barthes, Roland. "Rhetoric of the Image." In *Image, Music, Text*, 32–51. New York: Hill and Wang, 1977.

Batalla Rosado, Juan José. "Una aproximación a la iconografía tarasca a través de las ilustraciones de la *Relación de Michoacán*." In *Relación de Michoacán*, edited by Armando Escobar Olmedo, 143–172. Morelia, Mexico: Patrimonio Nacional, H. Ayuntamiento de Morelia; Madrid: Testimonio Compañía Editorial, 2001.

Beals, Ralph. *Cherán: A Sierra Tarascan Village*. Smithsonian Institution, Institute of Social Anthropology. Washington, DC: United States Government Printing Office, 1946.

———. "The Tarascans." In *Handbook of Middle American Indians*, vol. 8, *Ethnology*, pt. 2, edited by Evon Vogt, 725–773. Austin: University of Texas Press, 1969.

Beals, Ralph, and Pedro Carrasco. "Games of the Mountain Tarascans." *American Anthropologist* 46 (1944): 516–522.

Beals, Ralph, Pedro Carrasco, and Thomas McCorkle. *Houses and House Use of the Sierra Tarascans*. Smithsonian Institution, Institute of Social Anthropology. Washington, DC: United States Government Printing Office, 1944.

Beaumont, Pablo. *Crónica de la provincia de los santos apóstoles San Pedro y San Pablo de Michoacán*. Morelia, Mexico: Balsal Editores, 1969.

———. *Crónica de Michoacán*. Vol. 2. Mexico City: Talleres Gráficos de la Nación, 1932.

Becerril Patlán, René, and Igor Cerda Farías. "Recatón, casquillo y dardo: La lanza del petámuti y los nuncios sinodales cristianos." In *Catálogo de documentos históricos coloniales de Michoacán: Expedientes microfilmados y reproducidos*, 147–153. Morelia, Mexico: Universidad Michoacana de San Nicolás de Hidalgo, 2005.

Benavente, Toribio de. *Historia de los indios de la Nueva España*. Edited by Claudio Esteva Fabregat. Madrid: Dastin, 2001.

Bening, Simon, and António de Holanda. "Leaves from the Genealogy of the Royal Houses of Spain and Portugal, 1530–4." In *Illuminating the Renaissance: The Triumph of Flemish Manuscript Painting in Europe*, edited by Thomas Kren and Scot McKendrick, 460–463. Los Angeles: J. Paul Getty Museum, 2003.

Berdan, Frances. *Ethnic Identity in Nahua Mesoamerica: The View from Archaeology, Art History, Ethnohistory, and Contemporary Ethnography*. Salt Lake City: University of Utah Press, 2008.

Bernal García, María Elena, and Ángel Julián García Zambrano. "El altepetl colonial y sus antecedentes prehispánicos: Contexto teórico-historiográfico." In *Territorialidad y paisaje en el Altepetl del siglo XVI*, edited by Federico Fernández Christlieb and Ángel Julián García Zambrano, 31–113. Mexico City: Fondo de Cultura Económica and Universidad Nacional Autónoma de México, 2006.

Bhabha, Homi. "Of Mimicry and Man: The Ambivalence of Colonial Discourse." In *The Location of Culture*, by Homi Bhabha, 121–131. London: Routledge, 2006.

Blázquez, Adrián, and Thomás Calvo. *Guadalajara y el Nuevo Mundo: Nuño Beltrán de Guzmán, semblanza de un conquistador.* Guadalajara, Spain: Institución Provincial de Cultura "Marqués de Santillana," 1992.

Blethen, John. "The Educational Activities of Fray Alonso de la Vera Cruz in Sixteenth Century Mexico." *The Americas* 5, no. 1 (1948): 31–47.

Boone, Elizabeth H. "The Aztec Pictorial History of the *Codex Mendoza*." In *The* Codex Mendoza, edited by Frances F. Berdan and Patricia R. Anawalt, 35–54. Berkeley: University of California Press, 1992.

———. *The* Codex Magliabechiano *and the Lost Prototype of the Magliabechiano Group.* 2 vols. Berkeley: University of California Press, 1983.

———. *Cycles of Time and Meaning in the Mexican Books of Fate.* Austin: University of Texas Press, 2007.

———. *Stories in Red and Black: Pictorial Histories of the Aztecs and Mixtecs.* Austin: University of Texas Press, 2000.

Boone, Elizabeth H., and Michael E. Smith. "Postclassic International Styles and Symbol Sets." In *The Postclassic Mesoamerican World*, edited by Michael E. Smith and Frances F. Berdan, 186–193. Salt Lake City: University of Utah Press, 2003.

Borah, Woodrow. *Justice by Insurance: The General Indian Court of Colonial Mexico and the Legal Aides of the Half-Real.* Berkeley: University of California Press, 1983.

Born, Lester. "The Perfect Prince: A Study in Thirteenth- and Fourteenth-Century Ideals." *Speculum* 3, no. 4 (1928): 470–504.

Bourdieu, Pierre. *Distinction: A Social Critique of the Judgement of Taste.* Translated by Richard Nice. Cambridge, MA: Harvard University Press, 1979.

Boym, Svetlana. "Restorative Nostalgia: Conspiracies and Return to Origins." In *The Future of Nostalgia*, by Svetlana Boym, 41–48. New York: Basic Books, 2001.

Brand, Donald. "Ethnohistoric Synthesis of Western Mexico." In *Handbook of Middle American Indians*, vol. 11, *Archaeology of Northern Mesoamerica*, pt. 2, edited by Gordon Ekholm and Ignacio Bernal, 632–656. Austin: University of Texas Press, 1971.

———. "An Historical Sketch of Geography and Anthropology in the Tarascan Region." *New Mexico Anthropologist* 6–7, no. 2 (1943): 37–108.

———. *Quiroga, a Mexican Municipio.* Smithsonian Institution, Institute of Social Anthropology Publication 11. Washington, DC: United States Government Printing Office, 1951.

———. "Recent Archaeologic and Geographic Investigations in the Basin of the Río Balsas, Guerrero and Michoacan." In *Proceedings of the Twenty-Seventh International Congress of Americanists*, 140–147. Mexico City: Secretaría de Educación Pública, 1942.

Bravo Ugarte, José. "La *Relación de Michoacán*." *Historia Mexicana* 12, no. 45 (1962): 13–25.

Brown, Betty Ann. "Seen but Not Heard: Women in Aztec Ritual—the Sahagún Texts." In *Text and Image in Pre-Columbian Art: Essays on the Interrelationship of the Verbal and Visual Arts*, edited by Janet Berlo, 119–153. Oxford: BAR International Series, 1983.

Brumfiel, Elizabeth. "Ethnic Groups and Political Development in Ancient Mexico." In *Factional Competition and Political Development in the New World*, edited by Elizabeth Brumfiel and John Fox, 89–102. New Directions in Archaeology. Cambridge: Cambridge University Press, 1994.

Burrus, Ernest. "Cristobal Cabrera on the Missionary Methods of Vasco de Quiroga." *Manuscripta* 5, no. 1 (1961): 17–27.

Byland, Bruce E., and John M. D. Pohl. *In the Realm of Eight Deer: The Archaeology of the Mixtec Codices*. Norman: University of Oklahoma Press, 1994.

Campos, Leopoldo. "Métodos misionales y rasgos biográficos de don Vasco de Quiroga según Cristobal Cabrera, Pbro." In *Don Vasco de Quiroga y Arzobispado de Morelia*, edited by Manuel Ponce, 107–155. Mexico City: Editorial Jus, 1965.

Caso, Alfonso. "El calendario de los tarascos." In *Relación de Michoacán*, edited by Armando Escobar Olmedo, 533–558. Morelia, Mexico: Patrimonio Nacional, H. Ayuntamiento de Morelia; Madrid: Testimonio Compañía Editorial, 2001.

———. "Comentario al *Códice Baranda*." *Miscellanea Paul Rivet, octogenario dicata* 1 (1958): 373–389.

Castro Gómez, María Concepción. "Arte popular indígena colonial en Michoacán." Undergraduate thesis, Universidad Nacional Autónoma de México, 1984.

Castro Gutiérrez, Felipe. *Los tarascos y el imperio español 1600–1740*. Mexico City: Universidad Nacional Autónoma de México; Morelia, Mexico: Universidad Michoacana de San Nicolás de Hidalgo, 2004.

Cerda Farías, Igor. *En el pueblo de Tiripetío, en la provincia de Michoacán. La edad dorada. El siglo XVI.* Morelia, Mexico: Universidad Michoacana de San Nicolás de Hidalgo, 2005.

Certeau, Michel de. *The Practice of Everyday Life*. Berkeley: University of California Press, 1984.

Cervantes de Salazar, Francisco. "Crónica de la Nueva España," MS 2011. Biblioteca Nacional de Madrid, microfilm at the Ex-Convento de Tiripetío. 1560?

Chipman, Donald. *Nuño de Guzmán and the Province of Pánuco in New Spain, 1518–1533*. Glendale, CA: A. H. Clark, 1967.

The Chronicle of Michoacán. Translated by Eugene R. Craine and Reginald C. Reindrop. Norman: University of Oklahoma Press, 1970.

The Codex Borgia*: A Full-Color Restoration of the Ancient Mexican Manuscript*. Edited by Gisele Díaz and Alan Rodgers. New York: Dover, 1993.

The Codex Mendoza. Edited by Frances F. Berdan and Patricia Rieff Anawalt. 4 vols. Berkeley: University of California Press, 1992.

The Codex Nuttall*: A Picture Manuscript from Ancient Mexico*. Edited by Zelia Nuttall. New York: Dover Publications, 1975.

Códice Xolotl. Edited by Charles Dibble. Mexico City: Universidad Nacional Autónoma de México, 1951.

Corona Núñez, José. "Antonio Uitziméngari, primer humanista tarasco." In *Humanistas novohispanos de Michoacán*, 49–61. Morelia, Mexico: Universidad Michoacana de San Nicolás de Hidalgo, 1982.

———. "Estudio preliminar." In *Relación de las ceremonias y ritos y población y go-*

bierno de los indios de la provincia de Michoacán (1541), edited by José Corona Núñez, v–xx. Mexico City: Balsal Editores, 1977.

———. *Tres códices michoacanos*. Morelia, Mexico: Universidad Michoacana de San Nicolás de Hidalgo, 1986.

Cortés Alonso, Vicenta. "Un temprano testimonio de historia oral." In *Relación de Michoacán*, edited by Armando Escobar Olmedo, 75–88. Morelia, Mexico: Patrimonio Nacional, H. Ayuntamiento de Morelia; Madrid: Testimonio Compañía Editorial, 2001.

Cortez, Constance. "Gaspar Antonio Chi and the Xiu Family Tree." PhD diss., University of California, Los Angeles, 1995.

Cosentino, Delia. "Drawing Out the Truth in Colonial Nahua Courtrooms." Paper presented at the College Art Association annual conference, Seattle, 2004.

———. "Genealogías pictóricas en Tlaxcala colonial: Nobles afirmaciones del orden social." *Relaciones* 27, no. 105 (2006): 205–236.

———. *Las joyas de Zinacantepec: Arte colonial en el monasterio de San Miguel*. Mexico City: El Colegio Mexiquense and Instituto Mexiquense de Cultura, 2003.

———. "Zinacantepec's *Tree of Saint Francis*: Cross Cultural Roots and Colonial Blossoms in a Sixteenth-Century Mexican Mural." Master's thesis, University of California, Los Angeles, 1996.

Cosgrove, Denis. "Introduction." In *Social Formation and Symbolic Landscapes*, by Denis Cosgrove, 1–38. Totowa, NJ: Barnes and Noble, 1985.

———. "Introduction: Iconography and Landscape." In *The Iconography of Landscape: Essays on the Symbolic Representation, Design and Use of Past Environments*, edited by Denis Cosgrove and Stephen Daniels, 1–10. Cambridge: Cambridge University Press, 1988.

Covarrubias Orozco, Sebastián de. *Tesoro de la lengua castellana o española*. Edited by Martín de Riquer. 4th ed. Barcelona: Alta Fulla, 1998.

Crespo Chiapa, Raquel. "Fondo Mexicano de la Biblioteca Nacional de Francia, documento No. 081, El *Códice de Tepotzotlán*." Accessed September 10, 2013. http://www.amoxcalli.org.mx/presentaCodice.php?id=081.

"Cuarta Relación anónima." In *Memoria de los servicios que había hecho Nuño de Guzmán, desde que fue nombrado gobernador de Panuco en 1525*, edited by Manuel Carrera Stampa, 93–128. Mexico City: José Porrúa e Hijos, 1955.

Cuiri, Pablo. "*Codex Plancarte*." In *Tres códices michoacanos*, edited by José Corona Núñez, 41–90. Morelia, Mexico: Universidad Michoacana de San Nicolás de Hidalgo, 1986.

Cummins, John. *The Hound and the Hawk: The Art of Medieval Hunting*. New York: St. Martin's Press, 1988.

Cummins, Tom. "The Madonna and the Horse: Becoming Colonial in New Spain and Peru." In *Phoebus: A Journal of Art History* 7 (1995): *Native Artists and Patrons in Colonial Spanish America*, edited by Emily Umberger and Tom Cummins, 52–83.

Darras, Véronique. "La obsidiana en la *Relación de Michoacán* y en la realidad arqueológica: Del símbolo al uso o del uso de un símbolo." In *Génesis, culturas y espacios en Michoacán*, edited by Véronique Darras, 61–88. Mexico City: Centre Français d'Études Mexicaines et Centraméricaines, 1998.

Davidson, William, and James Parsons. "Robert C. West, Geographer." In *Historical Geography of Latin America, Papers in Honor of Robert C. West*, edited by William Davidson and James Parsons, 1–8. Baton Rouge: Louisiana State University Printing Office, 1980.

de Escobar, Matías. *Americana Thebaida*. Morelia, Mexico: Balsal Editores, 1970.

de la Rea, Alonso. *Crónica de la orden de N. seráfico P.S. Francisco, provincia de S. Pedro y S. Pablo de Mechoacán en la Nueva España*. Edited by Patricia Escandón. Zamora, Mexico: Colegio de Michoacán and Fideicomiso Teixidor, 1996.

de Las Casas, Bartolomé. *Brevísima relación de la destrucción de las indias*. Edited by Isacio Pérez Fernández. Bayamón, Puerto Rico: Universidad Central de Bayamón, Centro de Estudios de los Dominicos del Caribe, Instituto de Estudios Históricos Juan Alejo de Arizmendi, 2000.

De Wolf, Paul. *Seis estudios lingüísticos sobre la lengua phorhé*. Zamora, Mexico: Colegio de Michoacán, 1989.

Dealy, Ross. *The Politics of an Erasmian Lawyer, Vasco de Quiroga*. Malibu, CA: Undena Publications, 1976.

Dean, Carolyn, and Dana Leibsohn. "Hybridity and Its Discontents: Considering Visual Culture in Colonial Spanish America." *Colonial Latin American Review* 12, no. 1 (2003): 5–35.

Demant, Alain, and Dominique Michelet. *El proyecto Michoacán, 1983–1987: Medio ambiente e introducción a los trabajos arqueológicos*. Mexico City: Centre d'Études Mexicaines et Centraméricaines, 1992.

Díaz del Castillo, Bernal. *Historia verdadera de la conquista de la Nueva España*. Edited by Joaquín Ramírez Cabañas. Mexico City: Editorial Porrúa, 1999.

———. *Historia verdadera de la conquista de la Nueva España, II*. Edited by Miguel León-Portilla. Madrid: Dastin, 2000.

Diccionario grande de la lengua de Michoacán. Edited by J. Benedict Warren. 2 vols. Morelia, Mexico: Fimax Publicistas, 1991.

Diego Fernández, Rafael. *Antonio de Mendoza*. Colección Grandes Protagonistas de la Historia Mexicana. Barcelona: Cayfosa-Quebecor, 2002.

Diel, Lori B. *The Tira de Tepechpan: Negotiating Place under Aztec and Spanish Rule*. Austin: University of Texas Press, 2008.

Douglas, Eduardo de Jesús. *In the Palace of Nezahualcoyotl: Painting Manuscripts, Writing the Pre-Hispanic Past in Early Colonial Period Tetzcoco, Mexico*. Austin: University of Texas Press, 2010.

———. "Our Fathers, Our Mothers: Painting an Indian Genealogy in New Spain." In *Contested Visions in the Spanish Colonial World*, edited by Ilona Katzew, 117–131. Los Angeles: Los Angeles County Museum of Art, 2011.

Durán, Diego. *Historia general de las indias de Nueva España*. Translated by Doris Heyden. Civilization of the American Indian Series. Norman: University of Oklahoma Press, 1994.

Dyer, Richard. "Coloured White, Not Coloured." In *White*, by Richard Dyer, 41–81. New York: Routledge, 1997.

Escalante Gonzalbo, Pablo. "The Mixteca-Puebla Tradition and H. B. Nicholson." In *Fanning the Sacred Flame: Mesoamerican Studies in Honor of H. B. Nicholson*, edited by Matthew A. Boxt and Brian Dervin Dillon, 293–307. Boulder: University Press of Colorado, 2012.

Escobar Olmedo, Armando. "Introducción." In *Relación de Michoacán*, 11–40. Morelia, Mexico: Patrimonio Nacional, H. Ayuntamiento de Morelia; Madrid: Testimonio Compañía Editorial, 2001.

Escudero Buendía, Francisco J. *Antonio de Mendoza: Comendador de la villa de Socuéllamos y primer virrey de la Nueva España*. Pedro Muñoz, Spain: Perea, 2003.

Espejel Carbajal, Claudia. *Caminos de Michoacán . . . y pueblos que voy pasando*. Mexico City: Instituto Nacional de Antropología e Historia, 1992.

———. "Guía arqueológica y geográfica para la *Relación de Michoacán*." In *Relación de las cerimonias y rictos y población y gobernación de los indios de la provincia de Michoacán*, edited by Moisés Franco Mendoza, 301–314. Zamora, Mexico: El Colegio de Michoacán; Morelia, Mexico: Gobierno del Estado de Michoacán, 2000.

———. *La justicia y el fuego: Dos claves para leer la* Relación de Michoacán. 2 vols. Zamora, Mexico: El Colegio de Michoacán, 2008.

———. "Tarascan Ethnohistory and Archaeology." Foundation for the Advancement of Mesoamerican Studies, 2007. http://www.famsi.org/reports/06041/06041EspejelCarbajal01.pdf.

———. "Voces, lugares y tiempos: Claves para comprender la *Relación de Michoacán*." PhD diss., El Colegio de Michoacán, 2004.

Espinosa, Isidro Félix de. *Crónica de la provincia franciscana de los apóstoles San Pedro y San Pablo de Michoacán*. Edited by Nicolás León and José Ignacio Paulino Dávila Garibi. 2nd ed. Mexico City: Editorial Santiago, 1945.

———. *Crónica franciscana de Michoacán*. Edited by Nicolás León. Morelia, Mexico: Instituto de Investigaciones Históricas de la Universidad Michoacana de San Nicolás de Hidalgo and Morevallado Editores, 2003.

Faugère-Kalfon, Brigitte. "Venados y hogares sagrados en la *Relación de Michoacán: Reivindicación nórdica y construcción del estado en los pueblos tarascos*." In *Génesis, culturas y espacios en Michoacán*, edited by Véronique Darras, 89–99. Mexico City: Centre Français d'Études Mexicaines et Centraméricaines, 1998.

Fisher, Christopher. "Demographic and Landscape Change in the Lake Pátzcuaro Basin, Mexico: Abandoning the Garden." *American Anthropologist* 107, no. 1 (2005): 87–95.

Fisher, Christopher, Helen Pollard, Isabel Israde-Alcántar, Victor Garduño-Monroy, and Subir Banerjee. "A Reexamination of Human-Environmental Change within the Lake Pátzcuaro Basin, Michoacán, Mexico." *Proceedings of the National Academy of Sciences* 100, no. 8 (2003): 4957–4962.

Foster, George. *Empire's Children: The People of Tzintzuntzan*. Smithsonian Institution, Institute of Social Anthropology. Washington, DC: United States Government Printing Office, 1948.

Foucault, Michel. *The History of Sexuality*. Vol. 1, *An Introduction*. Translated by Robert Hurley. New York: Vintage, 1978.

Franco Mendoza, Moisés. "El discurso del petámuti en la estructura de la lengua P'urhépecha." In *Relación de las cerimonias y rictos y población y gobernación de los indios de la provincia de Michoacán*, edited by Moisés Franco Mendoza, 265–284. Zamora, Mexico: El Colegio de Michoacán; Morelia, Mexico: Gobierno del Estado de Michoacán, 2000.

———. "Ediciones de la *Relación de Michoacán*." In *Relación de las cerimonias y rictos y población y gobernación de los indios de la provincia de Michoacán*, edited by Moisés Franco Mendoza, 17–36. Zamora, Mexico: El Colegio de Michoacán; Morelia, Mexico: Gobierno del Estado de Michoacán, 2000.

Franco Mendoza, Moisés, and Salvador Pérez Ramírez. "Cuadro comparativo de voces p'urhépecha de la *Relación de Michoacán*." In *Relación de las cerimonias y rictos y población y gobernación de los indios de la provincia de Michoacán*, edited by Moisés Franco Mendoza, 735–796. Zamora, Mexico: El Colegio de Michoacán; Morelia, Mexico: Gobierno del Estado de Michoacán, 2000.

Gabany-Guerrero, Tricia. "Deciphering the Symbolic Heritage of the Tarascan Empire: Interpreting the Political Economy of the Pueblo-Hospital of Parangaricutiro, Michoacán." PhD diss., University at Albany, State University of New York, 1999.

Galván Villegas, L. Javier. *Las tumbas de tiro del Valle de Atemajac, Jalisco*. Mexico City: Instituto Nacional de Antropología e Historia, 1991.

Gerhard, Peter. *Geografía histórica de la Nueva España, 1521–1821*. Translated by Stella Mastrangelo. Mexico City: Universidad Nacional Autónoma de México, 1986.

Gilberti, Maturino. *Arte de la lengua de Michuacán*. Edited by J. Benedict Warren. Morelia, Mexico: Fímax Publicistas, 1987.

———. *Diccionario de la lengua tarasca o de Mechoacán (1559)*. Edited by J. Benedict Warren. Morelia, Mexico: Fimax Publicistas, 1990.

———. *Vocabulario en lengua de Mechuacán*. Edited by Agustín Jacinto Zavala, Clotilde Martínez, and J. Benedict Warren. Zamora, Mexico: Colegio de Michoacán; Mexico City: Fideicomiso Teixidor, 1997.

Gillespie, Susan. *The Aztec Kings: The Construction of Rulership in Mexica History*. Tucson: University of Arizona Press, 1989.

Goggin, John. "An Archaeological Survey of the Rio Tepalcatepec Basin, Michoacan, Mexico." *American Antiquity* 9, no. 1 (1943): 44–58.

Gómez Bravo, Eloy. "Glosario de voces en español." In *Relación de las cerimonias y rictos y población y gobernación de los indios de la provincia de Michoacán*, edited by Moisés Franco Mendoza, 727–734. Zamora, Mexico: El Colegio de Michoacán; Morelia, Mexico: Gobierno del Estado de Michoacán, 2000.

Gómez-Herrero, Fernando. "Good Places and Non-Places in Colonial Mexico: The Figure of Vasco de Quiroga (1470–1565)." PhD diss., Duke University, 1999.

———. "The Legal Reformation of Indian Subjectivities: Quiroga's Información en derecho (1535)." *Revista de Historia de América* 122 (1997): 25–107.

Gorenstein, Shirley. *Acambaro: Frontier Settlement on the Tarascan-Aztec Border.* Publications in Anthropology, vol. 32. Nashville, TN: Vanderbilt University, 1985.

Gorenstein, Shirley, and Helen Pollard. *The Tarascan Civilization: A Late Prehispanic Cultural System.* Publications in Anthropology, vol. 28. Nashville, TN: Vanderbilt University, 1983.

Greer, Margaret. "La caza sacro-política: De *El bosque divino* de González de Eslava a Calderón." In *El teatro en la Hispanoamérica colonial*, edited by Ignacio Arellano and José Antonio Rodríguez Garrido, 75–98. Pamplona, Spain: Universidad de Navarra; Madrid: Editorial Iberoamericana, 2008.

Gruzinski, Serge. *Painting the Conquest: The Mexican Indians and the European Renaissance.* Translated by Deke Dusinberre. Paris: Flammarion, 1992.

Guzmán, Nuño de. "Carta a la emperatriz, de Nuño de Guzmán, dando cuenta del estado en que se hallaba la conquista y población de la Nueva Galicia y quejándose de los daños que le hacían la Audiencia y el marqués del Valle. De la Ciudad de Compostela, a 12 de junio, 1532." In *Guadalajara y el Nuevo Mundo: Nuño Beltrán de Guzmán, semblanza de un conquistador*, edited by Adrián Blazquez and Thomás Calvo, 237–262. Guadalajara, Spain: Institución Provincial de Cultura "Marqués de Santillana," 1992.

———."Carta a S.M. del presidente de la Audiencia de Mexico Nuño de Guzmán, en que refiere la jornada que hizo a Mechoacan a conquistar la provincia de los Tebles Chichimecas, que confinan con Nueva España. A ocho de julio de 1530." In *Guadalajara y el Nuevo Mundo: Nuño Beltrán de Guzmán, semblanza de un conquistador*, edited by Adrián Blazquez and Thomás Calvo, 205–225. Guadalajara, Spain: Institución Provincial de Cultura "Marqués de Santillana," 1992.

———. *Memoria de los servicios que había hecho Nuño de Guzmán, desde que fue nombrado gobernador de Panuco en 1525.* Edited by Manuel Carrera Stampa. Mexico City: José Porrúa e Hijos, 1955.

Haskell, David. "History and the Construction of Hierarchy and Ethnicity in the Prehispanic Tarascan State: A Syntagmatic Analysis of the *Relación de Michoacán*." Master's thesis, University of Florida, 2003.

———. "History, Ideology, and Problematic Assumptions in the Ethnohistoric Inquiry into the Development of the Tarascan State." Paper presented at the annual meeting of the Society for American Archaeology, San Juan, Puerto Rico, April 2006.

Hassig, Ross. *Aztec Warfare: Imperial Expansion and Political Control.* Civilization of the American Indian Series. Norman: University of Oklahoma Press, 1988.

Hedberg, Mary Ann. "Conflicts and Continuities: Chapters in the History of Tuzuntla, a Town in Colonial Mexico." PhD diss., University of Minnesota, 1994.

Hidalgo Brinquis, María del Carmen. "Descripción material." In *Relación de Michoacán*, edited by Armando Escobar Olmedo, 41–74. Morelia, Mexico: Patrimonio Nacional, H. Ayuntamiento de Morelia; Madrid: Testimonio Compañía Editorial, 2001.

Historia tolteca-chichimeca. Edited by Paul Kirchhoff, Lina Odena Guémes, and Luís Reyes García. Mexico City: Fondo de Cultura Económica, 1989.

Hobsbawm, Eric. "Introduction: Inventing Traditions." In *The Invention of Tradition*, edited by Eric Hobsbawm and Terence Ranger, 1–14. Cambridge: Cambridge University Press, 1984.

The Holy Bible containing the Old and New Testaments. London: George Eyre and Andrew Strahan, 1817.

Hosler, Dorothy. *Los sonidos y colores del poder: La tecnología metalúrgica sagrada del occidente de México.* Translated by Eduardo Williams et al. Zinacantepec, Mexico: El Colegio Mexiquense, 2005.

———. *The Sounds and Colors of Power: The Sacred Metallurgical Technology of Ancient West Mexico.* Cambridge, MA: MIT Press, 1994.

Hosler, Dorothy, and Andrew Macfarlane. "Copper Sources, Metal Production, and Metals Trade in Late Postclassic Mesoamerica." *Science* 273 (1996): 1819–1824.

Hunt, Lynn. "Introduction: History, Culture, and Text." In *New Cultural History*, edited by Lynn Hunt, 1–24. Berkeley: University of California Press, 1989.

Hurtado Mendoza, Francisco. *La religión prehispánica de los purhépechas: Un testimonio del pueblo tarasco.* Morelia, Mexico: Linotipográfica "Omega," 1986.

Jacinto Zavala, Agustín. "Tres traducciones de la *Relación de Michoacán*." In *Relación de las cerimonias y rictos y población y gobernación de los indios de la provincia de Michoacán*, edited by Moisés Franco Mendoza, 121–138. Zamora, Mexico: El Colegio de Michoacán; Morelia, Mexico: Gobierno del Estado de Michoacán, 2000.

Jiménez, Nora. "Indígenas michoacanos y escritura fonética: Tres datos del siglo XVI." *Historias* 60 (2005): 37–41.

Jiménez Martínez, Érika. "Sobre una sentencia de 200 azotes, 100 en Michoacán y 100 en México, a un indio de Michoacán que decía era Dios y venía del cielo y además afirmaba que era el ánima del Caltzontzin, 1536." *Boletín del Archivo General de la Nación* 12, 6ª época (2006): 15–21.

Johansson, Patrick. "*Tira de la peregrinación* (*Códice Boturini*): Análisis de láminas, paleografía y traducción de textos en Náhuatl." "Edición Especial: Códices," *Arqueología Mexicana* 26 (2008): 17–73.

"Juicio seguido por Hernan Cortes contra los lics. Matienzo y Delgadillo." *Boletín del Archivo General de la Nación* 9, no. 3 (1938): 339–407.

Kelly, Isabel. *Excavations at Apatzingán, Michoacán.* Viking Fund Publications in Anthropology. New York: Viking Fund, 1947.

Kirchhoff, Paul. "Estudio preliminar: La *Relación de Michoacán* como fuente para la historia de la sociedad y cultura tarascas." In *Relación de las ceremonias y ritos y población y gobierno de los indios de la provincia de Michoacán (1541)*, edited by José Tudela, xix–xxxii. Madrid: Aguilar, 1956.

Klein, Cecelia F. "Editor's Statement: Depictions of the Dispossessed." *Art Journal* 49, no. 2 (1990): 106–109.

———. "Fighting with Femininity: Gender and War in Aztec Mexico." *Estudios de Cultura Náhuatl* 24 (1994): 219–253.

———. "The Ideology of Autosacrifice at the Templo Mayor." In *The Aztec Templo Mayor: A Symposium at Dumbarton Oaks, 8th and 9th October 1983*, edited by Elizabeth Boone, 293–370. Washington, DC: Dumbarton Oaks Research Library and Collection, 1987.

———. "Masking Empire: The Material Effects of Masks in Aztec Mexico." *Art History* 9, no. 2 (1986): 135–167.

———. "Rethinking Cihuacoatl: Aztec Political Imagery of the Conquered Woman." In *Smoke and Mist: Mesoamerican Studies in Memory of Thelma D. Sullivan*, edited by J. Kathryn Josserand and Karen Dakin, 237–277. Oxford: BAR, 1988.

Kraus, Theresa. "The Establishment of United States Army Air Corps Bases in Brazil, 1938–1945." PhD diss., University of Maryland, College Park, 1986.

Krippner-Martínez, James. "Invoking 'Tata Vasco': Vasco de Quiroga, Eighteenth–Twentieth Centuries." *The Americas* 56, no. 3 (2000): 1–28.

———. "The Politics of Conquest: An Interpretation of the *Relación de Michoacán*." *The Americas* 47, no. 2 (1990): 177–197.

———. *Rereading the Conquest: Power, Politics, and the History of Early Colonial Michoacán, Mexico, 1521–1565*. University Park: Pennsylvania State University Press, 2001.

———. "The Vision of the Victors: Power and Colonial Justice." *Colonial Latin American Review* 4, no. 1 (1995): 3–28.

Kubler, George. *Mexican Architecture of the Sixteenth Century*. New Haven, CT: Yale University Press; London: Oxford University Press, 1948.

Kuthy-Saenger, [María de] Lourdes. "Parentesco y matrimonio en la sociedad tarasca prehispánica." In *El matrimonio en Mesoamérica ayer y hoy: Unas miradas antropológicas*, edited by David Robichaux, 107–134. Mexico City: Universidad Iberoamericana, 2003.

———. "Strategies of Survival, Accommodation and Innovation: The Tarascan Indigenous Elite in Sixteenth Century Michoacan." PhD diss., Michigan State University, 1996.

Lacadena, Alfonso. "Vowel Length and Glottalization in Nahuatl Hieroglyphic Writing." *Revista Española de Antropología Americana* 38, no. 2 (2008): 121–150.

Lacas, M. M. "A Social Welfare Organizer in Sixteenth-Century New Spain: Don Vasco de Quiroga, First Bishop of Michoacán." *The Americas* 14, no. 1 (1957): 57–86.

Lagunas, Juan Baptista de. *Arte y diccionario con otras obras en lengua michuacana*. Edited by J. Benedict Warren. Morelia, Mexico: Fimax Publicistas, 1983.

Le Clézio, Jean Marie. "Universalidad de la *Relación de Michoacán*." In *Relación de las cerimonias y rictos y población y gobernación de los indios de la provincia de Michoacán*, edited by Moisés Franco Mendoza, 107–119. Zamora, Mexico: Colegio de Michoacán; Morelia, Mexico: Gobierno del Estado de Michoacán, 2000.

Leibsohn, Dana. "Mapping Metaphors: Figuring the Ground of Sixteenth-Century New Spain." *Journal of Medieval and Early Modern Studies* 26, no. 3 (1996): 497–523.

Leitz, Paul. "Don Vasco de Quiroga and the Second Audiencia of New Spain." PhD diss., Loyola University, 1940.

León, Nicolás. *Documentos inéditos referentes al ilustrísimo Señor Don Vasco de Quiroga*. Mexico City: Antigua Librería Robredo, de José Porrúa e Hijos, 1940.

———. "Testimonio de mercedes y tierras concedidas a la frontera de Guachichil, y el pueblo de San Francisco de Penjamo." In *Anales del Museo michoacano*, edited by Edmundo Aviña Levy, 251–257. Guadalajara, Mexico: Biblioteca de Facsímiles Mexicanos, 1968.

Leonard, Irving Albert. *Books of the Brave, Being an Account of Books and of Men in the Spanish Conquest and Settlement of the Sixteenth-Century New World*. Cambridge, MA: Harvard University Press, 1949.

León-Portilla, Miguel. "Fray Juan de Zumarraga y las lenguas indígenas en México." In *La utopía mexicana del siglo XVI: Lo bello, lo verdadero y lo bueno*, edited by Guillermo Tovar de Teresa, Miguel León-Portilla, and Silvio Zavala. Colección Arte Novohispano, 41–65. Mexico City: Grupo Azabache, 1992.

———. "Jerónimo de Alcalá y los primeros frailes etnógrafos en Mesoamérica, siglo XVI." In *Relación de las cerimonias y rictos y población y gobernación de los indios de la provincia de Michoacán*, edited by Moisés Franco Mendoza, 57–78. Zamora, Mexico: El Colegio de Michoacán; Morelia, Mexico: Gobierno del Estado de Michoacán, 2000.

———. "El tonalámatl de los pochtecas (*Codex Fejérváry-Mayer*)." "Edición Especial: Códices," *Arqueología Mexicana* 18 (2005): 18–107.

"Las Leyes Nuevas, 1542–1543." *Anuario de Estudios Americanos* 2 (1945): 811–835.

Lister, Robert. "Archaeology of the Middle Rio Balsas Basin, Mexico." *American Antiquity* 13, no. 1 (1947): 67–78.

———. *Excavations at Cojumatlán, Michoacán, Mexico*. University of New Mexico Publications in Anthropology. Albuquerque: University of New Mexico Press, 1949.

Lockhart, James. *The Nahuas after the Conquest: A Social and Cultural History of the Indians of Central Mexico, Sixteenth through Eighteenth Centuries*. Stanford, CA: Stanford University Press, 1992.

López Austin, Alfredo. *Cuerpo humano e ideología: Las concepciones de los antiguos nahuas*. Mexico City: Universidad Nacional Autónoma de México, 1980.

López de Gómara, Francisco. *Historia general de las indias: "Hispania Vitrix" cuya segunda parte corresponde a la conquista de Méjico*. Edited by Pilar Guibelalde and Emiliano M. Aguilera. Vol. 2. Barcelona: Editorial Iberia, 1965.

López Sarrelangue, Delfina Esmeralda. *La nobleza indígena de Pátzcuaro en la época virreinal*. Morelia, Mexico: Morevallado Editores, 1999. Originally published in Mexico City: Universidad Nacional Autónoma de México, Instituto de Investigaciones Históricas, 1965.

Lumholtz, Carl. *Unknown Mexico: A Record of Five Years' Exploration among the Tribes of the Western Sierra Madre; in the Tierra Caliente of Tepic and Jalisco; and among the Tarascos of Michoacan*. New York: C. Scribner's Sons, 1902.

Marcus, Joyce. *Mesoamerican Writing Systems: Propaganda, Myth, and History in Four Ancient Civilizations*. Princeton, NJ: Princeton University Press, 1992.

Márquez Joaquín, Pedro. "El significado de las palabras p'urhépecha en la *Relación de Michoacán*: Glosario de voces p'urhépecha." In *Relación de las cerimonias y rictos y población y gobernación de los indios de la provincia de Michoacán*, edited by Moisés Franco Mendoza, 693–726. Zamora, Mexico: Colegio de Michoacán; Morelia, Mexico: Gobierno del Estado de Michoacán, 2000.

———, ed. *¿Tarascos o p'urhépecha? Voces sobre antiguas y nuevas discusiones en torno al gentilicio michoacano*. Morelia, Mexico: Universidad Michoacana de San Nicolás de Hidalgo, El Colegio de Michoacán, Universidad Intercultural Indígena de Michoacán, and Fondo Editorial Morevallado, 2007.

Martínez Baracs, Rodrigo. *Convivencia y utopía: El gobierno indio y español de la "Ciudad de Mechuacan," 1521–1580*. Mexico City: Instituto Nacional de Antropología e Historia and Fondo de Cultura Económica, 2005.

———. "Etimologías políticas michoacanas." In *Autoridad y gobierno indígena en Michoacán*, edited by Carlos Paredes Martínez and Marta Terán, 61–90. Zamora, Mexico: El Colegio de Michoacán; Mexico City: Centro de Investigaciones y Estudios Superiores en Antropología Social, Instituto Nacional de Antropología e Historia; Morelia, Mexico: Universidad Michoacana de San Nicolás de Hidalgo, 2000.

Martínez Baracs, Rodrigo, and Lydia Espinosa. *La vida michoacana en el siglo XVI: Catálogo de los documentos del siglo XVI del archivo histórico de la ciudad de Pátzcuaro*. Serie Fuentes. Mexico City: Instituto Nacional de Antropología e Historia, 1999.

Martínez Ibáñez, Clotilde, and Carmen Molina Ruiz. "Diferencia de voces castellanas en la paleografía de la presente edición y las versiones de José Tudela y Francisco Miranda." In *Relación de las cerimonias y rictos y población y gobernación de los indios de la provincia de Michoacán*, edited by Moisés Franco Mendoza, 797–814. Zamora, Mexico: El Colegio de Michoacán; Morelia, Mexico: Gobierno del Estado de Michoacán, 2000.

McGuire, Thérèse. "The Symbol of Power in Suger's Tree of Jesse." In *The Propagation of Power in the Medieval West*, edited by Arjo Vanderjagt and Jan Veenstra Martin Gosman, 301–311. Groningen, Netherlands: Egbert Forsten, 1997.

Mendieta y Núñez, Lucio. *Los tarascos: Monografía histórica, etnográfica y económica*. Mexico City: Imprenta Universitaria, 1940.

Merback, Michell B. *The Thief, the Cross and the Wheel: Pain and the Spectacle of Punishment in Medieval and Renaissance Europe*. Chicago: University of Chicago Press, 1999.

Michelet, Dominique. "Histoire, mythe et apologue: Note de lecture sur la seconde partie de la *Relación [...] de Michoacán*." In *Enquêtes sur l'Amérique moyenne: Mélanges offerts à Guy Stresser-Péan*, edited by Guy Stresser-Péan and Dominique Michelet, 105–112. Mexico City: Instituto Nacional de Antropología e Historia, Consejo Nacional para la Cultura y las Artes, and Centre d'Études Mexicaines et Centraméricaines, 1989.

Miranda Godínez, Francisco. "Las láminas de la *Relación de Michoacán*: Una descripción." In *Relación de Michoacán*, edited by Armando Escobar Olmedo, 173–

204. Morelia, Mexico: Patrimonio Nacional, H. Ayuntamiento de Morelia; Madrid: Testimonio Compañía Editorial, 2001.

———. "Monumentos literarios del Michoacán prehispánico." In *Relación de Michoacán*, edited by Armando Escobar Olmedo, 101–142. Morelia, Mexico: Patrimonio Nacional, H. Ayuntamiento de Morelia; Madrid: Testimonio Compañía Editorial, 2001.

———. *La* Relación de Michoacán*: Estudio preliminar y notas*. Mexico City: Secretaría de Educación Pública, 1988.

Mirrer, Louise. "The 'Unfaithful Wife' in Medieval Spanish Literature and Law." In *Medieval Crime and Social Control*, edited by Barbara A. Hanawalt and David Wallace, 143–155. Minneapolis: University of Minnesota Press, 1999.

Mohar Betancourt, Luz María. Códice Mapa Quinatzin*: Justicia y derechos humanos en el México antiguo*. Mexico City: Comisión Nacional de los Derechos Humanos México, CIESAS, and Miguel Angel Porrúa, 2004.

Moreno, Juan Joseph. *Vida de don Vasco de Quiroga, ordenanzas, testamento*. Morelia, Mexico: Balsal Editores, 1989.

Mundy, Barbara. *The Mapping of New Spain: Indigenous Cartography and the Maps of the* Relaciones geográficas. Chicago: University of Chicago Press, 2000.

Nader, Helen. "The Mendoza in the Fifteenth-Century Renaissance." In *The Mendoza Family in the Spanish Renaissance 1350–1550*. New Brunswick, NJ: Rutgers University Press, 1979.

Navarrete, Federico. "The Path from Aztlan to Mexico: On Visual Narration in Mesoamerican Codices." *Res* 37 (2000): 31–48.

Nelson, Robert. "Appropriation." In *Critical Terms for Art History*, edited by Robert Nelson and Richard Shiff, 116–128. Chicago: University of Chicago Press, 1996.

Nesvig, Martin. "Review Essay: Recent Work on Early Western Mexico and the Revival of the Black Legend." *Journal of Social History* 39, no. 2 (2005): 531–538.

Nicholson, H. B. "The History of the *Codex Mendoza*." In *The* Codex Mendoza, edited by Frances F. Berdan and Patricia Rieff Anawalt, 1–11. Berkeley: University of California Press, 1992.

———. "Introduction." In Bernardino de Sahagún, *Primeros memoriales*, by Bernardino de Sahagún, edited by H. B. Nicholson et al., paleography of Nahuatl text and English translation by Thelma Sullivan, 3–14. Norman: University of Oklahoma Press, 1997.

———. "Pre-Hispanic Central Mexican Historiography." In *Investigaciones contemporáneas sobre historia de México: Memorias de la tercera reunión de historiadores mexicanos y norteamericanos (1969)*, 38–81. Austin: University of Texas Press, 1971.

"Ordenanza para el gobierno de Indios, 1546." *Boletín del Archivo General de la Nación* 11, no. 2 (1940): 185–186.

"Ordenanzas reales sobre los indios (Las leyes de 1512–1513)." *Anuario de Estudios Americanos* 13, no. 9 (1956): 434.

Osberg, Richard. "The Jesse Tree in the 1432 London Entry of Henry VI: Messianic Kingship and the Rule of Justice." *Journal of Medieval and Renaissance Studies* 16, no. 2 (1986): 213–232.

Osborne, Douglas. "An Archaeological Reconnaissance in Southeastern Michoacan." *American Antiquity* 9 (1943): 59–73.

Owst, G. R. *Literature and Pulpit in Medieval England: A Neglected Chapter in the History of English Letters and of the English People.* New York: Barnes and Noble, 1961.

Pagden, Anthony. "The Humanism of Vasco de Quiroga's *Información de derecho.*" In *The Uncertainties of Empire: Essays in Iberian and Ibero-American Intellectual History*, 133–142. Norfolk, UK: Galliard, 1994.

Panofsky, Erwin. "Painting in Italy and the Lowlands during the Fifteenth Century." In *Readings in Art History*, edited by Harold Spencer, 25–34. New York: Scribner, 1969.

Paredes Martínez, Carlos. "La estratificación social de los tarascos." *Arqueología Mexicana* 4, no. 19 (1996): 34–39.

———. *Michoacán en el siglo XVI.* Morelia, Mexico: Fímax Publicistas, 1984.

Paredes Martínez, Carlos, Victor Cárdenas Morales, Iraís Piñón Flores, and Trinidad Pulido Solís, eds. *"Y por mi visto . . .": Mandamientos, ordenanzas, licencias y otras disposiciones virreinales del siglo XVI.* Mexico City: Centro de Investigaciones y Estudios Superiores en Antropología Social; Morelia, Mexico: Universidad Michoacana de San Nicolás de Hidalgo, 1994.

Paredes Martínez, Carlos, and Marta Terán. *Autoridad y gobierno indígena en Michoacán: Ensayos a través de su historia.* Zamora, Mexico: Instituto Nacional de Antropología e Historia; Mexico City: Centro de Investigaciones y Estudios Superiores en Antropología Social, El Colegio de Michoacán, Universidad Michoacana de San Nicolás de Hidalgo; Morelia, Mexico: Instituto de Investigaciones Históricas, 2003.

Pasztory, Esther. "Identity and Difference: The Uses and Meanings of Ethnic Styles." In *Cultural Differentiation and Cultural Identity in the Visual Arts*, edited by Susan Barnes and Walter Melion, 15–38. London: National Gallery of Art; Hanover, NH: University Press of New England, 1989.

Pepper, George. *George Hubbard Pepper Papers 1895–1918: From the Latin American Library, Howard-Tilton Memorial Library, Tulane University, New Orleans.* New York: Norman Ross Publishing, 2000.

Pérez Martínez, Herón. "El arte literario de la *Relación de Michoacán.*" In *Relación de las cerimonias y rictos y población y gobernación de los indios de la provincia de Michoacán*, edited by Moisés Franco Mendoza, 79–105. Zamora, Mexico: Colegio de Michoacán; Morelia, Mexico: Gobierno del Estado de Michoacán, 2000.

Perry, Richard. *Blue Lakes and Silver Cities: The Colonial Arts and Architecture of West Mexico.* Santa Barbara, CA: Espadaña Press, 1997.

Peterson, Jeanette. "The *Florentine Codex* Imagery and the Colonial Tlacuilo." In *The Work of Bernardino de Sahagún, Pioneer Ethnographer of Sixteenth-Century Aztec Mexico*, edited by J. Jorge Klor de Alva, H. B. Nicholson, and E. Quiñones Keber, 273–293. Albany: Institute for Mesoamerican Studies, University at Albany, State University of New York, 1988.

———. *The Paradise Garden Murals of Malinalco: Utopia and Empire in Sixteenth-Century Mexico.* Austin: University of Texas Press, 1993.

———. "Synthesis and Survival: The Native Presence in Sixteenth-Century Murals of New Spain." In *Native Artists and Patrons in Colonial Latin America*, edited by Emily Umberger and Tom Cummins. *Phoebus: A Journal of Art History* 7, Arizona State University (1995): 14–35.

Pierce, Donna. "Identification of the Warriors in the Frescoes of Ixmiquilpan." *Research Center for the Arts Review* 4, no. 4 (1981): 1–8.

Pilar, García del. "Relacion de la entrada de Nuño de Guzmán, que dio García del Pilar, su intérprete." In *Memoria de los servicios que había hecho Nuño de Guzmán, desde que fue nombrado gobernador de Pánuco en 1525*, edited by Manuel Carrera Stampa, 177–193. Mexico City: José Porrúa e Hijos, 1955.

Pollard, Helen P. "Central Places and Cities: A Consideration of the Protohistoric Tarascan State." *American Antiquity* 45, no. 4 (1980): 677–696.

———. "Central Places and Cities in the Core of the Tarascan State." In *El urbanismo en Mesoamérica/Urbanism in Mesoamerica*, edited by William Sanders et al., 345–390. Mexico City: Instituto Nacional de Antropología e Historia; University Park: Pennsylvania State University, 2003.

———. "Ecological Variation and Economic Exchange in the Tarascan State." *American Ethnologist* 9, no. 2 (1982): 250–268.

———. "Ethnicity and Political Control in a Complex Society: The Tarascan State of Prehispanic Mexico." In *Factional Competition and Political Development in the New World*, edited by Elizabeth Brumfiel and John Fox, 79–88. New Directions in Archaeology. Cambridge: Cambridge University Press, 1994.

———. "The Political Economy of Prehispanic Tarascan Metallurgy." *American Antiquity* 52, no. 4 (1987): 741–752.

———. "Pre-Hispanic Urbanism at Tzintzuntzan, Michoacán." PhD diss., Columbia University, 1972.

———. *Taríacuri's Legacy: The Prehispanic Tarascan State.* Norman: University of Oklahoma Press, 1993.

Pollard, Helen P., Amy Hirshman, Hector Neff, and Michael Glascock. "Las élites, el intercambio de bienes y el surgimiento del área nuclear tarasca." In *Estudios cerámicos en el occidente y norte de México*, edited by Eduardo Williams and Phil Weigand, 289–309. Zamora, Mexico: Colegio de Michoacán; Morelia, Mexico: Instituto Michoacano de Cultura, 2001.

Popol Vuh: The Mayan Book of the Dawn of Life. Translated by Dennis Tedlock. New York: Simon and Schuster, 1996.

Puga, Vasco de. *Provisiones, cédulas, instrucciones de su magestad.* Vol. 1. Mexico City: J. M. Sandoval, 1878–1879.

Quiñones Keber, Eloise. "An Introduction to the Images, Artists, and Physical Features of the *Primeros memoriales.*" In *Primeros memoriales by Fray Bernardino de Sahagún*, edited by H. B. Nicholson et al., 15–51. Norman: University of Oklahoma Press, 1997.

Ramírez, Félix. *Ireti Khatape: Ensayo de una interpretacion de la "Relacion de Michoacan," personajes y dioses michoacanos*. Mexico City: Casa Ramírez, 1956.

Ramírez, Francisco. *El antiguo Colegio de Pátzcuaro*. Edited by Germán Viveros. Zamora, Mexico: El Colegio de Michoacán; Morelia, Mexico: Gobierno del Estado de Michoacán, 1987.

———. "Relación sobre la residencia de Michoacán (Pátzcuaro) hecha por el padre Francisco Ramírez." In *Monumenta mexicana, vol. 2 (1581–1585)*, edited by Félix Zubillaga, 474–538. Rome: Apud "Monumenta Historica Soc. Iesu," 1959.

Real Academia Española. *Diccionario de autoridades*. 3 vols. Biblioteca Románica Hispánica. Madrid: Editorial Gredos, 1984.

Reinhardt, Kurt. "Fray Alonso de la Vera Cruz and the Beginnings of Philosophic Speculation in the Americas." *The Americas* 1, no. 2 (1944): 207–214.

Relación de las ceremonias y ritos y población y gobernación de los indios de la provincia de Michoacán (1541). Edited by José Tudela, with revision of Tarascan words by José Corona Núñez. Madrid: Aguilar, 1956.

Relación de Michoacán. Edited by Leoncio Cabrero. Crónicas de América 52. Madrid, Spain: Historia 16, 1989.

Relación de Michoacán. Edited by Armando Escobar Olmedo. Morelia, Mexico: Patrimonio Nacional, H. Ayuntamiento de Morelia; Madrid: Testimonio Compañía Editorial, 2001.

Relación de Michoacán. Edited by Moisés Franco Mendoza. Zamora, Mexico: El Colegio de Michoacán; Morelia, Mexico: Gobierno del Estado de Michoacán, 2000.

Relaciones geográficas de la diócesis de Michoacán, 1579–1580. Edited by José Corona Núñez. 2 vols. Guadalajara, Mexico: Colección Siglo XVI, 1958.

Relaciones geográficas del siglo XVI: Michoacán. Edited by René Acuña. Mexico City: Universidad Nacional Autónoma de México, Instituto de Investigaciones Antropológicas, 1982.

Riley, G. Michael. *Fernando Cortés and the Marquesado in Morelos, 1522–1547*. Albuquerque: University of New Mexico Press, 1973.

Risse, Guenter B. "Medicine in New Spain." In *Medicine in the New World: New Spain, New France, and New England*, edited by Ronald L. Numbers, 12–63. Knoxville: University of Tennessee Press, 1987.

Robertson, Donald. *Mexican Manuscript Painting of the Early Colonial Period: The Metropolitan Schools*. Norman: University of Oklahoma Press, 1994.

———. "Tulum Murals: The International Style of the Late Post-Classic." In *Proceedings of the 38th International Congress of Americanists (Stuttgart and Munich, 1968)*, 77–88. Munich: Kommissionverlag K. Renner, 1970.

Roskamp, Hans. "El carari indígena y las láminas de la *Relación de Michoacán*: Un acercamiento." In *Relación de las cerimonias y rictos y población y gobernación de los indios de la provincia de Michoacán*, edited by Moisés Franco Mendoza, 235–264. Zamora, Mexico: El Colegio de Michoacán; Morelia, Mexico: Gobierno del Estado de Michoacán, 2000.

———. *Los Códices de Cutzio y Huetamo: Encomienda y tributo en la tierra caliente de*

Michoacán, siglo XVI. Zamora, Mexico: El Colegio de Michoacán; Zinacantepec, Mexico: El Colegio Mexiquense, 2003.

———. "Las 44 láminas de la *Relación de Michoacán*: Una propuesta de lectura." In *Relación de las cerimonias y rictos y población y gobernación de los indios de la provincia de Michoacán*, edited by Moisés Franco Mendoza, 323–691. Zamora, Mexico: El Colegio de Michoacán; Morelia, Mexico: Gobierno del Estado de Michoacán, 2000.

———. *La historiografía indígena de Michoacán: El lienzo de Jucutácato y los títulos de Carapan.* Leiden, Netherlands: Research School CNWS, Leiden University, 1998.

Rubín de la Borbolla, Daniel, and Ralph Beals. "The Tarascan Project: A Cooperative Enterprise of the National Polytechnic Institute, Mexican Bureau-Indian Affairs, and the University of California." *American Anthropologist* 42, no. 4 (1940): 708–712.

Ruiz Medrano, Ethelia. "Códices y justicia: Los caminos de la dominación." *Arqueología Mexicana* 7, no. 38 (1999): 44–50.

———. *Gobierno y sociedad en Nueva España: Segunda Audiencia y Antonio de Mendoza.* Zamora, Mexico: El Colegio de Michoacán; Morelia, Mexico: Gobierno del Estado de Michoacán, 1991.

Ruiz Medrano, Ethelia, and Perla Valle. "Los colores de la justicia, códices jurídicios del siglo XVI en la Bibliothèque nationale de France." *Journal de la Société des Américanistes de Paris* 84, no. 2 (1998): 227–241.

Russo, Alessandra. *El realismo circular: Tierras, espacios y paisajes de la cartografía indígena novohispana, siglos XVI y XVII.* Mexico City: Universidad Nacional Autónoma de México and Instituto de Investigaciones Estéticas, 2005.

———. "El renacimiento vegetal: Árboles de Jesé entre el viejo mundo y el nuevo." *Anales del Instituto de Investigaciones Estéticas* 73 (1998): 5–39.

Sachsen, Ludolf von. "De como el que muere ë Acabado de Batizar se va derecho a parayso." In *Vita Cristi Cartuxano Romanaçado por Fray Ambrosio.* Seville, Spain: J. Croberger, 1551.

Salazar Simarro, Nuria. "Relación de las ceremonias y ritos y población y gobierno de los indios de la provincia de Michoacán." In *Los siglos de oro en los virreinatos de América 1550–1700*, edited by Sociedad Estatal para la Conmemoración de los Centenarios de Felipe II y Carlos V, 208–211. Madrid: Brizzolis, 1999.

Sánchez Díaz, Gerardo. "Las ediciones de la *Relación de Michoacán* y su impacto historiográfico." In *Relación de Michoacán*, edited by Armando Escobar Olmedo, 205–238. Morelia, Mexico: Patrimonio Nacional, H. Ayuntamiento de Morelia; Madrid: Testimonio Compañía Editorial, 2001.

———. *Historiografía michoacana: Acercamientos y balances.* Morelia, Mexico: Universidad Michoacana de San Nicolás de Hidalgo, Instituto de Investigaciones Históricas, and Morevallado Editores, 2000.

———. "Los manuscritos y las ediciones de la *Relación de Michoacán*: Su impacto historiográfico." *Tzintzun: Revista de Estudios Históricos* 40 (2004): 11–50.

Sanz, María Jesús. "Algunas representaciones del Árbol de Jessé, durante el siglo XVI, en Sevilla y su antiguo reino." *Cuadernos de Arte e Iconografía* 2, no. 4 (1989): 123–124.

Scholes, France, and Eleanor Adams. *Proceso contra Tzintzicha Tangaxoan, el Caltzontzin, formado por Nuño de Guzmán, año de 1530*. Mexico City: Porrúa y Obregón, 1952.

Schöndube, Otto. "Los tarascos." *Arqueología Mexicana* 4, no. 19 (1996): 14–21.

Seler, Eduard. "Los antiguos habitantes de Michoacán." In *Relación de las cerimonias y rictos y población y gobernación de los indios de la provincia de Michoacán*, edited by Moisés Franco Mendoza, 139–234. Zamora, Mexico: El Colegio de Michoacán; Morelia, Mexico: Gobierno del Estado de Michoacán, 2000.

Sepúlveda y Herrera, María Teresa. *La medicina entre los purépecha prehispánicos*. Mexico City: Universidad Nacional Autónoma de México, Instituto de Investigaciones Antropológicas, 1988.

Smith, Michael. *The Aztecs*. Cambridge: Blackwell Publishers, 1996.

———. "The Aztlan Migrations of the Nahuatl Chronicles: Myth or History?" *Ethnohistory* 31, no. 3 (1984): 153–186.

Spiegel, Gabrielle. "Political Utility in Medieval Historiography: A Sketch." *History and Theory* 14, no. 3 (1975): 314–325.

Stanislawski, Dan. *The Anatomy of Eleven Towns in Michoacan*. Latin American Studies. Austin: University of Texas Press, 1950.

———. "The Political Rivalry of Patzcuaro and Morelia." *Annals of the Association of American Geographers* 37 (1947): 135–144.

———. "Tarascan Political Geography." *American Anthropologist* 49, no. 1 (1947): 46–55.

Stark, Barbara L., and John K. Chance. "Diachronic and Multidisciplinary Perspectives on Mesoamerican Ethnicity." In *Ethnic Identity in Nahua Mesoamerica: The View from Archaeology, Art History, Ethnohistory, and Contemporary Ethnography*, edited by Frances F. Berdan and et al., 1–37. Salt Lake City: University of Utah Press, 2008.

Stoler, Ann. *Carnal Knowledge and Imperial Power: Race and the Intimate in Colonial Rule*. Berkeley: University of California Press, 2002.

Stone, Cynthia. "A Fragile Coalition: The *Relación de Michoacán* and the Compiling of Indigenous Traditions in Sixteenth-Century México." PhD diss., University of Michigan, 1992.

———. *In Place of Gods and Kings: Authorship and Identity in the* Relación de Michoacán. Norman: University of Oklahoma Press, 2004.

———. "Rewriting Indigenous Traditions: The Burial Ceremony of the Cazonci." *Colonial Latin American Review* 3, no. 1–2 (1994): 87–114.

Stresser-Péan, Guy, and Dominique Michelet. *Enquêtes sur l'Amérique moyenne: Mélanges offerts à Guy Stresser-Péan*. Études Mésoaméricaines. Mexico City: Instituto Nacional de Antropología e Historia, Consejo Nacional para la Cultura y las Artes, and Centre d'Études Mexicaines et Centraméricaines, 1989.

Taube, Karl. "At Dawn's Edge: Tulúm, Santa Rita, and Floral Symbolism in the International Style of Late Postclassic Mesoamerica." In *Astronomers, Scribes, and Priests: Intellectual Interchange between the Northern Maya Lowlands and*

Highland Mexico in the Late Postclassic Period, edited by Gabrielle Vail and Christine Hernández, 145–191. Washington, DC: Dumbarton Oaks, 2010.

Terán Elizondo, María Isabel. "Elementos mítico-simbólicos." In *Relación de las ceremonias y rictos y población y gobernación de los indios de la provincia de Michoacán*, edited by Moisés Franco Mendoza, 285–300. Zamora, Mexico: El Colegio de Michoacán; Morelia, Mexico: Gobierno del Estado de Michoacán, 2000.

Terraciano, Kevin. "Competing Memories of the Conquest of Mexico." In *Contested Visions in the Spanish Colonial World*, edited by Ilona Katzew, 55–77. Los Angeles: Los Angeles County Museum of Art; New Haven, CT: Yale University Press, 2011.

———. "Crime and Culture in Colonial Mexico: The Case of the Mixtec Murder Note." *Ethnohistory* 45, no. 4 (1998): 709–745.

Tomás y Valiente, Francisco. "El derecho penal de la monarquía absoluta (siglos XVI, XVII y XVII)." In *Obras completas*, 201–246. Madrid: Centro de Estudios Políticos y Constitucionales, 1997.

Torquemada, Juan de. "De la solemnidad, con que se hacian los entierros, y obsequias de los reies de Mechoacan, que es capitulo de notar." In *Monarquía indiana*, by Juan de Torquemada, 523–526. Mexico City: Salvador Chavez Hayhoe, 1943.

Tortorici, Zeb. "'Heran todos putos': Sodomitical Subcultures and Disordered Desire in Early Colonial Mexico." *Ethnohistory* 54, no. 1 (2007): 35–67.

Toussaint, Manuel. *Pátzcuaro*. Mexico City: Universidad Nacional de Mexico, Instituto de Investigaciones Estéticas, 1942.

Tovar de Teresa, Guillermo. "La utopía del Virrey de Mendoza." In *La utopía mexicana del siglo XVI: Lo bello, lo verdadero y lo bueno*, edited by Guillermo Tovar de Teresa, Miguel León-Portilla, and Silvio Zavala, 17–39. Colección Arte Novohispano. Mexico City: Grupo Azabache, 1992.

"Tributes of Tzintzuntzan and Tlalpujava, recto, [1542–1552]." Garrett Mesoamerican Manuscripts, Manuscripts Division, Department of Rare Books and Special Collections, Princeton University Library.

Tudela, José. "Prólogo." In *Relación de las ceremonias y ritos y población y gobernación de los indios de la provincia de Michoacán (1541)*, edited by José Tudela, v–xviii. Madrid: Aguilar, 1956.

Umberger, Emily. "Ethnicity and Other Identities in the Sculptures of Tenochtitlan." In *Ethnic Identity in Nahua Mesoamerica: The View from Archaeology, Art History, Ethnohistory, and Contemporary Ethnography*, edited by Frances Berdan et al., 64–104. Salt Lake City: University of Utah Press, 2008.

Valle, Perla. "Códices coloniales: Memorias en imágenes de los Pueblos Indios." *Arqueología Mexicana* 7, no. 38 (1999): 6–13.

Warren, Fintan B. [J. Benedict]. *Vasco de Quiroga and His Pueblo-Hospitales of Santa Fe*. Washington, DC: Academy of American Franciscan History, 1963.

Warren, J. Benedict. "El autor, Fray Jerónimo de Alcalá." In *Relación de Michoacán*, edited by Armando Escobar Olmedo, 89–100. Morelia, Mexico: Patrimonio Nacional, H. Ayuntamiento de Morelia; Madrid: Testimonio Compañía Editorial, 2001.

———. "The Carvajal Visitation: First Spanish Survey of Michoacán." *The Americas* 19, no. 4 (1963): 404–412.

———. *The Conquest of Michoacán: The Spanish Domination of the Tarascan Kingdom in Western Mexico, 1521–1530*. Norman: University of Oklahoma Press, 1985.

———. *La conquista de Michoacán, 1521–1530*. Morelia, Mexico: Fimax Publicistas, 1977.

———. *Estudios sobre el Michoacán colonial: Los inicios*. Morelia, Mexico: Universidad Michoacana de San Nicolás de Hidalgo and Fimax Publicistas, 2005.

———. "Fray Jerónimo de Alcalá: Author of the *Relación de Michoacán*?" *The Americas* 27, no. 3 (1971): 307–326.

———. "Fray Jerónimo de Alcalá, autor de la *Relación de Michoacán*." In *Estudios sobre el Michoacán colonial: Los inicios*, 155–186. Morelia, Mexico: Universidad Michoacana de San Nicolás de Hidalgo and Fimax Publicistas, 2005.

———. "Fray Jerónimo de Alcalá, autor de la *Relación de Michoacán*." In *Relación de las cerimonias y rictos y población y gobernación de los indios de la provincia de Michoacán*, edited by Moisés Franco Mendoza, 37–56. Zamora, Mexico: El Colegio de Michoacán; Morelia, Mexico: Gobierno del Estado de Michoacán, 2000.

———. "Información del licenciado Vasco de Quiroga sobre el cobre de Michoacán, 1533." In *Ritmo del fuego: El arte y los artesanos de Santa Clara del Cobre, Michoacán, México / Rhythm of Fire: The Art and the Artisans of Santa Clara del Cobre, Michoacán, México*, edited by Michele Feder-Nadoff, 118–152. Morelia, Mexico: Morevallado Editores; Chicago: Cuentos Foundation, 2004.

———. "Minas de cobre en Michoacán, 1533." *Anales del Museo Michoacano* 6, 2nd ed. (1968): 35–52.

———. "Vasco de Quiroga y la fundación de Pátzcuaro colonial." In *Estudios sobre el Michoacán colonial: Los inicios*, 79–94. Morelia, Mexico: Universidad Michoacana de San Nicolás de Hidalgo and Fimax Publicistas, 2005.

Warren, J. Benedict, and Cristina Monzón. "Carta de los principales de Pátzcuaro al Obispo Vasco de Quiroga. 10 de marzo de 1549." *Relaciones: Estudios de Historia y Sociedad* 25, no. 99 (2004): 177–211.

Watson, Arthur. *The Early Iconography of the Tree of Jesse*. London: Oxford University Press, 1934.

Weckmann, Luis. *La herencia medieval de México*. Mexico City: El Colegio de México and Fondo de Cultura Económica, 1994.

Weigand, Phil. "La transición del formativo-clásico y del clásico postclásico en la zona jalisciense de Teuchitlán/Etzatlán." In *Evolución de una civilización prehispánica: Arqueología de Jalisco, Nayarit y Zacatecas*, 21–37. Zamora, Mexico: El Colegio de Michoacán, 1993.

West, Robert. *Cultural Geography of the Modern Tarascan Area*. Smithsonian Institution, Institute of Social Anthropology. Washington, DC: United States Government Printing Office, 1948.

Zavala, Silvio. "La 'utopía' de Tomás Moro en la Nueva España." In *La utopía mexicana del siglo XVI: Lo bello, lo verdadero y lo bueno*, edited by Guillermo Tovar de Teresa, Miguel León-Portilla, and Silvio Zavala, 67–94. Colección Arte Novohispano. Mexico City: Grupo Azabache, 1992.

Index

Page numbers followed by f indicate material in figures.